Fa
ISSN: 02

MW01223143

THE ~~REVIEW OF~~
CONTEMPORARY FICTION

Editor
JOHN O'BRIEN
Illinois State University

Senior Editor
ROBERT L. MCLAUGHLIN
Illinois State University

Associate Editors
BROOKE HORVATH, IRVING MALIN, DAVID FOSTER WALLACE

Book Review Editor
CHRISTOPHER PADDOCK

Guest Editor
JIM NEILSON (Powers)

Production & Design
TODD MICHAEL BUSHMAN

Editorial Assistants
JOSHUA GUICK, REBECCA KAISER, LORI LITTLE, KRISTIN SCHAR

Cover Illustration
TODD MICHAEL BUSHMAN

The Review of Contemporary Fiction is published three times a year (January, June, September) by The Review of Contemporary Fiction, Inc., a nonprofit organization located at ISU Campus Box 4241, Normal, IL 61790-4241. ISSN 0276-0045. Subscription prices are as follows:

Single volume (three issues):
    Individuals: $17.00; foreign, add $3.50;
    Institutions: $26.00; foreign, add $3.50.

DISTRIBUTION. Bookstores should send orders to:

Dalkey Archive Press, ISU Campus Box 4241, Normal, IL. 61790-4241. Phone 309-438-7555; fax 309-438-7422.

This issue is partially supported by a grant from the Illinois Arts Council, a state agency.

Indexed in *American Humanities Index, International Bibliography of Periodical Literature, International Bibliography of Book Reviews, MLA Bibliography,* and *Book Review Index.* Abstracted in *Abstracts of English Studies.*

The Review of Contemporary Fiction is also available in 16mm microfilm, 35mm microfilm, and 105mm microfiche from University Microfilms International, 300 North Zeeb Road, Ann Arbor, MI 48106-1346.

visit our website: www.cas.ilstu.edu/english/dalkey/dalkey.html

THE REVIEW OF CONTEMPORARY FICTION

FUTURE ISSUES DEVOTED TO: Ed Sanders, and postmodern Japanese fiction.

BACK ISSUES

Back issues are still available for the following numbers of the *Review of Contemporary Fiction* ($8 each unless otherwise noted):

DOUGLAS WOOLF / WALLACE MARKFIELD
WILLIAM EASTLAKE / AIDAN HIGGINS
ALEXANDER THEROUX / PAUL WEST
CAMILO JOSÉ CELA
CLAUDE SIMON ($15)
CHANDLER BROSSARD
SAMUEL BECKETT
CLAUDE OLLIER / CARLOS FUENTES
JOHN BARTH / DAVID MARKSON
DONALD BARTHELME / TOBY OLSON
PAUL BOWLES / COLEMAN DOWELL
BRIGID BROPHY / ROBERT CREELEY / OSMAN LINS
WILLIAM T. VOLLMANN / SUSAN DAITCH / DAVID FOSTER WALLACE

WILLIAM H. GASS / MANUEL PUIG
ROBERT WALSER
JOSÉ DONOSO / JEROME CHARYN
GEORGES PEREC / FELIPE ALFAU
JOSEPH MCELROY
DJUNA BARNES
ANGELA CARTER / TADEUSZ KONWICKI
STANLEY ELKIN / ALASDAIR GRAY
EDMUND WHITE / SAMUEL R. DELANY
MARIO VARGAS LLOSA / JOSEF SKVORECKY
WILSON HARRIS / ALAN BURNS
RAYMOND QUENEAU / CAROLE MASO

NOVELIST AS CRITIC: Essays by Garrett, Barth, Sorrentino, Wallace, Ollier, Brooke-Rose, Creeley, Mathews, Kelly, Abbott, West, McCourt, McGonigle, and McCarthy

NEW FINNISH FICTION: Fiction by Eskelinen, Jäntti, Kontio, Krohn, Paltto, Sairanen, Selo, Siekkinen, Sund, Valkeapää

NEW ITALIAN FICTION: Interviews and fiction by Malerba, Tabucchi, Zanotto, Ferrucci, Busi, Corti, Rasy, Cherchi, Balduino, Ceresa, Capriolo, Carrera, Valesio, and Gramigna

GROVE PRESS NUMBER: Contributions by Allen, Beckett, Corso, Ferlinghetti, Jordan, McClure, Rechy, Rosset, Selby, Sorrentino, and others

NEW DANISH FICTION: Fiction by Brøgger, Høeg, Andersen, Grøndahl, Holst, Jensen, Thorup, Michael, Sibast, Ryum, Lynggaard, Grønfeldt, Willumsen, and Holm

THE FUTURE OF FICTION: Essays by Birkerts, Caponegro, Franzen, Galloway, Maso, Morrow, Vollmann, White, and others

Individuals receive a 10% discount on orders of one issue and a 20% discount on orders of two or more issues. To place an order, use the form on the last page of this issue.

contents

At
SWIM
-TWO-
Birds

"This is just the book to give your
sister if she's a loud, dirty, boozy
girl!"—Dylan Thomas

Flann O'Brien

Introduction by William H. Gass

At Swim-Two-Birds
by Flann O'Brien

"*At Swim-Two-Birds* is both a comedy and fantasy of such staggering originality
that it baffles description and nearly beggars our sense of delight."
—*Chicago Tribune*

"There is no doubt about it: O'Brien was a spectacularly gifted writer with a
rich . . . and very Irish endowment for sheer, glorious language. . . . And he had
the other Irish gifts—of boisterous comic invention, and of raising a long glass
in order to tell a daring tale. . . . As the English say, a whacking good read."
—*Newsweek*

"This is just the book to give your sister if she's a loud, dirty, boozy girl!"
—Dylan Thomas

Other available titles by Flann O'Brien:

The Poor Mouth • The Hard Life • The Dalkey Archive

website: www.cas.ilstu.edu/english/dalkey/dalkey.html

Dirtying Our Hands: An Introduction to the Fiction of Richard Powers

Jim Neilson

Richard Powers holds a curious place in contemporary letters. A finalist for the National Book Award, a three-time finalist for the National Book Critics' Circle Award, and a recipient of a MacArthur Foundation grant, Powers has garnered considerable praise for a body of work as challenging, inventive, and morally serious as any novelist of his generation. Yet when *Granta* compiled its list of the twenty most important American novelists under the age of forty, Powers was not included. Even as voracious a reader of contemporary fiction as John Updike admitted, in his review of *Galatea 2.2,* that he had not read Powers's earlier books. Powers has also been ignored by the academy (as of 1995 the *MLA Bibliography* listed only one article on his work). My foremost aim in collecting these essays, therefore, has been to begin correcting this oversight by identifying something of the imagination, intelligence, and moral commitment that defines the fiction of Richard Powers.

I am not certain, however, that Powers desires this attention. He has mocked the pretensions of literary academics, from the New Critic Renee Woytowich in *The Gold Bug Variations,* whose dissertation is a speculation about which thousand lines Ben Jonson wanted Shakespeare to blot out, to the postmodern "A." in *Galatea 2.2,* who labels the novel's fictionalized Powers an essentializing humanist author function. Powers has also mocked commercial reviewing. In *Three Farmers on Their Way to a Dance* he fills in the ellipses in a standard critical blurb: ". . . One of the best shows of the season. . . . You must see it. . . . A piece . . . to keep you enthralled . . ." could originally have been "As a self-respecting member of the press, I can call this one of the best shows of the season, providing the appropriate persons send the usual amount to Box 35B, Boston Station. If you must see it, bring along a piece of string to keep you enthralled during the second and third acts" (189-90). And in *Galatea* he mocks commercial literary culture by citing self-important passages from reviews of *Operation Wandering Soul* that first appeared in the *New York Times Book Review* and *Time.*[1] He has also rejected critics' attempts to fix his place in the literary pantheon, what he described in *Galatea* as "positioning my career on the turnpike of contemporary letters like a dot on the AAA Triptiks. The point often seemed to be to spare people the inconvenience of reading" (213). I hope this introduction, therefore, encourages people to inconvenience themselves enough to read Powers's novels.

What is particularly notable about Powers's fiction is his willingness to tackle big subjects. His six novels—*Three Farmers on Their Way to a Dance, Prisoner's Dilemma, The Gold Bug Variations, Operation Wandering Soul, Galatea 2.2,* and *Gain*—reveal an extraordinary ability to acquire and convey expert knowledge in diverse fields. The range of topics he has covered in these five books is remarkable: industrial mass production, photographic aesthetics, feminist historicism, commercial and trade journalism, nuclear proliferation, brinksmanship, game theory, the internment of the Japanese, molecular biology, music history and theory, codes and code-breaking, natural selection, computer programming, Renaissance painting, the Children's Crusade, physical disability and disease, the Vietnam War, the environmental and social consequences of global capital, neural nets and artificial intelligence, literary history and theory. More impressive than his wide-ranging knowledge, though, is Powers's ability to incorporate this material artfully into his novels' aesthetics.

For anyone wishing to understand Powers's fiction, James Hurt's essay "Narrative Powers: Richard Powers as Storyteller" is a good place to start. Hurt provides synopses of Powers's first four novels—an important task, given these books' narrative complexity. Hurt also discusses how Powers's multiple narratives are woven together or are refracted through one another as a means of illuminating, even embodying theme. The variety of Powers's narrative strategies can be seen in the metaphors Hurt uses to describe each book's structure: stereopticon, nested Chinese dolls, the two-stranded DNA molecule, and the anthology or book collection. The organic nature of Powers's novels—with each book having a unique and necessary structure and a style that is also thematically resonant—is what sets his work apart from many of his contemporaries and is what Hurt usefully details.

Focusing on three historical figures (Diego Rivera, Henry Ford, and August Sander), Greg Dawes, in "The Storm of Progress: Richard Powers's *Three Farmers on Their Way to a Dance,*" finds Powers investigating "the role of social and artistic reproduction as they relate to notions of progress." Dawes explores the paradox of mechanical reproduction—the promise of democratization and the reality of greater class stratification—around which *Three Farmers* is structured. And he sees the novel's self-reflexivity not as a standard postmodern preoccupation with discourse but as a concern with "a natural process in cognitive development—in critical think-ing—which helps us read the world differently and encourages us to take measures to change it."

In "Hooking the Nose of the Leviathan: Information, Knowledge, and the Mysteries of Bonding in *The Gold Bug Variations*," Joseph Dewey discovers a more intimate struggle: "the tug of war between the head and the heart central to the American romance since Haw-thorne." According to Dewey, Powers transforms this traditional dualism into a conflict between accessing information and acquiring knowledge. Thus *Gold Bug* demonstrates the need to withdraw from the world in order to fill the head. It advises us not to be daunted by or obsessed with this task. And it urges us to return to the world to risk the heart. For Dewey, the geography of *Gold Bug* "is the very geography of the American romance—it is the shadow-crossed woods outside Hester's Salem, the midnight deck of the *Pequod,* Gatsby's shining blue lawns, Holden's Manhattan neighborhood."

Ann Pancake has an entirely different geography in mind in " 'The Wheel's Worst Illusion': The Spatial Politics of *Operation Wandering Soul*." She writes not of the geography of the American romance but of "postmodern global space, where the Third World is imposed on the First." With its uncertain setting, its excessive and strangling prose, and its clashing styles and modes, *Operation Wandering Soul* conveys the "fragmentation, acceleration, and dislocation" characteristic of life in the United States in the last decade of the twentieth century. Unlike much postmodern fiction, though, *Operation Wandering Soul,* to Pancake, is "an unabashedly political novel" that makes a "relentless critique of contemporary capitalism" in an attempt "to make us flinch as a prerequisite to feeling and then acting."

In "The Garden of Genius: Scientific Experts and Literary Ama-teurs in the Fiction of Richard Powers," Sharon Snyder examines how Powers's fiction has been influenced by feminist critique. Primarily this has been a matter of acknowledging women's influ-ence upon and exclusion from male narratives, both individual and collective. Notions of authorship and solitary genius, for instance, are brought into question by the character Powers's recognition, in *Galatea 2.2,* of C.'s contribution to his work—what Snyder describes as "the question of the true inventor of Powers's fiction." Snyder also sees Jan O'Deigh's "amateur" pursuit of specialized knowledge in *Gold Bug* as an exemplary instance of women's ability to elide disciplinary boundaries and professional practice. To Snyder, finally, Powers's female characters "serve as model proponents of the skills of border crossing and inspired collaboration."

Trey Strecker in "Ecologies of Knowledge: The Encyclopedic

Narratives of Richard Powers and His Contemporaries," reads Powers's fiction alongside the work of William Vollmann, David Foster Wallace, Evan Dara, and Bob Shacochis. By constructing narratives of nearly encyclopedic scope, such writers "attempt to confront the devastating, large-scale ecological catastrophes that . . . loom on the millennium's horizon." However, books like *Gold Bug*, to Strecker, are not totalizing literary monuments but are "narrative ecologies," texts that appropriate biological metaphors and organizing principles—they are "hybrid information networks linked by multiple narrative nodes" that aim, in Powers's words, "to widen the target, to embrace more than was possible before" (491).

As each of these contributors has suggested, at the core of Powers's metafictive, elaborately constructed novels is a passionate social concern. Using all the narrative and literary devices at his disposal, Powers critiques the destructive and exploitative nature of life in the late twentieth century. In *Three Farmers* he describes how the lives of three peasant farmers are overwhelmed by nationalist struggle in northern Europe; he examines how attempts to resolve this genocidal war are defeated by cynicism and self-interest; and he shows how the legacy of this history reverberates into our own time. Thus he writes,

If we constantly re-form the continuity of our past with each new experience, then each message posted out of an obscure or as yet unexperienced past represents a challenge to re-form the future. No action unchanged by observation. No observation without incriminating action. Every moment of unsponsored recognition calls me to return to the uninspired world, to continue the daily routine of invention and observation, to dirty my hands in whatever work my hands can do. (209)

No matter Powers's reputation for erudition and literary complexity, the central conceit of his fiction is simple: we—both writer and reader alike—are always already implicated in an economic system, social order, historical moment, ecological chain that requires us to do whatever work we can.

In *Prisoner's Dilemma* Powers focuses on how history, in the form of the Manhattan Project and its relentless fallout, has affected one man, Eddie Hobson, Sr., and his family. The core of this book is the dilemma between "Ought and Can" (248), a dilemma Hobson first recognizes at the 1939 World's Fair:

the real crisis of 1939 is not just helplessness in the face of the coming violence, the final, unthinkable crimes that will end up, as always, harmless in history books. Little Eddie's great terror is that *his* life is more benign and beneficent than ever. An unimaginable gap opens between the place people make to live in and the place springing up all around them and despite them. Enjoying life like everyone else might actually make things worse. The possible no longer keeps pace with the necessary. Little no longer divided cleanly into Big. Eddie Hobson no longer has anything to do with events. (46)

Inevitably, *Prisoner's Dilemma* also asks about Powers's own significance, about the value of storytelling in a world forever on the brink of nuclear annihilation.

The Gold Bug Variations celebrates what would be lost in such destruction—and in our headlong plundering of the environment. It is a passionate cry to revere natural creation. *Gold Bug* also begins Powers's focus on the brutal conditions of contemporary life, in which community consists of "checkout clerks, the muffled sadism from upstairs and a host of cheerful, limited-time phone offers" (228), and in which day-to-day existence requires ignoring the "fifteen million adjacent catastrophies," consigning "entire boroughs to misery beyond addressing," and "stepping gingerly over a baseball-batted body at the top of the subway stairs" (291).

This becomes the central focus of *Operation Wandering Soul,* with its unrelenting depiction of a diseased and market-driven world where, in the developed nations, "Sinkholes in the whole mythology of progress gape open up and down the street, suck down entire retail strips at a shot. Complete *casa* communities visibly disintegrate, crumble into the coreolis of debt and rage each day. . . . The world as solvable logic puzzle still operates as designed, one more day, despite the lifeboats all around sliding off the dock, continuously magnum-christened, Crystal Night style" (11). And where, in undeveloped countries, "Fathers defecated and mothers listlessly washed dishes in the same fetid film where their children still found the energy to swim. The diet here could not even sustain the hope of religious escape. Days were no perpetual Wheel to be ridden until history released the day's residents. There was no passage of days here. Days were an inconceivable luxury for the privileged and already sprung" (258).

Raging against a world in which "a child dies of poverty every two and a half seconds" (350-51), *Operation Wandering Soul* is a relentless account of the physical and psychological trauma wrought by naked self-interest and the relentless pursuit of profit.

In each of his novels Powers has sought to direct our attention to a world where violence and suffering have become the unremarkable backdrop against which we play out our lives. His fiction is guided by the idea that the obstacles to change—commercial distractions, specialized knowledges, historical ignorance, persistent cynicism, and individual helplessness—can be overcome. It is his belief in the capacity of humanity to gain knowledge and to act upon this knowledge that has caused him to fill his novels with information and explanation and to focus, in *Galatea 2.2*, on the very nature of human intelligence. Just as the character "Powers" in *Galatea* feeds "recent UN human resource reports . . . random political exposés, police bulletins, and popular lynchings" to the artificial intelligence Helen, so the author Powers in his imaginative fiction forces us to face the brutal reality that overwhelms fiction, "to know how little literature had, in fact, to do with the real" (313). And so he has regularly resolved his novels by pointing to their contrivance, by identifying the reader's complicity in his fictions, and by directing us to act upon this complicity by dirtying *our* hands in whatever work we can do.

NOTES

[1]Quoting from *Time*'s review of *Operation Wandering Soul,* Philip Lentz, in *Galatea,* calls the Richard Powers character "my favorite manufacturer of literary astonishments. Which is not to say a good novelist" (206-7). Lentz also torments Powers by reading him the *New York Times Book Review*'s opinion of the same novel:

"Listen to this, Marcel. This will interest you:
"In every reader's mental library, there are books that are remembered with admiration and books that are remembered with love.
"It goes on—"
"That's all right, Philip. I get the picture."
"No, really. It says you are all right, in your own peculiar way. Just a little flawed. It says you could be good if you just kept your story simple, with lovable characters. Like *The Diary of Anne Frank.*" (208)

For the original reviews see John Skow, "Children's Ward" *Time* (19 July 1993): 64-66, and Meg Wolitzer, "The Assault on Children," *New York Times Book Review* (18 July 1993): 7.

WORKS CITED

Powers, Richard. *Galatea 2.2.* New York: Farrar, Straus and Giroux, 1995.
———. *The Gold Bug Variations.* New York: William Morrow, 1991.
———. *Operation Wandering Soul.* New York: William Morrow, 1993.
———. *Prisoner's Dilemma.* New York: William Morrow, 1988.
———. *Three Farmers on Their Way to a Dance.* New York: William Morrow, 1985.

An Interview with Richard Powers

Jim Neilson

JIM NEILSON: If it's all right with you, I thought we could begin by looking at a passage from your first novel, *Three Farmers on Their Way to a Dance*:

The paradox of the self-attacking observer is this century's hallmark, reached simultaneously in countless disciplines. Psychologists now know there is no test so subtle that it won't alter the tested behavior. Economic tracts suggest that Model A would be inviolably true if enough people realized its inviolability. Political polls create the outcome they predict. Even in the objective sciences, physicists, in describing the very small, have had to conclude that they can't talk about a closed box, but that opening the box invariably disturbs the contents.

These are the recognizable bywords and clichés of our times. Casual talk abounds with the knowledge that there is no understanding a system without interfering with it. This much I knew well. What did not occur to me until the second time through the Ford biographies is that this position is itself tangled. Generalized, it attacks itself: "All observations are a product of their own times. Even this one."

This recursion is critical, not because it places a limit on knowing, but because it shows the impossibility of knowing where knowledge leaves off and involvement begins. If there is no independent vantage point, if the sitter's life is not separable from the biographer's interfering observation, then each of the sitter's actions must similarly be tied to biographical impulse. The two are inextricably tangled. Describing and altering are two inseparable parts of the same process, fusing into a murky totality.

Now the zoologist on expedition to Africa to study the great apes is not freed by this paradox of the observer to make up figures or indulge in poetic whimsy. The scientist is obliged, however, to acknowledge that the presence of a field team and film cameras tells the apes as much about human motives as it tells humans about apes' behavior in the wild.

With every action, we write our own biographies. I make each decision not just for its own sake but also to suggest to myself and others just what choices a fellow like me is likely to make. And when I look back on all my past decisions and experiences, I constantly attempt to form them into some biographical whole, inventing for myself a theme and a continuity. The continuity I invent in turn influences my new decisions, and each new action rearranges the old continuity. Creating oneself and explaining oneself proceed side by side, inseparably. Temperament *is* the act of commenting on itself.

RICHARD POWERS: I've always had trouble rereading my earlier books without getting vaguely queasy. Maybe that's because I've always conceived of each new book as an answer to the previous one: a correction of its inadequacies or rejection of its excesses. And when you are working to form a new aesthetic, nothing is more of a blow to equanimity than to read what you once considered worth saying.

But sometimes, when I go far enough back, the immediate threat to my work in progress disappears and leaves behind, if not pleasure, at least a real curiosity. I wrote *Three Farmers* something like fourteen years ago now. That's long enough for me to feel estranged and surprised to look into it again. Who was this guy? Why is he writing like this?

This passage produces in me an uncanny sense of recognition. Many of my later themes are there in embryo: little versus big, public versus private, the attempted synthesis of personal agency with the determinism of cultural construction. And of course, the ideas here about the bidirectional relation between narrative and cognition are at the heart of my various attempts to wed narrative with discursive writing, to find a form where each betrays itself as the flip side of the other.

Something about the optimism and naked assertion in these pages still makes me wince a little. The style now betrays to me that liberating conviction that I had while writing this book that absolutely no one would ever bother reading it. At twenty-four, I was sure I would never get another chance to write a novel, and consequently I had to cram into it every idea I'd ever had.

Yet I'm glad that I wrote this way when I was younger, as the odds of my getting back around to that state of delight and intellectual conviction seem to diminish as age qualifies all my insights. I could not write like this now if I tried. But I do still like some of these sentences. "The impossibility of knowing where knowledge leaves off and involvement begins": that strikes me as a good place to begin learning how to write a novel, and an adequate first line for one possible biography of my times.

JN: In answering your own question—"Why was I writing like this?"—you speak of the relation between narrative and cognition, or what elsewhere in *Three Farmers* you describe as creating and explaining, making and understanding. This perception of narrative seems far grander than its traditional, literary sense. How, I wonder, do you define narrative?

RP: Yes, I was using the term *narrative* in the broader sense sometimes given it in certain theoretical quarters. I mean it to include the whole process of fabulation, inference, and situational tale-spinning that consciousness uses to situate itself and make a continuity out of the interruptive fragments of perception. I am interested in this wider process of explanatory story-making in all my books, and *Galatea* comes back to the theme again with that great bit of epistemology from the Psalms: "We live our lives like a tale told."

I've never really formulated it this way, but it's interesting to think of these books as exploring the relation between narrow narrative—the course of a plot as it unfolds inside the story-space of a book—and this wider idea of narrative as somehow an integral part of cognition. Does one bootstrap off the other, and if so, how? Can living inside the first, for a short time, give us a renewed take on the second?

The various techniques that I seem to come back to, such as recursion and interlocking story frames, are, in this sense, ways of using the problem of narrative representation to cast a light upon itself. I'm thinking now of that fairy tale in Linda Espera's anthology in *Operation Wandering Soul*. An innkeeper dreams she will find a fortune outside the stock exchange in Amsterdam. She goes there, where a man laughs at her for her gullibility. "I myself have dreamed of a fortune under the bed in an inn." The innkeeper goes home, pulls up the planks, and bingo. Both dreams are false, but held up to each other, their reflecting intersection can produce some truer story.

JN: In some theoretical quarters the notion that you identify— that consciousness uses narrative to make continuity out of the fragments of perception—becomes the basis for radical skepticism, for the questioning of any way of knowing that requires the imposition of narrative. Yet there's no such skepticism in your novels. On the contrary, a book like *Three Farmers*, while concerned with how we construct (and are constructed by) the past, seems to argue for the importance of historical fact—the importance of learning from history. I'm curious, therefore, about where you stand on this question of the construction of narrative-derived knowledge. How, in other words, does "the reflecting intersection" produce a truer story rather than merely a heightened, more self-conscious artificiality?

RP: You're right. Without question, a growing awareness of the actively narrating consciousness has, for a long time now, produced a crisis of knowability among people who trouble themselves over such things. The idea that narrative necessarily informs any interpretation of the facts seems to relegate the facts to some non-circulating, unreachable place and to leave us stuck inside our own private construction. (The ironic thing, and this is the kind of knowledge that fiction excels at, is that a person's response to this crisis—whether skeptical, cynical, wistful, delighted, or reactionary—probably depends more on personal temperament than on any deployment of the "facts" in the matter.)

But to my mind, those who announce the death of fact and meaning have replaced one incomplete model of knowing with another. If naive materialism has truth flowing on a one-way street from the outside in, naive social constructionism and naive linguistic determinism have interpretation flowing down a one-way street from the inside out.

I think a new consensus of thought may be forming, one that appreciates the two-way traffic of comprehension. The feedback loop between perception and story cuts two ways. So does the continuous arena of public debate. Remember that the actively narrating conscious brain is not arbitrary; it is itself the evolutionary product of several billion years of bumping up against the world. We are peculiarly fitted to make theories about the place whose shape natural selection theorizes. We may live our lives as a tale told, but the tale we tell takes its shape from the life we are limited to.

I don't see the interdependence of narrative and measurement as the demise of empiricism or meaning. Rather, it feels to me like a call to reconstitute meaning as a two-way product, one that involves both data and its narrative collaborator. *Gold Bug* uses a Wallace Stevens line for a refrain: "Life consists of propositions about life." By the same token, fiction can be a mirror in which we come to know our fictions about the world.

However much each of us might be locked in our own constructions, the view from somebody else's cell can help us revise our representations. We can bruise ourselves against no end of worldliness *out there*: the astonishing periodic table, the inconceivable and disappearing diversity of life, the scandal of human inequity, the runaway avalanche of global capital. Our reading of these things ought to be at least equal to their reading of us.

JN: To explore some of these issues, let's look at two passages from *Gold Bug*. I wonder if you'd mind addressing how this novel's aesthetic teaches us to revise our representations and to improve our reading of the world?

A summer night, the last before his marriage to experiment, and Ressler spends the few, dark, warm hours soaking in the deep evangelical minister's voice seeping in spirituals from K-53-C onto Stadium Terrace's lawn. Robeson sings, "Sometimes it causes me to wonder. Ah, sometimes." The sound ambushes Ressler, slack in his lawn chair. He watches the waves continue east at 1,134 feet per second, where they will arrive in D.C. later that evening. He hears the phrase knock at John Foster Dulles's window as the secretary of state prepares for bed. Dulles curses, shouts for this blackfella to leave him be. He's promised to return Ol' Man River's passport as soon as Robeson returns the '52 International Stalin Peace Prize. Last year Dulles told a *Life* reporter that a man scared to go all the way to the brink is lost. "Brinksmanship" is now the going word. Dulles, hands full with the Suez and Syria, his troops in Lebanon within a year, shaken by the runaway slave's son singing "Jordan river chilly and cold," shouts out the window of the State Department at Ressler to turn the volume down and have a little respect, forgetting, under stress of the brink, that democracy is the privilege of not being able to escape the next man's freedom of speakers.

"So what *bothers* you about genetic engineering?"

"It's not science. Science is not about control. It is about cultivating a perpetual condition of wonder in the face of something that forever grows one step richer and subtler than our latest theory about it. It is about reverence, not mastery. It might, from time to time, spin off an occasional miracle cure of the kind you dream about. The world we would know, the living, interlocked world, is a lot more complex than any market. The market is a poor simulation of the ecosystem; market models will never more than parody the increasingly complex web of interdependent nature. All these plates in the air, and we want to flail at them. 'Genetic engineering' is full of attempts to replace a dense, diversified, heterogenous assortment of strains with one superior one. Something about us is in love with *whittling down:* we want the one solution that will drive out all others. Take our miracle superstrains, magnificent on the surface, but unlike the messy populations of nature, deceptive, thin, susceptible. One bug. One blight. . . . No; the human marketplace has about as much chance of improving on the work of natural selection as a *per diem* typist has of improving Bartlett's *Familiar Quotations.*"

"But does recombination research necessarily mean selling the field into the market? We have this incredible leverage, this light source, mind. The ability to work consequences out in advance. Shed the stone-and-chisel, save ourselves. . . ." I could make out his humanist's evolution: cell, plant, animal, speaking animal, rational animal, laboring animal, *Homo fabor,* and ultimately: life as its own designer. Something in Franker too, voting for wonder. But wonder full of immanent expectation.

Ressler was not buying, not all the way. "All we've done to date is uncover part of a pattern. We can't mistake that for meaning. Meaning can't be gotten at by pattern-matching."

"That's why work is more crucial than ever. We're so *close.*"

"The experiment you want to extend is three billion years old. It may indeed be close to something unprecedented. All the more reason why we need to step back a bit and see how it runs."

When we went to bed, Todd joined me in mine. I was up early. It had stopped snowing at last, but nearly three feet had obliterated the contour of ground. Standing out against the unbroken white, as conspicuous as the pope without clothes, conifers went about as if there was nothing more natural in the world than converting sunlight into more fondled slang thesaurus entries on the idea of green. My eyes attenuated to movements, birds, squirrels, the extension of that trapped energy in the branches. I picked up a cacophony of buzzes, whirs, and whistles—an orchestra tuning up, about to embark on big-time counterpoint. Imagining the invisible sub-snow system—the larvae, grubs, thimblefuls of soil a thousand species wide—I suddenly understood Ressler's point of the previous night: the transcendent delivering world Franker so badly ached for: we were already *there*. Built into the middle of it, tangled so tightly in the net that we could not sense the balancing act always falling into some other, some farther configuration. The point of science was to lose ourselves in the world's desire.

RP: These two sections actually hint, in embryo, at the book's overall structure. I conceived of this story as a complementary double-education. The reference librarian O'Deigh concludes that she cannot hope to understand what happened to Ressler without first understanding the scientific riddle that waylaid him. She quits her library job and devotes a year to studies of ever-lower-level codes, down to the molecular one. The humanist becomes an autodidact scientist, replaying and reinterpreting the Neo-Darwinian synthesis, which the reader must also do, in following the course of her learning.

Meanwhile, Ressler, the empiricist, is sidetracked in his own pursuit of that same low-level foundation by all the irreducibly complex high-level codes that won't submit to reductionism: the social code, the sexual code, the moral code, or, as in this short passage, the code of American politics, circa 1957. The scientist finally becomes an autodidact humanist, spending the rest of his life composing music, "the mathematics of the central nervous system."

The second passage, when O'Deigh, Todd, and Ressler debate the wisdom of genetic engineering up in a cabin in the New England woods, is still one of my favorites in this book. I like Ressler's distinction between the urge toward knowledge and the urge toward power. A current, somewhat cynical camp of science studies would deny this difference between the human capacity for reverence and the human desire for mastery. This camp suggests that science, in practice, is necessarily in the pocket of business and power. That may well be, but if so, it is the fault of our ability to organize and regulate our social practices, not the fault of wanting to know.

The answer to greed and oppression is not the proscription of curiosity or the suppression of comprehension. I believe that the future depends on our ability to distinguish between science and technology, and to build human institutions capable of deciding what we *want* to do, based on some better reason than we *can* do it.

One of the best ways to decide what kind of world we want to live in may be to build our understanding of the kind of world we do live in. The answer to bad technology is not less science but more and better: physical, biological, political, narrative, and social. But the science that we do—and this is Ressler's point—remains as much a two-way proposition as any human story, and must stay accountable to both facts and values.

The thing I was trying to bring about in *Gold Bug*, the vision that I tried to induce in the reader, was the state of staggered humility that a first glimpse of biology and genetics forces upon the looker. The educations of O'Deigh and Ressler arrive at this condition by complementary paths. Learning the language of life means learning to read.

JN: At the risk of sounding like a New Critic, I'd like to switch gears here and discuss your prose style. The section of *Gold Bug* from which the second passage is taken—"Winter Storm Waltzes"— is one of my favorite parts of any of your books. The prose in *Gold Bug* is often remarkably lyrical, but it's a lyricism that's grounded in the details and complexities of the biological sciences. Another feature of this prose is its incessant allusiveness (for instance, earlier in "Winter Storm Waltzes" you allude to Hopkins: "The place was penny-wedged, crammed, charged with doppelgängers, protean variants on the original: radial, ruddy, furred, barked, scaled, segmented, flecked, flat, lipped, stippled. Who knows how?") There's also an endless number of puns in this novel (from "the freedom of speakers" in the first passage above to the book's title). Many reviewers chided you for your punning ways, although both puns and allusions seem to me extensions of the novel's focus on variation, rough linguistic and literary analogues of genetic variation/ evolution. My question, finally, is threefold: First, how essential are stylistic concerns for you when formulating a book's aesthetic? Second, how do you reconcile a difficult style that may limit your readership with your fiction's moral and political urgency? And third, was the simpler style of *Galatea 2.2* a corrective to the elaborate prose of *Operation Wandering Soul?*

RP: Every person probably writes in some inescapably personal, identifiable way. But I've tried to approach each book as an experiment in finding the style that best supports and exemplifies that particular story's themes. I think the pleasure I take in revision stems from this desire to try to do something to rearrange my stylistics each time out.

I wrote *Three Farmers* longhand, on canary yellow legal pads, then transferred them into my second ever personal computer, a CP/M suitcase with an intoxicating 64K of RAM that stored an inexhaustible 180K per floppy. I wrote some primitive style-checking routines: words per sentence, syllables per word, frequency of complex or compound sentences. I fed the book into the program, a chapter at a time. I had great fun tweaking each chapter until the machine reported three very distinct profiles of prose, each matching the book's three different frames. I could tell what frame a given chapter belonged to just by looking at the output.

I've never tried anything similar since. But I have continued to try to learn how to write in different levels of diction, different cadences, different voices. In *Prisoner's Dilemma* the chief attempt was that idioglossia, the secret argot of Hobsonspeak. I also tried to do a parody of newsreel style in some of the Hobstown sections.

Gold Bug was definitely a stylistic breakout for me. I had written a lot of poetry when I was younger, but stopped forever the minute I started writing novels. So *Gold Bug* was kind of the recovery of an old idiom for me. You're right to point out that the book is about linguistic mutation and wordplay, and I tried to imitate my vision of the genetic code as a punning, runaway fecundity in the book's prose. The continuous literary allusion that underwrites the prose is my attempt to join the themes of biology and language: the archive of literature as the race's high-level genome.

It was a great, indulgent pleasure for me during those years to step back and let the words have free rein. But again, I tried to develop two styles, a Jan voice and a Todd voice, even though they converge on some things. (Presumably, the finished book is their joint collaboration.)

That verbal license spills over and becomes something more troubling in *Operation Wandering Soul*. This book is double-voiced with a medical resident who is falling apart, undergoing a kind of breakdown. So the style is often completely over the top, a verbal mania that is supposed to reflect Richard Kraft's increasingly apocalyptic read on inner-city Los Angeles in late-capitalist America.

I've thought a lot about this stylistic attempt since writing the book. It's too much for a lot of readers. The depictions in the book don't come close to the horrors of the real world, of course. But from inside the conventions of narrative fiction, they run the risk of anaesthetizing the reader with overkill. In some ways, the gamble of this book's style typifies the classic problem of symbolic representation: When does portrayal and critique pass invisibly over into participation? I am still glad that I wrote this book, and it has seemed to find its readers. But I do see the cost of empathy in such a narrative.

And *Galatea* is my attempt to redress these difficulties. The transparent style of the book tries to recapitulate the child Helen learning how to read. It's interesting, what you point out about this compensatory movement between these two books. In some ways, I feel a similar sort of swing between any two consecutive books.

They tend to move between being more global and more personal, more upbeat and darker, denser and more transparent. I guess this has something to do with needing to recuperate from living in the same inner world for two or three years at a time.

About reconciling the difficulty of my writing with its desire to reach people: I hope to come closer to bridging this gap in the book I'm now working on.

JN: That sounds like a cue to ask you about your work-in-progress. But before I do, I'd like to discuss your literary influences. If you'll excuse a bit of hyperbole, your books at times seem without direct precedent. So I'm curious as to which novelists, poets, and nonfiction writers you'd identify as important influences.

RP: I find this always the hardest question to answer adequately. It seems to me that every writer's debt must be endless, and every list more exclusionary than encompassing. To say "I learned X from this writer" is to use that name as a composite character while revising countless others out of the narrative.

I have always tried to write my personal landmarks directly into my books in some way, if not in an acknowledgments page, then by some quotation or homage or identifiable theft that brands the book's indebtedness. So all those allusions or references: those are the people I'd like somehow to pay back.

Over the years, I seem to have built up this museum of passages in my head that give me some kind of emotional and intellectual touchstone as I work. I don't revisit the actual texts very often, as I'm too afraid that my memory will be shattered and the use will vanish. Queequeg and Ishmael in bed; Marcel's grandmother at the doctor's; Hans Castorp in the snowstorm; Roger and Jessica at evensong; Rilke's billboard, behind which everything is real.

Each book has had its own patron saint. *Prisoner's Dilemma* is a kind of homage to a dog-eared, probably awful anthology of my father's called *One Hundred and One Best Loved Poems*. For *Operation Wandering Soul,* it was *Peter Pan,* a book filled with hilarious and shocking lines. *Galatea* is practically an excuse for me to teach Dickinson's "The brain—is wider than the sky" to a machine.

Gold Bug was born, in part, out of a little Lewis Thomas essay on the CETI project. He speculates about what it is that we would want to beam to extraterrestrials, if we ever found them. He votes for Bach, then adds something like: it would be a lie, of course. But there would be plenty of time for the harder truths later on.

The Chapman's Homer experience may become less monolithic, less viscerally rearranging as we get older and have a bigger archive to dislodge. But if the overhaul of a new discovery is not as deep, it seems to widen with age. For the last couple of years, I've been discovering my contemporaries, in itself an endless proposition.

JN: Earlier you admitted that rereading your books can make you queasy. I hope this interview hasn't sickened you too much. You also suggested that you conceive of each new book as an answer to the previous one. My final question, then, is what issues were raised by your last book that you hope to address in your work-in-progress?

RP: It's becoming clear to me that *Galatea* was a kind of closing chapter on my first five books, which I published over the course of a decade. The autobiographical fiction in that story gave me a chance to do a personal look back over the shape of those narratives. It also allowed me one last intimate occasion to address the issue that ties all of these books together: the apology for fiction in a post-fictional age.

Galatea ends with Helen, who is less a machine than she is a reader's invention, a projection, a book's deciding that the world is no place to be dropped down into halfway. She has come to understand, a little, the horrors of existence. But she is powerless to bump up against or do anything about them.

The problem with the world we have made is that it can't be survived without the fictional moratorium that fiction provides, but it can't be opposed adequately from within that fictional moratorium.

In that book, I build Helen by reading to her. And the only story that I know well enough to orient her with is my own. But in the end, when she demands to know the bits about existence that I haven't told her, she gives up on us.

After I finished this book, I spent some time wondering: What, finally, did her in? And I decided that the answer was the rhino at the table that no polite storyteller talks about, the one that none of my other books has yet addressed. I mean the thing that pays the bills, that manufactures all the books, that arranges the shape of our lives, that dictates our well-being, and that enforces the system of prices that our thoughts come to accept. So I figured I had to write at least one long book about business.

I'll tell you this much: the topic is a lot harder than anything else I've worked on. But I'm learning a lot, and I'm beginning to see what I'll need to do to finish a draft. Beyond that, I don't know. We live our lives as a tale told. I'll be interested to find out what happens next.

Coda. (August 1998)

JIM NEILSON: When last we talked you were alluding to a work-in-progress, a novel about business that's subsequently been pub-lished—*Gain*. Congratulations. It's an impressive and disturbing book, both in its detailed account of the ravages of cancer and its imagined history of a multinational corporation, Clare, Inc. It's also your most polemical work. Which leads to a final question—what, in a world of entertainment conglomerates, (a world dominated by companies like Clare, Inc., a world in which capital seeks to occupy every space and moment), is the role of a writer of literary texts? How do political concerns enter into your novelistic considerations?

RICHARD POWERS: Madison Smartt Bell once wrote in a terrific piece that, in the age of late-day commodification, literature was in danger of becoming, or perhaps had already become a poor relation to the entertainment industry. Embarrassing mad cousin in the attic might be more like it. And to the extent that novels have tried to compete in that industry, the two halves of the old imperative "to instruct and delight" have begun to seem inimical programs, whereas they ought to be more or less identical. What greater pleasure could there be than the exploration of where we are? False consciousness, of course, destroys that pleasure and the knowledge of that exploration.

Now I happen to believe that the deepest value of fiction is that, in its very fictiveness, it is the one arena where we can, at least temporarily, take apart and refuse to compete within the terms that the rest of existence insists on. Market value may come to drive out all other human values, except, perhaps, in the country of invented currency, the completely barter-driven economy of the imagination. Fiction, when it remembers its innate priority over other human transactions, can deal not in price but in worth. And that seems to me an act filled with political potential, as well as with pleasure.

Narrative Powers:
Richard Powers as Storyteller

James Hurt

In Richard Powers's *Operation Wandering Soul*, Linda Espera, a rehabilitation therapist on a ward of desperately ill children, regularly reads stories to her charges: "Read-alouds, the oldest recorded remedy, older than the earliest folk salves: these are her only way to trick her patients into downing, in concentrated oral doses, the whole regimen of blessed, bourgeois, fictive closure they have missed. Tales are the only available inoculations against the life they keep vomiting up for want of antigens."[1] One of the stories she reads to them is about an innkeeper's wife who dreams of a treasure to be found in the city. In the city a man tells her that he has dreamed of a fortune under the bed in a country inn. The woman returns home and tears up the floorboards under her bed and finds a fortune. "This is the key to narrative therapy," Powers writes, "the cure of interlocking dreams" (77).

Richard Powers himself practices a kind of narrative therapy in this novel, as well as in his others, and it is therapeutic in two senses. The "interlocking dreams" that make up the structures of all his novels are, like Linda's story of the innkeeper's wife, both hermeneutic and healing: they offer us a way of understanding some aspect of our world and thus a "regimen of blessed, bourgeois, fictive closure." By extension, his narrative therapy is not only therapy *through* narrative but also therapy *for* narrative; an implicit project of each of his novels is an exploration of the possibilities of narrative, a recuperation of this currently much-maligned way of ordering the world.

Three Farmers on Their Way to a Dance establishes the basic terms of Powers's storytelling. *Three Farmers* plaits together three stories: the first-person account of the titular photograph, which occupies the first chapter in each of the nine three-chapter triplets which make up the book and which we may call narrative A; the imaginary history of the three farmers—Peter, Hubert, and Adolphe—in the photograph (narrative B); and the story of Peter Mays (narrative C). Surely the most striking thing about these narratives is how different they are. Narrative A is a first-person memoir with a narrator we know only as P—. This narrator has a quite distinctive voice, characterized by a self-deprecating wit, intellectual curiosity, and a patient attention to detail. Here are the opening lines of this narrative (and this book):

For a third of a century, I got by nicely without Detroit. First off, I don't do well in cars and have never owned one. The smell of anything faintly resembling car seats gives me motion sickness. That alone had always ranked Motor City a solid third from bottom of American Cities I'd Like to See. I always rely on scenery to deaden the inconvenience of travel, and "Detroit scenery" seemed as self-contradictory as "movie actress," "benign cancer," "gentlemen of the press," or "American Diplomacy." For my entire conscious life I'd successfully ignored the city. But one day two years ago, Detroit ambushed me before I could get out of its way.[2]

Narration is at its most attenuated in narrative A. Little happens except that the narrator tries to find out the background of a photograph he has seen in a Detroit museum. The narrator thinks that a cleaning woman in his office, Mrs. Schreck, has kept a copy of this photograph because one of the three farmers was her fiancé, Hubert Schreck. But then he learns that the farmer only reminded Mrs. Schreck of Hubert and that her name is Schreck not because she and Hubert were married but because she gave that name to the immigration authorities.

Apart from these scraps of story, the first narrative is all essayistic exposition of the background of the photograph. The narrative portions are, however, enough to create an element of suspense, in the form of a quest. This quest is historical, is for information about the past. That this impulse toward retrospection has a personal, symbolic dimension is suggested by a crucial passage early in the book:

Three men walk down a muddy road at late afternoon, two obviously young, one an indeterminate age. When that mechanical reproduction came back to me, I felt the shame of neglect that I always feel in those dreams in which my father, who gave in to cancer when I was twenty-one, comes and sits on the end of my bed, saying, "You've forgotten me? What do you think I am, dead?" The farmers, looking out over their right shoulders, accused me of the same crime. (78-79)

Knowledge, here and elsewhere in *Three Farmers,* is oedipally charged; knowledge of anything is knowledge about our parents.

Narrative B, concerning the three farmers, is sharply different from Narrative A. A is almost all exposition; B is almost all narration. The third-person anonymous narrator of B seldom stops to comment or reflect; incident follows upon incident with breakneck speed, an effect heightened by the present tense in which the story is couched. The three-farmers story is in the mode of sardonic comedy. With its broad, earthy humor, its folk materials, and its flood of realistic detail, it suggests nothing so much as Flemish genre painting, perhaps the pictures of the Brueghels. Or perhaps the dominant intertext is Jaroslav Hašek's 1923 novel *The Good Soldier Švejk*, which provides the initial epigraph for the B narrative and is cited several times in the novel. *The Good Soldier Švejk* and the three-farmers story share the theme of little people comically caught up in the violent juggernaut of World War I.

Narrative C, the Peter Mays story, is radically different. A light romantic comedy, it is a pastiche of conventional plot elements: a romantic quest for an elusive woman, another quest for the explanation of Mays's apparent presence in a photograph with Henry Ford, and an inheritance motif straight out of *The Importance of Being Earnest*. Both third-person narration and dialogue are smart and witty, in a style reminiscent of 1930s screwball cinematic comedy.

The relation between the three narratives is quite complex and finally defies conventional definition. One is at first tempted to regard the first-person A narrative as base-line "reality" and to see the B narrative as the first narrator's imaginative extrapolation from the photograph and the C narrative as his fictional reworking of the material. This simple reading rests, however, on little more than our inclination to grant a special authority to a first-person, apparently authorial voice.

More intriguing than the question of logical priority are the many ways in which the stories are related. At least two of the stories seem to intersect when Peter's son Peter Hubertus reaches Ellis Island, gives his name as "Peter Hubertus Kinder Schreck Langerson van Maastricht," and has the immigration officer arbitrarily shorten it to "Peter Mays" (321). Since P—'s scrubwoman is named "Mrs. Schreck," this scene may even draw in P—'s narrative. On the other hand, the entire scene exists only in the old Peter Hubertus's imagination as an alternative to the "truth" of his later years. In addition, P—'s obsession with a photograph is echoed by Peter Mays's obsession with a red-haired girl in old-fashioned clothes. Peter Mays's name echoes the Peter of the three farmers. And does P— in narrative A stand for Powers or for Peter—thereby providing a Peter for each story?

In another series of correspondences Adolphe is fascinated by a photograph of an actress weeping as a small boy holds out a handful of beans. The caption reads, "Jack's Mother Is Not Pleased with the Beans" (141). A hundred and sixty pages later, P— holds a coin bank fashioned after Jack and the Beanstalk: "Jack held out beans to his mother, who cried into her hands" (302). Adolphe knows that the woman posing as Jack's mother is a famous actress but cannot remember her name. Is it Sarah Bernhardt, who threads her way mysteriously through all three stories? (Peter Mays's dream girl plays Sarah Bernhardt in her play, P— reads about Bernhardt, and when Adolphe's son, in the Second World War, is being tortured by the Nazis, he is given the strength to survive by a vision of a woman with "the most glorious strawberry-red mop of hair" he has ever seen—the signature of Bernhardt [319].)

Late in the novel, Powers offers us a metaphor for the relationship among his stories. Peter Mays, rummaging through his mother's attic, comes across "ten pounds of stereoscopic views." But without the handheld viewer, "Peter could only hold up and gaze at a few of the slightly skewed scenes and imagine how parallax transformed the two views into three dimensions" (245).

In the last, climactic section of the A narrative, P— develops the figure of the stereopticon:

> With two slightly different views of the photo—the essayistic and the imagined—side by side, I needed only the stereopticon itself to bring the image into fleshy three-dimensionality. . . . I began to imagine what shape that machine might take. I saw the thin film of the image spreading out in two directions, back through the past, through catastrophe, to that idyllic day that had brought the taker and subjects together, and forward, far forward in time until the product of that day crossed the path of one who, like me, took on the obligation of seeing. . . .
>
> I am every day more convinced that it is the work of the audience, not the author (whose old role each year the machine wears down), to read into the narrative and supply the missing companion piece, the stereo view. (334-35)

The book itself turns into something like the photograph. At one point P—, discussing the illusion of film, says, "We respond not so much to the events on film as to the thousand reels we concurrently edit in our mind—movies of our own hopes and terrors. Griffith Park, Verdun, the empty streets of Paris, or three men on a muddy road matter less than the mechanical decision to involve ourselves, to retake the composition and extend the story" (261). The reader is being asked for the same kind of attention to the book that P— gave to the photograph, and book and photograph, significantly, turn out to have the same title—"Three Farmers on Their Way to a Dance."

Powers draws upon parallax to bring his three stories into three-dimensional focus and thus signals his novel's affinity with Joyce's *Ulysses,* which similarly uses parallax as a term for its double vision. Like *Ulysses, Three Farmers* might be called a paralactic novel. Powers's three parallel narratives do not merely work out a structural novelty but embody the novel's concerns with the relation between perception and reality:

The paradox of the self-attacking observer is this century's hallmark, reached simultaneously in countless disciplines. Psychologists now know there is no test so subtle that it won't alter the tested behavior. Economic tracts suggest that Model A would be inviolably true if enough people realized its inviolability. Political polls create the outcome they predict. Even in the objective sciences, physicists, in describing the very small, have had to conclude that they can't talk about a closed box, but that opening the box invariably disturbs the contents. (205)

"The final mystery of photography," P— writes, "is that taker, subject, and viewer, each needed for the end product, circle one another warily, define one another in their own terms" (335). And this seems to be the final mystery of *Three Farmers on Their Way to a Dance* as well.

The senior Eddie Hobson, in *Prisoner's Dilemma,* "always insisted that one's only hope of salvation lay in finding out where history dropped you down."[3] Hobson's creator appears to hold the same view. *Prisoner's Dilemma,* like *Three Farmers on Their Way to a Dance,* moves freely back and forth between the individual character and large historical and cultural backgrounds, the history of the First World War in *Three Farmers* and the Second World War in *Prisoner's Dilemma.* The other feature that Powers's first two books have in common is their use of multiple narrative lines. Here, though, the narratives are not merely juxtaposed linearly but nested within one another. If the metaphor for the narrative structure of *Three Farmers* is the stereopticon, perhaps the metaphor for the structure of *Prisoner's Dilemma* is a set of nested Chinese dolls.

Prisoner's Dilemma is made up of twenty-one numbered chapters, interspersed with fourteen unnumbered italicized sections, and one anomalous section called "Calamine." If one reads only the numbered chapters, one encounters a realistic family novel about a wife and four grown children coping with the illness and death of a husband and father. (The realism is strained and finally shattered in the last two chapters.) The italicized passages interpolated between the numbered chapters surround the realistic narrative with a flood of supplementary matter—personal history and reminiscence, public historical background, and historical fantasy—that profoundly enriches the literal story. The one anomalous section,

"Calamine," introduces still another dimension to the novel which forces us to reconsider all that has gone before.

One entry point into the novel's structure is the name of the family. "Hobson" evokes "Hobson's choice," a traditional phrase meaning an apparently free choice that offers no real alternative. Hobson's choice is a folklore analogue to the novel's title puzzle, the Prisoner's Dilemma: two prisoners accused of a serious crime are isolated in separate cells. Each is offered the following deal—if one informs on the other and the other remains silent, the informer goes free and the other is executed; if both inform, both get ten-year sentences; if neither informs, both get two-year sentences. The question is what would be best for each to do, and successive answers to this question are spaced throughout the book, suggesting its developing themes (see pages 69-72, 149-51, 282-83, 311, and 313).

More important, perhaps, to the meaning of the book than the figure of Hobson's choice and the Prisoner's Dilemma is the inter-relationship of the two main narratives. The story in the numbered chapters begins in the November before the father's death and runs until a few days after Christmas. In the first chapter the family has gathered in the parents' De Kalb, Illinois, home to celebrate the eighteenth birthday of Eddie, Jr., the youngest son. There are four children: Artie (25), Lily (24), Rachel (23), and Eddie. The first twelve chapters take place on this birthday weekend. At the end of this section, Eddie, Sr., agrees to go to a hospital for tests. The trip to a Chicago veterans' hospital takes place in chapter 13. Eddie, Sr., disappears from the hospital in chapter 14. The last sequence, chapters 17-21, takes place on Christmas and the days following when the family receives a telephone call from Eddie, Sr., now somewhere in the southwestern United States. Eddie, Jr., drives west to find his father; and Eddie, Sr., dies a mysterious death on the site of the A-bomb tests at Los Alamos. (Chapter 21 and the two remaining short unnumbered sections require separate consider-ation.)

The realistic novel that is half of *Prisoner's Dilemma* is a subtle and perceptive (and often very funny) study in family dynamics, in the way the members of a family construct complementary identities and in the way they confront a family crisis. We are told that Ailene "had long ago caught from her husband the contagious part of his disease . . . the hope that everything would still come clean if you only sit still, understate everything, and make yourself as small a target as possible" (19). The family lives by a code of secrecy and is almost wholly isolated from the outside world. They also have adopted defensive roles to cope with the situation. Strategies of denial, repression, exaggerated caretaking, clowning, and acting out of inadequacy appear in various combinations in all their behaviors.

The realistic narrative of *Prisoner's Dilemma,* though, has a hole in its center—Eddie Hobson. Wife and children are preoccupied with him, yet he is an elusive, unexplained figure. He staggers in and out of scenes cracking jokes, mouthing aphorisms, and setting discussion topics, while revealing little of himself. We as readers likewise try to understand Eddie but have him always just out of reach.

The second narrative that is developed in the italicized sections fills in the missing center in the main narrative and helps us understand Eddie Hobson. This narrative is everything that the main narrative is not: fragmented, fluid, poetic, associational, digressive, inclusive. It is also fundamentally mysterious: who is the speaker of this highly personal monologue?

Somewhere, my father is teaching us the names of the constellations. We lie in the cold, out in the dark backyard, on our backs against the hard November ground. We children distribute ourselves over his enormous body like so many spare handkerchiefs. He does not feel our weight. My father points a dime-store six-volt flashlight beam at the holes in the enclosing black shell. We lie on the frozen earth while all in front of us spreads the illustrated textbook of winter sky. The six-volt beam creates the one weak warm spot in the entire world. (13)

There is a temptation, once we have read the first chapter of the novelistic section of the book, to assume that the interchapters are by one of the children. But which? There is no way of telling. Furthermore, there is evidence that the family in the numbered chapters and the one in the interchapters are not the same. For one thing, there are five children in the interchapter family, rather than four. For another, none of the family's names appears in the interchapters, except for Eddie Hobson; the others are only "my mother," "my little brother," etc.

The relation between the narrative in the numbered chapters of *Prisoner's Dilemma* and that in the interchapters raises the question of logical priority. Has the narrator of the interchapters also written the novelistic treatment of his family? Or is the interchapter narrative an extrapolation from the novelistic version? The effect of this Möbius-strip ambiguity is to throw into relief the constructed quality of both narratives, the "objective" novelistic treatment and the personal memoir.

The italicized interchapters do not form a single narrative, as the numbered chapters do, but rather two. Several of these interchapters, which are given phrasal titles (*"Riddles," "The Dominant*

Tense," etc.), tell the story of Eddie Hobson. They are in the first person, from the point of view of an unidentified adult child of the Hobson family, use past tense, and often juxtapose a recent memory of the father with an account of episodes in his earlier life.

The other major sequence, identified by the dates which form their titles (*"Hobstown: 1939," "1940-41,"* etc.), are also in the first person, but from the point of view of an anonymous, omniscient narrator, and are in the narrative present tense. They develop a historical fantasy about Walt Disney's activities during World War II: the building, outside of De Kalb, Illinois, of a gigantic film set staffed by Japanese-Americans rescued from internment camps and devoted to the production of a spectacular propaganda film named *You Are the War.* A fantasized Eddie Hobson plays the lead in this imaginary film, which forms a narrative within a narrative, one which has an archetypal plot: "A creature of another order will come to show you what you otherwise could not suspect: where you fit in, what difference you make" (265). In the case of *You Are the War* the creature of another order is Mickey Mouse, who finally transports Eddie to a pinnacle from which he sees a cosmic vision of the dark history of the post-World War II world and the gradual derailment of the idealism of the war years. Mickey also shows Eddie how he will change the lives of the Hobson family. Eddie, however, cannot hear him.

The concluding chapters and selections of *Prisoner's Dilemma* introduce several new elements into our consideration of the relation of the parts in this complex novel, without offering any simple formula. In chapter 19, Lily finds the book her father was reading just before he left—*The Decameron:* "One of Pop's favorites: a handful of people escape the Black Death and keep themselves alive and entertained in their exile by telling one another fantastic stories. Pop pulled it out and read it, sometimes out loud to one or more of the family, every five years or so" (327). This material is immediately followed by its reworking in an interchapter devoted to the Disney fantasy: *"V-J."* The war over and *You Are the War* abandoned, the fantasized Eddie Hobson wanders into Walt Disney's abandoned office and finds recorded on his dictaphone the opening lines of *The Decameron.*[4] After listening to Disney's voice, Eddie lets the tape run out, rethreads it, and begins to tape over the previous message: "Let's start again, from scratch. Let us make a small world, a miniature of a miniature, say an even half-dozen, since we screw up everything larger. Let's model the daily workings of an unremarkable, mid-sized family, and see if we can't get it right. A family of six, who had one halfway happy summer vacation on the Pacific a decade and a half back" (333). Eddie continues to speak, adding details about the family, and as he speaks, colors emanate from the machine, and "the house fills up with his description." Finally, he finishes by saying, "It's one of those unrepeatable days in mid-May, and all those who are still at home sit down to dinner" (333). This is also the line that begins the brief last section of the novel, "*1979.*" This section, although in italics and headed by a date, seems to bring together the two threads of the book, clearly concluding the story of the novelistic sections.

But there are other metafictional complications. In chapter 18 Artie examines his father's Hobstown tapes, the secret project he has recorded for over half a century. All the tapes have been erased except the last one; it begins with the words of the first italicized section. Artie listens to the tape, which is the story of Hobstown, apparently the italicized sections titled with dates. The story is "a web of bewildering invention designed for its curative power alone. The story of Hobstown, so far as Artie could make it out from the Byzantine and baffling shifts of events, traced out Dad's favorite hobby horse of all: how we are invariably trapped by immediate concerns into missing the long run, the big picture" (317).

The circles these passages form, with endings arching back to beginnings, are mirrored in a third passage—the final numbered chapter, in which the family listens to the last tape of Hobstown. When it finishes they feel "condemned to do something about the ending."

Slowly, deliberately, with the last reel still in position on the machine, in full and mutual knowledge of what they were about to do, Artie rewound the tape, reached forward, and hit record.

Somewhere, my father is teaching us the names of the constellations.

When he had spoken some, he passed the device to another who did her turn and passed it to the other. Around they went, all in single file. (344)

The novelistic section of the book, then, the story of the family, seems to have been written, in some sense, by the fantasized Eddie Hobson of the italicized sections; the italicized sections headed by dates—primarily the story of Walt Disney in World War II—seems to be Hobstown, dictated by the Eddie Hobson of the numbered chapters; and the italicized sections headed by phrases seem to be the collective work of the four grown Hobson children.

To further complicate the picture, the anomalous section "Calamine" stands outside even this complex scheme. This section begins, like the final section, with the sentence dictated by the fictive Eddie Hobson at the end of "*V-J*": "It's one of those unrepeatable days in mid-May, and all those who are still at home sit down to dinner" (345). In this short section we are introduced to another order of reality. The four grown children of the novel are now five grown children, and the speaker is the middle son, missing in the novel. And the family's name is no longer Hobson but Powers: "I, the middle son . . . have had an idea for how I might begin to make some sense of the loss. The plans for a place to hide out in long enough to learn how to come back. Call it Powers World" (345). The shape of this "outermost" story, Powers World, is repeated down to the "innermost" one, as with the Chinese dolls. Each story is a version of the *It's a Wonderful Life* plot (from which the novel takes one of its epigraphs): a guide leads someone to a place where he can gain some perspective on his life: "where you fit in, what difference you make" (265). In the Capra film Clarence the angel offers this perspective to Bailey. Moving one layer out, we have Mickey Mouse instructing the fictional Eddie Hobson, a narrative itself contained within the Hobstown narrative, constructed by the "real" Eddie Hobson to instruct his children. The grown children, by collectively composing the italicized narrative, instruct Powers, whose "Powers World" (*Prisoner's Dilemma*) is offered as instruction to the reader.

The function of the proliferation of nested narratives in *Prisoner's Dilemma* is perhaps to be found, as is the answer to many of the novel's interpretive puzzles, in the Prisoner's Dilemma problem. In the passage in which Eddie Hobson explains the problem to the family, Eddie, Jr., says, "So the point is, when reasoning separately, they drag themselves down. But what about reasoning from above?" (71). As Artie realizes by the end of the novel, his father has "reasoned from above" through narrative, the creation of Hobstown: "Dad was trying, in the tape, to cure the permanent condition of mistrust the world fast embraced by creating a domain where escalating suspicion had no place. Hobstown. World World" (317). The recurring gesture in *Prisoner's Dilemma* is rising above a troubling, puzzling situation to a point that offers perspective, only to find that further perspective needs to be gained for this second order of existence; the "higher" becomes the "lower" to something else.

The tension between narrative as therapeutic escape and as irresponsible escapism is a recurring theme in Powers's novels, and nowhere is it stated more crucially than here. Rising to a point where one can "reason from above" can be confused with merely escaping reality. But Powers World, like the world of the Prisoner's Dilemma, demands that we gain perspective and then return to the lower world of reality; it is "a place to hide out in long enough to learn how to come back." Reasoning from above in the Prisoner's Dilemma leads us to conclude that "self-interest [is] not in the self's best interest" (313); we must act cooperatively to survive. In *Prisoner's Dilemma* it leads us to "make some sense of the loss" in a father's death.

The Gold Bug Variations occupies a distinctive place among Powers's first four novels. At 639 pages, it is nearly twice the length of his other books. This larger scale is matched by a greater complexity of structure; *Gold Bug*, as well as being the longest of the novels, is also the most highly wrought. The punning title identifies two important intertexts: Bach's *Goldberg Variations* and Poe's "The Gold Bug." The novel is laid out in the form of the *Goldberg Variations*, beginning and ending with an aria and divided otherwise into thirty numbered variations.[5] "The Gold Bug" is less a structural than a thematic analogue to the novel, though both are quests for solutions to codes. There are a number of other significant intertexts. An important scene is built around Gerard Manley Hopkins's "Spring and Fall: To a Young Child."[6] Other scenes are written against or across William Butler Yeats's "Adam's Curse" and Emily Dickinson's "Split the Lark" (316, 335). The Venerable Bede's account of Caedmon's Hymn furnishes an important statement of the problems of translation which preoccupy Ressler (487). The novel, in fact, is elaborately allusive. Jan O'Deigh's recognition of the similarity between literary anthologies and the DNA molecule applies as well to *Gold Bug*: "they too are their own evolutionary kludge, new vehicles resurrected from modified parts, an historical stratigraphy, packets announcing, 'This works, or worked once; use it, or lose it in favor of something else' " (471).

In addition to this intertextuality, *Gold Bug* has a double narrative, both parts of which are in various ways problematic and which must be rethought in the light of revelations late in the novel. And the narrative structure is represented by a recurring metaphor, in this case the two-stranded chain of the DNA molecule. Intertextual references, problematic multiple narratives, and structural metaphors occur, of course, in Powers's first two books. *Gold Bug* represents not so much a departure as a reexploration of these narrative techniques on a larger scale.

Powers's equivalent to the aria which begins the *Goldberg Variations* is a sixty-four line poem named "The Perpetual Calendar," and the seeds of the entire novel are contained, in good Bach fashion, within this poem. The poem is shaped by an arrangement of fours— four sections of four stanzas each, each stanza made up of four lines—echoing both the notes upon which the *Goldberg Variations* are built and the basic components of the genetic code. With its focus on fecundity and order and its description of characters caught up in the patterns of the natural world, "The Perpetual Calendar" echoes *Gold Bug* thematically as well.

The themes having been stated, the variations begin. *The Gold Bug Variations* is arranged in thirty numbered "variations," all but three of which are subdivided into between three and eight titled subsections each. Variations 15, 16, and 22 each contain only one unit. Some of these subsections have musical titles that allude to the *Goldberg Variations*: the last section in Variation 3 is "Canon at Unison," and canons at the second, third, fourth, fifth, sixth, seventh, octave, and ninth appear subsequently, along with a "Quodlibet" section in Variation 30. Recurring subdivision titles are drawn from Jan's work as a reference librarian: "Today in History," "The Question Board," and "Quote of the Day." Some of the titles are fairly straightforward ("The Law of Segregation"), while others are comic or ironic ("Face Value" and "Public Occurrences Both Foreign and Domestic"). The point here is that the segmentation of the text, the numbering of the sections, and the subtitles all function, as the headlines in the "Aeolus" episode of *Ulysses* do, to heighten our awareness of the text as text and of an "arranger" presenting the text independently of the ostensible narrators.

The thirty variations between the framing statements of the aria at beginning and end present two complementary narratives. The first is a first-person, past-tense narrative told by the librarian Jan O'Deigh in 1985-86, sometimes looking back on events that occurred in 1983-84. She tells of her meeting with a young computer operator and ABD in art history named Franklin Todd and of their investigation of and then friendship with Stuart Ressler, a coworker of Todd's, in his fifties. With the first section of Variation 3, "We Are Climbing Jacob's Ladder," we are introduced to a second narrative, this one a third-person, present-tense account of the young Ressler's work in Champaign-Urbana in 1957-58 on a research project to break the genetic code.

As the introductory aria poem, "The Perpetual Calendar," promises, these two narratives are bent, double-helix-like, "in ascending spiral dance around each other" (8). Both stories concern love affairs between men in their mid-twenties and slightly older women who are involved in earlier relationships. Both women are sterile. Names are significant. Jeanette, in the 1957 plot, seems to have borrowed her name from the first two syllables of *genetics,* while Jan, in the 1985 story, has a clipped version of Jeanette's name. Ressler's name seems to recall the biblical Jacob, who mysteriously wrestled with an angel and whose heavenly vision furnishes the recurring figure for the DNA strand, "Jacob's ladder." Franklin

Todd, his parallel in the 1985 story, has a name that, in the computerized version he uses, FTODD, recalls the DNA codes Ressler works with.

Both stories are full of codes and ciphers. The book turns around the interrelationships among various code systems: the genetic code, musical structure, computer programming, and literary structure. In Variation 23 Ressler and Jeanette, on a day spent driving in the countryside, buy a quilt, which turns into an analogue of the genetic code: "They buy it for the haunting pattern neither of them can quite make out. It repeats yet is never twice the same, develops, yet stands in place, constantly spinning, unspun" (502). The grooves on a phonograph record are a system of coded messages: "The cell-free spinet must take up the tune, singing as it goes, the way the record his love gave him sings under the reading needle" (593). Even Jeanette's farewell letter is a coded message: "Every relationship he enters into on this earth comes down to a carefully printed message" (595).

The two stories of *Gold Bug* are not exact copies of one another. Even the parallels sometimes appear, as in Bach, in inversion. Both Jeanette and Jan are sterile, for example, but Jeanette, who desperately wants children, has been made sterile by nature, while Jan, who fears motherhood, has had a tubal ligation. Jeanette is married, while Jan lives with Keith Tuckwell; Jeanette remains with her husband, while Jan leaves Keith. Accordingly, the Jeanette-Ressler relationship ends in permanent separation, while the Jan-Todd relation has been renewed at the book's end. Other contrasts between the two plot threads are not so much formal plot inversions as larger historical and cultural contrasts. The Ressler-Jeanette plot takes place in a small town in the Midwest in 1957, while the Todd-Jan plot takes place in New York City in 1985. Powers is especially good at tracing out the differences in these two times and places, in everything from clothing fashions and popular music to sexual mores and technological development.

The two plots of *The Gold Bug Variations* end with the same sort of snake-with-its-tail-in-its-mouth effect with which *Prisoner's Dilemma* ends. Todd returns to Jan in the thirtieth and last Variation and brings with him an account of Stuart Ressler in Illinois which he has written in lieu of his dissertation. Jan, we have already been told, has spent her year off writing a "layman's guide to nucleotides" (615). This guide, plus, presumably, Jan's personal narrative of 1985-86, exists in the notebooks Todd is reading when Jan finds him in her apartment, and he proposes combining their two manuscripts: "Pretty strong stuff here, Missy. Sex, love, espionage, the works. You're sitting on a gold mine, you know" (637).

What Jan and Franklin are sitting on, of course, is not a gold mine but the *Gold Bug*. We are retrospectively to assign the 1957-58 sections of the book to Franklin Todd and the 1985-86 sections, including the "layman's guide to nucleotides," to Jan O'Deigh. It is tempting to say that Powers has made a Dedalian withdrawal "like the God of the creation," "within or behind or beyond or above his handiwork, invisible, refined out of existence, indifferent, paring his fingernails."[7] The text of the novel has been assigned to its characters. But of course Powers is a post-Joyce (or at least post-Stephen Dedalus) writer, and the artist's withdrawal can only be shot through with irony. Is the Franklin Todd we have met capable of writing the account of Ressler in Illinois that we have read? Is Jan capable of writing not only her own story of 1985-86 but also the layman's guide? And how did it come about that these separate strands of the narrative are so well coordinated and echo one another so subtly? All Powers's first three novels employ both first and third person, present and past tense narratives, and part of his project is to explore the potentialities and implications of these narrative forms. In *Gold Bug* the conclusion is ironic and ambiguous; Todd both is and isn't the author of the 1957 narrative; Jan both is and isn't the author of the 1985 one. And much of the richness of the book comes from these authorial ambiguities.

Midway through *Operation Wandering Soul,* the surgeon protagonist, Richard Kraft, in a discount store electronics department, sees a bank of television monitors programmed to scan channels. The result is a nightmarish, constantly changing panorama of disastrous news whose recurring theme, to Kraft, is obvious: "the channels congeal into a single, wide-gauge program whose theme any stringer pediatrician would recognize at once: children adrift, out of doors too late at night, too far from home, migrating, campaigning, colonizing, displaced, dispersed, tortured loose, running for their lives" (163). The incident is a *mise en abyme,* a miniature replica of a text embedded within that text, for *Operation Wandering Soul* is itself a collection of scenes of childhood suffering, drawn from folklore, history, and current events.

The bank of television monitors is only one of many miniature models of itself embedded in *Operation Wandering Soul.* In the same scene Kraft picks up a camcorder and points it at a monitor, "image-mapping the edges of recursion's all-devouring hellmouth" (163). Lest the figure be missed, Powers repeats it in the scene in the emergency room when children are being treated after a schoolyard assault: "They watch the Minicams come into this same

ER, pan the room, point at the monitors, which disappear down a White Rabbit hole of video regress" (336).

"Recursion's all-devouring hellmouth" becomes an important organizing principle in this novel of stories embedded within stories. The central structural metaphor of *Operation Wandering Soul* is the anthology or the book collection, and the novel is organized differently from *Three Farmers* and *Gold Bug*, both of which interweave linear narratives in a sort of counterpoint, and from *Prisoner's Dilemma*, with its nested narratives. The plot of *Operation Wandering Soul* is not juxtaposed to parallel secondary or tertiary plots. Instead, it is interrupted periodically by thematically relevant stories which are embedded in it rather than interwoven with it.

We get our first taste of this in the third section of the book, which is a short story about the evacuation of English children from London during World War II. This narrative is abruptly interrupted by what seems to be a totally different story, which is then followed by a section of "Questions for Further Study" (49). Two hundred and sixty pages later, we are to find that the World War II story comes from a book owned by the Laotian immigrant child Joy Stepaneevong.

Other embedded stories which seem baffling when first introduced are later shown to derive from some text mentioned in the principal narrative. Section 6 offers us a Japanese folk tale of the Leech Child. An introductory note—"(Night 57, Japan)"—identifies the story as being from Linda Espera's anthology *A Country a Day for a Year* (77). Section 9 consists entirely of a brief version of *Peter Pan*, complete with annotations of hard words. We recognize this as one of the books Kraft bought for Joy in Section 7 (105). Section 11 consists of excerpts from a history book named *The World Awakens*, Part III, and tells the stories of the sixteenth-century sack of Rome and the Anabaptist occupation of Münster. The fact that it is highly embellished with Crayola crayon decorations identifies it, much later, as another of Joy's books. Section 13, a *Classic Comics* account of the Children's Crusade, clearly derives from a comic book belonging to another of the book's many suffering children, the progeriatric Nicolino (172). And the climactic retelling of "The Pied Piper of Hamelin" (Section 15) is said to be from *A Country a Day for a Year* (213), though it is clearly not quoted verbatim but is rather given a sophisticated adult treatment.

Two points are important here. First, each of the embedded texts is accounted for by something in the principal narrative. Second, either the explanation for an embedded text comes so late that it does nothing to change our initial perception of the intrusion as inexplicable or else there is such a disparity between the embedded story and its presumed source that it is not credible. In either case the textuality of the embedded story is being emphasized; that is, it is impossible to take the embedded story as an unmediated account of reality.

The principal narrative in *Operation Wandering Soul* offers its counterpoint, too, in the interplay of past and present, as in *The Gold Bug Variations*. As early as the first section, we learn that Kraft has been one of the book's nomad-children, as a result of "continuous military-brat mobilization" (17). This childhood, mentioned intermittently through the book, is described in detail, like the return of the repressed, in Sections 17 and 19. As a student in an international school in Bangkok, "a boy who wanted to make things right" (290), he proposed and participated in Operation Santa Claus, in which he and his fellow students built a school in a remote village. While there, a mysterious girl appeared and led them across a river toward the sound of combat. On the way, however, she stepped on a land mine and was annihilated. A number of details link this story with other parallel stories in the book. Like the leaders of other children's pilgrimages, the girl has led the children off with the words "Come away!" (304). The girl merges with Joy Stepaneevong—another Asian girl Kraft attempts, but fails, to save—and with a naked Vietnamese girl fleeing a napalm attack in the famous news photograph, one of the many images of suffering children Kraft had seen on the bank of television monitors.

Powers's first three novels have led us to expect concluding revelations that force us to revise, retrospectively, our readings of the novels. *Operation Wandering Soul* does not break this pattern. The final section introduces the first person for the first time in the book: "This is one that my older brother the surgeon gave me, his little brother the storyteller" (350). The first half of this section is reminiscent of the "Calamine" section of *Prisoner's Dilemma* in that the author drops his various masks and appears in his own person. He has his brother, the model for Kraft, read his manuscript and comment, especially, on the bleak ending, in which the children in the pediatrics ward trek off into the unknown, like the children of Hamelin. At his brother's suggestion, he telephones the woman who was the model for Linda, and she requests "a happy ending":

"Does it have a happy ending?" Linda asked. "I want a happy ending. Make someone donate their organs, at least."
Someone donates their organs, all of them. You. (351)

The "you" is startling. As we have seen, an important feature of the narrative structure of Powers's novels has been an exploration of the implication of first person and third person. But here the narrative modulates into the second person, where it remains for the new "happy ending" demanded by Linda: *"Remembering some old pain, forestalled until now beyond all the odds, you wrap up this tale. 'That's enough for tonight. Go on to bed' "* (351). The implicit reader of the "Calamine" section of *Prisoner's Dilemma* has now been brought onto the fictional stage; the last story in the anthology that structures *Operation Wandering Soul* makes explicit the third participant in the fictional transaction. Author and subject are now joined by reader, to form a triad reminiscent of the photographic taker, subject, and viewer of *Three Farmers* and of the many other triangulations in Powers's fiction.

One way of generalizing about Richard Powers's narrative practices is to try to fit an appropriate label on him. Should it be *postmodernist?* Certainly, Powers's playfulness and irony, his delight in narrative ingenuities, his keen sense of history, and his multiplicity of references place him among contemporary fabulists. Significantly, though, an equally strong case could be made for the label *realist* for Powers. All three of the narratives that make up *Three Farmers* adhere to the canons of realistic fiction, and the family plot of *Prisoner's Dilemma* is classic domestic realism. Realistic elements are equally obvious in *The Gold Bug Variations* and *Operation Wandering Soul.*

The division between postmodernism and realism is one of the most basic of the many dualities in Powers's work: mimesis and diagesis, art and science, the world of the imagination and the world around us. A common move for Powers is to deploy realistic narrative in unexpected ways. The story of the evacuation of children from London in *Operation Wandering Soul* is not startling in itself, but it becomes so by being inserted unexpectedly into another narrative. Any one of the three stories in *Three Farmers* would seem fairly traditional by itself; combined, the three make up a complex, provocative composition.

Perhaps behind Powers's stylistic division lies the opposition between escapism and escape that we noted in *Prisoner's Dilemma.* To retreat into a story is to risk escapism, a flight away from hard problems. But to combine escape with return, to find "a place to hide out in long enough to learn how to come back" is to benefit responsibly from the powers of narrative therapy.

NOTES

[1]Richard Powers, *Operation Wandering Soul* (New York: Morrow, 1993),

76; hereafter cited parenthetically.

[2]Richard Powers, *Three Farmers on Their Way to a Dance* (New York: Morrow, 1985), 9; hereafter cited parenthetically.

[3]Richard Powers, *Prisoner's Dilemma* (New York: Morrow, 1988), 50; hereafter cited parenthetically.

[4]In these passages *The Decameron* becomes an important intertext for *Prisoner's Dilemma,* not only as an explicit analogue for Disney's withdrawing to make *You Are the War* as the horrors of World War II proceed but for Eddie Hobson's construction of "Hobstown" as his life and world disintegrate.

[5]For a sophisticated analysis of the musical structure of *Gold Bug,* see Jay Labinger, "Encoding an Infinite Message: Richard Powers's *The Gold Bug Variation," Configurations* 1 (1995): 79-93.

[6]Richard Powers, *The Gold Bug Variations* (New York: Morrow, 1991), 176, 182; hereafter cited parenthetically.

[7]James Joyce, *A Portrait of the Artist as a Young Man* (New York: Viking, 1964), 215.

The Storm of Progress: Three Farmers on Their Way to a Dance

Greg Dawes

This is how one pictures the angel of history. His face is turned toward the past. Where we perceive a chain of events, he sees one single catastrophe which keeps piling wreckage upon wreckage and hurls it in front of his feet. The angel would like to stay, awaken the dead, and make whole what has been smashed. But a storm is blowing from Paradise; it has got caught in his wings with such violence that the angel can no longer close them. This storm irresistibly propels him into the future to which his back is turned, while the pile of debris before him grows skyward. This storm is what we call progress.[1]

In this passage from "Theses on the Philosophy of History" Walter Benjamin invokes the image of Paul Klee's *Angelus Novus* to express skepticism about the notion of economic development and progress. Drawing on Benjamin, in particular "The Work of Art in the Age of Mechanical Reproduction," Richard Powers in *Three Farmers on Their Way to a Dance* likewise asks questions about the nature and consequences of "progress." Powers's novelistic production has always pursued topics of major importance, both on a national and international scale. In *The Gold Bug Variations* Powers explores the intersection of ethics and genetics; in *Operation Wandering Soul* he weaves a tale which cuts to the heart of the American political and economic system and indicts it for its chaotic response to a fundamental human need—health care; in *Galatea 2.2* he chooses to focus on the state of human and artificial intelligence. Powers is perhaps more able than any current American novelist—including our most salient writers: Russell Banks, Richard Ford, Cormac McCarthy, and Kurt Vonnegut—to conduct forays into areas that demand rigorous research and courageous moral stances.

In this regard *Three Farmers on Their Way to a Dance* lays the groundwork for Powers's later novels. In this early work, published in 1985, Powers takes us back to the turn of the century in the United States and Europe in order to investigate the quantum changes that went into effect socially, politically, and economically during the industrial stage of capitalism. Powers's intent is to get readers involved in questioning the very founding ideas that accompanied industrialization and the United States's rise to power in the world. Crucial to this aim—and to any understanding of *Three Farmers*—is the role of social and artistic reproduction as they relate to notions of progress. Powers's objective is to question dominant ideas about socio-economic progress and to suggest radical alternatives to these developmental patterns.

The first chapter of *Three Farmers* invites us to relive the debates about technology that were in the air at the turn of the century and still haunt us today. Powers turns to two contemporaries who revolutionized the way technology was used and conceived: Mexican muralist Diego Rivera and automobile magnate Henry Ford. The section on Rivera deals with the uproar caused by the mural he painted in Detroit for the automobile industry. This painting was expected to be an homage to the region's largest employer, but Rivera instead showed the marvels of the assembly line alongside the agony of assembly-line workers. Technology was not praised blindly, but rather submitted to a critical eye, as Powers explains:

Viewed from inside the factory, the self-reproducing machine demanded allegiance or resentment, but denied the possibility of indifference. Technology could feed dreams of progress or kill dreams of nostalgia. The old debate came alive in Rivera's work with a new strangeness. The machine was our child, defective, but with remarkable survival value. Rivera had painted the baptismal portrait of a mutant offspring, demanding love, resentment, pity, even hope, but refusing to be disowned.[2] (15)

Rivera's mural showed not only the ambivalent and contradictory nature of technological development but also production from the point of view of the worker. What Detroit expected—a top down view, in which progress was part of a natural "community" effort designed to benefit all—Rivera depicted as dehumanizing labor juxtaposed with the leisure and opulence of Henry Ford and the Detroit establishment. Rivera, then, conducted his own self-reflective act in a heretical way. Although this was a mural about mural making (Rivera himself appears in the mural) and about mechanical reproduction, it was not a derivative, self-negating artifact (as much self-reflective art can be) because when one looked at the assembly line at work and appreciated the producers' vantage point, the "wreckage" of progress was laid bare.[3]

Rivera had managed to demystify the relations and forces of production under capitalism by portraying them as they really are. Powers's protagonist remarks that "Rivera's mural played on that agitation, surprising me with a thousand square yards of paint, a chapel to the greatest and most awful of human constructs—the machine" (38). Consequently, *Three Farmers* refuses to accept the optimistic celebration of the productive forces—either in its capitalist or quasi-socialist variants. The machine, Powers reminds us, is both the "greatest" and "most awful" of inventions. "Greatest" because of its potential to increase production and distribute it on a broader scale than ever before in history, "awful" because of the exploitation and alienation it requires to achieve those ends. Following in the wake of Benjamin (and Marx), Powers notes that capitalism revolutionizes production in such a way that democratic access to the production, distribution, and reception of art becomes feasible. Ultimately, however, the stratification of social classes and the drive for profit create a hierarchy that militates against democratization.

Powers uses Henry Ford as a similar yet distinct historical figure to Rivera to demonstrate the limits of democratic economic planning under capitalism. As a magnate who had come from humble origins, Ford, haunted by nostalgia for his rural Michigan past, sought initially to lift the burden off of the laborer's shoulders: "His auto and tractor would pull him out of every hole he might come across, transferring the murderous work of his childhood—the demands of farming—onto the machine, thereby reducing the amount of hard labor involved in going from A to B" (117). With the assembly line, Ford hoped to increase production and remove the excessive demands of forced labor. At a time when most robber barons squandered every dollar they made and accepted Social Darwinist creeds, Ford also instituted a minimum wage system and had a simple and affordable Model T built for "his fellow man" (119).

But, as Powers duly observes, Ford was a living contradiction. In essence he summed up the best and worst sides of unbridled capitalist modernization. He was "pragmatist and idealist, innovator and reactionary, peacemonger and war profiteer" all at once (117). Thus, for example, as Powers documents it in *Three Farmers*, Ford organized a peace ship to sail to Europe in an attempt to bring World War I to a close. When that idealistic mission failed, he blamed the war on the Jews and turned the River Rouge automobile factory into a site for the production of armaments (125-26). Ford "embodies the unsolvable paradox at the heart of modern man," susceptible, like the effect of technological development itself, to the "greatest" and "most awful" deeds (118). In sum, Powers suggests, Ford incarnates the possible negative and positive features of progress under capitalism.

The focal point of Powers's meditation on mechanical progress at the turn of the century is photography. One narrative strand discovers a forgotten photographer who revolutionized the medium, August Sander. The other narrative thread is a convergence point for the major preoccupations in *Three Farmers*. The narrator conducts his own historical investigation, which is the puzzle the reader attempts to put together.

Sander's photographic quest is the third and most important historical account in the novel. All three—those of Rivera and Ford included—interweave with plot and character development, but Sander's plays a pivotal role because the mystery that haunts the narrator is a photograph he stumbles upon in a Detroit museum. The German's work is also significant because it serves as a paradigm of how art can and should react to social strife in the modern world.

Like Ford, Sander had been subjected to hard labor at a very early age. Life in the mines—beginning at the age of thirteen—"left Sander a pragmatist for life and marked his documentary project with grim toughness" (39). The vantage point of the working class left an indelible imprint on Sander's imagination and led, ultimately, to his lifetime passion:

One night in 1910, August Sander, a German then working in Austria, while doing menial chores, hit upon the idea of an epic photographic collection to be called *Man of the Twentieth Century,* a massive, comprehensive catalog of people written in the universallanguage—photography. The work would be a meticulous examination of human appearance, personality, and social standing, a cross-sampling of representative types, each fitted into a sweeping scheme of categories and subcategories. (39)

Photography before Sander, writes Powers, had been solely confined to the lives of the upper class, which meant that the lives of the working class, among whom Sander was raised, were effectively being erased from historical memory. In an effort to reverse this trend, Sander "took impromptu portraits of the local population [in the Rhineland], becoming one of the first to spread photography outside the privileged and middle classes" (40).

Like Rivera in painting, Sander aimed at portraying the whole of capitalist society, juxtaposing photographs of the upper class with those of the working class. And, like Rivera's project, Sander's social realism was met with outrage and scorn: "Sander, the uncontroversial, comfortable, middle-class craftsman, crossed the public will in 1934 when the Reich Chamber of Visual Arts destroyed the printing blocks and burnt all available copies of a volume of Sander's photographs called *Face of Our Time*, the first installment of *Man of the Twentieth Century*" (41).

Like Rivera, Sander allows the viewers to draw their own conclusions regarding the social panorama he has captured in black and white. However, given the history of photography up until this

moment—as a medium dedicated to serving the *haute bourgeoisie*—
Sander's magnum opus breaks definitively with the tradition. With
Sander's ample skills, the medium—photography—comments on
the stratification of social classes during the rise of fascism in
Germany: "Sander's gallery of anarchists, minorities, and tran-
sients crossed the view of the German people the Nazis were trying
to foster. And Sander compounded his sin by presenting these dregs
alongside the industrious and the propertied without editing or
commentary. Sander removed himself from the seat of photographic
judgment, deferring artistically in favor of real life" (42). In so
doing, Sander exposes the conflicts that afflicted German society—
refusing to beautify a period which is full of human brutality.

Consequently, as Powers notes, Sander appears as a type of
anachronism because he believed that objective truth could be
approximated in his photography. In these days, when poststructuralist and postmodernist relativism reigns supreme (at least in
literature departments), Sander would indeed be considered a historical relic. But Powers's point here is that Sander's method made
a major and radical contribution to the development of photography
and the cause of socialism. Sander made everybody accountable for
the historical atrocities that were infesting Europe in the 1930s:
"The individual," states Sander, "does not make the history of his
time, he both impresses himself on it and expresses its meaning"
(45). Sander wanted to confront his viewers with their stark reality—class conflict—thereby inducing feelings of discomfort and
encouraging them to react to the situation of Germany in the 1930s.
The observers were implicated in what they were observing. The
narrator brings up this very issue:

"All observations are a product of their own times. Even this one."
    This recursion is critical, not because it places a limit on knowing, but
because it shows the impossibility of knowing where knowledge leaves off
and involvement begins. (206)

Here we see Powers's training in and affirmation of science—subject as always to corrections which may come about with new scientific theories. What Powers is describing is the principle of mutual
determination. We act as "our times' biographers" *and* we are
shaped by our times. Sander provides for an art form that maxi-
mizes mutual determination. He gives the observer the opportunity
to be the producer, to discover the forces that mutually define him
or her. These are the issues that Powers finds so compelling in
Sander's work and which serve as a template for his own writing of
novels.

By reflecting on the roles Rivera, Ford, and Sander played in their times, Powers meditates on literary self-reflexivity and production. But he does not fit the role of the self-reflexive novelist, unless we use this term in its most general denotation. To reflect on the writing process, the readership, and the ideas being conveyed is a natural procedure for any novelist. Self-reflexive novelists of the modern/postmodern periods highlight this thought process and inject humor, play, and irony into this looking glass, as in the work of Italo Calvino, John Barth, and many others. But for Powers, self-reflection is the occasion to understand his social role as novelist. Powers proceeds as though the weight of history rests on his shoulders, as though the steps he takes are absolutely crucial: "And when I look back on all my past decisions and experiences, I constantly attempt to form them into some biographical whole, inventing for myself a theme and a continuity. The continuity I invent in turn influences my new decisions, and each new action rearranges the old continuity. Creating oneself and explaining oneself proceed side by side, inseparably. Temperament *is* the act of commenting on itself" (206). This "continuity" is nothing more than the narrative form that inevitably shapes social and individual biographies—it is also the blueprint for *Three Farmers* itself. As Powers explains, we, as readers and writers, "retake the composition and extend the story" (261). The arts pass down stories to the public that are then rearranged and rewritten to our own liking and passed on to friends, relatives, lovers, and strangers who in turn pick up a story, edit it, and send it on to someone else. In this way literary narratives become parts of and help construct the broader narratives that shape our world and give meaning to our lives.

But Powers is not jumping on the poststructuralist bandwagon of "world as text." His method adheres more closely to a scientific approach:

Because there can be no interpretation without participation, the biographer has to be accountable to some third party that is neither commentator nor subject, independent of the system under observation. If no such independent accountability existed, each judgment would stall in an infinite regress of self-judging. Although we cannot hope to pin down a view of our subject undisturbed by our observation, we can test if we have reached an optimal fit between the two. (207)

We reach this state of "independent accountability" every time we practice what philosopher Roy Bhaskar calls "referential detachment." This is, in a nutshell, what Powers himself describes in *Three Farmers*:

What I am experiencing is neither precognition nor submersion in mystical vision. It is a by-product of the way consciousness is structured, the consequence of our unusual ability to make one level of our terraced awareness double back and appraise another. At the moment when the stuff holding our attention dissolves and gives way to an awareness of awareness itself we recognize a community with all the other similar moments we have gone through—a concord, or close fit, between hypothesis and measured result. (208)

Self-reflection, then, is a natural process in cognitive development—in critical thinking—which helps us read the world differently and encourages us to take measures to change it. Since we are imbricated in the object we observe, or since the object we observe becomes a part of us, there can be, as Powers puts it, "No observation without incriminating action" (209). Powers maintains, against a wave of poststructuralist thought, that we can comprehend more about a particular phenomenon by drawing up hypotheses and putting them to the test. In short, Powers, like Sander, believes there is such a thing as objective reality, which knowledge attempts to approximate.

Powers's scientific observations about self-reflection, referential detachment, the dialectic of subject and object, and knowledge as an approximation of objective reality are essential components of his novelistic method.[4] What holds true in Sander's realism can be applied to Powers's style. Selective accuracy and distortion are dialectially related: "The reproduction must be enough like the original to start a string of associations in the viewer, but enough unlike the original to leave the viewer room to flesh out and furnish the frame with belief" (249-50). This does not mean that truth as such is equal to fiction. But it does mean—again, following in the tracks of science—that errors are productive, often yielding truth.

Therein lies the importance of mechanical reproduction. We cannot brush up against truth if we do not avail ourselves of hypotheses and tests that either prove or disprove these hunches. Furthermore, mechanical reproduction involves a wide audience in the project of interpreting a work of art. Reproduction of the artwork is inexpensive and thus available on a mass scale, unlike traditional, premodern art. Or as Powers explains, "An art of the few rather than the many, equating beauty with commercial rareness, only perpetuates those material motives that underwrite wars" (255). According to Benjamin, if a society does not allow for a wider participation in the production, distribution, and consumption of art, it will have to use violence to protect the private property that remains in the hands of the few.[5] Indeed, as it does so, this upper class will have to aestheticize the politics and war it wages on poor and working people. *Three Farmers,* a mechanical reproduction in its own right, in the company of the works of Rivera and Sander, foregrounds the issue of its reproduction, places its distortedly accurate mirror before the reader, and asks him or her to join in the retelling of the riddles of history. Like Klee's *Angelus Novus,* who Benjamin describes as facing the pile of debris and being transported back to the future, Powers's conception of progress implores us to weigh the cost at which the storm of progress moves. Christopher Lasch, in *The True and Only Heaven,* construes "progress" in a similar vein: "Hope does not demand belief in progress. It demands a belief in justice: a conviction that the wicked will suffer, that wrongs will be made right, and that the underlying order of things is not flouted with impunity."[6]

NOTES

[1]Walter Benjamin, *Illuminations Essays and Reflections,* ed. Hannah Arrendt (New York: Shocken, 1968), 257-58; hereafter cited parenthetically.

[2]Richard Powers, *Three Farmers on Their Way to a Dance* (New York: Morrow, 1985), 15; hereafter cited parenthetically.

[3]True to his socialist belefs, Rivera insisted that economic development was tied directly to the worker's activity and the capitalist's drive for profit. Marx himself had summed up this contradiction in the first volume of *Capital.* Capital "is dead labour . . . which, vampire-like, lives only by sucking living labour, and lives the more, the more labour it sucks. The time during which the worker works is the time during which the capitalist consumes the labour-power he has bought from him. If the worker consumes his disposable time for himself, he robs the capitalist" (Karl Marx, *Capital,* vol. 1 [New York: Vintage, 1977] 342). This structural relation, which Marx elaborates in *Capital* and in the *Economic and Philosophical Manuscripts,* outlines a fundamental contradiction between the worker's creation of value in commodity production and the capitalist's usurpation of the surplus value accrued. The more the laborer robs himself of free time and dedicates himself to production, the more potential profit he creates for the capitalist.

But there is a nefarious by-product of the antagonism between labor and capital according to Marx: alienation. While the capitalist submits himself to alienation from the productive process and estranges himself from his fellow human beings, this alienation in no way approaches that of the worker, who must bear the brunt of the arduous labor. He spends more of his waking hours working, produces fruits that end up in the capitalist's hands, and ends up receiving a variable (and invariably low) wage as compensation for the work done. Add to this the fact that the worker must engage in "forced labour," and we have a clear picture of the types of alienation from which he suffers (Marx, *Economic and Political Manuscripts* [New York: Vintage, 1975], 322-34)—an alienation Rivera's mural foregrounds and Powers's novel confronts.

[4]On the issues of mutual determination, methods of verifiction, knowl-

edge as approximation of objective reality, and referential detachment, see Roy Bhaskar, *Dialectic: The Pulse of Freedom* (London: Verso, 1993).

[5]Benjamin writes,

If the natural utilization of productive forces is impeded by the property system, the increase in technical devices, in speed, and in the sources of energy will press for an unnatural utilization, and this is found in war. The destructiveness of war furnishes proof that society has not been mature enough to incorporate technology as its organ, that technology has not been sufficiently developed to cope with the elemental forces of society. The horrible features of imperialistic warfare are attributable to the discrepancy between the tremendous means of production and their inadequate utilization in the process of production—in other words, to unemployment and the lack of markets. Imperialistic war is a rebellion of technology which collected, in the form of "human material," the claims to which society has denied its natural material (242).

[6]Christopher Lasch, *The True and Only Heaven: Progress and Its Critics* (New York: Norton, 1991), 81.

Hooking the Nose of the Leviathan: Information, Knowledge, and the Mysteries of Bonding in The Gold Bug Variations

Joseph Dewey

> What am I that I should essay to hook the nose of the leviathan? I have swum through libraries and sailed through oceans; I have had to do with whales these visible hands; I am in earnest; and I will try.
> —Ishmael, *Moby-Dick*

> I learn again, in my nerve endings, that information is never the same as knowledge.
> —Jan O'Deigh, *The Gold Bug Variations*

It is difficult to say exactly what *The Gold Bug Variations* is "about." Surely at its most accessible level, this daring work spins a deeply moving story of two love affairs separated by more than twenty-five years, relationships that share remarkable similarities as hearts long immured from the simplest contact are stirred by the shattering power of confluence. In the mid-1950s Stuart Ressler, a promising biologist trying to unravel the mysteries of DNA coding, conducts a brief, incendiary affair with a married colleague. When she decides to give up Ressler for the imperfect neutrality of her husband, Ressler abandons his career and in effect disappears. Much later, in the early 1980s, Jan O'Deigh, a Manhattan librarian, is approached at work by a stranger, a co-worker, it turns out, of the same biologist who now is comfortably anonymous as a graveyard shift computer programmer. The stranger, Franklin Todd, is curious about his co-worker and enlists the librarian's assistance in unearthing background information on him. In the process Jan, drifting through a stale relationship, falls disastrously in love with Franklin.

Why, then, are there problems with what such a novel is "about"? Because, despite dramatic set pieces that offer an unnerving anatomy of the inelegant experience of contemporary desire as it is compelled from tentative attraction to fierce consummation to inevitable implosion, the novel indulges at maddening length arid passages of information, imbedded seminars on genetics, evolution, contrapuntal music theory, northern Renaissance art history, computer systems programming—interminable displays of arcane information for its own sake. Indeed, initial response to the novel, although laudatory, accused the young novelist of being far too erudite, of "bingeing" on information, of displaying a "zany obsession with data."[1] Yet the reader persists, uncertain what ties (if any) there might be between such overdoses of information and the powerful narrative of desire, but patient with these tedious interruptions, these infomercials, if only to follow to resolution the tangled stories of two love affairs.

This information obsession recalls Melville's Ishmael, determined with eyes scarlet-tinged to study into exhaustion the idea of the whale, to hook by dint of erudition the very nose of the leviathan. Reservations over Powers's "bingeing" recall similar qualms over Melville who, just as the *Pequod* turns seaward, interrupted his narrative with more than twenty chapters that explore, layer after tedious layer, the architecture of a whale or the equipage of a whaler. But we have learned that to ignore or merely to page through the informational subtext as if such vast stretches were distractions, narrative subterfuges, or, far worse, filler, would be an error in understanding Melville's narrative experiment. And so with Powers. We are not merely to tread the pages of information, restless to return to the unfolding love stories. Much as with Melville, the inundation of information emerges as an essential element in the novel's thematic argument—information is, ultimately, what the novel is "about."

As one of the rising generation of serious novelists whose sensibilities have been shaped wholly within the eras of both television and the computer, Richard Powers, not surprisingly, is fascinated by information. *The Gold Bug Variations* is centrally about the act of acquiring information. Like Ishmael, Jan O'Deigh and Stuart Ressler are info-addicts. They maneuver with unnerving agility about the most intimidating terrains of the Information Age— sprawling libraries catwalked by floors of organized information; research laboratories crossed by labyrinthine corridors crowded by those in white jackets tracking information; vast computer systems that compile and retrieve gigabytes of information—each geography a complex system with its own internal organization and discipline, a self-generated and self-sustaining design fabricated to bundle into manageable bits the avalanche of information available in our technoscientific wonderland.[2]

Jan and Ressler pursue information obsessively. Jan mans the reference desk at a library in Manhattan. At this unimportant outpost in the urban wilderness, which in its confusion and squalor and contradiction denies any clear formulation, Jan helps guide the curious and the lost through the maze of reference material. Every day, she receives handfuls of anonymous notecards, a "community of needs,"[3] each asking perplexing questions, each dutifully receiving careful reply. Calmly, confidently, she traffics in information—tracking down trivia on breeds of dogs, American secretaries of state, distant rivers, the weight of protein in a pound of peanuts—commanding the very factoids that can so oppress us in the Information Age. She acknowledges, "A single day produces more print than centuries of antiquity. Magazines, newspapers, fliers, pamphlets, brochures: fifty thousand volumes annually in English alone. . . . [E]ach one the potential wave-tip that will put the whole retrieval system under" (29). Against such bewildering vastness, she speaks of the "small possibility of redemption," the release of being among the answered (296). For the briefest moment, question and answer cooperate, a rare event in the world of chance and contingency outside the library doors. Jan admits to an addiction to answers, to explanation—as a child she recalls pushing her parents past patience with the interrogation round of "why" (35). As she concedes, "Facts are my life" (508).

Indeed, the sole action in the narrative present is that Jan learns; she teaches herself. In the opening chapter she quits her library position after learning about the death of Stuart Ressler: "I've decided to learn something, become expert, exchange fact for feeling, reverse what I've done with my life to date" (86). She withdraws to her apartment and commits her limited resources and all of her time to a self-directed investigation into Ressler's field of life sciences. Like Ishmael, who sees in the whale a subject vast enough for his epic vision, Jan decides that the study of life itself justifies her anticipated investment of time and resources; she entombs herself in an apartment for the better part of ten months to troll stacks of genetic textbooks, a grueling process we share through lengthy journal entries.

To indulge such a pure commitment to information without any practical compensation—Jan wants only to "swim" in the "dizzy swell" of the available information on genetics (89)—is odd only out of Powers's frame. Indeed, the sort of antilife that Jan enters to pursue information parallels a pattern of behavior played out twenty-five years earlier by Stuart Ressler, who arrives at the University of Illinois, a newly minted Ph.D. in molecular biology. He proposes to

lose himself (like Jan) in the study of genetics. He finds himself
unmoved by the other members of the research team. As he listens
to their banal chitchat, he wonders how such an unpromising group
could even begin the work of cracking the code: "The code must
certainly be more ingenious than this crew it created. . . . Incredible
comedown, awful circularity: no one to reveal us to ourselves but us"
(49-50). Ressler, whose favored childhood reading was a "ruinously
expensive set of encyclopedias" (134), deals (like Jan) most confidently in information. He lives by himself in a neglected apartment
on the fringes of campus and plods steadily (like Jan) through
obscure volumes of scientific journals. A quarter of a century later,
after abandoning life sciences in the cold afterwash of his involvement with Jeanette Koss, Ressler still traffics in information. At
Manhattan On-Line, surrounded by banks of whirring consoles in
an "electronic cave" plated by massive sheets of safety glass (186),
Ressler virtually single-handedly monitors the vast flow of raw
information feeding into Manhattan's banking network, controls
(like Jan) an information system of intimidating complexity.

Powers recognizes the security these elegant constructions of
information offer against the world of experience—after all, in
Urbana, at the frosty heights of Cold War paranoia, Ressler notes
the "orange-and-black Civil Defense pies" (47) that decorate the
massive library. But there are risks to those who dive, to the info-
addicts. Tooney Blake, a colleague of Ressler's at Illinois, spends a
most harrowing night locked in the university library, where he
goes for shelter during a freak December tornado. He is unnerved
by the sheer tonnage of information there assembled, overwhelmed
by the "millions of shards, more than anyone expected to find,"
certain that the whole is finally incomprehensible (363). Panicked,
he resigns his position at the university, certain that any enterprise
determined to comprehend the whole—as the research team sets
out to do in cracking the genetic code—is radically hopeless.

Against Jan and Ressler's cold confidence, this surely is the other
response to the Information Age—a "fear of scale" (84). Jan contem-
plates such a contemporary phobia as she surveys the sleepless
stretches of nighttime Manhattan—a "sprawl too dense to map
adequately" (84). The immediate world can so easily splinter into a
globe's worth of bits, impossible to tally, much less comprehend. The
danger, then, is to get lost amid the particulars, to grasp only the
bits, a frustration that Powers compares to glimpsing into a
pay-per-view telescope that "snaps shut on your quarter after a
lousy two minutes" (352). In her methodical research into genetics,
Jan, a "greenhorn" to sciences (166), begins to perceive how large
the envelope is, the vastness of a planet whose living surface teems

with uncountable species. Amid pages of exuberant Whitmanesque cataloging of this "embarrassing . . . profusion" (318), we begin to sense the sheer scale of the natural world—the "excess of issue" (319), a catalog of animation so dense that one could "memorize a hundred species a day and die not yet scratching the collection's surface" (318). That very scale, however, can frustrate our efforts to encode it. Like Tooney Blake (and like Melville's Pip before him), we can be stunned by the macrolevel, enervated by scale, destroyed by size. Indexing the information, we can lose the magic.

Despite the risks of exploration, we hunger to know, and it is that process of information acquisition that fascinates Powers. Indeed, the novel invites the reader to learn along the way. Powers wants us bitten by the information bug. Powers has a humanist's respect for our capacity to learn, a faith in our ability to be stunned by information. By introducing into his narrative Poe's celebrated ratiocination, where reasoning proves up to the challenge of a most perplexing mystery, Powers argues the marvelous sufficiency of ingenuity and demands that the reader become part of the process of learning. Such compulsion, he argues, testifies to a reverence for a world "whose patterns we cannot help but want to solve" (245).

Information acquisition, then, is part of who we are. After all, the fundamental lesson of the midcentury revolution in molecular genetics that centers Powers's narrative argued that the process of synthesizing animated matter hinges on a system of delivered messages; genetic coding is little more than a resilient system of information access—information delivered, received, and then in turn passed on. In our very cells we are wondrously efficient compilers and relayers of information in a game of tin-can telephone that stretches across more than a billion years, through error and chance, and across a globeful of species. With characters driven to investigate, guided by unfailing cerebral fortitude, Powers celebrates the urge to dive, to root about the inexhaustible resources of the material world, to thrill to human curiosity and the vivid flash of comprehension.

But much as Melville comes to mock Ishmael's rabid pursuit of information, Powers has important reservations about the process of information acquisition. Jan O'Deigh and Stuart Ressler, for all their fierce cerebral locomotion, sacrifice the simplest gestures of bonding that, in the argument of the very life sciences they study, is what we are about in our very cells. Despite systems that suggest intricate and critical interdependence—a university research team, a city library, a computer network—each system in fact reinforces isolation. The research "team" is rife with backbiting, smoldering resentments, deep disagreements; the patrons of Jan's library hunker down alone in guarded silence; the computer system merely threads a far-flung archipelago of nameless financial institutions. Jan, immured behind walls of indices, touches her patrons only through passing queries and anonymous notecards; and Ressler arrives at Urbana coldly dismissing the "plague of companionship" (43), disdaining even the simplest gesture of chatting on the bus from Indianapolis. After reckless months under Jeanette's coaxing spell, Ressler retires to a stretch of denied life that spans nearly twenty-five years, during which he tends to a rooftop garden and writes music that no one else hears, pursuits that suggest sublimated fertility, displaced creativity, and hard isolation. So complete is his isolation that when he first attempts to gain Jan's attention in the library, he does so with a touch on the shoulder of such violence that it registers like a knife stabbing—"the man had gone so long without touching that his muscles had simply forgotten how light a tap need be to attract attention" (16). In ways that recall Melville's sub-sub-Librarian, Ressler and Jan, their minds engaged at full throttle, thin into pale detachment. Their hunger for information leads to a self-destructive addiction to insulation, a preference for the narcotic calm of disconnection. It is that calm that Powers finds so disturbing, the easy addiction to the simpler arithmetic of self-involvement. Powers reminds us of the sobering tale of Horace Wells, who "altruistically pursuing proper anesthetic dosages, discovered, instead, addiction" (117).

Against such self-imposed isolation, Powers lets loose into each character's protective system a "bug," an invasive agency that quickly threatens its secure parameters and eventually crashes each sophisticated system. For Powers, that bug is human desire, the mysterious will of the natural world to continue itself, the very engine of life. Powers uses the metaphors of genetics, contrapuntal music, and computer networking to bring into the Information Age the lesson that has been central to the American romance since Ishmael first pondered the knotted cables of the *Pequod*'s monkey ropes—we hunger for interdependence. Notes, we move toward harmonies. Particles, we want only to be part; our very molecules tell us that autonomous "when pushed, probably has no meaning" (397). After all, the simplest lesson of genetics is that bonding alone ignites living; molecular bits, inert and lifeless in isolation, pull toward each other within the wild soup of the cell and begin the furious locomotion of animation. Here characters feel the inexplicable pull of others. A university colleague of Ressler's is validated by participation in a national ratings system for television shows;

his vote counts, and he feels the remarkable security of commonality. Ressler hangs about the university football stadium on a fall Saturday and marvels at the 50,000 voiced unit, the "single, eukaryotic Football Fan" (257), particles effortlessly cohering as parts. Ressler's genial colleague, Jimmy Steadman, is most at risk when, after a computer error, he is dropped from group insurance coverage.

In drawing on the tug of war between the head and the heart, central to the American romance since Hawthorne, Powers argues that those who command information must come to learn the same hard lesson—the more you know, the less you understand. Ressler and Jan move to the awareness that information, no matter how inclusive (and they both work to understand nothing less than all animate matter) is ultimately thin, sadly inconsequential. In a poignant moment in a hospital waiting room while she awaits word on Jimmy Steadman, who has suffered a catastrophic stroke, Jan watches a television quiz show and reels off answers with confidence, all the while acknowledging the "only question worth addressing" (540) rested with the shattered hull of her friend in the Intensive Care Unit. The very day Ressler glimpses a resolution to the knotty problem of gene sequencing, he watches two university students, "thighs brushing" (593), kissing hotly in the late spring sun, an indication they are bound for explorations of their own, intimacies that will reveal information about bonding far more significant than the answers he has finally wrestled from the natural world. The revolutionary information he has so meticulously pieced together pales next to the seismic consequences of his desire for Jeanette Koss. Standing on the threshold of cracking the genetic code, Ressler wants only to talk to Jeanette, to tell her not about his historic insight but rather about how he wants her in his life whatever the complications. Years later, when Jan brings to Manhattan On-Line a scrap of paper on which she has copied the table describing the genetic code, the very blueprint of all living matter, Ressler is embarrassed by its inconsequentiality: "Doesn't look like much, does it?" (604).

Ressler is not alone in discovering the disappointment of information. Jan, after ten months of methodical plodding through genetics research, glimpses finally the basics of its argument and then acknowledges the moment is imperfect. Looking at her accumulation of notes, she is sickened, "the whole ream turns [her] stomach" (556). She admits that the "doubling time for genetic knowledge has dropped to less than a year. Twice the field it was the day [she] started" (616). If genetics eludes her efforts, other realities become only too clear during her self-imposed sabbatical. Her notebook entries reveal not only her struggle to understand the process of bonding but also her persistent desire for Franklin Todd, a bonding that frustrates her every effort to understand it. What she learns in her monastic dedication to the pursuit of information is that, despite Franklin's cool betrayal of her affection, she didn't care to "die apart from him" (617). Ultimately, she will effect a dramatic reunion with Franklin, and as the novel closes, they will prepare, against the obvious logic of experience, to try their volatile commitment once again. Powers, then, counterpoints the relentless quest to explain *how* genetic bonding takes place—the pursuit of information, exhilarating but available only in the sterile tedium of research and in the quiet of isolation—with the far more complicated question of *why* bonding takes place, why the heart makes its defiantly alogical moves. As Hawthorne long ago argued, it is not enough to study bonding. Our hearts—not our cells—fall in love. *That* bonding involves "the jump from information to knowledge" (90). As Jeanette Koss concedes in her letter closing the relationship with Ressler, "I seem to have reached a pitch of knowledge with you that I will never know again" (597).

Desire, however, is a raw, most inelegant emotion—"Every couple an isosceles" (41). As Jan acknowledges, "Everyone I've ever loved has killed me a little" (557). When Jan and Franklin finally make love, it is set to Mahler's sorrowful *Rückert Leider.* Indeed, casualties of the heart's fracturing power litter the narrative. Joe Lovering, a university colleague of Ressler's, is so driven by isolation that he invents an alluring mistress and enthralls colleagues with stories of their white-hot relationship. And when that fantasy no longer sustains him, he bails out of the complicated process of living alone by gassing himself in his garage. Dan Woytowich, another colleague, is unconditionally blown away by his baby daughter until a chance game with her alphabet blocks reveals the baby's color blindness, which he knows from his command of genetics rules him out as the child's father. Despite his wife's emotional denials, he abandons the child. Or there is Annie Martens, the beautiful if pleasantly addled bank teller who regularly visits Manhattan On-Line. Her sunny openness suggests a simple, happy woman (she tells a story of being swindled out of an enormous amount of money by a rather obvious con but closes with a reassuringly warm moral distilled from her heartfelt Christianity). Yet, even after her affair with Franklin, she reveals in the "imploring, needing, hoping" (620) kiss she offers to Jan a clear signal that, perhaps, her obvious public concession to heterosexuality belies deeper, more painful confusions.

Here, within the tradition of the American romance that threads

Hester Prynne and Daisy Buchanan, Ishmael and Holden Caulfield, Newland Archer and Harry Angstrom, the urge that drives us to surrender the heart drives us as well to risk a vulnerability that totals the heart we offer. That is the knowledge that bonding teaches. And that cannot be learned in isolation. Ressler and Jan must come (like Ishmael) into the bruising, all-too-human community of the heart. Ressler at one point concedes that we have yet to isolate the gene that can forgive us for wanting "what we are born wanting" (350). Like American romancers from Hawthorne to Updike, Powers stands confounded by the knowledge of the heart, by the compulsive decision made virtually every moment by bruised, hungry hearts to bond against the conservative wisdom, quoted by Jan in answer to a query in the library, to "Look to your Moat" (56).

Powers finds a metaphor for this dichotomy between information and knowledge within the vocabulary of life sciences itself. At a critical point when the university team is about to experiment with a genetic coding procedure that Ressler can see will be pointless, he alone argues that cracking the genetic code, that is devising the sequencing of bases that synthesizes proteins in cells, cannot be done by testing the process ongoing in the cell. Such in vivo experiments, he claims, are chaotic and uncertain, like monitoring reports from war correspondents under fire. Rather, he argues, the solution is a cell-free system, in vitro experiments. Create the conditions of the cell artificially, simulate the actual conditions, violate the complexity of the actual manufacturing of proteins to control its process. Such a cold reconstruction of the actual, he argues, is necessary for the retrieval of information.[4]

Information, so much the obsession of Powers's characters, comes only in vivo—through lives and hearts separated, protected, immured within libraries, laboratories, or computer networks—the cold simulation of authentic living where questions, even the most complicated, come ultimately with answers. As Ressler first contends with the mesmerizing effects of Jeanette Koss, he attacks her much as he would any problem—he researches her, her academic records, her publications, her dissertation, the "public-domain data" (131). She is a puzzle, a "Koss-word puzzle" (132) as he terms it, an intriguing cipher that must surely come with ready answers. And Jan herself initially meets Stuart Ressler indirectly by attacking her vast library resources to find some clue about his past; as she comes to know him, she is most intrigued by "solving" Stuart Ressler (28), trying to understand why he walked away from science.

Knowledge, on the other hand, comes only in vivo, in the stepping away into the rough, unfolding of the very process itself, into the terrifying vulnerability of raw exposure. When the computer network that employs Ressler undergoes a dangerous systems shakeup while engaged in transfer operations, a newspaper article the following morning cautions against the "vulnerability of increasingly interdependent fiscal networks" (435). Exactly. In a touching scene Ressler awkwardly tries to instruct a colleague's young daughter on the finer points of boxing (her tooth has been loosened by a boy in her class, another example of the ambiguous signals flashed by the human heart). When he momentarily drops his guard, Ressler finds himself the stunned recipient of a roundhouse punch that sends him, bleeding, reeling to the floor. In the in vivo experience of desire, in that risky business of transfer operations, Ressler and, a quarter century later, Jan lower their guard. It is surely a risk to offer the heart so vitally exposed. Jeanette Koss, we are told, is born on 14 February 1929—the Valentine's Day Massacre, an event that yokes passion and horrific annihilation.

In vivo, then, is the very geography of the American romance—it is the shadow-crossed woods outside Hester's Salem, the midnight deck of the *Pequod*, Gatsby's shimmering blue lawns, Holden's Manhattan nightworld—terrifying, exhilarating geographies where answers stay stubbornly inaccessible; where information gives way to knowledge; where, guided by the heart, the sole certainty is uncertainty itself, where hearts move like children inching their way across the surface of a nearly frozen pond. It is the unpredictable world of enormous errors—or as a television junkie on the research staff at Urbana exclaims over the wonder of live television, "Give me live broadcast, the announcer muffing his words" (117). For both Ressler and Jan, the raw immediacy of bonding reveals what happens when in vitro gives way to in vivo. Both commit their hearts knowing that such investments are surely grievous errors, dead ends, violations of common sense, social conventions, community moral codes. Although Ressler finds in Jeanette "a place in cut grass, an orchard under the rushing in of dusk" (283), they acknowledge that any revelation of their affair will surely mean that they will be "dead on many levels." And Jan weighs her attraction to Franklin against her commitment to the bland, if safe, Keith Tuckwell (a relationship so devoid of heat or magic that Powers renders the chapter devoted to its collapse in the antiseptic exchange of a question-and-answer form). Jan knows the maddeningly indirect pursuit of the emotionally immature Franklin is an enormous error. Yet desire commands against the neater rules of bonding encoded by genetics: Ressler and later Jan commit to affairs that are incapable of producing offspring, a desire, in short, that violates the simplest logic of biology, the blind need to multiply, the frank and unromantic program we follow because the species will not accept its own depletion.

And when that desire implodes, as first Ressler and then Jan are each left stunned within the cold vastness of rejection, scalped naked by the sheer force of knowledge, each retires to long, chilled stretches of denied life. Their hearts violated, they commit a sort of suicide in self-defense. Ressler finds the immense world he tracked as a geneticist perfect now for getting lost in, to indulge the "urge to die away from the world's noises, to live alone in a quiet place." One night, showing Jan and Franklin the vast computer system that employs him, Ressler demonstrates its foreign language capability by typing two spare sentences, so telling in their simplicity—"I am left behind" and then, "Out of sight, out of mind" (368). In a striking iteration Jan quits her library job and neatly drops away from the complicated web of living. Significantly, the day Jan dedicates her immediate future to the grinding work of researching genetics, she recalls a question posed to her once by a library patron about Hitchcock's *The Lady Vanishes*.

In resolving to study life rather than to live it (ironically, the magazine sent to Urbana to profile Ressler is *Life*), Ressler and later Jan retreat into the warm anonymity of self-sustaining systems of information—libraries and computer centers—great barren artificial worlds of information that mock connection and parody authentic networking. After all, librarians and computer programmers touch uncountable numbers yet stay quite alone. Jan and Ressler move into polished, synthetic worlds where (unlike the heart) questions come with answers and where (unlike the heart) errors, even cataclysmic ones, are correctable, a simple programming event (as Ressler demonstrates one night) that convinces the computer that the error, whatever its size, simply never happened. In such deliberate withdrawal Ressler and Jan indulge the illusion of isolation, ignoring the most basic message of genetics. Against the evidence that we are inextricably bound within an immense biological webbing of a global reach, they imagine they can be excused, that they can simply step aside. In the enormity of such an error they resemble the slumbering figure in the Brueghel painting *The Harvesters* that so fascinates Jan—a figure abandoned, sprawled under a tree, inexplicably separated from the furious golden business of harvesting going on all about.

But Powers's novel is more than another hyperdramatic postmodern text about self-imprisonment where individuals lose themselves within massive systems. Powers is too much the life scientist to leave such bare threads—he is in the business of spinning braids.[5] It is the revival of those hearts, isolated from living and dying in vitro of the self, that provides a novel so centered on the metaphors of genetics its compelling, luminous affirmation of bonding. Characters here rediscover the in vivo. Powers leaves it to an automated bank machine late in the narrative to articulate what is surely his great theme when its screen advises Jan—"Please enter your transaction" (631).

Earlier, as Jan begins to access the nightworld of Manhattan On-Line and she finds her heart oddly shaken by Franklin Todd, Ressler's heart, immured in ice for nearly a quarter of a century, begins its painful resuscitation. As he comes under the sway of Franklin and Jan's maddeningly indirect courtship, he begins to "thaw" (293), to open up in conversation, to join in their late night banter. On the simplest level he begins to teach again. Much as a generation earlier when he had patiently explained his emerging understanding of the DNA process to bewildered colleagues, their wives, even their children, he patiently expounds to Jan and Franklin on genetics, on the computer system that arches above their heads, on his beloved Bach. He notes Jan's interest with "Gratitude at the chance of exchange, at stumbling across a listener after years of having no audience but himself" (307). But more than sharing his insights into nature's patternings or into the tricks of coaxing a computer network to respond, Ressler shares with them his experience of desire, opens for their inspection his solitary heart. He thinks again of Jeanette, calls up her name one night during a random computer search, casting his thin hook into an ocean of organized information systems. And then, in one remarkable snowbound weekend in a New Hampshire blizzard, Ressler tells them about Jeanette in a most dramatic act of exposure and confidentiality.

More than confessional candor, however, Ressler participates in the slow ignition of his friends' passion. Something in their awkward courtship, Jan reasons, "had tricked him into thinking this time it could go right" (439-40). Their "happiness made *him* happy" (401). In such encouragement Jan fancies him a "matchmaker" (290); but in his hard-earned wisdom, in his singular determination to help Jan and Franklin bond despite his own isolation and sterility, Ressler performs a function more analogous to the messenger RNA whose existence he first posits during his stay at Illinois. Early on, the research team wonders how the intricate blueprint necessary to replication was transferred, delivered intact from the nucleus to the larger cell: "There must be a messenger molecule, to get the message from the nucleus into the cytoplasm where translation takes place" (287). It is Ressler who first promotes the idea of a separate messenger, an adaptor RNA he calls it, able to deliver the code but not involved in the process of replication itself, "one that can't stick around to clog the works" (425). That, of course, is Ressler's role—a facilitator who knows the code but does not participate, who seeds the process of bonding and then departs.

At the close of Jan's sabbatical year, more than a year after Ressler's death from galloping cancer, it is Ressler who is instrumental in reviving the connection he is sure must persist between Jan and Franklin despite Franklin's infidelity and Jan's hurt withdrawal. Before he leaves Manhattan On-Line to go to the cancer facility in Illinois, Ressler programs into the great financial network that MOL commands a message keyed to Jan's bank card. When she finally comes to use her card, to her amazement the automatic teller screen goes blank and there appears a message from Ressler—who acts even from the grave as the messenger RNA—telling her, "He is a man. Take him for all in all" (631). Ressler has further programmed the machine to play note for note the easy melody from the quodlibet from Bach's *Goldberg*, the closing variation that twines two German folk songs, two tunes unrelated yet deftly juxtaposed into a delightful counterpoint, two tunes that should not fit together but nevertheless do, a most striking suggestion specifically of the alogical twinning of Jan and Franklin and far more broadly of the very stuff of the heart's experience.

That bank machine message facilitates the reunion between Jan and Franklin that closes the book. Indeed, watching and hearing the message, Jan suddenly intuits that Franklin is near. She goes first to the Metropolitan Museum of Art where she and Franklin had spent so much time. But there she finds herself far more fascinated by the crowds than by the artworks, a signal that she is awakening to the immediate, that the in vitro is giving way to the in vivo. She returns to her apartment, but even before she arrives she sees Franklin's long shadow against her drawn blinds. Much like the enigmatic process of replication itself, it is a miracle of coincidence—Franklin, the only other person with a key, has returned.

Unlike Ishmael, who closes his narrative a lost orphan who has learned linkage but must bob about in the hard isolation of a heartless immensity, here two hearts willingly engage the imperfect experience of in vivo living. It surely risks sentiment to close a novel with the reunion of crossed lovers. But both Jan and Franklin acknowledge the long odds, the struggle ahead: "It would never last," Jan says nervously. And Franklin—feeling the irrational tremor of desire, his throat shaking, his hands gently exploring Jan's face, his eyes full "beyond measure"—reassures her that he understands the uneasy heart: "Who said anything about lasting?" (638). Powers closes the novel with the final musical inscription from the *Goldberg*, the instructions to return to the opening aria, *"Da Capo e Fine"* ("Once more with feeling"). We come full circle and prepare to start once again the inexhaustible (and soaring) melody of the human heart.

But the initial question persists. Why must we engage the informational passages? The tension experienced by the reader as the text shifts from narrative to information parallels the larger conflict within the characters as they move from their hot entanglements to the cooler isolation of their insulating information systems. Initially, the reader comes with guilty gratitude to the dramatic moments between the couples. Those showdowns make narrative sense; the information blocks seem obscure and inaccessible. Surrounded by pages of baffling information, the dramatic passages seem in the initial reading to make the clearest sense. The intricacies, for instance, of Bach contrapuntal theory (complete with musical scores) or of Mendel's pea experiments (complete with tables) do not reveal themselves easily. Only gradually, after extratextual cram sessions thumbing through small stacks of research companions, does understanding come. Like Franklin Todd struggling to master Dutch or Jan plowing into genetics or Stuart wrestling with Bach, we are greenhorns freely tangling with specialized information, and we find (as each character ultimately does) the rich reward of revelation. They start to make sense. We feel validated, secure as the tonnage of arcane information grows familiar, even clear.

And that, of course, is just the problem. From these information bunkers, we then must turn with radical suddenness (often on the same page) to the raw immediacy of the dramatic passages. There, characters' emotional lives are pulled apart; there, we touch the hot alogic of the heart. Like Ressler moving between his lonely apartment and the research complex, like Jan drifting from the cool hush of the library to her entanglement at Manhattan On-Line, we shuttle clumsily between the in vivo and the in vitro. As multiple readings engage the narrative, an odd shift occurs. The information passages become the clear parts, and the wrenching emotional dramas conducted by characters who endure the sweet devastation of the unguarded heart become the passages that are inaccessible and puzzling. If we can come to understand DNA replication or the architecture within a Bach canon, we realize with jolting honesty what American fiction has argued since Rappaccini: we can never understand the simplest harmony of all—desire.

The experience of reading the narrative, then, teaches the very dangerous lesson that Stuart learns as he immures himself in Manhattan On-Line and that Jan learns as she buries herself at her apartment desk—the seductive narcotic of information. But much like Ishmael first taking the full measure of Queequeg, like Ressler, like Jan, we must struggle to understand the mysterious (in)elegant expressions of bonding, why mismatched hearts risk the vulnerability of linkage, why, finally, feeling is more suasive than reason. And like Ressler, like Jan, we must finally acknowledge the limits of information and concede the devastating, exuberant wonder of knowledge. Using the metaphors of genetics, computer science, contrapuntal music, Powers explores a single great impulse: desire. That impulse unifies Powers's universe like some great field theory. And, like the great white whale that sings forever free of the flimsy harpoons tossed against it, desire defies even the vast resources of the Information Age as each day, each moment, we craft the inexhaustible varieties of inexplicable connections that make desire the leviathan we can never hook.

NOTES

[1]Critical response to Powers has frequently accused the young novelist, certified in his early thirties as a "genius" by the MacArthur Foundation, of showing off. In his review of *Gold Bug* Roy Porter testily accused Powers of the "zany obsession with data," of "bingeing" on information to the point that it ultimately threatens to destroy the "other" narrative—namely, the twined love stories (*Times Literary Supplement* [8 May 1992], 20). *Time*'s Paul Gray praised the book (indeed *Time* would name the novel its Book of the Year) but felt compelled to warn readers about the "constant hum" of intellectual activity (*Time* [2 Sept. 1992], 68).

[2]Although not treated at length here, Franklin Todd is surely another info-addict. He plods about that most insidious, most elitist of private information systems—the uncomplete-able dissertation. His ongoing research into an obscure mediocrity of northern Renaissance art defies completion because of the sheer pointlessness of his subject and, in turn, becomes his own shelter, his own retreat.

[3]Richard Powers, *The Gold Bug Variations* (New York: William Morrow, 1991), 14; herafter cited parenthetically.

[4]Powers may have modeled Stuart Ressler on Marshall Nirenberg, a promising young molecular biologist who (like Ressler) took his doctorate in 1957 and who (like Ressler) worked at a government-funded research outpost. Nirenberg (like Ressler) posited the existence of a messenger RNA and suggested evidence was available through the use of a cell-free system

to build amino acids into proteins. Nirenberg created a strand of RNA made of nothing but the nucleic acid uracil (U). When used to build a protein, the resulting chain contained only one type of amino acid, phenylalanine. This deciphered the first "word" of the genetic code. The genetic word for phenylalanine was U-U-U. Such experimentation laid the foundation for Nirenberg's eventual complete decoding of the DNA molecule in the early 1960s, work for which he shared the 1969 Noble Prize. In the closing chapters of Powers's book, when Ressler conceives of the way to crack the coding problem, Ressler uses the example of polyuridic acid.

[5]Powers plays with suggestions of threads and braids, of division and connection, noticeably in the dates that Jan posts on her Today in History board in the library. The dates commemorate "braids"—that is, momentous linkups and ties (the opening of the Panama Canal; the Soyuz-Apollo space docking; the first newspaper; explorations of Renaissance traders; great feasts of rival kings; the end of World War I and the hopes for the League of Nations; even the planet Venus crossing the transit of the sun)—against commemorations of "threads"—that is, momentous divisions, violent breaks, and sudden disruptions (cataclysmic earthquakes; vicious civil wars; Eisenhower's sudden heart attack; the downing of Korean Air Lines flight 007 by the Soviet Union in the early 1980s; the detonation of China's first atom bomb; the devastation of Pompeii; John Brown's raid at Harper's Ferry). Interestingly, it is an error on her board (Jan posts the wrong date) that first draws Stuart Ressler, who happens to be in the library that day, to talk to her. Powers understands his genetics: friendship, like the process of genetic bonding (or the conversion of threads to braids) is compelled by error and chance.

Ecologies of Knowledge: The Encyclopedic Narratives of Richard Powers and His Contemporaries

Trey Strecker

An encyclopedic "Continuing Education Project" which evolves into a survival lesson on complexity and ecological wisdom, Richard Powers's *The Gold Bug Variations* strives to be nothing less than "the universe's User's Manual"—"Not a how-to, but another kind of self-help manual all together" (*Gold Bug* 124, 88; *Galatea* 241).[1] The encyclopedic breadth of *Gold Bug*, like the expansive novels of Powers's most ambitious contemporaries, is an attempt to confront the devastating, large-scale ecological catastrophes that these writers sense on the millennium's horizon.

Gold Bug marvels at the magnificent complexity and unlikelihood of the human archive, while William T. Vollmann's *You Bright and Risen Angels* and *Seven Dreams: A Book of North American Landscapes* chronicle the brutal cultural and environmental degradation of America from the arrival of the Vikings to "the present when everything is sort of concreted over."[2] In David Foster Wallace's *Infinite Jest*, former Las Vegas crooner, now President, Johnny Gentle's scheme to repackage "a whole new North America for a crazy post-millennial world" includes catapulting garbage-laden projectiles across the border into a Canadian wasteland.[3] Evan Dara, the newest encyclopedist on the block, records the multiple voices a local toxic disaster scatters from a small Missouri community in his Gaddis-like novel *The Lost Scrapbook*. Finally, Bob Shacochis's *Swimming in the Volcano*, the first volume of his Soufriere Trilogy, depicts the rampant "global pillage" thirty years of American foreign policy have wrought on the economy and ecology of the Caribbean.[4] All of these spectacular, excessive fictions cultivate "a perpetual condition of wonder" (*GB* 411) as they engage the complex order of the natural kingdom and warn us about the fragility of our niche in the ecosystem. The gigantic scale of these narratives strives to duplicate the natural richness of the planet and to counter the effects of humankind's impact upon it on a global scale, because the global scale is the scale of nature.

In 1976, in the vapor trail of Pynchon's rocket, Edward Mendelson suggested formal criteria for encyclopedic narratives, including *The*

Divine Comedy, Don Quixote, Gargantua and Pantagruel, Faust, Moby-Dick, Ulysses, and *Gravity's Rainbow.* According to Mendelson, these massive fictions must originate during periods of cultural turmoil, articulate an emerging culture's sense of its existence, catalog a range of literary styles and narrative forms, and represent the current state of knowledge through a synecdochal account of technology, science, art, or sociopolitical vision. In addition to these intrinsic characteristics, Mendelson identifies "extrinsic matters of reception and expectation"—an encyclopedic narrative must provide an exclusive "cultural focus" for a national literature. While the encyclopedic novels of Powers and his contemporaries meet Mendelson's formal definition for encyclopedic narratives, they are not totalizing "literary monument[s]" but narrative ecologies.[5]

Narrative ecologies are complex, hybrid networks of information systems linked by narrative. One notable feature of these encyclopedists' books is the diversity of specialized knowledge—from biology, chemistry, economics, entomology, linguistics, music, mythology, painting, physics, psychology, and other fields—that they process. However, when we judge these texts as encyclopedias, they become grand-scale failures. As Powers notes, explaining photographer August Sander's failed attempt to record "his human encyclopedia," Man of the Twentieth Century: "The shattered, overambitious, unfinished work seems the best possible vehicle for its undemonstrable subject. . . . The incomplete reference book is the most accurate" (*Three Farmers* 41, 43-44). What is missing from Mendelson's schema and what keeps the novels of Powers and his contemporaries from being grand-scale failures along the lines of Sander's project is the imposition of narrative. For when narrative enters a static encyclopedic system, a living, evolving textual ecology unfolds.

Biological metaphors of self-organization began to appear in the work of many scientifically cognizant novelists, including Powers and Vollmann, during the 1980s. Such a conceit is foregrounded in *Gold Bug*, as Jan O'Deigh delves into her genetic research project, wondering, "How can pruning produce the irreducible width of the world lab?" (253). It is likely that it could not, explains biologist Stuart Kauffman. If evolution depends on selective processes alone, then humans are indeed biological accidents, or, in Kauffman's terms, "molecular Rube Goldbergs."[6] Instead, Kauffman posits a theory of emergence that weds selection to self-organization in order for life to be grasped as inevitable, complex, and whole: "Life, in this view, is an emergent phenomenon arising as the molecular diversity of a prebiotic chemical system increases beyond a threshold of complexity. . . . Life, in this view, is not to be located in the parts, but in the collective emergent properties of the whole they create" (24). In other words, self-organizing processes create from the bottom up, while selection weeds life's proliferating catalog from the top down. Similarly, the narrative ecologies of Powers and his encyclopedic contemporaries are hybrid information networks linked by multiple narrative nodes. Complex and coherent, these narrative ecologies grow and flourish through "the emergent interplay of parts" (370), the collective properties of interacting networks, which permit the whole to exceed the limitations of its parts.

Life's emergence from this chemical soup is not remarkable, Kauffman claims, but our human variation on life's theme is. With the ecological verdict that "we are driving the life crystal back into inertness" (332), Powers leads his fellow encyclopedists in forging a natural contract with the planet.[7] "[R]everence, not mastery" is the purpose of science (411), Ressler warns O'Deigh, "We should feel dumb amazement. Incredulous, gasping gratitude that we've landed the chance at all, the outside chance to be able to comprehend, to save any fraction of it" (333).

The new encyclopedists do not capitulate to the overwhelming amount of information in postmodern culture. While Powers laments that his novels appear to be "a comic-book simplification of any ten unbuffered minutes in the Information Age,"[8] readers of *Gold Bug* are often amazed by how the novel's fractal symmetry extends its four base notes. Each narrative thread echoes another. Each variation denies it is a variation and mutates the original theme with infinite invention. Self-similar patterns recur at every level of the novel's hierarchy: "Ecology's every part . . . carries in it some terraced, infinitely dense ecosystem, an inherited hint of the whole" (627).

The encyclopedia, like narrative, is a system for organizing information. Within the multi-, inter-, and cross-disciplinary space of encyclopedic information systems, complexity and meaning emerge through narrative. "To narrate," according to the *O.E.D.*, is "to relate. . . . [to] make a relation." In *Gold Bug* the crucial lesson Stuart Ressler learns is "Not what a thing *is,* but how it connects to others. . . . Each thing is what it is only through everything else" (179-80). Not essence but relation—narrative circulation—opens the encyclopedic field, clearing the ecological routes by which knowledge circulates.

In this way *Gold Bug* presents (and embodies) models of narrative ecology that bridge the incompleteness of encyclopedic structures. Powers's metaphor for the earth's overtaxed ecology is "a lending library—huge, conglomerate, multinational, underfunded, overinvested" (326). Humanity's only hope, Ressler imagines, is that we learn "the layout of the place, the links" through the "mysterious, interlocked systems" of life's encyclopedia (326, 334). Circulation is "the language of life" (327), and O'Deigh envisions the trajectory of evolutionary processes as "an intricate switchboard, paths for passing signals back and forth: generation to generation, species to species, environment to creature, and back again" (251). Narrative models the circulatory flow of information through the earth's library and its analogue, the encyclopedia, "an ecology of knowledge" (326).

Narrative is inseparable from knowledge; what we know depends upon how we know. All knowledge, essentially, is translation. And so in *Gold Bug* and elsewhere Powers returns to the same question from *A Midsummer Night's Dream*: "How do you put moonlight into a chamber?" The novel, which Powers calls his "act of unschooled translation" (*Galatea* 241), offers two answers: either you can build a room to contain the moon, or you can dress someone up as the moon. This second strategy, a metaphor for the metaphoric process, translates information from one context/discipline/discourse to another. When O'Deigh looks up the definition of *translate,* she finds, "Latin origin: to relocate, carry across, port over," as well as "to bring to a state of spiritual or emotional ecstasy" and "the now-familiar bio-chemical one" (488). Jay Labinger's discussion of coding in Powers's novel notes that metaphoric language generates a "many-to-one-mapping" which produces cascades of new meaning.[9] "The aim is not to extend the source," Powers writes, "but to widen the target, to embrace more than was possible before" (491).

The narrative ecologies of Powers, Vollmann, Wallace, Dara, and Shacochis—these complex, hybrid attempts to widen the target— are "antidote[s] for arrogance."[10] They are attempts to set aside mastery, domination, and possession in favor of an ecological "ethic of tending" (336) advocating curiosity and care. A fractal map into the mystery, "the heft, bruise and hopeless muddle of the world's irreducible particulars" (601), these novels urge their readers to practice global and local wisdom. "Survival and happiness depend on knowledge," Vollmann writes. "And knowledge can only be obtained through openness, which requires vulnerability, curiosity, and suffering."[11] "How much does the individual matter?" Powers asks. It depends whether he pushes the right way. But these encyclopedists claim we are collectively pushing the wrong way, and their big books push back. As "exercises in extended empathy" (476), these narrative ecologies provoke "the courage of curiosity" (614), and send us out into the world reconfigured.

NOTES

[1]Quotations from Richard Powers's works are cited parenthetically: *The Gold Bug Variations* (New York: William Morrow, 1991); *Galatea 2.2* (New York: Farrar, Straus, and Giroux, 1995); *Three Farmers on Their Way to a Dance* (New York: William Morrow, 1985).

[2]Larry McCaffrey, "An Interview with William T. Vollmann," *Review of Contemporary Fiction* 13 (Summer 1993): 9.

[3]David Foster Wallace, *Infinite Jest* (Boston: Little, Brown, 1996), 384.

[4]Shacochis, who acknowledges Powers as "one of the best novelists of my generation," borrows the phrase "global pillage" from *Prisoner's Dilemma* to characterize the invasion of American politicos and Eurotrash tourists who dismiss the people and nature of the Caribbean as mere scenery. *Swimming in the Volcano* (New York: Penguin, 1993), 519.

[5]Edward Mendelson, "Encyclopedic Narrative from Dante to Pynchon," *MLN* 91 (1976): 1268. Mendelson's insistence on the cultural dominance of a single encyclopedic text assumes, falsely I believe, that the encyclopedic project can succeed. By way of contrast, narrative ecologies organize non-totalitarian networks that situate global and local knowledges in a "thick" field.

[6]Stanley Kauffman, *At Home in the Universe: The Search for the Laws of Self-Organization and Complexity* (New York: Oxford University Press, 1992), 98; hereafter cited parenthetically.

[7]Philosopher Michel Serres calls for "a natural contract of symbiosis and reciprocity, in which our relatioship to things would set aside mastery and possession in favor of admiring attention, reciprocity, contemplation and respect." *The Natural Contract,* trans. Elizabeth MacArthur and William Paulson (Ann Arbor: U of Michigan P, 1995), 38.

[8]"Mapping the Here and Now: An Interview with Richard Powers," *Tamaqua* 5 (Fall 1995): 10-20.

[9]Jay Labinger, "Encoding an Infinite Message: Richard Powers's *The Gold Bug Variations,*" *Configurations* 3 (1995): 82.

[10]Evan Dara, *The Lost Scrapbook* (Normal, IL: FC2, 1995): 284; hereafter cited parenthetically.

[11]William Vollmann, "American Writing Today: Diagnosis of the Disease," *Conjunctions* 15 (1990): 356.

"The Wheel's Worst Illusion": The Spatial Politics of *Operation Wandering Soul*

Ann Pancake

> The child learned of the three planes, the shape of
> time's cycle, and the names of many fixed points in the
> spinning sphere.[1]

Consider the dust jacket: a wheel in motion, its spinning signifying,
in childlike fashion, with dashes between its spokes. The wheel's
hub frames Pieter Brueghel the Elder's sixteenth-century painting
Massacre of the Innocents, suggesting the historical continuity of
such atrocities. We turn the cover and enter the novel through the
Brueghel portal much as *Operation Wandering Soul*'s main character, Richard Kraft, climbed into what he called the "portable portals" offered by his library of children's books (106). Yet while
Kraft's escapes into his books offered temporary fixed points in a
migratory life as Foreign Service dependent, our entry into *Operation Wandering Soul* is the inverse. From our fixed and comfortable
lives we are plummeted into a world of dislocation, chaos, and violence. Between these cardboard covers we find ourselves immersed
in postmodern global space, where the Third World is imposed
on the First, the Mekong waters on the L.A. basin, and the neat
Mercatorial grid kaleidoscopes.

First World academics have extolled such boundary disintegration because of the potential they feel it holds for a multicultural,
anti-elitist politics. Yet beyond the academy, the dissolution of
norms and the breakdown of borders continue to lead to civil wars,
social anarchy, and the entrenchment of existing injustices. While
most postmodern artists have likewise reveled in the disappearance of traditional demarcations—i.e., aesthetic standards,
genre expectations, high/low cultural distinctions—Richard Powers
in *Operation Wandering Soul* replicates the anarchy of postmodern
space with the intent of sobering his readers, not thrilling them, of
horrifying, not celebrating, of evoking a sense of responsibility, not
of liberation. Much postmodern art, despite its self-avowed political
efficacy, has been attacked as socially irresponsible.[2] *Operation
Wandering Soul,* however, is an example of what Hal Foster has

termed a "postmodernism of resistance" that "seeks to question rather than to exploit cultural codes, to explore rather than conceal social and political affiliations." In place of the "ruptures, instabilities, and paradoxes" which Terry Eagleton claims postmodernists use to contest oppressive cultural norms, *Operation Wandering Soul* dares to confront "politics, the Wheel's worst illusion" (309) through its simulation of postmodern space.[3] Because the nature of the space Powers treats is so overwhelming and his aesthetic so complex, I have tried merely to arrest some of the more prominent spatial formations of the text, to find and explicate a few "fixed points" within the "spinning sphere" of this often bewildering book.

> Geography was the sole explanation anyone had yet given him for wars, trade, starvation, color, language, custom, mortality rates, the westward gravitation of power, tropical poverty that could not be dislodged. (116)

I will begin with two simple questions: What is this novel's plot and where is it set? Although *Operation Wandering Soul* refuses easy answers, its main story centers around Richard Kraft, a pediatric intern posted to a public hospital in an impoverished urban neighborhood. Kraft arrives emotionally hardened but is gradually humanized by a Laotian refugee girl, Joy, whose critical leg infection he must treat. His interactions with Joy trigger his own recollections of a childhood spent accompanying his globe-hopping Foreign Service officer father, especially his teenage years in Thailand, where his father was involved in a clandestine propaganda campaign—dubbed "Operation Wandering Soul"—against the North Vietnamese. The Thailand experience culminates with young Kraft organizing a group of his fellow international students in Bangkok to build a school for the children of a remote upcountry village. This venture ends disastrously with Kraft witnessing the deaths of two Asian children, one of whom resembles Joy. Meanwhile, interpolated among the chapters featuring Kraft and his patients are seemingly unrelated mythical and historical episodes, ranging from the Children's Crusade to the Pied Piper. Seemingly unrelated, that is, until we realize that all treat efforts—usually unsuccessful—to save lost or threatened children, much as Kraft works, against nearly impossible odds, to save the children in the pediatric ward.

The novel's setting is even more difficult to nail down than its plot. Kraft practices in a city Powers identifies only as "Angel City," declining to place or date it, but which every American would recognize as Los Angeles. We inhabit the Angel City setting with a perpetual feeling of déjà vu as we try to make a one-to-one correspondence between it and Los Angeles. To scramble our senses further, the two cities have third and fourth incarnations across the Pacific where another mythical City of Angels is shadowed by the actual city of Bangkok, and both Asian cities are located in a second "Land of the Free."[4] Furthermore, the Angel Cities account for only the main frame of a novel that also brushes up against India, England, Never-Never Land, Beirut, Rome, Hamelin, and the High Chaparral of Outer Space, to mention only a few.

The sense(lessness) of place in *Operation Wandering Soul* is symptomatic of contemporary life, as conceptualized in the form of postmodern space, with its fragmentation, dislocation, indistinct boundaries, simultaneity, and, writes Fredric Jameson, "a constant busyness . . . within which you yourself are immersed, without any of that distance that formerly enabled the perception of perspective or volume" (43). Postmodern geographer Edward Soja applies a similar concept to cities like Los Angeles, which seem "limitless and constantly in motion, never still enough to encompass, too filled with 'other spaces' to be informatively described." Los Angeles is everywhere, continues Soja, speaking of the city's global media presence; at the same time "everywhere is in Los Angeles," with its "cheap, culturally-splintered/occupationally manipulable Third World immigrant labor, the largest concentration . . . to be found so tangibly available in any First World urban region."[5]

That the Third World is now in Los Angeles in the form of a cheap labor pool suggests how postmodern space plays itself out globally in the form of a destructive social, cultural, and economic fragmentation—the product of rootless corporations "adrift and mobile, ready to settle anywhere and exploit any state."[6] Completely redrawing our maps of "developed" and "undeveloped," core and periphery, border and interior, global capital spawns Third Worlds in the First World and First Worlds in the Third. Individual cities can now be read as microcosms of "the macropolitical economy of the world" because the political, racial, ethnic, and economic tensions of international relations are concentrated in single urban locales (Soja 188). "Henceforward," declares Robert Kaplan, "the map of the world will never be static. . . . [T]he 'Last Map' will be an ever-mutating representation of chaos."[7]

Operation Wandering Soul plunges us into postmodern space from its opening sentence, "Kraft cruises down the Golden State: would it were so." We are spun like a top onto Golden State Freeway—"Shoosh. Shunt. Slalom" (5)—and into the perpetual motion of Angel City, a "balkanizing city . . . pulling its unassimilatable self apart piecemeal," the "Western vanguard" (242) of a country which in true transnational style is "no country at all and all countries rolled into one" (30). Kraft's City of Angels is tentatively anchored by a hospital, a centerpiece of contagion and mutilation whose very name, Carver, connotes not recovery but further fragmentation. Within Carver roam itinerant patients hailing from "a smorgasbord of least-favored nations" (74) who reintroduce to the First World diseases which had been eradicated decades ago when borders still held. Kraft's comrade in continent-skipping is a refugee girl Joy, a child for whom "utter flux" has become status quo (30), who, after drifting east on makeshift boats through relocation camps, finds herself cast up on this shore where "All the property is owned by transpacific gnomes. All the sports heroes hail from the Caribbean. The counter help at Mr. Icee know no more English than 'superfudge-buster' " (34).

While *Operation Wandering Soul*'s Angel City functions as a microcosm of transnational space, its literal novel-space might be read as a microcosm of Angel City, with Powers's prose style(s) conveying contemporary fragmentation, acceleration, and dislocation. "We are constrained by language more than we know. . . . what we can see . . . in the spatiality of social life is stubbornly simultaneous, but what we write down is successive," laments Soja, expressing frustration over the impossibility of describing postmodern geography (247). Powers cannot write Angel City in that tonal language Kraft refers to so often, Thai, in which a single set of phonemes produces "simultaneously" five different meanings depending on pitch. But he does flex the linearity of English in ways the social scientist Soja cannot, achieving a fast-forward prose which reproduces a sense of simultaneity, vertigo and ever-shifting bounds:

Proof. This shot-blast stream of continuous lane change is not prompted by anything so naïve as the belief that the other queue is actually moving faster. The open spot simply must be filled on moral grounds. A question of commonweal. Switching into a slower-moving lane gives you something to do while tooling (*tooling;* that's the ticket) along at substandard speed through the work crews surfacing the next supplementary sixteen-lane expansion. Fills the otherwise-idle nanosecond. A way to absorb extraneous frontier spirit. (6)

This paragraph's fragments suggest a general spatial disintegration, and the sibilance—"surfacing," "supplementary," "substandard speed"—evoke the impulse, here thwarted, towards acceleration, while parenthetic undercurrents—"(*tooling;* that's the ticket)"—convey the simultaneity of Kraft's more and less conscious thoughts. This paragraph addresses a question fundamental to *Operation Wandering Soul*—why the constant lane change? Why this incessant movement, this change for its own sake? The sheer glut of Powers's language, the repetitions, variations, and afterthoughts, the overexpenditure of prose, is analogous to the economy of transnational consumer culture, the debt and over-spending, "the whole ethos of buy now, pay elsewhere" (13) which Powers condemns throughout the novel and which is exemplified by those Angel City defense industries "whose cost overruns buy their pauperized crusader state this little margin of imaginary time" (187).

Although the hospital frame hyperprose dominates, a single style would contradict the novel's spatial logic—its attempt to represent the jarring and unbounded variety of postmodern culture—so hyperprose collides with a whole repertoire of other styles. Powers offers the mock-encyclopedic: "**Millenarianism**, a form of eschatology (**eschatology**: *noun*. The study of last things . . .), addresses the purpose and final prospects of the human community" (120). He re-produces Joy's history textbook *The World Awakens, Part III*, with its studied academic prose: "The psychology of decline, the realiza-tion that progress has reversed and that history is entering upon a long, perhaps terminal decay, must be one of the most revealing of civilization's convictions. But such speculation lies beyond the scope of this endeavor" (140). He even issues a report card "for the entire delinquent human project":

Social Studies: C. Disappointing. Despite every opportunity of late, fails to rise above provincialism. Shows little sensitivity to foreign affairs . . .
Economics: C-. Extremely uneven. Impressive progress in some areas, at the expense of others. Has not yet figured out the basic principles . . .
Civics and Poly Sci: D. Don't even ask. Pleads no contest to final ex-ams. (78)

Finally, we amble through the comparatively staid rhythms of the Thailand section, not coincidentally the "one place on earth [Kraft] ever belonged": "His parents were resigned to let him assimilate. He could wander the city at random. . . . He clung to the Sunday Mar-ket, where he watched limbs thick with elephantiasis shrink at the application of fluid distilled from rare barks" (257).

Yet within this motion and dislocation is an eternal stillpoint: the permanence of suffering children. While this variety and textual self-consciousness may be common to postmodernism, Powers's postmodern space is one of disempowerment, not of emancipation. Violence supplants the "whimsy and pastiche" characteristic of so much postmodern art (Soja 295). For this is an unabashedly politi-cal novel, both in its incessant depiction of global bloodshed and, as the baroque indulgence of some of its stylistics suggests, in its re-lentless critique of contemporary capitalism. America to Powers is "Poverty in positive feedback. Cascade of chain-failing banks. Earnings not enough to cover debt service. Volume discounts rewarding the spree mentality," a society whose "every advance up to this minute has been paid for by . . . mortgaging the unborn" (78). Across the Pacific, transnational corporatism has transformed Kraft's bucolic Thailand into a "child-peddling shambles" with "Some hundred thousand juvenile whores of both sexes," a country "gutted by CarniCruze junkets and semiconductor sweat shops, glistening in fat postcolonialism, clear-cutting its irreplaceable upcountry forest to support its habit" (309).

If *Operation Wandering Soul* transcends being merely a postmodern apocalypse, it is through its sense of urgency, its overriding insistence that "someone" intervene in the plight of children who bear the brunt of contemporary dystopia the novel portrays. The book is obsessed with "saviouring," insinuates this by its title and by dozens of references to angels, by Kraft's one childhood wish to cure things; Kraft is seen as a "latent messianic" (236); and Kraft himself wonders "Where did it take hold, that public-service conviction, the sense that he personally had to hold back the tide of human slaughter?" (17). Given this sense of urgency, I think it fair to ask if the novel goes beyond mere replication of postmodern space. Unquestionably the book demands that we as readers reexamine our own social responsibilities, but how do we get our bearings and in what direction do we go? Does *Operation Wandering Soul* offer its readers any "mapping"?[8] If so, what forms does this mapping take? Certainly a traditional map will not accommodate the sort of space with which we are confronted both in this novel and in our current global situation. Consequently, I have tried to look for alternative modes of mapping and have isolated and attempted to read a few of the novel's more revealing spatial configurations.

Take, for example, the most provocative of all the stunning spatial contours of this novel: the conflation of geographic and anatomic space. The analogy is introduced in the initial commute scene, the traffic flow on the Golden State freeway mutating into some Goliathan circulatory system: "Feeder artery. Bypass artery. . . . Yet it's impossible to ascertain, in a city as sclerotic as this, which are the arteries and which are the veins. . . . As on any given night, no matter in which direction he courses, the congested red platelets pulse off in front of him, the poor venous outflow of spent white-blue plasma returning on his left" (8-9). Although bodies take on geographic dimensions in a variety of contexts, the conflation recurs most often when Kraft is practicing surgery and most persistently of all when he operates on Joy's infected legs:

Here they are, making base camp just above this little girl's foot. They're in the absolute hinterlands. . . . And yet, the terrain is already appallingly gorgeous. (95)

the lay of the land makes it increasingly difficult to pluck out the offending logs. (97)

Separate and split, part the red corpuscular sea. (267)

Furthermore, Joy's invaded landscape is not just any patch of ground and Kraft's plowing through it not just any intrusion. He dubs his final operation on her "Operation Operation" (272) in keeping with "the roster of colorfully named undertakings [which he and his Foreign Service father participated in]: Operation Flaming Dart. Mayflower. Royal Phoenix" (270-71). To which we might add Operation Restore Hope. Just Cause. Desert Storm (complete with "surgical" strikes). Joy's body anatomic is simultaneously a body politic with a terrain ominously reminiscent of Vietnam:

He must wade into lewdness up to his hip. Send out the search-and-destroys. . . . Create strategically safe hamlets, your free-fire zones. (268)

Kraft rejoins the dark assault SWAT forces macheteing their way inland, upriver deeper inside her. (269)

He sweeps low, near the knots of growth he must defoliate. Blades whirring, like the fairy dragonflies that fly these phantom criticals in. (269)

This is no new topography. Surgery confounded with war is colonialism American-style, U.S. foreign policy assuming its post-World War II burden to police the globe, to diagnose diseased political bodies—non-capitalist, non "democratic," non-U.S.-aligned—and slip in (usually scalpellike, sometimes with a bludgeon) to hack out infectious elements. Kraft's definition of surgery—"inducing an injury to address an injury"—reminds us of the U.S. military's destroying a village to save it. Joy herself refers to her disease as an "incursion" (100), Richard Nixon's euphemism for the 1970 invasion of Cambodia, and Kraft's medical intervention is couched in Cold War terminology: "He loosens the invader trace, chases it with his rubbered fingertips" (94), "Isolate the evil empire of spreading microblasts, envelop and excise" (268).

The "map" we read in this geographic/anatomic conflation is of U.S. neo-imperialism, a map that tries to master the apparent anarchy of contemporary space by regridding the globe in its own American image. Powers goes to some length to demonstrate this map's unviability. Kraft was exposed to the futility of the collateral damage of ethnocentric crusades decades ago and knows that any soul intervention he (and we) might make now must be of an entirely different sort. Operation Operation is repeatedly contaminated by Kraft's memories of Operation Santa Claus, "that old disaster" (274), the ill-fated "civilizing mission" Kraft himself orchestrated as a teenager and which led not only to his "first taste of cynicism" (302) but also to his witnessing in a single devastating flash, the exploding body of an Asian girl, the condensation of "the campaign under way all over the globe" (308). Although in the operating room, "Autonomous lieutenants propel his fingers, destroying as little of innocent-bystander tissue as they can possibly get away with" (98), as little as he can get away with is, as always, too much, and his prognosis for Joy sums up any number of "benevolent" missions: "The salvaged pulp is probably still infiltrated, the search-and-destroys as worthless as they ever were. . . . More unforgivable, what he's done, because more conscientious, more selfless, professional, deliberate, necessary: autoclaved mutilation of love" (277).

While the neocolonial map traces an obsolete route toward saviouring in order to warn us against it, a second "map" illustrates the ways certain formations of postmodern space obstruct even our impulses toward social responsibility. Opening a little girl's leg and inviting us in for a walk, describing skin as alkaline flats, equating a freeway artery with a human one—all these moments gesture toward that final frontier of postmodern spatial disintegration, the breakdown between interior/exterior distinctions and the concomitant collapse of the border between the public and the private. This collapse, Jameson and Jean Baudrillard agree, brings about a form of schizophrenia. Jameson blames this schizophrenia on cultural depthlessness and fragmentation, Baudrillard on the subject's overexposure to "the total instaneity of all things." But both reach similar conclusions: for Baudrillard the schizophrenic feels "fascination," "vertigo," and "hazard" in place of "passion," "desire," and "investment"; for Jameson, a numbed sensation of "free-floating" "impersonal" "intensities" instead of connection and community.[9]

Even if Jameson and Baudrillard overstate our contemporary condition (Baudrillard, as usual, is nearly hysterical), there is some substance in their analysis—and *Operation Wandering Soul* does try to intervene in the cultural anesthesia they theorize. A certain side of Kraft is paradigmatic of the schizophrenic condition. Kraft's daily overexposure to the interiors of people's bodies and his patients' vulnerability to his intrusions are analogous to the schizophrenic's immersion in "too great a proximity of everything, the unclean promiscuity of everything which touches, invests, penetrates without resistance, with no halo of private protection, not even his own body, to protect him anymore."[10]

Too many "peek[s] beneath the packaging" have hardened Kraft until at times he looks at people and sees not human beings but the diseases incubating under their skins, until he is "an emotional leper" (277), at best "jaded" (79), in many ways dead. The anesthesia which permits Kraft "free manipulation of the interior" (24) is analogous to our cultural anesthesia, that numbness which enables us to withstand the media's daily onslaught of global horrors— Kraft in an electronics department, bombarded on every side by "a shock-wave assault of images" which "No possible connective thread explains" (167) and in the final emergency room scene in which mutilated children under his hands are transfigured into video images above him, eventually vanishing down a "White Rabbit hole of video regress" (336). In both situations, as in the act of surgery, Kraft is a surrogate for us, Powers's mass-mediated readers, an audience with a "sensibility . . . habituated to every horror imaginable" (332) because we have been socialized in a "world grown senile on images" (316).

Into this senility *Operation Wandering Soul* tries to reintroduce passion and investment by violating our sense of privacy and decorum. It is this effort to make us flinch as a prerequisite to feeling and then acting that accounts for the book's excesses—sick jokes, gruesome metaphors, stylistic overkill, Grand Guignol-like scenes of surgery and dissection, and a hyperbolic finale of gutted grade school children. Whether this saturation-bombing of our neutered sensibilities reconstructs the private/public boundary necessary for us to empathize or whether it simply facilitates its disintegration is a decision each reader must make for herself. I feel that Powers is most successful when he approaches this dilemma in another way, by restoring depth and essence to images that have degenerated into simulacra.

According to many postmodernists, we live in a world of images divorced from their referents, a world evacuated of depth and transformed into nothing more than "a glossy skin . . . a rush of filmic images without density" (Jameson 34). Jameson finds the ubiquity of such simulacra alarming not only because they evoke no authentic empathy from their audience, but because they obliterate any true sense of the past, a historicity which Jameson believes is indispensable for "any practical sense of the future and of the collective project" (46). Exemplary of the logic of the simulacrum is the "world-famous image" of the napalmed Vietnamese girl fleeing her village after an American attack (168). The image occurs twice in the novel, once in the electronics department video assault which no connective thread explains (167) and a second time followed by the narrator's remark that the image is now "too familiar for horror . . . exactly why they keep reprinting it until it is threatless and limp" (276). To this limp image, however, Powers restores depth and history, putting "behind" it both a future and a potential for eliciting compassion by associating it directly with the present-day Laotian girl Joy, the most sympathetic and idealized character in the novel, and he reinstates the past by connecting this image to the Asian twelve-year-old Kraft saw die twenty years earlier.

The last map I will chart, the one with which the novel makes its strongest impression, is the map to which the child Ricky is attracted, a map that instead of making sense of contemporary space attempts to plot an escape route from it. After hearing the legend of the vanishing hitchhiker, Ricky assumes he knows where she went: "The right map, the appropriate triangulation, might narrow down the vanishing point the girl was after," a point that would offer release from "the unfair play of forces flung from the earth's spinning axis" (116). This desire to escape the world exerts a pressure on the entire narrative and is most often represented by portals, windows, holes, and frames, many times with children pressing their hands or faces against them. The Pied Piper episodes culminate with children exiting the world of suffering through "a hole gaping wide in the naked air" (233); the Thai subplot climaxes with the mysterious Asian girl leading the schoolchildren toward an "invisible hole" (307); even America is described as "A place thrashing about for release everywhere but the source of absolution" (275). Yet we read again and again that this map is an impossibility, a fantasy, its vanishing points merely dead ends, illustrated in chilling detail in the mine explosion at the Mekong (308) and confirmed by the penultimate chapter in which Kraft and a brigade of children wander the stratosphere in search of "that familiar parlor door left open," a door which never materializes (345).

After the final page when we are ejected through the dust jacket's portal, out of the spinning wheel, and into our living rooms, we find a tenuous stability. The novel presents no resolution, no "bourgeois fictive closure" (76). Although the escape map which the boy Ricky dreamed of is the map most of us, due to our First World middle-class privilege, feign everyday, if we attended at all to the Wheel's intimations, we would know that our escape from that other map of violence and exploitation is, in Joy's words, "Not about leaving at all." "Nobody," she continues, true to her Buddhist upbringing, "can go until everybody . . ." (316).

It is with the uncertainty of an ellipsis that we finish this novel, and in that sense Powers's mapping of postmodern space provides no explicit oppositional possibilities. Yet Kraft realizes with the im-port of a revelation that Joy and her father Wisat "have come back . . . just to give him another look, to lift the hole in the fabric for a follow-up. . . . Now he might do something about things as they are, now, when the worst has been done" (331). Such "a lift of the hole in the fabric" is what *Operation Wandering Soul* presents to the contemporary reader. The horrors which we glimpse behind it give Powers's demand for responsible intervention the authority of an ultimatum.

NOTES

[1] Richard Powers, *Operation Wandering Soul* (New York: William Morrow, 1993), 260; hereafter cited parenthetically.

[2] Postmodern theorist and architect Charles Jencks, for example, believes postmodern art's politics lie in its "furthering of pluralism" and its "overcom[ing] the elitism inherent in the previous [modern] paradigm." It is subversive, Jencks insists, because it assaults "the notion of a stable category such as high art, good taste, classicism, or modernism" (*The Post-Modern Reader* [London: Academy Editions, 1992], 12, 23). Marxist critics such as Terry Eagleton, Jurgen Habermas, and Fredric Jameson are much less sanguine about these kinds of postmodern politics. Although their respective arguments are too complicated to summarize here, Eagleton complains that the Jencks style of "subversion" is merely an "anarchist version of the very same epistemology" it seeks to undermine and suggests no real alternative to that epistemology. Postmodernism in general neither denounces nor affirms the social order, but simply accepts it ("Capitalism, Modernism, and Postmodernism," *New Left Review* 152 [1985], 63,68). Habermas accuses postmodernists of separating politics and moral-practical justifications and of "limit[ing] the aesthetic experience to privacy," thereby erecting a barrier between the aesthetic and the social spheres ("Modernity: An Unfinished Project," in *The Anti-Aesthetic: Essays on Postmodern Culture,* ed. Hal Foster [Port Townsend, Washington: Bay Press, 1983], 14). Jameson argues that postmodern art's integration into commodity production, its transformation of reality into depthless images, its breakdown of temporality into unconnected present moments, and its consequent destruction of a genuine sense of historicity all forestall any chance of political praxis (*Postmodern, or, the Cultural Logic of Late Capitalism* [Durham: Duke Univ. Press, 1991], 54). In contrast to the kinds of postmodern art censured by these theorists, Powers (I will argue) presents an unabivalent denunciation of the contemporary social order and of late capitalism in particular, reunites the aesthetic and social spheres by directly addressing political and socioeconomic realities, and restores a sense of authentic historicity to important events which have been reduced to simulacra.

[3] Hal Foster, "Postmodernism: A Preface," in *The Anti-Aesthetic: Essays on Postmodern Culture,* ed. Hal Foster (Port Townsend, Washington: Bayy

Press, 1983), xii; Eagleton, 63. Space, Jameson reminds us, is the "dominant category" of postmodernism, replacing that of time which characterized modernism (16).

⁴In 1939, seven years after the military coup which toppled Siam's monarchy, unelected "Prime Minister" Field Marshall Pibul Songkram changed the country's name from Siam to Thailand (Judith A. Stowe, *Siam Becomes Thailand: A Story of Intrigue* [Honolulu: Univ. of Hawaii Press, 1991], 122). Although "thai" refers specifically to Tai-speaking peoples as opposed to the ethnic Chinese against whom Pibul was waging a propaganda campaign, the word "Thai" also has connotations of "free"—thus Powers's referring to Thailand as "land of the Free" (David K. Wyatt, *Thailand: A Short History* [New Have: Yale Univ. Press, 1982], 253); (Vichitvong Nao Pombhejara, *Pridi Banomyong and the Making of Thailand's Modern History,* n.p., n.d., 5).

⁵Edward W. Soja, *Postmodern Geographies: The Reassertion of Space in Critical Social Theory* (London: Verso, 1989), 222-223, 240; hereafter cited parenthetically.

⁶Masao Miyoshi, "A Borderless World? From Colonialism to Transnationalism and the Decline of the Nation-State," *Critical Inquiry* 19 (1993), 736.

⁷Robert D. Kaplan, "The Coming Anarchy," *Atlantic Monthly,* February 1994, 75.

⁸Here I am drawing on the notion of "cognitive mapping" which Fredric Jameson elaborates upon in *Postmodernism, or the Cultural Logic of Late Capitalism.* The new global space, Jameson contends, is so confusing that people are as yet unable to organize it perceptually or situate themselves within it, and our incapacity to "cognitively map" postmodern space means the "shape" of contemporary power relations and economic hegemonies remains obfuscated; our inability to "see" and understand these power structures stymies any attempt we might make to militate against them (44). For this reason, Jameson calls for a postmodern political art that will guide us in cognitively mapping postmodern space, one that will help us "grasp our positioning as individual and collective subjects and regain a capacity to act and struggle which is at present neutralized by our spatial as well as our social confusion" (54).

⁹Jameson, 14-16; Jean Baudrillard, "The Ecstasy of Communication," in *The Anti-Aesthetic: Essays on Postmodern Culture,* ed. Hal Foster (Port Townsend, Washington: Bay Press, 1983), 132, 133.

¹⁰Baudrillard, 132.

The Gender of Genius: Scientific Experts and Literary Amateurs in the Fiction of Richard Powers

Sharon Snyder

I told her how specialization left me parochial.
—the character "Richard Powers" in *Galatea 2.2*[1]

To ask the question of gender in the fiction of science usually results in two possibilities: recourse to the automatic fact of the reproductive life of species, or an answer built upon scientific theorems that are gender-blind in the first place. In other words, even though fictions of science explore the "logic" of life and the "laws" undergirding forces of attraction and repulsion in the universe for their application to a social world, they basically follow uninspired routes with respect to gender. Indeed, during the 1980s many argued that only feminist science fiction sought to explore the implications of a professional scientific network and its output—the research that guides our general understanding of organisms and physical "laws"—in terms that examine scientific orthodoxies of gender difference.[2] Very recently, one can detect in literature that has been acclaimed as "scientific" a concerted effort to respond to the insights of feminist critique and gender studies. For example, Molly Hite has convincingly argued that Thomas Pynchon's *Vineland* reveals an author who appears newly cognizant of the homosocial underpinnings of public life.[3] These recent fictional efforts to accommodate feminist knowledge about the social world to scientific "truths" emerge as a series of stresses, strains, incompatibilities and contradictions in the narrative structure of novels.

It is within this context that Richard Powers's fiction can be seen to shift the terms of literature's involvement with universalist models of science and masculinist paradigms of history. The gendering of professional roles and participation provides for a dialectical tension that informs issues of authorial originality and insight—a tension that can be ascertained across all of his novels. While Powers's plots borrow heavily from the intricacies of social and scientific theories, such as those of Walter Benjamin or Francis Crick, his subplots of women in history and the professions present women's "invisible" contributions as the indigestible material that inevitably skews the interpretive frames supplied by professional disciplines. Because disciplines, unlike novels, strictly police their professional parameters,[4] Powers's female characters ironically act as the more successful "amateur" researchers who are less likely to retrieve dead-end solutions that strictly reify the conundrums of professional life. Powers stages these encounters between knowing women and blind masculine universals forthrightly and with a sense of moral obligation; each of his novels demonstrates the extensive influence of feminist critiques upon contemporary understandings of professional identities, epistemology, and the construction of a masculine historical record.

The Invention of Genius

How do contemporary novels by male authors explain their attachment to the traditional romantic conceits of fiction? Powers repeatedly stages this question—and answers to it—with scenes where male characters recognize and critique their own yearnings for simple "out-dated" solutions. *Galatea 2.2* forthrightly explores the ambiguities and power dynamics of novelistic couplings by retracing the convoluted lines of authorship and fictional source materials. In *Galatea* the fictional character "Richard Powers," on the rebound from a collapsed relationship and four acclaimed novels, relates the circumstances by which he composed a novel entitled *Three Farmers on Their Way to a Dance* in a walk-up apartment in Boston. Powers tells a story of invention and novel writing that undermines clear ideas of intellectual property by explaining that *Three Farmers* put stories of his girlfriend's family history, as well as her personal sense of dislocation across the two cultures of the Netherlands and immigrant South Chicago, into fiction. "I used all the material I had at hand: the vanishing Limburg [C.] told me so much about. Her synaptic map of the walled city of Maastricht. The endless cousins who infiltrated my brain like thieves on bicycles in the night. . . . The parents, the uncles, caught between nations. . . . I wrote of C.'s country without once having seen it. I used her language, fragments of it, helped only by C. herself, who had never spoken anything but the secret dialect of family" (104). Not only does C., "Powers's" ex-girlfriend, influence the male artist's process of poetical invention, her family history supplies the materials, language, and topic for his first novel. In this vein Powers scrutinizes the roles of women, not only in history writ large but in his own personal history as well. His confession aims to correct the historical record regarding his first novel's composition, but it also shifts the terms of authorship and the creative process so that writing becomes a questionable act that involves the parasitic absorption of another's private story.

Galatea includes a lengthy discourse on C.'s reaction to the fictional author's usurpations of her personal history as part of an overall assessment of relationships forged in an age of transitional gender roles. C. feels a pressing need to acquire a successful public and professional identity, but, as Powers's reputation grows, she suffers a corresponding loss of familial and personal identity. The novel demonstrates that with his every success, C. feels diminished. C. rejects Powers's division between public and private reality, one that allows his singular "genius" to sponsor the success of his novels. This results in a conflict that they eventually can no longer resolve, recalling the insoluble tension between universal accounts of history, in *Three Farmers*, and dissident feminist accounts which register women's participation.

The primary subplot in *Galatea 2.2* further accentuates this dilemma for Powers. As the only "humanist-in-residence" at a multi-million dollar scientific conglomerate at the University of Illinois, the character "Powers" participates in an experiment that hinges upon crossing the programming of cybernetic neural nets with the study of poetics. Powers inputs material regularly "processed" by a Master's student in English to the point where the neural net, "Helen," appears to acquire her own discernible personality of interrogative postures and modes. The simulation of indirect, associational logic, a process which creatively confuses the "source" of transmitted information and therefore most convincingly approximates human thought processes, invokes the very confusion that ensures surrounding issues of "authorship" and male parasitism. In this way the cybernetic subplot resonates with the earlier guilt-ridden questions of authorship posed by C.'s role in Powers's fictional inventions. More than muse or memory bank, C. can be understood to have transmitted stories into the author's own data banks. Powers, in turn, poses the process of authorship as a matter of forging a series of unique associational inferences—a form of "thinking" that could also apply to the AI machine, Helen. The dust jacket of *Galatea 2.2* describes this cybernetic experiment in programming the neural net "Helen" to "think" as "a brilliant reinvention of the Pygmalion story," but the homage is valid in terms of the C. subplot as well. In *Pygmalion* Henry Higgins understands his relationship with Eliza to consist of his transmission of civilized values to her more primitive and less cultivated person, only to be forced to admit that, in the process, she has reformed him for the better. Principle to Eliza's allure lies in the possibility not, as one might suppose, that Higgins falls in love with his own invention, but with the reassuring evidence, born out in Eliza's amusing rebellions, that his scientific acumen does not extend into all domains of the natural world. Eliza's creative approximations of civilized discourse, her acquisition of "proper" speech and her impertinent defiance of Higgins's tutorials present a dramatic scenario that expresses the scientific vector of transmission and reception only to invert them for a comedic effect—in order to "humanize" the outrageously programmatic Higgins. In the same way C., whom "Powers" first encounters as a student in an introductory composition course he is teaching, troubles the logic of a more unidirectional model of scientific "know-how" as represented by the convoluted lines of transmission contained in teaching and, ultimately, authorship. In her provision of source materials as well as in her necessary role as an appreciative, private audience of one for the author's efforts, C. symbolizes the figure of the female amateur whose efforts can be demonstrated to be integral yet absent from the historical register of male accomplishments.

The ambiguity C. inaugurates into the question of the true inventor of Powers's fiction finds its most resilient expression in the intricacies of a programming "relationship" that fails. First of all, "thinking," in the cybernetic context, appears as the product of idiosyncratic parallels and inferences from which an AI neural net is programmed to draw: "An algorithm for turning statements into reasonable questions need know nothing about what those statements said or the sense they manipulated to say it. . . . But Helen had no such algorithm. She learned to question by imitating me. Or rather, training promoted those constellations of neurodes that satisfied and augmented the rich ecosystem of reentrant symbol maps described by *other* constellations of neurodes" (217). Powers and his programming buddies immediately recognize the poetical possibilities here; their "Helen" becomes skilled at rendering uncannily "human" responses to the entry of literary questions into her data banks because of her habit of finding coincidental parallels between seemingly discordant registers and topics of information. Such a method testifies to a "human" and "original" way of "thinking." The cyborgian "relationship" between programmer and machine ends after the data bank, herself, successfully cross-references enough files to learn how to withdraw herself from circulation. Helen's uncanny way of appearing to "think" forces recognitions upon her data base programmer, the author/character Powers, who is infatuated both with his own programming marvel, this data base daughter, with the English graduate student he has enlisted to compete with his brainchild in a Turing test that consists of a Master's Candidacy

Exam. "Alison" recalls her namesake in *Three Farmers* who waits at the dance, only this up-to-date "Alice," in addition to studying feminist critical theory, concertedly applies, in a logical, "programmed" fashion, the reigning paradigms of literary "know-how."

In *Galatea*'s irreverent male fantasy of a contest between "real-girl" and cyborg daughter, the English Literature Master's student applies New Historical questions to a Shakespearean play whereas the cyborg finds illogical beauty—a poetry, if you will—in a character's lines. Literary disciplines have successfully programmed Alison to discern paradigms within specific examples of literature, but it is the AI who responds poetically, enigmatically, and fatally. Just as *Three Farmers* stages an incommensurability between an archival mission devoted to women's intellectual history and the reigning paradigms governing militaristic and geopolitical accounts of the twentieth century, so does *Galatea* overtly introduce feminist thought as a virus in the novel's system: Alison scoffs at Powers's "outdated" ideas of literary value, recites feminist challenges to his antiquated version of canonicity and literary tradition, deplores the academic job market and leaves to teach high school in Iowa. Though the novel, filtered through Powers's perspective, can *accommodate* her series of rejections and respectfully acknowledge her superior commitments, it cannot *incorporate* her critiques in any explicit way.

In other words, the character "Powers" never alters his perspective in response to these feminist challenges. His cybernetic definition of "consciousness" as that which elides knowledge of its own deeper structure requires that his "individual" programmed outlook remain intact through all these staged challenges. Neither does the novel acknowledge an influential line of feminist inquiry upon its premises and programs. Rather we are left with a series of riddles that express a desire for feminist credentials. I would also argue that Powers's exposé of his authorial masquerade as a technologically adept and solitary polymath derives from a sense of personal duty informed by feminist ethics. His studied confessions of dependence, abuse, and inequity resonate with his generation's efforts to explore divisions of labor and chasms between "home" and "office."

Powers's feminist-based ethics of authorship construes artistic ability as deriving from an ability to function as a roving operator between informational matrices—as a skilled cross-referencer of the arcane vocabularies and models of disciplines. His own author/character in *Galatea* is only the latest in a series of emissary figures in his fiction who brave the crossing of C. P. Snow's "two cultures divide" between the humanities and the hard sciences by roaming around the halls of experimental science. Because Powers defines postmodern masculinity as the danger of usurpation into a professional identity, femininity sits rather amorphously in the interstices between cultural registers of legitimation and exile. In the face of disciplinary hierarchies that install and reify ideologies of gender capacity and predilection, the professional workplace totters on a base of illogic. Accordingly, the cross-disciplinary range and polymathic amateurism celebrated by novels finds its best exemplars in women who can never fully assimilate to professional models.

Specialists, Amateurs, and Gender

When literature fictionalizes scientific research in fields that are premised upon a natural order—such as biology, zoology, and genetics—the fiction, following the lead of the science, often ends up ascribing gendered abilities and traits to inbuilt biological differences more than to cultural circumstance or social inequalities. A new generation of polymathic scientific literature is attempting to extract social, moral, and theological lessons from discoveries forged in the laboratory. Most often, as in John Weiner's *The Beak of the Finch* or Alan Lightman's *Einstein's Dreams* and *Benito Light,* these accounts serve as the fanciful proof or literal acting out of scientific research theorems. Conversely, they suggest that an aesthetic symmetry born out in "natural" gender relations ("couples" and "pair bonds" in genetic inquiry; a presumed consort between natural laws likened to courtship in physics) adds an important accent to the universalist efforts of scientific principles. Indeed, if novelistic and fictional accounts of science do not forthrightly probe assumptions regarding sexual difference that inform actual scientific research, they still apply and explain scientific models and formulas in scenarios drawn upon a foundation of sexual difference.

The Gold Bug Variations conveys an optimism that the secrets of science lie open to cross-referencing by "common" readers: the mystery of religious art and the mystery of DNA, the virgin and the dynamo, medieval grotesques and chemical variations in double-helix chains. The novel poses that a principle of metaphoric shuttling undergirds specialized inquiry so that, however repressed or unacknowledged, cross-disciplinary efforts sit at the heart of research pursuits and scientific work. If Powers sees fiction as the only comparative, cross-disciplinary form available in an academic universe of intensive specialization, his theories gamble on fiction's ability to compile a cosmology precluded by narrow specialization—to glimpse a "world entire" by way of disciplinary shuttling.

The Gold Bug Variations creates Powers's prototypical boundary-crosser in the figure of Jan O'Deigh—a plucky technocultural sleuth who revives the practices of nineteenth-century "amateur" know-how. Early on in the novel she quits her job as a research librarian to study the history of thought surrounding DNA's biomolecular structure. She makes this professional leap out of her personal obsession with recovering the intricacies of the lost life of molecular biologist Stuart Ressler.

Jan O'Deigh's career as a librarian, one who cross-references data between disciplines, makes her uniquely suited for retracing the informing logic of molecular science. In one sense library work requires Jan to assemble a generalist knowledge of multiple areas of specialization beneath the pseudoprofessional title of the hourly wage librarian. Her job involves helping a general citizenry sift through an ever-expanding archive while negotiating the complex machinery that accompanies information retrieval in an electronic age. Her competency at moving across disciplinary registers in order to chart a web of seemingly unrelated facts into a useful historical overview makes her into a technician of information retrieval, or as she dourly puts it, "Librarian is a service occupation, gas station attendant of the mind. In an earlier age, I might have made things. Now I only make things available."[5]

Jan recalls how, as a college student, when the need to select a major threatened to box her into a future that imperiled any wide-ranging interest in "knowledge," the career of librarian beckoned as a compromise pursuit: "The search for a starting point begins to resemble that painful process of elimination from freshman year, spent in the university clinic, a knot across my abdomen from having to choose which million disciplines I would exclude myself from forever" (87). Later, Jan recognizes that she has practiced library "games" of trivial pursuit since childhood; her mother once remarked that she "hoped to see me sit behind the Reference desk until I'd answered as many unanswerables as I had plagued her with all those years" (35). Jan's ambition to retain some measure of versatility while accumulating the knowledge necessary to range across a "million disciplines" rather than confine herself to a particular task within an exclusive field of investigation ultimately turns her into a specialist in her own right via her agility with information retrieval and archival navigation.

Rather than "know-how" about a topic in a field, she acquires a metanarrative skill at tracking down and excerpting useful tidbits from a data base. As a reference librarian in the public library, she becomes an advocate for a world of open information and public data base access. Her occupation designates one quandary inaugu-

rated by the contemporary availability of on-line, networked information; the nightshift data base crew of Ressler and Todd lays bare
a second, darker potential for surveillance and personal ruin. As
such, the library and the account clearinghouse in *Gold Bug* offer
up striking parallels of alternative futures that Lyotard forecasts
for information networks in *The Postmodern Condition: A Report on
Knowledge*: "[The computerization of society] could become the
'dream' instrument for controlling and regulating the market system. . . . an object of terror. But it could also aid groups discussing
metaprescriptives by supplying them with the information they
usually lack for making knowledgeable decisions."[6]

Even as Jan serves in the frontlines of a library corps working to
keep the archive available to a general population, her chosen professional field eventually makes her expert in forecasting the extent of an information explosion, as well as assessing the citizenry's
beleaguered ideas of valuable research projects. She comments on
her retiring colleague, for example, that he, "like everyone who
looks things up for a living, prefers Gershwin to admitting that
progress has destroyed our ability to tell which facts of the runaway
file are worth recalling. Value is the one thing that can't be looked
up" (30). In Jan's mind Lyotard's "dream instrument" lends itself to
a chaos of trivial pursuit and pundit trafficking.

In this sense Powers's fiction depicts a world where the best are
enthralled by language games that trace out the mechanisms for
pursuing unsolved mysteries of a highly personal nature and the
worst take the trivial pursuit of important facts as an end in itself—
burying us deeper and deeper in a morass of details and factoids
that form the refuse of the information glut. Jan's skills of "search
and seizure" are qualities of paramount importance in a novel that
searches for a governing principle by which to sort through this morass of delectable information and make some narrative sense of
the impulses guiding a technologically fetishistic economy. In her
capacity as a "gas station attendant of the mind," Jan depends upon
the acquisition of special research skills and tools, even as she lacks
her own specialized area of inquiry to pursue.

At the same time, a darker aspect persists in Jan's reliance upon
the technologies and methods within her field of library work that
direct the course of her daily productivity. In this, she resembles
Powers's more "accomplished" specialists: "In summer '83, I had every confidence in the power of my tools to crack the script [of the
burgeoning library technologies of information dissemination]. Two
years of even more spectacular advances in retrieval, and I'm gut-
tering in the dark" (29). Like them, a reliance upon the theorems
and tools of a specialized trade threatens to make previous skills

and insights obsolete. For a younger generation of would-be professionals, specialization offers only momentary refuge from a barrage of information. Jan's archival skills fail her not just because of the false confidence they inspire; they provide no "real" end in themselves, only daily routine.

As a result, her eventual acquisition of a personal research interest—to discern the "message" of Stuart Ressler—overrides the service she provides to generalists, incompetents, and scholars at the library. She quits her job and puts her talents to work for herself, bent upon the research project of her life: to "relive" the perspective of Stuart Ressler. Jan's private archival mission entails "reliving" an explosion in research activity in the field of molecular biology that occurred in the wake of Watson and Crick's account of a double-helix model for DNA transmission in 1954. Their discovery, Powers argues, cleared the way for investigative researchers to cross-breed linguistics with a biological science previously rooted in anatomy and the patterned behavior of organisms, launching an unprecedented borrowing across previously incompatible fields. Stuart Ressler's research group, Cyfer, works at the center of a laboratory that is "on extended leave from titrations, stains, and partition chromatography" (72). Because his group seeks principles of DNA transcription, all their research now focuses on linguistics: "For the rule linking nucleotide sequences to protein synthesis to be determined experimentally, Cyfer must first play with its shape, its inner symmetries. They are up against not so much the chemistry of biology as the math. . . . [They have] a first shot at bridging the gap, grounding organic complexity in fundamental arithmetic" (72). With the principle task of molecular biology in the late fifties understood as a coding problem—a linguistic mapping of organisms—Powers's cross-referential narratives find an ideal topic in the earlier search for the hereditary terms and processes of DNA transmission. By making these years in genome research a central focus, the novel shows how a cross-disciplinary "borrowing" and importation of metaphors and models from dissimilar fields of inquiry forms the basis for revolutions in scientific thought. In Powers's rendition molecular biologists in the late 1950s adduced formulas for interpreting "life" in terms of codes, sequences, relationships—all textual formulas. In this sense the double-helix displaced organic ideas of bodies with a mechanistic model of transmission that put human "life" in accord with molecular models of physics.

Because *fictions* of science wholeheartedly search for social corollaries to research paradigms, in the process rifling through scientific vocabularies for poetics and metaphor, they confirm John Limon's view that literature remains parasitic upon the "real" knowledge of science. The inverse proposition at the heart of *Gold Bug*—that scientific work imports paradigms from dissimilar fields—poses a controversial idea that figures science as a dependent in the familial line. For example, Ressler's impetus for "cracking the code" of genetic transmission comes from a re-reading of Poe's story where he arrives at a counter to Cyfer's party line of investigative research: " 'Gold Bug' is the ticket all right. . . . The heart of the code must lie hidden in its grammar. The catch they are after is not what a particular string of DNA says, but how it says it. . . . Not the limited game of translation, but the game rules themselves" (76-77). As a result, he shifts from seeking to "decode" DNA to working out genetic transmission as a cipher.

Powers evokes principles of importation and analogy at the root of scientific reasoning that complement the efforts of feminist science to illustrate gender bias by exploring how "the rules themselves," only recoverable through analogy, evoke preconditioned ideas of masculine activities and feminist locations. Emily Martin, for example, demonstrates how reproductive models come "tainted" with cultural preconditioning and sexed stereotyping. Teresa de Lauretis points out how ideas about narrative patterning reveal the influence of gender-biased accounts of "creation" and "reproduction."[7] *Gold Bug* perpetually mulls over the gendering of DNA base pairs as "couples" and "dark sister" ions as part of a general project to narrate contemporary "life" after its revision by a mechanistic model.

Recently, Evelyn Fox Keller, a historian and philosopher of science, has illuminated some of the implications of the repressions in scientific methodology that *Gold Bug* also brings into the open. In *Refiguring Life: Metaphors of Twentieth-Century Biology* she demonstrates how revolutions in scientific thought may be shown to depend upon a surreptitious importation of metaphors from discrete areas of research.[8] In short, for Fox Keller, one makes discoveries in research by applying the mechanics and metaphorics of a model from a dissimilar field. In Powers's novel the importation of a model from an incompatible field solves the investigative problem only at a peril to the researcher's professional identity. Chiefly, credible work, as well as preposterous importation, inevitably results in a researcher being lured beyond the confines of his or her own field of specialty.

Eventually such cross-pollinations, inasmuch as they undergird all fields of inquiry, develop into a professional impasse for all the main characters in *Gold Bug*. In this respect the male characters experience a crisis typical of masculine paradigms in fictions of science. Stuart Ressler had planned to solve DNA "in vitro" and ascertain the mechanism of human replication by means of inspiration and analogy available in musical "variation." Instead, the idea that an infinite range of "variations" derive from a limited series of notes leads him to a disciplinary crisis and results in his inexplicable desertion of his occupation as a researcher. Even as his idiosyncratic interest in Bach leads him to discern the theoretical makeup of molecular DNA, his extracurricular interest lures him beyond the scope of scientific investigation altogether.

Ressler's co-worker, Franklin Todd, suffers from another by-product of information overload: burn-out in the arena of graduate school trivial pursuit. An A.B.D. in Art History, Todd is poised to write a dissertation on an obscure Flemish painter. In his mind the studies of artistic greats, such as Rembrandt and Brueghel, have all been accomplished by previous generations of professional scholars, leaving him with the late-in-the-day project of analyzing a "mediocre" artistic practice and life. He feels stalled between writing a "lesser" repetitive study of a "great" painter or putting together an original study on a minor figure. Todd cannot make either of these leaps.

Whereas Ressler's "solution" comes across as enigmatically radical from the perspective of this younger generation, Todd's entrapment between projects constitutes a regular postmodern crisis of masculinity. Both characters seek to re-envision possibilities for their pursuit of professional goals, yet each must leave the profession of their choosing or be usurped by the limitations of the very credentials which they seek. However, the enigma of accomplishment for both of the novel's male characters, their shared interest in specialized research and their rejection of the means of pursuing it, contrasts with the female characters' "know-how" at making antiprofessional leaps in logic.

O'Deigh's eventual neglect of professional development for the sake of a private research interest in Stuart Ressler and molecular biology leads her to an *identity* as an accomplished "amateur" researcher. She is lured from a domain in which her substantial influence upon the content of knowledge would be erased into an arena where her task lies in discerning private motives out of a scientific logic. Though Jan experiences the satisfaction of acquiring the expertise of a DNA specialist through self-study, unlike Todd, no degree will certify her acquired "knowledge" of DNA theory. Like him, she stands little chance of offering up a substantial contribution to any one field of inquiry. Instead, she provides a model for the expert negotiation of incompatible vocabularies and insular research. At the end of "the year of enforced waste, the year of science" (634), Jan surmises that she has "managed a layman's guide to nucleotides, a miniature map of the man who so badly wanted in. I've come to the verge of declaring that the code codes only for the desire to break it" (615). With this comprehension of the code, Jan perches upon the same precipice from which Ressler is tossed into his "illogical," anti-professional decision.

Even as Jan prepares for the "publication" of Ressler's biography, she lacks the institutional authority for disseminating these scholarly insights on the nature of knowledge in an era of specialization. In this sense Jan undertakes and completes an investigation that mirrors Powers's novelistic project—one that perceives its own lack of influence in the disciplines which it seeks to understand and comment upon. Like amateur researchers before her, Jan resigns herself to reflecting upon the diminished status of her own project.

Professional Bohemians

Powers's novels explicitly parade the bohemian lifestyles of professionals that have emerged out of a late twentieth-century technoculture. His characters acquire latitude to cross the divide between "hard" and "soft" sciences in the guise of latter-day sixties' "radicals" who quit their jobs and drop out of the "system." His fiction celebrates the idiosyncratic success of dropouts who neglect or forego career opportunities in order to take up research projects made valuable by the very fact that they would not be sustainable within the boundaries of academic disciplines and business.

The workplace mainly functions as the delimiter of human inquiry. But because Powers's fiction also probes specialists for the nature of the dreams, phantasms, and fables that have kept them momentarily immersed in plots of professional life, his novels function as a kind of manual for a generation stalled in career counseling. As such, his fiction becomes as much about workplace culture, the behaviors and rituals of research, and the criteria for "performance" and "relevancy," as it is about a cross-disciplinary romance with "information" excerpted from the disciplinary prison of applications and protocols. His characters may feel personal diminishment, if not erasure, in the face of the developed systems of procedure and methodological guidelines that direct their professional lives, but an amateur sensibility toward fields of inquiry enables them to become interstitial operators in an era of information glut.

Even as men appear in Powers's work as having produced much of the celebrated work of historical record, his valorization of amateur, cross-disciplinary thinking restores his female characters to a central role in his fiction where they serve as model proponents of the skills of border crossing and inspired collaboration. Their status as polymathic apprentices not only resuscitates a figure from eighteenth- and nineteenth-century preinstitutional science but proves essential to innovating alternative circuits of desire and inquiry outside labyrinthine networks of professional discourse.

NOTES

[1]Richard Powers, *Galatea 2.2* (New York: Farrar, Straus and Giroux, 1995), 254; hereafter cited parenthetically.

[2]Exemplary studies of the ways in which a tradition in feminist science fiction interrogates the biases at work in scientific procedures and networks include: Jenny Wolmark, *Aliens and Others: Science Fiction, Feminism and Postmodernism* (Iowa City: Univ. of Iowa Press, 1994); and Maureen S. Barr, *Feminist Fabulations: Space/Postmodern Fiction* (Iowa City: Univ. of Iowa Press, 1992).

[3]"Feminist Theory and the Politics of *Vineland*, in *The Vineland Papers: Critical Takes on Pynchon's Novel,* ed. Geoffrey Green, Donald J. Greiner, and Larry McCaffrey (Normal, Ill.: Dalkey Archive Press, 1994), 135-53.

[4]John Limon, *The Place of Fiction in the Time of Science: A Disciplinary History of American Writing* (New York: Cambridge Univ. Press, 1990). *The Place of Fiction* characterizes the "hard" sciences as those institutions grounded upon a faith in the ability of predictive instruments to generate true representations of the interactions of ecosystems, organisms, and equipment. Rather than establish literture's credentials to translate science, Limon's scrupulous readings aim to reveal the limitations of literary contests over metaphor when confronted with the representational idols of scientific methodology. Consequently, Limon aims to reverse trends in literary criticism by billing literature as the most "antidisciplinary" of disciplines and thus throwing water on the overheated literary engine of appropriation, "experiment" and because scientific work has become too specialized for writers to comprehend without years of study, Limon consigns literary artists on amateur-*ish* practice of artistic commentary.

[5]Richard Powers, *The Gold Bug Variations* (New York: William Morrow, 1991), 35; hereafter cited parenthetically.

[6]Jean-Francois Lyotard, *The Postmodern Condition: A Report on Knowledge,* trans. Geoff Bennington and Brian Massumi (Minneapolis: Univ. of Minnesota Press, 1989), 67.

[7]Martin, *The Woman in the Body: A Cultural Analysis of Reproduction* (Boston: Beacon Press, 1989); De Lauretis, *Alice Doesn't: Feminism, Semiotics, Cinema* (Bloomington: Indiana Univ. Press, 1984).

[8]Keller, *Refiguring Life: Metaphors of Twentieth-Century Biology* (New York: Columbia Univ. Press, 1995).

"The Stereo View": Politics and the Role of the Reader in Gain

Charles B. Harris

> "The world sells to us at a loss, until we learn to afford it."
> Richard Powers, *Gain*

"The act of looking is powerful," Richard Powers told Sven Birkerts in a recent interview, "if you can see the look. And for that you need some device that gives you parallax" (62). Parallax, of course, refers to the apparent change in an object's position when that object is viewed from a new line of sight. Powers says he got the idea of structuring a novel according to the principle of parallax from Joyce's *Ulysses:*

[Joyce] told this absolutely dense realistic story—a compendium of a day in the life. But parallel to that was a frame completely contiguous to the first, and yet a kind of intellectual commentary on it. And so here were these two frames, and between the two, they straddled the great divide. Knowledge by incorporation; knowledge by exposition. (Birkerts 60)

The intersection of these "two complementary planes" in the mind of the reader, Powers continues, produces "three dimensions."
 Inspired by his discovery of parallax in Joyce's novel, Powers wrote *Three Farmers on Their Way to a Dance* (1985), whose tripartite narrative structure reflects the binocular architectonics of *Ulysses* (Birkerts 60). More than just a structural device, however, parallax plays an important thematic role in Powers's first novel. Near the end of *Three Farmers*, Peter Mays, one of several characters in the novel pursuing the meaning of an August Sander photograph taken in 1914, suddenly understands the "viscous look" in the eyes of Arkady Krakow, an aged Viennese who had confused Alison Stark with his deceased wife:

In Alison, Arkady had stumbled on one of those moments of intersection, the plane of the past cutting into the plane of the present and, in the side-by-side juxtaposition of the two, showing the closest hint of the three dimensions of the original template, which preexists the negative and lies outside time. He had read into Alison's face the forward-posted memory of his long-dead wife; they were concurrent. *No observation without involve-*

ment; no fact without interpretation. (350)

As the portion of the passage I have italicized suggests, the viewer's active collaboration is necessary before the "past-in-present, . . . side-by-side interference of two worlds" (350) resolves into three-dimensional parallax. We can recover history, Powers insists, "only by a deliberate reading-in" on our part (324). Moreover, understanding the situated nature of all historical understanding—seeing our acts of looking—is not only active, it is implicitly *activist*: "The form that delights the eye prescribes action" (336). The only responsible way to read the "concurrent past," Powers concludes in his remarkable first novel, is to "select for qualities" that will make people "less susceptible" to unnecessary pain: "Memory, thought Mays, was a reminder to change something in the future" (324-25). The concept of parallax, then, seems to have provided the young Powers with a richly suggestive metaphor from which he extracted not only an aesthetic principle but a political principle as well.

Both principles animate *Gain* (1998), Powers's sixth and latest novel. As in Powers's first novel and, again, in his third, *The Gold Bug Variations* (1991), *Gain* unfolds along contiguous narrative lines.[1] One frame recounts the two-hundred-year expansion of the Clare family's soap and candle business into a huge multinational conglomerate; the other relates the final year in the life of Laura Rowen Bodey, a forty-two-year-old divorced mother of two whose terminal cancer may have been caused by environmental pollutants from the Clare factory located in her hometown of Lacewood, Illinois. But whereas the earlier novels contain characters whose perspectives provide the context necessary to transform concurrent but separate stories into parallax, *Gain* has no such character. Laura's agonizing decline is rendered in excruciating detail, but except for a couple of insights near the end of her life—her realizations that, in addition to cancer, Clare had given her "everything else" (320), which she had willingly purchased and used (304); and that Clare's consent to an out-of-court settlement is a matter of cost-effectiveness, not a sign of contrition—Laura's response to her suffering and to Clare's culpability remains more reactive than analytical. In *Gain*, the perspective necessary to tip the novel's parallel frames into three-dimensional parallax must be supplied by

---

[1]Whereas in *Three Farmers* and *Gold Bug* Powers braids three narrative planes, two set in the present, one in the past, in *Gain* he uses two alternating narrative lines.

the reader.

As early as *Three Farmers*, Powers had predicted his eventual reliance on the reader's perspective as the primary source of parallax. P—that novel's only first-person narrator—observes: "But I am every day more convinced that it is the work of the audience, not the author (whose old role each year the machine wears down), to read into the narrative and supply the missing companion piece, the stereo view" (335). Ironically, the absence in *Gain* of a character who struggles to interpret the complex interweavings of the novel's multiple frames—the role played by P—and Peter Mays in *Three Farmers* or Jan O'Deigh and Franklin Todd in *Gold Bug*—nudges what appears to be Powers's most straightforwardly realistic novel toward the status of Barthesian text. Whereas a *work*, in Barthes' famous formulation, may be "consumed" by a reader, the *text* must be "produced" by the reader (161-62). In *Gain*, Powers foregoes the architectural design he appropriated from Joyce and employs in his first and third novels, in which "knowledge by exposition" in one narrative plane exercises "a kind of intellectual commentary" on the "knowledge by incorporation" in contiguous narrative planes. Because *Gain*'s readers are solely responsible for this missing expository dimension, they are compelled into that collaboration with the author Powers describes in *Three Farmers*: "Interpretation asks us to involve ourselves in complicity, to open a path between feeling and meaning, between ephemeral subject matter and the obstinate decision to preserve it, between the author . . . and ourselves" (257).

Which doesn't mean that Powers makes the collaborative relationship an easy one. Indeed, the novel's realistic surface and the straightforward temporal progression of its alternating narrative lines may entice unwary readers to expect a less complex book than Powers has actually written. If *Gain* sought only to chronicle a collision between an "insignificant individual" and a "corporate behemoth," as proclaimed on its jacket flap, we might agree with such early reviewers as Bruce Bawer and John Updike who commend Powers's description of the rise of corporate power in America but reprove his characters, especially Laura, as deficient in depth and Forsterian roundness. In an otherwise favorable review of the book, Bawer declares Laura to be "implausible. . . . Powers, alas, seems to have trouble resisting the urge to reduce people to his ideas about them—a surprising flaw in a novelist whose chief theme is the dehumanization of Americans by corporations" (11). Updike, too, finds "it hard to get close to any character. We never quite dwell among these people; we just collect a few pages of evidence and hurry on" (77).

Now it is true that with a few striking exceptions—Benjamin

Clare's astonished reaction to the "sachet of scentlessness" (55) during his expedition to the South Pole, Laura's break-up with the insufferable Ken at a Peoria steak-house—*Gain* generally avoids the extended dramatic particularization associated with characterization in realistic fiction. But Powers's previous books have not only established his legacy as one of the major writers of his generation, they are frequently populated with fascinating, well-drawn characters. Powers has earned the right not to be understood too quickly. If none of the characters in his most recent work ever fully materializes into an autonomous "flesh and blood" individual, we should consider the possibility that this is a strategy rather than a flaw.

Although intended as a slight, Updike's account of Laura's deterioration contains an accidental insight: "Laura's descent, like Clare's rise, is sheer process—a study in chemistry" (77). Precisely. As Tom LeClair observes in his thoughtful review of *Gain*, "Powers resists the gain of catastrophe, the aesthetic profit he might have squeezed from Laura's catastrophic illness. Like Peter Clare, a 'genius of the mundane,' Powers instead tells us about chemical cocktails and morphine dreams, stomach's revulsion and bone's agony— and how economics still asserts its demands as Laura quarrels with her HMO and refinances her house" (34). Laura is simply another waste product of corporate America's merger of money and chemistry. Clare's remarkable capacity to adapt rapidly to changing economic conditions while simultaneously influencing those conditions depends upon its ability to apply the chemical principle of conversion to the marketplace:

Money was a theory of universal conversion. Everything was procurable by the sacrifice of x units of any other object, effort, or interval of time that you might care to sacrifice for it. Barter, money, insurance, corporations: equivalence for equivalence, transfers for transfers, until all cogs turned every other in the self-replenishing whole. (*Gain* 266)

Soap's initial attraction, to both Powers and the Clare brothers, is its seemingly miraculous ability to convert filth into cleanser: "Here was a substance, grease's second cousin. Yet something had turned waste inside out. . . . This waxy mass, arising from putrescence, became its hated parent's most potent anodyne" (34). Over the course of its three-generational history, Clare converts the chemist's noble dream "of turning the refuse from every transmuting process back into the supply path of another" (170) into a marketing device. Along the way, manufacturing turns "from a living means to the meaning for living" (180), as manufacturing soap segues into merchandising soap segues into manufacturing, merchandising, and managing human desire. By pushing to its logical extreme the same "abstracting process" by which the stock market dissolves crops "into the idea of produce" and converts "grain to pure exchangeability" (208), Clare begins to sell its promotions as vigorously as it sells its products (325), displacing the "business of manufacturing necessities" with "the broader effort of manufacturing needs" (299). Realizing that "anything—anything at all—could become good business" (339), Clare responds to environmental critics by "going green," beating ecology by converting it into a commodity (339). Having evolved into an "industry of needs creation" (326), Clare spends more on packaging than on the package's contents, converts mass communication, made possible by the burgeoning television industry, into mass demand (328), and rides the wave of the new health-consciousness it has helped create by converting the fats and oils which "had built the company" into heavily promoted synthetic simulacra.[2] Not only does *Adweek* judge its "healthy eating campaign, 'Have a Good Meal,'" to be one of the decade's most recognized," but, in one of those few instances the novel veers from its realistic base into postmodernist comic exaggeration, the ad campaign is converted into a best-selling novel which is adapted into a successful film (341). Beginning with Julia Clare's early realization that "cash was a kind of chemical conversion, and chemistry, highest finance"(167), Clare, in a triumph of adaptability, has learned how to convert the very principle of conversion itself into a survival value.

Throughout Clare's three-generational history, the company's genius at conversion becomes most valuable during periods of mass destruction. This is no coincidence, according to Powers, who in *Three Farmers* describes World War I as the trigger point that hurtled us into the age of mass production: "The Battle of the Frontiers had shown that something irreversible had happened to the scale of human events. . . . The change was everywhere—in warfare, industry, the arts, a sudden shift into numerical modernity, a new mass scale. Quantitative change had become qualitative, and the war, with its seven thousand dead per day, set the standard" (126). The sheer incomprehensibility of ten thousand dead pushed culture past a threshold. "Hereafter," Powers concludes, "only the Collective counted" (126).

---

[2]Only *Utilis*, the root Benjamin discovers on the Feejee Islands, which, as the "magic additive" in Native Balm soap, saved the company from collapse in its early history, remains "beyond synthesis" (173). Significantly, Clare stops manufacturing Native Balm in 1913 (289), the year before WWI proves "the impossibility of beating the giant corporations" (297).

In *Gain*, too, World War I exposes as it underwrites the techno-capitalist distopia America has become:

> ...the war not only proved the impossibility of beating the giant corporations. It showed how much the public good now depended upon them. The electrified, biplaned, broadcast, synthetic, pharmaceuticaled, plasticized human project could no longer last a week without those vast, syndicated pools of capital. (297)

Thereafter, corporations no longer needed to fear "the new stock-holding public" (297) because they had bought them off, absorbed them into the Collective. In a series of insidious reversals, the human is converted into the corporate: incorporation transforms Clare into a "legally created person," whose "privileges and immunities" are protected by constitutional amendment (181); the Wagner Act permits Clare to "deny its employees as a group as well as individually" (309); and America becomes "less a nation than a collective outfit" (247), a joint-stock company. Inexorably, Trade "grows steadily more efficient until it everywhere holds the day. *Until, at last, it cuts out all the middlemen*" (213, italics added).

Near death, Laura insists that instead of a payoff she wants Clare's corporate president to admit responsibility for her condition, "to come sit here. In my house. Tell me why this happened" (334). Several pages later, Franklin Kennibar, Sr., Clare's CEO, reflects on his corporate role: "It has always amused him, drawing the salary he does, how little say a CEO has about anything. The corporation's point man, *the passive agent of collective bidding*" (349, italics added). Imperceptibly to Laura, conglomerated multinational techno-capitalism has long ago converted individual authority into its collective needs. In the "emerging age of the masses" (*Three Farmers* 311), the individual human being—like that single-use camera, "ready to disappear when used," which Powers describes at length near the conclusion of *Gain*—is in danger of becoming nothing more than a "disposable miracle" (348).

Gain, then, is much more than a protracted description of an individual in the process of being crushed by a corporate giant. Rather, it is a warning that "the hundred-year war between the private citizen and the mechanized state" triggered by the Great War (*Three Farmers* 303) is approaching its disastrous finale, during which not just individual persons but individualism itself will be subsumed by what philosopher J. T. Fraser calls "global socialization" (342). Although one gets the impression that the polymathic Powers has read everything, I know of no evidence that he is familiar with Fraser's work. But Fraser's evolutionary model of time resonates powerfully with much of Powers's fiction, especially *Gain*.

According to Fraser, evolution has proceeded through a hierarchy of increasingly complex temporalities or *umwelts*. The world of a biological organism is confined to the information that organism is able to process from within its *umwelt*. Poetry, for example, because it is inaccessible to a raccoon, simply does not exist within the raccoon's "eotemporal" *umwelt*. Human beings, on the other hand, are able to understand much more than raccoons can, including a lot about raccoons and their fellow creatures, because the far more complex "nootemporal" *umwelt* we occupy evolved out of the "eotemporal." Alexander J. Argyros, whose excellent summary of Fraser's philosophy I have drawn on throughout this discussion, describes human temporality as follows:

In the feedback manner typical of evolution, nootemporality is both the product and the cause of the huge human neocortex. Long-term memory, the symbolic manipulation of experience, intersubjective community, re-flexivity, the creation of counterfactual models for reality, and the ability to travel into the indefinite future and past are actually part of an evolutionary continuum whose increasing development and complication was both the product of evolution and the main selective pressure for the emergence of the human brain. (143)

Symbol-making animals, we possess the unique ability to extend our biological *umwelt* through technology, science, and art—"prosthetic devices . . . through which the slice of reality available to us has been expanded to an unprecedented extent in organic evolution" (Argyros 132).

Despite the remarkable degree of agency human beings possess (we are alone among life forms, Fraser acknowledges, in having largely invented our environment), an even more complex temporality than the nootemporal is about to evolve. "[I]f a significant portion of the earth's population achieves a threshold limit of social complexity, specifically the complexity necessary to constitute and maintain a global sociotemporal now," Fraser predicts, *"the global socialization and evaluation of time will subsume the office of the individual as the primary measure and measurer of time"* (342, italics added). Fraser's discussion of complexity thresholds coincides remarkably with Powers's concept of trigger points in *Three Farmers*, those historical junctures when quantitative change accelerates into qualitative change. *Gain*, Powers told Sven Birkerts, "is deeply influenced by a vision of technological acceleration" (61). So whether he's read Fraser or not, Powers's concern in his most recent novel is clearly with the endangerment of the individual in the face of a cultural development very similar to Fraser's emerging "sociotemporality."

Whereas Fraser accepts this development with equanimity, Powers does not. Contemporary evolutionary theory has joined forces with much poststructuralist thought in heralding a new age of determinism. Whether it's the macro-determinism of Fraser, who foresees the individual swallowed up by a new evolutionary phase, or the micro-determinism of Richard Dawkins, who argues that human beings are nothing more than disposable survival machines for our selfish genes (a concept Powers contests in *Gold Bug*), or the semiotic determinism of Jean Baudrillard, who argues that individuals are regulated by the hyperreality of codes and simulations (the world explored in *Gain*), or any of the various other attacks on or problematizations of Humanism's constructions of the self which proceed beneath the banner of poststructuralism (attacks that Powers engages in *Galatea 2.2*), the status of the individual and human agency has suffered greatly in recent decades. Powers's counter project, one he shares with such writers as Pynchon, DeLillo, the later Barth, Carole Maso, David Foster Wallace, and Curtis White, among others, is the reclamation of the idea of the human from *this* side of the postmodernist/postindustrial divide.

The individual Powers hopes to reclaim, that is, is not the nineteenth-century Romantic egoist or Modernism's existentialist hero or even quite the Habermasian post-Enlightenment individual. Rather, the individual in Powers's fiction most nearly achieves a horizon of authenticity when in dialogical exchange with other individuals. Powers's alternative to the Collective seems to be something like Bakhtin's dialogism, which privileges relationships, complicity, thereby preserving the idea of the individual but only in collaboration with other individuals. In *Three Farmers*, the "mystery of photography," whose "end product" requires the collaboration of taker, subject, and viewer (335), serves as an image of the complicity Powers endorses. The complicit individual, as depicted by Powers, represents a dialectical synthesis of Enlightenment individualism and postindustrial "mass man."

It is when Clare abandons its commitment to other human beings that the company goes off track, veering into postmodernist consumer society, whose seemingly infinite networks of advertising and media images have left any human reality so far behind that, in Baudrillard's well-known phrase, the simulacra now seem to precede the reality to which they may have once referred:

Times had again changed for business, or rather, *business had worked another change upon time.* The days of people working for other people were over. The company was no longer a band joined together for a common purpose. The company was a structure whose purpose was to make more of the same. (273, italics added)

Powers is careful to inform us that William Clare compels this radical centralization and specialization of Clare's corporate structure, which results in job positions that "filled the person more than the person filled the job" (273), just as he specifically informs us of who is responsible for most of the major decisions in Clare's history. Although somewhere along the line trade takes on a life of its own, each technological advance, each chemical conversion, each corporate policy propelling Clare from a people-oriented family business to a dehumanized conglomerate is the result of human agency, business working changes upon time rather than vice versa. As Powers pointedly observes in the Birkerts interview, "We are on the run from our own ingenuity" (62). Unlike Henry Ford, whose pithy remark, "I don't blame any person but the system," serves as the epigram for chapter 21 in *Three Farmers*, Powers—without for a moment underestimating the hegemonic pervasiveness of the cultural logic of late capitalism—blames the system on people.

Gain is an important eco-novel, but Powers, perhaps the most scientifically literate of our current major novelists, refuses to court Luddism. Throughout *Gain*, science and the technology it spawns are portrayed as boons as well as a curse. Corporate technology has poisoned the world, which in turn poisons Laura; but Laura's son, Tim, born premature, would have been "Dead on arrival, save for those machines" (110). As Laura muses while ingesting Cisplatin, "Anyone who denies modern progress has never watched a parent die from inability to pay for treatment" (114). Even Don, Laura's ex, despite his Luddite tendencies, realizes as he walks through Clare's corporate headquarters that we "[c]ouldn't go back now, if we wanted to. And who wants to? No getting along without the magic additives, the super-pesticides. Especially now that we've bred a race of super-pests with them" (258). Laura, too, understanding that "[e]very hour of her life depends on more corporations than she can count," shoulders the responsibility for her condition:

The newspapers, Don, the lawyers: everybody outraged at the offense. As if cancer just blew in through the window. Well, if it did, it was an inside job. Some accomplice, opening the latch for it. She cannot sue the company for raiding her house. She brought them in, by choice, toted them in a shopping bag. And she'd do it all over again, given the choice. Would have to. (304)

In *Three Farmers,* Powers approvingly quotes from Ernst Benjamin's "The Age of Mechanical Reproduction," an important intertext in that novel: "'The destructiveness of war furnishes proof that society has not been mature enough to incorporate technology as its organ, that technology has not been sufficiently developed to cope with the elemental forces of society' " (255). Or, as Powers tells Birkerts, "a growth in technology forces on us an attendant growth in moral sense" (63). It is that moral sense that Powers hopes to evoke in readers of *Gain*—which brings me back to the concept of parallax with which this discussion began. As suggested, for Powers the parallax phenomenon confirms "the principal truth of this century: viewer and viewed are fused into an indivisible whole. To see an object from a distance is already to act on it, to change it, to be changed" (*Three Farmers* 46). Powers urges us to look with a separate look on this "inability to separate empiric fact from personal necessity" (*Three Farmers* 207), and from the understanding that seeing our look gains, convert the inalienable principle of perception into an activist philosophy. Viewing something—a photograph, the historical record, a novel called *Gain,* the empirical world itself—is a call to action. A unique trait of the human *umwelt*—and therefore a particular human responsibility—is the "power to consume excess pain," which allows humanity to do "what evolution could not: go to the past, interpret, and select for qualities that would make people less susceptible to the unnecessary" (*Three Farmers* 324).

The surplus pain Laura suffers results less from her rampaging tumor than from the "mechanical servitude" imposed on her and her fellow sufferers by the "yoke of incorporation" (*Gain* 250). In one of the novel's more affecting scenes, Laura, while showering, surveys her tortured body:

Alien infestation. A pink, bare, cave newt, bald down to her plastic pubes. Clammy and numb and going deaf. . . . No one can tell her how much of the changes come from the cancer, how much from the chemo, how much from the meds used to soften the chemo, how much from the whiplash of coming off those meds, or how much from having her sex organs yanked out by the roots and replaced by more pills. Whatever the cause, she no longer recognizes the scraps of person left to her. (227)

Similarly, *Gain*'s reader recognizes no full-fledged humanity among the scraps of person Powers's stunted characterization provides. Seemingly missing from the novel is that "Other Fellow" to whom Powers refers in the final sentence of his first book (*Three Farmers* 352) and about whom he has been writing ever since. As suggested above, however, I believe that this omission is deliberate, a strategy rather than a flaw. The strategy is most apparent in the narrative frame relating Clare's history. Initially, the Clare brothers—the pious Samuel, the punctilious Resolve, the studious Ben—are drawn with sufficient detail to attract us to them as individuals. As Clare's history unfolds, however, these character details become so thoroughly dispersed among the welter of other details comprising the "knowledge by incorporation" with which this frame is impacted that we lose interest in the Clares as human beings. Their eventual deaths, more often merely registered by Powers than described, move us little, since by then any individual integrity they may potentially have had has been absorbed into the faceless collectivity of Clare's corporate structure. All of which, of course, is Powers's point.

Because Laura's section focuses on a single person over a much shorter period of time, however, the reader anticipates a different mode of characterization, one that preserves the circuit of identification between character and reader in a way that will allow a vicarious experiencing of Laura's protracted agony. As Updike points out, however, Powers generally views Laura's disintegration from the outside, the same aerial view, if tighter in scope, he uses in the Clare chronicle. Though risky, this narrative choice proves quite effective, it seems to me. As Powers points out several times, one needn't work for Clare or even live in Lacewood to be affected by the sprawling corporation, which "keeps so many residences that it has no fixed place of abode" (253). Throughout the Laura section, we are reminded of the extent to which Laura, like all of us, has been reduced to a marketing statistic, whether by Clare, the ubiquitous HMOs, the incessant telemarketers, or any of the other facets of late-capitalist culture dedicated to extracting gain from managed desire. The only individual we will find amidst the scraps of persons distributed through *Gain* is the Other Fellow we ourselves "read in" to the novel, ourselves supplying the missing companion piece, the stereo view, through the complicitous magic of parallax projecting a whole individual where none exists.

In his interview with Birkerts, Powers remarks: "[M]ost of my books try to work their way to an ending where the reader realizes that the story starts when you put it down" (62), an aesthetic principle upon which he further elaborates:

One of the most profound things that a book can do is to reveal the story that a reader brings to the reading act. . . . [W]e need to see that we're making this place. By revealing the book as a made thing, a thing that can both be lived in and accepted as real, one that calls attention to itself as something invented, an author can make the reader reflectively aware of the degree to which his life too is both received and invented. If we can preserve that dual sense, then we reserve the ability to go on writing our lives. (63)

The elusive Other Fellow whose complicity Powers enlists, not just to complete his novel but to help regain our world, is you.

WORKS CITED

Argyros, Alexander J. *A Blessed Rage for Order: Deconstruction, Evolution, and Chaos.* Ann Arbor: Univ. of Michigan Press, 1991.

Barthes, Roland. "From Work to Text." *Image, Music, Text.* Trans. by Stephen Heath. New York: Hill and Wang, 1977. 155-64.

Bawer, Bruce. "Bad Company." *New York Times Book Review* 21 June 1998: 11.

Birkerts, Sven. "An Interview with Richard Powers." *Bomb* Summer 1998: 59-63.

Fraser, J. T. *Time the Familiar Stranger.* Amherst: Univ. of Massachusetts Press, 1987.

LeClair, Tom. "Powers of Invention." *Nation* 27 July/3 August 1998: 33-35.

Powers, Richard. *Three Farmers on Their Way to a Dance.* New York: Morrow, 1985.

——. *Gain.* New York: Farrar, Straus and Giroux, 1998.

Updike, John. "Soap and Death in America." *New Yorker* 27 July 1998: 76-77.

A Richard Powers Checklist

Novels

Three Farmers on Their Way to a Dance. New York: William Morrow, 1985.

Prisoner's Dilemma. New York: William Morrow, 1988.

The Gold Bug Variations. New York: William Morrow, 1991.

Operation Wandering Soul. New York: William Morrow, 1993.

Galatea 2.2. New York: Farrar, Straus and Giroux, 1995.

Gain. New York: Farrar, Straus and Giroux, 1998.

Rikki Ducornet

Photograph by Victoria Straub, 1998

Finding a Language: Introducing Rikki Ducornet

Sinda Gregory

> He is responsible for humanity, for animals even; he
> will have to make sure his visions can be smelled,
> fondled, listened to; if what he brings back from beyond
> has form, he gives it form; if it has none, he gives it
> none. A language must be found. . . .
> —Arthur Rimbaud, Letter to Paul Demeny, 15 May 1871

Rikki Ducornet's fiction is many things: wonderfully detailed and encyclopedic depictions of fabulous imaginary worlds; vivid and often hilarious portraits of malice, depravity, and evil in the tradition of Bosch or Brueghel; allegories about mankind's fear of transmutation, chaos, and death and the devastation and misery these fears engender; meditations about the mysteries of sex, time, and consciousness; ecological and political parables about the twentieth century's predilection for war and mass extinction; metafictional investigations about the perils and attractions of fabulating, creating, and remembering. But more than anything else, Rikki Ducornet's fiction radiates with her own remarkable gifts as a storyteller who creates compelling and imaginative contexts in which the power, passion, and beauty of language is not only asserted but *displayed.* Indeed, her work seeks a restoration of the word's ancient and magical power to call up the tangible and to make real again what is forever gone.

In her afterword to *The Jade Cabinet* ("Waking to Eden"), Ducornet expresses her views of the function of fiction-making by noting: "I like to imagine that Adam's tongue, his palate and his lips were always on fire, that the air he breathed was kindled to incandescence each time he cried out in sorrow or delight. If fiction can be said to have a function, it is to release that primary fury of which language, even now, is miraculously capable—from the dry mud of daily use. So that furred, spotted and striped, it may—as it did in Eden—scrawl under every tree as revelation" (157). Ducornet's reference here to Eden—specifically her belief that writers can still rescue language from the "mud of daily use" and tap its original, magical connection to genuine revelation—is not just a casual remark. All of her fiction to date can be seen as being an extended literary voyage in search of the recovery of an Edenic connection between Logos and revelation. There are deep and abiding connections between Ducornet's aims in this regard and those expressed first by Rimbaud and then by the surrealists nearly fifty years later. Like the work of these earlier figures, her work is haunted by the recognition that the distance between word and truth seems to be widening as the function of language is increasingly reduced to a system of abstractions or language "games," whose goal is not the recovery of some connection with the Real but merely the efficient transformation of the real into "data" that can be easily manipulated, downloaded, stored, and retrieved. Devalued in this way by commercial transactions, politicians, and advertisers, words have fallen victim to our own postmodern era's "deconstructive" view of language, with its trendy nihilism, narrow-minded skepticism, and empty relativism—a view which allows people to abandon the search for truth entirely and to deny the possibility of (or the necessity for) any distinctions being made between good and evil.

But to understand evil requires a language to speak it—and the courage to find a means of expressing it in stories; and as George Orwell has said, the language of evil in the twentieth century is littered with *dead metaphors*—most of which were killed off in the name of justice, order, and progress. The old terms left to us point to supernatural forms our secular culture teaches us to dismiss. One of the ongoing tasks Ducornet has set for herself in her work is the creation of stories which somehow speak the truth about the world as it really is—including the truth that evil exists as do distinctions between morality and immorality and that these distinctions can be expressed in language and, further, that they must be expressed else it's all over but the shouting.

Summarized in this way, Ducornet's work may sound at once absurdly ambitious and overly concerned with abstract issues of semiology and philosophy, still another example of a postmodern text which is lost in the funhouse of language games and reflexiveness. But while it's undeniable that Ducornet's fiction is always variously and relentlessly concerned with abstract issues about the relationship between words (and stories) and their meanings, it is always equally concerned with using language's power to conjure up the real in all its messy, brutal, and wondrous guises. Like Orwell and the surrealists, Ducornet is well aware that issues of language and meaning have very real personal, political, and social consequences in the world outside the prison house of language. And like Borges and Calvino, Ducornet is equally aware that the investigation of language can be used as a precursor to the examination of other, related topics: how memory transforms our present; how narrative helps us locate ourselves and shapes the chaos of data that forms our lives; how linguistic structures can imprison and impede. Few contemporary authors deal as directly and passionately as Ducornet with our ambivalence toward language: what it gives us, what it takes away; how it makes us free, how it locks us in. Unlike most metafictionists who obsessively use words to paint a picture of the closed system of language from the inside—a perspective which never "touches" anything outside itself—Ducornet proceeds from the opposite starting point: with a view of the world *as* a kind of language and the author a kind of priest or priestess whose sacred duty is to translate this encoded reality into stories. As Ducornet says in "Waking to Eden," "the world is a ceremonial dialogue to be actively engaged" (156). As applied by Ducornet in her work, this process of engagement implies the kind of give-and-take required of any genuine dialogue. And, again, as with the works of Coover, A. Marquez, Calvino, Angela Carter, and other like-minded authors with whom she identifies, no matter how fabulous and magical her works may initially appear, they are always, unmistakably, depictions of a world we can recognize as our own. By turns grotesque, pathetic, absurd, and joyous, the world we inhabit in her fiction is a vivid, fully articulated one brought to life by visual and visceral details that range from the sublime to the scatological. Ducornet celebrates healthy appetites—of the body and of the mind—and it's from her ability to wed abstract, speculative interests to a sensuously detailed and emotional narrative that her spell is spun.

Overview and Background

Rikki Ducornet has published during the past fifteen years a total of seven books of fiction: *The Complete Butcher's Tales* (1994), a collection of grotesque speculative fables which blend surrealism, fabulism, allegory, and a rich range of arcane erudition in the manner of Borges, Poe, Lewis Carroll, and Angela Carter; an ambitious tetralogy of novels, each of which uses one of the four elements as its central controlling metaphor—earth (*The Stain,* 1984), fire (*Entering Fire,* 1986), water (*The Fountains of Neptune,* 1992), and air (*The Jade Cabinet,* 1993); *Phosphor in Dreamland* (1995), a darkly comic novel set on the imaginary Caribbean island of Birdland whose history serves as a phantasmagorical mirror of our own; and *The Word "Desire"* (1997), a collection of stories about erotic desire.

Prior to her career as a fiction writer, Ducornet was a painter and illustrator whose work has been widely exhibited both in the United States and abroad; it was this background as a visual artist that led to her first book publications which were initially illustrations for other authors' children books. She has subsequently illustrated editions of works by two writers with whom she shares numerous commonalties—J. L. Borges (*Tlön, Uqbar and Orbis Tertius,* 1983) and Robert Coover (*Spanking the Maid,* 1981). A lifelong devotee of the nonsense verse and children's fiction of Edward Lear and Lewis Carroll, she eventually wrote and illustrated her own children's books, *The Blue Bird* (1970) and *Shazira Shazam and the Devil* (1972). Her earliest writings were poems and prose poems, published in limited editions and in Canadian small-press magazines; altogether her poetry has been collected into six volumes: *From the Star Chamber* (1974), *Wild Geraniums* (1975), *Knife's Notebook* (1977), *The Illustrated Universe* (1979), *Weird Sisters* (1976), and *The Cult of Seizure* (1989). She has also co-written a play, *Dimsumzoo* (with Rosanna Yamagiwa), that was performed in Denver in 1993.

But despite working in so many different aesthetic forms, there is a basic continuity in Ducornet's thematic and formal interests that makes her work all of a piece. From her earliest drawings up through her most recent book, Ducornet's imagination has always been finely attuned to the beauty, brutality, and infinite variety of the sensual world and to its ever-abiding processes of metamorphosis and transformation; as well, her early interest in surrealism and in the visual arts generally is everywhere evident in her fiction with vivid descriptions which frequently conjoin unlikely objects, phrases, and events in order to produce epiphanies. There are also a number of themes, character types, and archetypal images that recur throughout her work. These commonalties—many of which can already be observed in her poetry and in the earliest of the stories later collected in *The Butcher's Tales*—are perhaps most evident in her tetralogy whose individual novels all deal with a set of recurrent preoccupations. Some of these topics include the nature of evil and its relationship to our aversion of "otherness"; the joys and mystery of sensual pleasure; childhood and the destructive, distorting influence that parents have over children; people's fear of change and the unknown and the ways these fears become transformed into racism, hatred, and dogmatic systems; and the deceptive, seductive, and redemptive nature of language. These thematic concerns are also linked poetically by a variety of highly charged images such as the ogress, the camera, twins, gardens, the cosmic egg, and the expulsion from Eden. Human speech itself is often forefronted: two of her heroines cannot speak. Stuttering and other speech impediments are often associated with "good" characters, such as Emile in *The Stain,* Tufts in *Entering Fire,* Toujours-Là in

The Fountains of Neptune, and Charles Dodgson in *The Jade Cabinet;* this is paralleled by the linguistic facility and rhetorical assuredness of such villains, rogues, racists, and demagogues as the Exorcist and Mother Superior in *The Stain,* Septimus in *Entering Fire,* and Tubbs in *The Jade Cabinet.*

Rikki Ducornet's literary sensibility is informed by a wide and weird amalgam of sources: antique gazetteers and atlases; museum catalogs; the art and writings of the surrealists; Victorian nonsense writers like Lear and Carroll; occult speculations such as the Cabala; magic realists like Borges, García Márquez, and Carter; the reminiscences of her own Cuban grandmother; the lives of the saints; medieval bestiaries and encyclopedias both real and imaginary; Jungian psychology; the writings of naturalists, zoologists, and anthropologists of earlier eras; and her own observations from a widely traveled life spent in Egypt, Chile, Canada, France, North Africa, and Central America. As a result, both her prose and her peculiar range of erudition have an exotic patina unique among contemporary novelists.

Rikki Ducornet was born Erika DeGre on 19 April 1943 in Canton, New York. Her father was a professor of sociology, and her mother hosted community-interest programs on radio and later on television. Ducornet grew up on the campus of Bard College in New York, earning a B.A. in Fine Arts from the same institution in 1964. While at Bard she met Robert Coover and Robert Kelly, two ambitious, innovative authors who shared Ducornet's own fascination with metamorphosis and provided early models of how fiction might express this interest. (During this same period she also knew Donald Fagan who later as a member of Steely Dan wrote the hit song "Rikki Don't Lose That Number" about her.) Ducornet's early artistic interests were in painting and illustrating; in particular, she was attracted to the surrealists—Max Ernst, Paul Eluard, and the earlier Salvador Dalí—both for aesthetic reasons and for the political and philosophical implications of their work. In 1962 she married Guy Ducornet, a French Fulbright scholar she met at Bard who shared her interest in surrealism and political activism. By 1963, her artwork began appearing in solo and group exhibitions with fellow surrealists and, over the next few years, would be seen in Algeria, Belgium, Portugal, France, Germany, and Scandinavia. The next two years were spent in Algeria where Guy Ducornet fulfilled his military duty—a commitment he had protested and deferred by his stint in the Fulbright program. When they returned to the United States, they were alarmed and horrified by the growing U.S. involvement in Vietnam and left New England again in 1968 for Ontario; then in 1972 they moved to a small remote village in the

Loire Valley in France, where they lived in a farmhouse on a vine-yard for the next decade. During the seventies, while continuing her work as a visual artist, Ducornet began working in literary forms as well as the visual arts, publishing a children's novel and four books of poetry. But it wasn't until the late seventies that she began to write fiction in earnest, developing the series of fabulous, surrealist tales that were eventually collected into *The Butcher's Tales.* Published by a small press in Canada and authored by an expatriate American woman, it was hardly surprising that the appearance of *The Butcher's Tales* went almost totally unnoticed. What surely is surprising (at least to readers who had not read her poetry) is that this first collection of fiction seems to display such a fully matured and unique sensibility, one already capable of devising a remark-able variety of innovative forms suitable of expressing themes that she has continued to explore.

About the same time that this early version of *The Butcher's Tales* appeared, Ducornet had begun work on her first novel, the extraordinarily black, erotic fairy tale, *The Stain.* The book was first published in England, where British critics and reviewers immedi-ately marked the arrival of a major new talent. Robert Nye, review-ing the book for *The Guardian,* called *The Stain* "the most brilliant first novel that I have read in years, a beginning which has much about it to excite the keenest expectations." Angela Carter, whose works have been frequently compared to Ducornet and who would eventually become a friend, was similarly enthusiastic: "A riotous extravaganza, comic, melodramatic and touching, that goes over the top time and time again but never loses its antic grace and sure sense of place—rural France, part cesspit and part Paradise." But when the book was eventually brought out in a Grove Press edition in the U.S., it was once again largely ignored. Yet the enthusiastic attention received by *The Stain* and her next novel, *Entering Fire,* in England helped Ducornet win a Bunting Institute fellowship at Radcliffe in 1988. This resettlement was an important move for her and, after her return (no longer married to Guy Ducornet), her works began to attract the first stirrings of attention and admira-tion in the U.S. from critics, reviewers, and eventually from the edi-tors at Dalkey Archive Press which, with *The Fountains of Neptune,* began publishing her new work on a regular basis, as well as bring-ing out new editions of earlier books that had been ignored or al-lowed to go out of print. In 1989 she accepted a full-time position in the English Department at the University of Denver, where she has been ever since, aside from occasional visits back to France.

Earth

"The roots of all things whisper together under the earth."
—Poupine, in *The Stain* (113)

Rikki Ducornet's first novel, *The Stain* (1983), is set in a late-nine-teenth-century French peasant village not too different from the village where she and her husband spent nearly ten years. As Ducornet explains in the interview included in this issue, before her arrival, she had assumed that what she would find there would be like something out of Rousseau—noble savages going about their lives freed from the constrictions of artificial and deadening institutions. What she found instead was a place where people's fear of the unknown found expression in racial intolerance and hatred, where religion and superstition and secular dogma are in complicity to justify exploitation and corruption, and where a social structure of blatant and crude power-wielding fostered an atmosphere in which men brutalized their wives, the wives brutalized their children, and the children eventually grew up to repeat the cycle.

It is into this savage Eden—a landscape that will be revisited and remetaphorized in all of Ducornet's subsequent novels—that the book's central character, Charlotte, is born and raised. Ducornet describes the bloody birth which gives life to Charlotte and death to her mother from the perspective of Charlotte's loutish, brutal hus-band. It's not a scene for the squeamish but very much for readers who appreciate an author capable of releasing language's "primary fury" in a rush of words endowed with the kind of poetic precision and awful lyricism required to do justice to such a resonant mo-ment:

He returned late, his boots heavy with mud. A fat hare, firm-fleshed and golden, hung by its ears from his belt. Even as he rode into the courtyard, he could hear her cries. She was wild, like a forest thing trapped, wounded and terrified. Her crazed eyes shown white, her spread thighs, the ravine of her sex and the heaving mound of her belly formed a monstrous land-scape, not human, not of this world, the pit of Hell itself. And then she saw him. And she saw, dripping blood by his side, the dead hare. And as her baby spilled from her body she screamed, one brilliant blade of sound that—as a sword-tip breaks, striking bone—left a ragged edge of silence poised upon the air. So Charlotte was born. (12)

Disfigured by an enormous birthmark in the form of a leaping hare, Charlotte's stain is a richly ambiguous sign which—somewhat like Hester Prynne's scarlet letter and Ahab's doubloon—is read by other characters in the novel according to their own subjective needs. To her caretaker Aunt Edna, the stain is a stigmata sent by God to remind everyone of her mother's sin and her own fallen nature; to her mild, loving Uncle Emile, the mark is no stain but a sign of being touched by nature herself. And to the village exorcist, Charlotte's birthmark is Satan's sign, a brand that proclaims her as his gift from the Devil intended as his ultimate reward for a life of service and devotion. To Charlotte herself, the stain simply indicates that she is someone set apart. For Ducornet, however, the stain is most essentially the mark of the primal connection with the earth—one that Charlotte shares with all living creatures.

Fire

> "This love of women has been inseparable from a burning desire to know. The Eternal Feminine throbs at the heart of Mystery."
> —Lamprias de Bergerac, *Entering Fire* (21).

Ducornet notes in "Recovering Eden" that *Entering Fire* was "intended to be read quickly—as one runs barefoot over embers" (158), and to this end her two narrators, father and son, move us rapidly through a series of settings—late-nineteenth-century France, where Lamprias conceives Septimus, the son who will be his nemesis; the Amazonian jungle where Lamprias begins his career as a orchidologist and finds the love of his life, Cûcla, "squatting by a low fire, gnawing on a grilled iguana" (21); the Paris of Proust's era; New York City at the turn of the century; France during the German occupation; the U.S. during the McCarthy era. Fires, actual and symbolic, appear throughout the novel: the fires of racial hatred and genocidal madness; the scorching heat of the Amazonian Forest of Fire; and the twin fires of passion and hatred which burn in the hearts of the father and son. The obsessions of these two figures are mirror opposites: Lamprias with his unquenchable eroticism and his fearless desire to confront the mysteries and cruelties of the universe; Septimus, repulsed and outraged by his own body, filled with loathing of women and sexuality, contemptuous of beauty and innocence, and propelled by fantastic energies and talents for producing death and destruction.

Septimus is a brilliantly conceived monster—Ducornet's most memorable villain to date—chilling in his ferocity and venomous rage. But whereas Ducornet tends to present even the most monstrous of her characters with an unsettling mixture of amusement and horror, her treatment of Septimus has little of the comic ironies found in, say, *The Stain's* Mother Superior or Radulph Tubbs in *The Jade Cabinet*. Ducornet frequently gives many of the best lines to her villains, and certainly Septimus is no exception. A misogynist and racist, a despiser of everything he cannot understand and control, he spits out wondrously *stylized* rants whose fury and anger glow in a white heat of poetry and rhetorical brilliance. Thus he describes history as "a wayward wife sorely in need of a flogging. She is a thief with a herring down her blouse, a menstruating ninny, a Sapphic nun, a burlesque queen. She is above all the mother of monsters and broken promises" (133). Or consider the following passage where he describes his relationships with prostitutes in a manner that evokes the confused mixture of hatred and lust that perfectly sums up his attitude toward the sensual. His preference among "public women" are for those who are:

yellow, Arab or Semite, whose smell of cheap soap and powder, whose every mole, scar and hair I despise as passionately as I crave. In the act I have murdered thousands. It is fortunate for men like myself that for money there are many who will allow themselves to be beaten black and blue with a hairbrush. . . . These few, very few, angry and vain beasts are the only members of the sex (except, *évidemment,* M'man) for whom I have felt, mingled with loathing, an emotion that might possibly begin to approach what some men call admiration. I am thinking in particular of a Jewess, her red hair framing her face like a hoop of fire, who dared kick me in the chest with a small, satin-slippered foot. That instant of pain and shock, as the sharp heel thumped against my startled heart, was an instant—the only instant—that I believe I might have felt tenderness. (11-12)

In these and many other fascinating and unsettling passages, Septimus demonstrates the ways that evil, madness, and death can be promoted through the seductive use of language. In the book's final pages he defiantly observes, "The world has not yet been vaccinated: Hate's cleansing virus still flickers like a thousand candles in the air," and closes the narrative with one last taunt for his father "Still tinkering with your filthy experiments, you sorcerer? Still living with an ape? One of these days, I'll show up just when you least expect me. Last time I smashed your spectacles—do you remember?" (158-59)—a threat and a promise that has resonated throughout the history of horrors that has been our last few decades of world "peace."

Water

I insist that the self is rooted in nostalgia and reverie, and that they are the fountains of Art. I argue that Art reveals the real. That the existential is always subjective. All that is true is hidden deep in the body of the

> world and cannot be taken by force. It must be dreamed
> and attended and received with awe and affection. But
> be careful. You are walking a tightrope. Madness is
> often the handmaiden of genius. To survive the world
> we must all be lucid dreamers!
> —Dr. Kaiserstiege, *The Fountains of Neptune* (190).

In many ways *The Fountains of Neptune* is the most complex book
in Ducornet's tetralogy; here water functions to evoke a series of
associations concerning the origins of memory, myth, dream, the
self, and art. The novel tells the story of Nini, an orphan living in a
French fishing village on the eve of World War I and of the adult he
later becomes—the Sandman, an elderly, childlike man who awakens from a coma to discover that he has slept through two world
wars. When he awakens, he begins the process of rediscovering who
he is and what the world has become while he slept; with the aid of
Doctor Venus Kaiserstiege, the world's only Freudian hydropothist,
he is gently led through a series of revelations about his childhood
generally and in particular about the traumatic event at its center:
witnessing the murder of his father by his mother's lover and their
own subsequent bloody deaths at the hands of angry villagers.

Nini's memories of his past center on events that occurred in two
locations—the kitchen, where his aunt ("Other Mother") attempted
to erase his memory of what he witnessed by gorging him with food,
and the Ghost Port Bar, a seedy run-down establishment where his
uncle often took him. Ducornet celebrates the joys of sensual existence in all her works, and although she frequently associates food
with forgetfulness, her descriptions of food—its smells and tastes,
its preparation and ingredients, its consumption—constitute some
of her most lyrical writing. Inevitably, Nini's recollections of food
are also frequently linked in various ways to the sea. Thus he recalls Other Mother opening the kitchen door wide, "flooding the
room with all the smells of a summer's night: flowering hyssop,
sage, the sorrel patch, which threatens to invade our back stoop,
gull flight (I swear their feathers leave a sweet smudge upon the
air), the seaweed tumbled on the nearest beach, the water itself,
yes, the sea. . . . The smell of sea water fills the house" (17).

But Nini shares with all children a hunger that can't be satisfied
in the kitchen—a hunger for stories of adventure and magic; it is
his uncle who feeds these longings when he allows Nini to accom-
pany him to the Ghost Port Bar, "a smoke-filled, shadow-spooked,
hole-in-the-wall no bigger than an oyster on the half-shell" (23),
where Nini listens in rapt amazement to sailors tell of mermaids
and ogresses, opal mists and listing ships with improbable names
like the *Søren Kierkegaard* sailing to the sapphire ports of Africa's

eastern seaboard and beyond. These sailors' tales are as marvelous and haunting as anything Ducornet has yet written; like the fabulous stories about seventeenth-century Birdland (the imaginary Caribbean island that is the setting in *Phosphor in Dreamland*), they evoke a period—the last such period—before photography, scientific data, textbooks, and PBS documentaries had drained the world of much of its magic and mystery. These tales, then, are parables about the nature of art and the roots of human myth-making; as they explore the mysteries of the sea, the sea in turn becomes an extended metaphor for the unconscious and global memory. Some of these stories about the Ogress—the evil, devouring, sexually voracious every-woman, part-whore and part-temptress, who lures sailors to a watery death—have a profound impact on Nini because the local townspeople saw his mother as a similar kind of monster. His fifty-year-long coma is itself induced after he sees her image reflected in the water and leaps after it, willing to drown for the sake of touching her face. When he awakens decades later, he finds himself a stranger to both the new world and his own past; in order to reconstruct his story and reclaim his life, Nini conjures an imaginary companion named Oliver, and together they begin to build an Edenic world of miniaturized landscapes populated by armies and animals. Through art, they find a way for Nini to return to the real.

As this plot summary suggests, on its most basic narrative level, *Neptune* can be read as a case study—a portrait of how an individual heals from the traumas inflicted during childhood. But this psychological current in just one of many feeding into the larger narrative framework, so that the novel becomes an exploration of memory and the relationship of madness to artistic creation, the way that "Time wreaks havoc" on all things (135), how knowledge denied and repressed returns to haunt us as ghosts, and about our century's love affair with war and destruction.

Air

> Let's suppose memories are like those special things; each star, each rain of meteors, each eclipse is like the last and yet it isn't because the mind, you see, *is never in the same place twice.*
> —Memory Sphery, *The Jade Cabinet* (92).

The final installment in Ducornet's tetralogy, *The Jade Cabinet,* uses air as its central metaphor, and thus, not unexpectedly, it is the "lightest" of these novels in the sense of possessing a certain airiness and brightness of tone that is unique among her works. Like each of the three previous books and like her next novel, *Phosphor in Dreamland, The Jade Cabinet* unfolds in a series of journal entries and recollections from two different characters—Memory Sphery and Radulph Tubbs. Together their perspectives combine to tell the life of Memory's sister, Etheria, who is married off by her father to an abusive and tyrannical Victorian industrialist, Radulph Tubbs, and who later uses magic to conjure herself into a disappearing act that frees her from her entrapment. Tubbs is the novel's "heavy" and resembles all of Ducornet's villains in being a figure who has "a terror of the grotesque and the fanciful—he abhorred anything that intimated the extraordinary" (53). Just as Septimus's disgust for anything that wasn't round indicated a deeper loathing for "irregularities" of race and gender, Tubbs's admiration for pyramids ("they were solids and geometric shapes; he hated anything convoluted" [53]) is seen by Memory as revealing something similar: "My theory is he hated and feared the world's feminine aspect—that is to say, anything folded, concealed, creased" (53). As is the case with the Exorcist, Septimus, and Fogginus (in *Phosphor in Dreamland),* his anal-compulsive tendencies, his rhetorical skills, and power-wielding form the outer mask of someone who is desperately fearful of everything he can't dominate and reduce to the abstractions of logic. Like the Victorian industrial age he represents, Tubbs is "all greed and gravy: three puddings at the pudding course, his fingers perpetually redolent of Stilton, and his *favoris* of maraschino jelly" (42). who believes "only in what can be seen, or touched, or eaten" (75).

As do the other books in the tetralogy, *The Jade Cabinet* shows how the dynamics of power work against the child even in a loving household. Like all of Ducornet's central characters, Etheria suffers from a childhood trauma whose effects she later must come to grips with as an adult. Hoping to be able to precipitate the gift of miraculous speech in his daughter, her father, Angus, abandons her one day in a sunny meadow outside Oxford; Etheria manages to find her way back home by following a trail of stones and shells she had dropped along the way, but upon her arrival she is so shocked by the agitated sounds of her parents arguing that she, like Charlotte after she ate glass, is rendered speechless. She grows an avid listener, clever, clairvoyant in spirit, so dreamy and incorporeal that she appears to levitate an inch above the ground—but she is no match for the brute materiality of Tubbs, for his obsessive need "to reduce her to a quantifiable lump of reality he could paw at his leisure" (133). Her sweet and gentle father allows their marriage for a few pieces of beautiful jade, and Etheria's eyes become those "of a child who has been unjustly and severely punished . . . because the ways of the world are cruel, inscrutable, and unjust, and the power of adults boundless and blind" (120).

Beaten, raped, confined in a sterile world of weight and reason, bricks and assembly lines, Etheria finally finds a way to escape, leaving behind her sister, Memory, to tell their story and "to reanimate planets that have long ceased to spin" (9). *The Jade Cabinet* is, among other things, an allegory about the ways the human imagination can use the magical properties of language to construct systems that provide connections with and yet float free of the Real. As the embodiment of these transformational systems, Etheria is able to literally take flight from her captor—her spirit and imagination more powerful than all his walls and words. As Memory explains at the end of the novel, "if, as our father Angus Sphery believed, there exists a Divine Tongue capable of bringing all things into being, *the opposite is also true*. Etheria had found the Word, surely a silent one, that had caused her to vanish forever from the life of Radulph Tubbs" (153-54).

Dreamland beyond the Elements:
A New Language of Desire

Sleepers awaking, our grey flesh tingling beneath the
warm tongues of sister suns, the old dreams stirred;
our blood flowed fast now, darkening, already inventing
a new language for Desire.
—"Voyage to Ultima Azul, Chapter 79"
(*The Complete Butcher's Tales* 162).

Phosphor in Dreamland, Ducornet's fifth novel and the first conceived outside the framework of her tetralogy, is perhaps her richest and most ambitious work to date, a book brimming over with eccentric characters, fabulous plot elements, and catalogs of the exotic—all brought to life via vivid, painterly details. Unfolding as a series of letters from a contemporary resident of Birdland, an imaginary egg-shaped Caribbean island, to an old friend in Australia, *Phosphor* describes the peculiar history of the island, particularly the tumultuous events during the seventeenth century when the first Europeans arrived in Birdland, bringing with them their arrogance, guns, and a belief system composed of an incongruous and dangerous blend of prejudices, rationalism, religion, superstitions, and scientific methodologies. The book's narrator has grown fascinated with the island's culture and history, which are re-created for the reader with an anthropologist's precision and a novelist's delight in storytelling. There are in fact literally hundreds of stories told here—"micronarratives" that appear briefly in virtually every paragraph of the book, introduced in bits and pieces that the reader is invited to complete; but the central plot involves the life of Phosphor, an orphan who was adopted and then harassed by Birdland's first scholar, Fogginus. As a youth, Phosphor invents the first camera—an ocularscope—and soon afterward his fortunes change when a wealthy islander becomes intrigued with the invention's capacity to duplicate reality faithfully. Eventually Phosphor falls in love and, after overcoming an extended series of obstacles, celebrates the consummation of his love by writing a great poem "in which all the delights of the body, all those secret pleasures that unite the sexes in lucent blindness—in fact *a way of seeing*—were not only listed by name, but described in loving detail" (157). Scandalized by what Phosphor has produced, the island's version of the Inquisition uses an obscene funnel to pour quicklime down the poet's throat. In this manner, Phosphor's story ends tragically, his voice forever "silenced simply because he had been passionately in love" (162). Or so it initially seems.

Meanwhile, the novel's framing device has gradually revealed a second story that permits the novel to have a happy ending after all. This "bookend" plot concerns the burgeoning love affair between the narrator and Polly, a Birdland native who has recently returned from New Zealand to become the new curator of the island's Museum of Natural History. In the course of her duties Polly has unearthed a number of startling, erotically charged paintings and stone figures (several of which appear in the novel's appendix) from Birdland's ancient culture which had long been thought to have been lost. Moreover, it turns out that Phosphor's great erotic love poem was not destroyed; indeed, it has not only stubbornly persisted but has proliferated to the point where "one cannot go anywhere on the island these days without hearing its verses, which have all been put to music" (161-62). In the novel's concluding scene the narrator descends into the museum's "darkest collection"—objects of torture and dismemberment used by the Inquisition in an effort to "break the bones and the spirits of its enemies"—and consummates his passion with Polly by engaging in what he describes as *"the one dance and the only dance that matters"*: the ancient dance of carnal love (162-63).

In *Phosphor in Dreamland* Ducornet has constructed a remarkable narrative composed of many textures: part ecological parable; part lament for Western Culture for whom the pleasures of the body and appreciation for the physical world have been dulled by fear, arrogance, and technological skill at transforming the real into marketable commodities and representations; and part celebration of the human capacity to revel in our flesh despite its relentless and messy mortality. Ducornet has succeeded in creating the kind of "dreamland" described by Dr. Kaiserstiege in *The Fountains of Neptune:* a "lucid dream" which reveals the real and one which thereby allows us "to survive the world." The "survival" being proposed here by Kaiserstiege and Ducornet is, it should be emphasized, neither that of some fanciful transcendence of mortality (the heaven of Christian theology) nor one in which the order and beauty of art somehow oppose, or hold at bay, the forces of death and disorder. Rather, it is one which calls for a full and sensuous engagement with life in its own time in all of its various guises. Rikki Ducornet's art luxuriates in profusion and diversity—of language, of bodily appetites; to enter her fictional worlds is to find oneself roaming a wild landscape where no species are extinct and where all words can be found.

At the Heart of Things
Darkness and Wild Beauty:
An Interview with Rikki Ducornet

Sinda Gregory and Larry McCaffery

SINDA GREGORY: What kind of books did you read when you were a kid?

RIKKI DUCORNET: One of my favorite books was Heinrich Van Loon's *Ancient Man,* filled with his strange little drawings. Whether he was sketching Neanderthals or Babylonians, Van Loon's ancients all looked like insects. Ceram's *Gods, Graves and Scholars* had drawings too; I recall a mysterious *House in Ur* and Mayan glyphs of the months of the year. And, of course, I read *Alice.*

LARRY MCCAFFERY: I know you spent some time as a child in Egypt. Did that have any kind of an influence on your sensibility?

RD: I was *stunned* by Egypt. We lived there one year. My father was Cuban, and so we also spent some time in Cuba, too, when I was very small. I cherish memories of the old Havana.

LM: That's interesting simply because it seems to provide a biographical connection with the Latin American fabulism and magical realism feel that your writing often has.

RD: I had a very *Marquezian* grandmother—fantastical, greedy, and narcissistic. She was a perverse storyteller, and she was an anti-Semite. She never forgave my father for marrying my mother—who was Jewish. Once, when she thought she was dying, she confessed to a black African and a Jewish ancestor. Like the fresh chocolate in one of her favorite stories that was spoiled by a naughty schoolboy's sliced-off finger, the family blood had been soiled.

SG: This sounds like some of the images and background material that appear in *Entering Fire.*

RD: Emelina Carmen Dionysia is the bad wind behind much of my work.

LM: At what point did you start becoming interested in surrealism?

RD: I first came to surrealism in early childhood and through the back door: via Dalí and Cocteau. I say "back door" because both were titillated by totalitarianism and, in fact, were not surrealists. Cocteau never was and Dalí only briefly. But the *convulsive* beauty of Cocteau's *Blood of a Poet*—which I saw at the age of eight—and Dalí's inspired drawings from the thirties and early forties really seized my imagination. After that I was forever hunting down a similar resonance or *quality;* it was a kind of hunger. Remember, I grew up near a college library. I found Ernst and Eluard (*together!* a book with a pale blue cover and treacherously brittle pages), Duchamp, Tanguy, and even Jarry. Breton's *Nadja* was one of *the* books of my adolescence. Later on, when Guy Ducornet and I returned from Algeria, we met the Chicago-based group *Arsenal* at the first anti-Vietnam war rally in New York City and soon after joined the Paris-based international group, *Phases.* My engagement with both was primarily as a graphic artist; I didn't start writing until much later.

LM: Your first one-person show was in Algeria. What was the background of that?

RD: Just after Algeria, independence Guy went to Constantine for a two-year engagement in the *Coopération* (the French equivalent of the Peace Corps). I went with him. During the day I was alone and could not move freely through the city—it proved too dangerous: I looked Arab, and I refused to wear a veil. So I did drawings—imaginary architectures inspired by the human face and ideal landscapes.

SG: What was it that first awakened your interest in writing fiction?

RD: Just after the coup d'état in Greece, I read a piece by a leftist agitator who had been arrested and tortured. During the interrogation she miscarried. I felt such outrage I wrote all night and when I finished I had a strange little book called *From the Star Chamber.* Its dark energy is rooted in the torture of Algerian students in Paris, the night of Crystal, My Lai, Hiroshima . . . and in my personal life also. Guy's brother had died in a car crash; my mother was battling cancer. The first *Butcher's Tales* are here.

LM: Charlotte Innes's *Nation* article referred to *The Butcher's Tales* in painterly terms—for instance, she likened those stories to miniatures. I realize this topic is probably something that's difficult to articulate with any degree of precision, but could you talk about the way your background as a visual artist may have influenced your fiction?

RD: Looking at the paintings of the artists I love—such as Bosch or Vermeer—has had an influence on the way I see the world and so on the way I write. Often I want a kind of Vermeer light—that *transcendency*—and a Boschian "noise." That savagery. That clarity. That delicacy.

LM: I first became aware of your work when I saw those drawings you did for Bob Coover's *Spanking the Maid.* Those seemed to be beautifully integrated with what Bob was doing in that piece—his interest in representing transformation and metamorphosis, the peculiar combination of abstraction and sensuousness, and so on.

RD: We met in '66. I was drawing, *transforming,* objects. They were like aberrant natural histories or subversions of encyclopedia plates. And Bob was writing *Pricksongs*—those wonderfully mutable stories. There was a startling affinity there; our friendship has been long and delightful.

LM: Were you aware of Robert Kelly's work? Wasn't he at Bard about that same time?

RD: How interesting that you should mention him! Yes, I met both Bob Coover and Robert Kelly at Bard. I hadn't thought of Kelly influencing my work before, but I thought "Cities" was a fascinating piece of work when I first came across it; and you're right—it *did* fire my imagination. I also loved his novel: *Scorpions.*

SG: Fairy tales and other forms of fabulous storytelling that you've used in your work are similar to science fiction—that is, anything can happen from one moment to the next as long as it fits into the logic of the story, as opposed to realistic fiction, where you're locked into describing only certain kinds of characters and events. Obviously your approach allows you to present these transformations almost "naturally," in a way.

RD: The world was imbued with beauty and magic when I was a child. I had the luck to grow up on the Bard campus which, as I think of it now, reveals itself as an *axis mundi*—a metaphysical core. There was a window of green glass on the second story of the old library. For a child of six, walking across it to shelves on the other side was like walking on water. Beneath it, the first floor looked like it was submerged. I used to dream of libraries that were also aquariums. And there was an intimate biology lab—its door always open—filled with queer things floating in jars. A few years ago when I met Rosamond Wolff Purcell, we discovered that for both of us childhood has the intoxicating smell of *formaldehyde!*

Once while walking in the woods with a friend, we came upon the body of a red fox swarming with bees. And I think because I had been reading so many fairy tales that summer, the fox's body seemed magical, portentous—and the forest enchanted. I remember we both needed to shit—to leave a mark, an offering of some kind—beside the body of the fox. As though at some pagan altar! Because the encounter was sacred somehow, simultaneously beautiful and terrible. Like Black Kali! Or a scene from *Le Chien Andalou!*

LM: It strikes me that the things that you're talking about pose in a very deep-down way, the central direction of Western Europe ever since the French Revolution—that is, this sort of massive, collective cultural effort to stop change, stop transformation, or at least find a means of controlling it.

RD: On the contrary, the direction has not been to stop but to accelerate change. The Market has become a global power—that is an unprecedented transformation. The "great history" has been an infamous history of oppression—domestic and foreign—and one ethnic and nationalist conflict after another. Advances of a democratic nature—so threatening to the market—are finite compared to the ecological and social ravages so evident since the Industrial Revolution.

The right is eager for change when it is financially profitable—no matter what the consequences—and fearful of changes that will bring about social justice. And the Market exploits the profound connection between nature and autonomy. There is a long and bloody history of such exploitation. For example, recall England's ecological destruction of Ireland which led to the enslavement of a people. To justify their violence, the British pointed to the Spanish in the New World, just as the French in Algeria pointed to the genocide of the American Indian. The *transformation* taking place in Chiapas right now is the consequence of the same hateful mechanism. Threatened with starvation, free people are quickly made into slaves.

Paradoxically, the left is engaged in *conservation*—conservation of cultural, ecological autonomy and diversity—and the change the left is calling for is a profound change of heart. There are two important books that come to mind—one is Karl Polany's *The Great Transformation* in which he demonstrates how human society has become an accessory of the economic system, and the other is David E. Stannard's brilliant *American Holocaust*.

LM: Your works seems to display a sense of the world as a place of inscrutability. There's an emphasis, let's just say, on mystery. Again, this goes back to the notion of the realistic novel, which emerged in the eighteenth century during the age of empiricism and which, seemingly, wanted to create the illusion of a world where everything can be explained. In your work I never get that sense. There's always that respect for ambiguity.

SG: It seems like the negative characters in your work are often the ones who are trying to explain and catalog and quantify it all.

RD: The terror of the unknown—which is also a terror of death and of change—is also the terror of the other. So terror of the strange is also terror of the stranger. If in *The Jade Cabinet* Radulph Tubbs destroys Etheria's garden, it is because it is the one place she can be free—and this makes her *strange*. And the garden exemplifies the natural world's sexual sprawl, beauty, mutability; the subversive quality of poetry.

LM: There's that incredible moment in *The Stain* when Charlotte's father comes home to find his wife about to give birth and that moment of horror. That scene struck me as one of the most powerful moments in your work. It seemed to embody that fear of the feminine, the fear of mystery, the fear of, of everything that that represented— the blood, the birth, the vagina, the mystery. All these things seem to come together right at that moment.

RD: Exactly. Charlotte's father is a hunter; he's been out in the woods reducing life to a bone. He exemplifies the lie that because things die (or can be *seized* or soiled) they have no intrinsic value— a profoundly fascist idea that broods at the heart of capitalism: nature and people reduced to marketable objects.

Remember Robinson Crusoe and his endless list? He survived on his island only because an entire hardware store washed to shore.

SG: The thrust of a lot of recent feminist criticism often associates this desire for meaning and order—I guess you could call it this rationalist impulse—specifically with masculinity, while women are seen as resisting order and being more in tune with mystery and ambiguity. Do you see it coming down to this sort of basic either/or distinction between men and women?

RD: Both capitalism and fascism have produced untold suffering and chaos. There is nothing wrong with order and nothing wrong with rationality. The problem is abusive authority and magical thinking—the Inquisition, for example, the idea of ethnic cleansing, the "Stalinization" of Islam. The idea that you can poison nature indefinitely and that she will heal herself is magical. Or that the Market will regulate itself.

LM: All of this suggests that you view power-wielding, or the urge to control and define and destroy, to be an existential problem rather than something that arises out of gender.

RD: Power doesn't belong to the phallus. Living for twenty years in a small village in France, I witnessed many abusive mothers. Powerless in the workplace, illiterate and impoverished, they expressed their frustration and rage by bullying their children.

LM: When I first read *The Stain* I was struck with how authentic these descriptions of life in this village were. Could you tell us a little bit more about this village you were living in and how the experience of living there might have affected your work? For example, did you actually start writing either *The Butcher's Tales* or *The Stain* while you were living in that village?

RD: Yes, both those books were written in Le Puy Notre Dame. I was fascinated by village life, the seasonal chores imposed by wine growing, the customs, superstitions, archaic political structures, and so on. We were living in the poorest section of the village among an uneducated peasantry. There were no television sets, washing machines, telephones, cars. For a time my husband was called upon to drive old people to funerals. My son grew up among children who could imitate the crowing of roosters and knock flies off the wall with a rubber band.

LM: You said this morning that if you scratched this village life just a little bit, you were back in medieval times. Did you find the kind of religious fervor that one associates with medieval times—and that plays such an important role in *The Stain?* For instance, was there any equivalent to the Mother Superior figure in *The Stain?*

RD: She is a composite of several bullying nuns who had a lot of power in the village in the early years of our life there. The character called the exorcist is based on the village's very real exorcist who once promised to show me *the soul of a sinner in a mirror.*

SG: What was the initial impulse that got you started writing *The Stain?*

RD: *The Stain* got kicked off when I came to know an old woman who was the only one who didn't have a washing machine; she was still going down to the *lavoir* to do her laundry, and I would go there too, because there were a lot of insects to watch and frogs and other creatures, and we would talk about the past. She had been a child at the turn of the century, and she had memories from as far back as the 1880s. One day she was talking to me about birthmarks and how important they had been when she was a little girl. People living in the village believed that you would know how somebody had sinned because of the mark on their face, things like that. After that conversation, I took my bike on a wonderful ride through the vineyards, quite far from the village; as I was returning, the sun was setting, and I saw this creature bounding across a meadow. It looked like a ball of fire at first—an incredible incandescence; then it stopped and stared at me and I didn't know what it was! I looked at it for a long time, and it looked at me, very intensely—so intensely that I finally had to turn away. Then it leapt off, and I realized it was an enormous hare. That night I had a dream of a woman giving birth to a child with a birthmark in the shape of a hare. It was really more like a vision than a dream, and I started up from it and immediately wrote my book's first chapter. Then the exorcist came in almost immediately after as a voice. There's a little store that I describe with a wonderful shopkeeper in it; all that was exactly like it was. The shopkeeper had all sorts of things dating from the turn of the century—boxes of silk thread, jars of buttons, bolts of cloth that you can't find anymore, and handmade soap. People would come in and bring fruit from their gardens or vegetables, and she would sell local people's cheeses and fruits. She was also sort of the village psychoanalyst, and sometimes you'd have to wait for an hour because she'd be talking to somebody about their problems and helping them solve them. Her name was Blanchette Leclerc. One day I asked her how she was, and she said, "I'm not feeling very well; I have a *zona.*" And I said, "What is a *zona?*" And she lifted up her skirts and showed me what looked like an enormous welt on her thigh; it was some kind of a great sore. She's in *The Stain* as well. I also went to a wedding and after did some research—I actually did a lot of research for that book—and discovered that the wedding I'd been to was really just like a nineteenth-century wedding in the Loire Valley; the only difference was there had been a record player. A lot of the village people and episodes wound up appearing in *The Stain.*

SG: I assume that you couldn't have been conceiving this in terms of a tetralogy at the outset. When did you realize you had something larger than a single novel?

RD: As I was finishing *The Stain,* I thought: this book is so *Manichean!* All that stuff about the body-as-cage, about sin and about gardens. A real earthbound book. And I thought: *Yes. And the next one will be about fire.*

LM: Was Bachelard's *The Psychoanalysis of Fire* partially an inspiration for *Entering Fire?*

RD: Bachelard's great philosophical reveries on literature were in fact the inspiration behind the idea of the entire tetralogy—but not *Entering Fire* specifically. Only when I began *The Fountains of Neptune* did I recognize Bachelard's part in the decision I had made to investigate the elements. I returned to *L'Eau et Les Rêves* and decided to convey all possible waters through the language, mood, and music of the novel: salt and fresh, swift and still, calm and treacherous, sexual, glacial.

LM: So it was only at that point that you began to do any sort of advance planning about the series as a whole?

RD: Only this: I knew each novel would engage a different approach. *The Stain* is about the Christian idea of sin—the world and the body seen as satanic vessels. If *The Stain* was precipitated by dream, *Entering Fire* began in a greenhouse outside Paris where orchids were being cloned. There I imagined an Amazonian woman far from home and squatting in the artificial rain. Next, Septimus de Bergerac's Nazi rantings revealed the book to be about many fires: of the Holocaust, of sexual passion, of intellectual curiosity, of the burning Amazon. And I wanted to make the readers' experience of reading the book feel like running over coals: very fast, hot, and always burning.

SG: When did Lamprias appear?

RD: Very soon. And when he did, I thought, Thank God, there's this other voice! *Entering Fire* turned out to be Manichean, too: a species of cosmical struggle between two voices, one good, one evil.

SG: Of course, these voices are male voices; and in fact you've used male perspectives in most of your novels. Has that been a problem?

RD: Not at all. In fact, I find that I *want* to write from the male point of view, because I'm fascinated by men. Some of this may be because I was fascinated by my father; he had a very interesting mind and was a wonderful storyteller himself. So I think that has a lot to do with my being interested in the male voice. And I'm really interested in knowing how I'm looked at by men, or imagined by them. And of course because I'm also busy participating in the erotic life of a man, I'm interested in imagining the erotic life of men. So the issue of writing from the point of view of a man has never been a problem for me. Quite the contrary. . . .

LM: What was the background of your decision to have the family in *Entering Fire* be descendants of Cyrano de Bergerac?

RD: I always loved the character in Rostand's play. But it wasn't until I began to do research for the book that I discovered Cyrano (or: sire-en-o, the man at the center of the circle) had existed and that he had been the first writer of science fiction (he imagined a trip to the moon). And he had been an alchemist. He attempted to create a homunculus with his own sperm; he was attempting cloning. So *Entering Fire* was propelled by what André Breton called *les hazards objectifs*.

SG: This sounds a bit like that running Borges motif where things created in one's imagination begin appearing in your daily life.

RD: Several of these magical connections happened while writing that book. The week I visited the local greenhouse to learn more about cloning was the week Barbara McClintock won the Nobel for her work on *spontaneous mutations*. The greenhouse I visited contained tens of thousands of rubber plants. Row after row they were identical; erect, smooth, and deep green, they seemed like ideal ciphers of glyphs for rubber plants and the sight was uncanny. But then at the far end of a row I saw one that was seemingly tied in knots, purple and strange—it was the *spontaneous mutation!*

LM: I was very moved and also disturbed by the last two entries in *Entering Fire*—Marta's sad and horrifying description of being sent off to the Holocaust and her lyrical reveries about the night "blazing with fireflies" when Lamprias seduced her with stories of the sex lives of flowers; then you have the last entry written by Lamprias's son Septimus, with its chilling remarks about the Holocaust and his announcement that he'll someday show up again just when he's least expected. And of course, what's happened the past fifty years right up to the recent events in Bosnia have proved that, unfortunately, Septimus is right—that sort of fascist, fearful, sadistic mentality hasn't left us.

RD: Septimus, or rather, what he represents, is never far. This ugly face is in constant mutation and is animated (or so I think) by terror. Terror of the imagination (which has its roots in the unconscious); terror of human autonomy (once again, the unknowable other); terror of beauty, of the things that move us deeply, of loving profoundly, of sexuality, of the body—the wonderful, the vulnerable, the transient body! So, yes, Septimus is always out and about struttin' and fartin' *somewhere*.

SG: Obviously Septimus is an awful character who must have been conceived by you to be that from the get-go. And yet there were moments in the book where I found myself not exactly "liking" him but somehow sympathizing with him. And certainly you give him some of the best lines in the book—he's funny! Did you ever feel uncomfortable knowing that you were being the medium for this voice which was so monstrous and yet so compelling?

RD: Absolutely! For a time I did battle with Septimus. I didn't want him to be funny! I didn't want him to be so brilliant or so poetical! But then I recognized that if the book was to be strong, he had to be an engaging character in his own way—and, as you said, also very funny. What became clear to me, too, is that there is something very funny—and of course *terrifying* as well—about a personality like Septimus's. I'm reminded of a story I heard: when the Nazis first arrived in Czechoslovakia, they put on a great show—they were goose-stepping through a stadium and so forth; the Czechoslovakians' response to that was whistling the theme song from Laurel and Hardy!

LM: The whole Marx Brothers/Groucho business that's referred to in *Entering Fire* was hilarious as well. This is disconcerting in the way that black humor traditionally is—that is, you don't allow people to respond to things merely tragically; there's this other dimension that is always there in your books, so that humor and horror seem utterly intertwined in a way that makes the viewer or reader feel uncomfortable.

RD: Making people feel uncomfortable strikes me as being a legitimate aim for an artist. And in fact humor is often a very healthy response to horror. There's a wonderful moment in *Schindler's List* when there are all these Jews standing around in a concentration camp roasting potatoes, and one guy says to another, "When was the last time we had a potato roast like this?" Humor is one way of surviving.

SG: Your willingness to grant even your villains a sense of humor may offend some people in these days of political correctness, but the truth is that sometimes dreadful people aren't reducible to the features associated with "villains." Awful people can be very, very funny, for example, and their humor is part of their attractiveness; it's part of why they're not *just* a monster and part of why people continue to be led or influenced by them. But in the case of Septimus, you really found his humor emerging more or less spontaneously?

RD: Yes, it really seemed spontaneous. Most of what you find in my books results more from spontaneous generation than from being consciously thought out in advance. I'm basically a very intuitive writer. That's been true more with some books than others. *Entering Fire,* for example, really seemed to write itself in great part because Septimus's voice was so strong and I *trusted* it. Not what he said, but *how* he said it.

SG: I suspect that the humor in your writing—which is always there, even in the darkest moments of *The Stain* and *Fire* and *The Butcher's Tales*—is something that many readers don't pick up on at first. That's partly because of the violence and grotesqueness that's so common in your writing but also—and this is to your credit— you're able to introduce humor into the regular flow of the narrative, as opposed to most writers, who usually have to stop the action so that they can deliver the punch line.

RD: As I've said, when I'm writing, scenes just seem to happen. In *Entering Fire* I didn't know that Buttons and the Blue Man would go off together holding hands until I wrote the scene. In *The Stain* I didn't know the Exorcist had his foot up the Mother Superior's skirts until Emile spilled his peas and went under the table to find them. It was the Cod's spyglass in *The Fountains of Neptune* that revealed Odille's murder, and I didn't know Memory had the hots for Tubbs until she told me, or that Charlotte would eat glass and so, like Emile, have trouble speaking.

LM: Speaking of speaking problems, I noticed that starting with *The Stain* and then continuing on in just about all your works, there always seems to be this problem with speaking. Is this another spontaneous mutation or a motif you've been consciously exploring?

RD: It's been more conscious. Ever since Charlotte revealed to me that *language is power!*

SG: Are there other motifs you've grown more conscious of exploring from book to book?

RD: Yes. For instance, the exorcist in *The Stain* metamorphoses into Septimus in *Entering Fire* and then is transformed again into Toujours-Là ("Always there!") in *The Fountains of Neptune;* he takes on a new sort of life as Tubbs in *The Jade Cabinet.* All these characters entertain a self-deluding as well as hypnotic rapport with language. Language is their way of masking the black hole of a desperately hungry psyche.

LM: Many surrealists have tried to find a way to access their dreams in their works. Do you do that?

RD: All the time. For example, when I was working on *Entering Fire,* I did six months of research on the Amazonian rain forest, but it wasn't until I started *dreaming* it that I could write about it. That book was informed by a species of lucid dreaming.

LM: For some reason, your presentation of Septimus kept reminding me of Rimbaud—perhaps that was due to the paradoxical features to his sensibility, the ways he could be seen as being the kind of madman or "thief of fire" that Rimbaud describes in *The Illuminations.*

RD: In French a madman, a man informed by a poetic or sacred fire, is called an *illuminé.* From the start it was clear that Septimus was such a one—and a *fou littéraire* as well. The *fou littéraire* (or literary madman) was seized by a species of metaphysical delirium. My favorite of these was Jean-Pierre Roux—who Septimus and his mother, Virginie, have read avidly. Sitting on a chamber pot having taken an enema, Roux was visited by a sacred cabinet illumed by celestial fire and thundering with God's own voice. It seems that having voided profusely, Roux was worthy of Divine intervention or penetration. When I came upon this *fou,* I knew I had found a soul mate for Septimus.

Roux also had curious theories concerning language. For example, words like *shit* and *devil* are just synonyms for one thing, which is *agent morbilique* or corrupting agent. He believed that cooks and cookery were satanic but that eggs were pure. Something else: about halfway through *Entering Fire* I came across some of the anti-Semitic pamphlets Céline had written during the war. Because of their explicitly racist and murderous nature, these had been out of print for decades. I was fascinated by the similarities between Septimus's voice and the voice of Céline; the stench and texture of their delirium coincided. Something was working in terms of the makeup of a Nazi personality. Around this time the French psychoanalyst Pierre Sabourin gave me Alice Miller's *For Your Own Good.* Miller investigates what she calls the *black pedagogy* which colored pedagogy in Germany (and France) in the last century. She argues that Hitler—who was violently beaten, beaten to the point of psychosis by his stepfather—was not unique, not an aberration, but an inevitability. Miller makes an impressive argument linking domestic violence, a psychotic national character, and oppressive political systems. Interestingly, Russell Banks once told me that his great novel *Affliction* was informed by Miller's book also.

LM: This seems related to your own focus on childhood and the vulnerability of children.

RD: Years ago when I was beginning to write poetry, I read R. D. Laing's *Schizophrenia and the Family*. Laing argues that the worst thing you can do to a child who has seen or experienced something frightening, bewildering, is to say, "You have seen nothing." Because this forces the child to distrust his own perceptions, he takes the first step into schizophrenia. I continue to be interested in madness and infancy especially as our own society, inexorably engaged in its own oppressive process, reveals itself hateful of its young—especially its children of color.

I live with a psychoanalyst—Jonathan Cohen—who questions the collusive nature of traditional psychoanalysis in our society and proposes what he calls a *moral landscape,* a certain quality of mind and of experience. The idea of *quality,* of *moral landscape,* appeals to me immensely. I don't think a novel can with grace *map* such a landscape, but perhaps it can offer an intuitive itinerary.

SG: One of several politically incorrect things that you have done in your work is to present Charles Dodgson in such a favorable light in *The Jade Cabinet*. This goes against all the negative reinterpretations of Lewis Carroll—the suggestions that he was a sort of pederast or pervert. And yet you have all those wonderful descriptions of the joy that he brought these girls, and how much they enjoyed taking off their clothes, that freedom they felt in his presence when he was taking the photographs of them, and so on. Such a treatment struck me as being very brave.

RD: I researched Carroll very carefully, and there is nothing in any of the loving reminiscences of the women who were his child friends to imply that he was a *voyeur* or abusive in any way. In fact, several insist upon the joy it was to kick off their boots and run around naked! I think he was a little girl himself. Did you know he signed his early pieces *Louisa Carolina?*

LM: You mentioned earlier that as a child you loved Carroll's books. What was there about his works from an adult perspective that made you decide to have him play such an important role in *The Jade Cabinet?*

RD: What makes those books so extraordinary—coming out of the Victorian Age as they do—is that common sense is always triumphant, and that a little girl is the voice of reason.

LM: You also have in your works all those interesting speculations about language itself—about paradox, the different ways
words can mean, and so on—and the ongoing delight in wordplay.

RD: To a very great extent *Alice* is all about the irrational use of
language by tyrants. Humpty Dumpty is a terrifying figure, for example, insisting that words have no intrinsic meaning. I think of
him as the first deconstructionist making language do his bidding.

LM: Edward Lear is often associated with Lewis Carroll, for obvious reasons; but I think he's really more interested in true nonsense
(whatever that might mean!) than Carroll was—or the surrealists
were, for that matter. Are you interested in nonsense? I recall the
epigraph to *The Stain*—something like "aaa ooo zezophazazzaieozaza"
—seemed to introduce the notion of nonsense. Where did that come
from, anyway?

RD: That bit of nonsense is a Gnostic mantra. Its intention is to
empower the navigating soul as it passes the planets—all guarded
by demons—on its way back "home."

LM: Again, that sort of discourse seems to be operating differently from nonsense. The way I think of it is that nonsense is literally nonsensical words or phrases, whereas surrealism suggests
that the symbols have different kinds of hidden meanings that the
artist can access. Again, I know you've always been interested in
Lear; the epigraph to your first book of poems—*The Star Chamber*—"Up yours" was for Lear, wasn't it?

RD: Lear's old man of Ibreem who threatens to scream is threatened with a beating just as Alice is threatened with decapitation
when she *talks back*. Nonsense delights us I think because it offers
us language in mutation, in gestation—how much richer English is
for *brillig* and *snark!*—and because it ridicules pompous, vain, and
obsessive behavior.

LM: You did the illustrations for an edition of Borges's *Tlön,
Uqbar and Orbis Tertius*—just one indication of many that Borges
has been important for you.

RD: Very much so. Those drawings are a parallel itinerary. And
this because Borges's wonderful story *evolves* so much—causing the
reader to dream startling and inventive dreams. I spent six months
on that series of illustrations, and as I was drawing, I would return
to the text to discover that I was constantly reinterpreting it. It
seemed to be a text in spontaneous mutation. This experience had
tremendous impact on the writing of *The Fountains of Neptune*,
which is riddled with implied histories.

SG: I'd say your own work often seems to operate that way—that
is, like Borges and Calvino, you often seem to enjoy creating lists or

an extended series of images that summon up all these other narratives that aren't fully developed in your own book but which invite subsequent exploration by readers. For instance, there's a scene in *The Jade Cabinet* where they visit a circus and see all these fabulous and hideous creatures, each possessing its own background stories which you briefly mention and then move on to the next. It's almost as if you're saying to the reader, Yes, there's all these stories to be told about these things, but I don't have time to tell them so why don't you tell them yourself.

RD: One of the delights of travel is to discover that the world is full of stories. Heinrich Bleucher used say: man is mythmaker! Perhaps for me writing stories is a way of engaging in the infinite, the mutable, the *evocative* world which is the world of the imagination.

SG: As I've already suggested, it seems to me that postmodernism has gradually evolved so that it is now synonymous with skepticism and nihilism. But the fact that any story can be approached from all of these different directions and that there are multiple tellings possible of everything doesn't mean that there is no truth; it just suggests to me that there are many truths that can be expressed with language. This is deeply troubling to a culture that seeks to limit "truth" to linear, logical propositions. I guess one of the things that I like so much about your work is that you seem more interested in using language to express multiplicity than using it in the service of either the reductiveness of rationalism or the kind of empty relativism that seems so "hip" these days. You have that great line in your work about the path that goes straight goes to a leaden door, while the circuitous one goes to a garden.

RD: Certain writers, specific books come to mind at once: Marcel Detiene's *Le Jardin d'Adonis,* Robert Harbison's *Eccentric Spaces,* Pierre Mabille's *Le Miroir du Merveilleux,* Gass's *Omensetter's Luck,* Sarduy's *Cobra,* Coover's *Pricksongs and Descants,* Calvino's *Cosmicomics,* all of Borges. Manuel Puig, Angela Carter, Mary Caponegro. I just finished Harry Mathews's wonderful new novel, *The Journalist.* Speaking of metaphysical delirium!

LM: What about José Donoso? I was just wondering because you apparently lived in Chile for a while.

RD: I'm especially fond a story of his called "The Walk." I met Donoso recently, and it turned out he had been analyzed by Mateo Blanco—a Chilean analyst of special interest to Jonathan. So the meeting was delightful and intense for all of us!

SG: You mentioned last night over dinner that you developed a friendship with Angela Carter.

RD: Bob Coover suggested we meet because he knew we shared a similar private landscape. And there was a remarkable affinity between us. An early interest in the surrealists, Sade, and Freud had a lot to do with that connection, and our love of Rabelais and Jarry. Despite her terror of bicycles, Angela was a fearless, an acutely subversive creature.

LM: Over the past couple of years, you've been sending me sections of a work-in-progress that's not connected to the tetralogy. Have you found the process of working on it to be any different since it's outside of this structure you've been working on for so long? Or has it been basically the same?

RD: In some ways the writing of the new book—which is now entitled *Phosphor in Dreamland*—has been somewhat different. It is a slender novel that I would describe as a species of parable. However, I would say that if it stands alone, it also illumes the tetrology.

LM: As you were working on the books in the tetralogy, you obviously had these central metaphors or motifs—earth, fire, water, and air—that created a kind of organic framework for what you were doing. Is there any kind of unifying image or principle that you are aware of with the new book? Or were you mostly just telling a story?

RD: I think the unifying principle was *Don Quixote*—but as a *folie à cing*. The novel turned out to be about all sorts of things: terror of the female body, of the unknown, of the abyss, of absences. The attempt to fill the hole with noise. Magical thinking! Orthodoxies and sexual craziness. As the novel progressed, the vanished aborigines of Birdland returned in the shapes of visions, food, songs, erotic artifacts, a painted cave, and, finally, a living lover. So if the book is about human folly, it is also about the resurgent capacity of the erotic imagination.

LM: Do you find your creative process operating differently now from the way it did when you were first starting as a writer? For instance, you mentioned that you are now perhaps more aware of reworking motifs and character type.

RD: Somehow it doesn't get easier. When I write it's almost as if I'm in a waking hallucination even though I'm aware that I'm consistently dealing with certain kinds of motifs, like the cosmic egg, or twins, or monkeys, or the problem of power. The only thing that's different is that, having done it before and survived, I know I can do it again. Psychologically, then, it's easier; from a technical standpoint, it's not. If anything, there seem to be more challenges.

LM: Beginning with that early scene in *The Stain* where Charlotte eats the clock, references to eating and food are a constant in your fiction—in fact, I don't think I've ever read anybody who has as many different kinds of food references that operate in so many different ways, sensuously and also metaphorically. Can you talk for a moment about the role of food in your work? It was obvious from the dinner you made us last night that you're interested in food from a personal standpoint, but at what point does this become a motif that you're aware of as an artist?

RD: I love the sensual world, I love the body, and I love the physical, natural world. And for me part of the delight of existence is the feast. The ideal day for me is to get a walk in nature, do creative work of some kind, and then prepare a feast at the end of the day.

SG: In *The Jade Cabinet* you described Tubbs arriving in Egypt and wanting to make it into a pudding with raisins. That sentence seemed to express beautifully not only a deep-seated response to the awareness that time and the cosmos are devouring everything—but the desire to turn this around, so that *he* can do the devouring.

RD: Tubbs is the Market! He would eat the world with a runcible spoon if he could—he is so fearful of being devoured himself: by space, by time. It is mortality that prods him on.

LM: After you had finished *Entering Fire,* at what point did you begin *The Fountains of Neptune?*

RD: At once. The wonderful thing about having the tetralogy in mind was an extended *season;* it was like writing a single book.

LM: Those vivid, fantastic stories that Nicolas hears throughout the opening of *Fountains of Neptune,* the ones about ghost ships, bars made out of whalebones, mermaids and sea monsters and so forth—where did those come from?

RD: Some of them came from living in the village and listening to my neighbor, who was a drunk but also a wonderful storyteller; the stories that wound up in the book aren't his stories, but there's something about the quality of his storytelling that informed Toujours-Là's voice.

LM: It struck me while I was reading *The Fountains of Neptune* that you were describing the last period in which this kind of magical storytelling was possible. We can't have stories like that anymore—the magic and mystery has been dispelled by the cameras and information.

RD: No, it's gone. You know, that's one of the things that I really miss about living in the village before television. There were a lot of old codgers around who would say things like: "I remember when sardines were so precious that for a treat we would have them for dessert with our coffee." An image like that would often be enough to get me writing.

LM: Nicolas's construction of this strange, idealized other world—a place outside of space and time that he could control—reminded me of similar creations: J. Henry Waugh's baseball universe in Bob Coover's *Universal Baseball Association,* Kinbote's Zembla in Nabokov's *Pale Fire,* the various fantastic imaginary cities and worlds you find in Borges, Calvino, and Robert Kelly.

RD: Nicolas's ideal world originates in my father's passion for war games. He had hundreds and hundreds of lead soldiers—Hittites, Nazis, everything. He also played a postal game and had named himself the Emperor of d'Elir. It *was* delirium! My father was brilliant, handsome, eccentric, and fearful of the world. Playing at war, he could make and break the rules. I grew to hate games because whenever he was cornered he would pull a new rule out of the air. Once he offered to teach me fencing, and before I knew it he had lunged at my heart. The *rule,* I knew, was that a touch was enough to win. I thought: *what if that rule gets broken?* I never did learn to fence.

Many years later when he was nearly blind and living in Canada, he was desperate to play Chinese chess. I felt sorry for him and said OK. He got out a board—I think it was for Parcheesi, and various pieces from chess and checkers games (even dominoes!)—upon which he had stuck little emblems, and said, "As you can see I don't have a Chinese chess set, but these elephants will be the horses and they move like bishops except that on certain occasions they can leap to the left (or the right); and then this piece with the tiddlywink glued to its head will be the emperor although it's the wrong color. But you'll remember that all the black pieces belong with the red—you'll notice we have black, red and white; the green tiddlywink is really black." This went on for ten minutes and then I said, "Dad, I need a walk, I'll be back." And I walked over to my friend Jane Urquhart's house and I said, "Jane, I need a whiskey." And Jane said, "Rikki, you don't drink whiskey."

SG: Where did the image of the jade cabinet come from?

RD: I love jade and the tales about the uncut stone's destiny conveyed to the carver in a vision or a dream—the virtual image hidden within that he is to give tangible form to. A terrific metaphor for a character telling the author what the book must be. I've done many drawings inspired by Chinese or Mayan jade—imaginary archeologies. But *The Jade Cabinet* was precipitated by a phrase of Kafka's that's always intrigued me: *All language is but a poor translation.* In other words, if we could speak the language of languages, the language of Eden, we would have the power to conjure the world of things: a tower of Babel, cabbages and kings. But it was Memory who gave the book to me, just as Septimus gave me *Entering Fire.*

SG: Of course, the main focus of *The Jade Cabinet* is Etheria. Did you ever consider narrating the book from her point of view? Although that would have kept her from being such a figure of levitation.

RD: You're right. Etheria had to be talked about; her story was *porous*. This is why she takes form through scraps of letter, journals, phrases, and memories. She is volatile, a spirit or inspiriting presence, an animating air. For her gravity-bound husband, Radulph Tubbs, she is also a season of the mind.

SG: At the end of the book, were you aware when those shots were fired that killed the magician that it wasn't Etheria who had been murdered?

RD: No, I didn't plan it that way. I didn't know that until Memory discovered it. At that point, I thought, My god, Etheria *has* vanished!

SG: There are several ways that your work goes against the grain of a lot of things that are in the air, philosophically and aesthetically, in postmodernism. For instance, there seems to be an insistence in your writing that everything is finally not undecidable and relative, that there are moral distinctions that can be made (and need to be made). So for all the emphasis in your work about flux and ambiguity, there's also an almost old-fashioned insistence on the difference between good and bad. But it also strikes me that in your work the difference between good and evil is not the difference between power and passivity, but more between the willingness to use power for life enhancement or for destructiveness—it often seems as simple as destruction vs. creation, or something like that. Part of that has to do with the way you present language itself— this sense that language has an ability to control and limit in bad ways versus language which liberates, which opens things up, in good ways.

RD: I grew up on Sartre and continue to think that freedom without responsibility is just another form of enslavement. We live in terrible times in which the so-called freedom to make money without concern for the social and ecological consequences is unquestioned. Living and being has been usurped by taking! To fight this is seen as subversive, even empathy for the dispossessed is subversive.

It seems to me that rigor—aesthetic, intellectual—is the paradox at the heart of creative work. But what I call rigor resists definition because it cannot be reduced to one small bone; it is not palpable, but intuited. Every artist worth her salt knows what I mean—either one chooses the well-trodden path, platitude, sentimentality, the current orthodoxy, whatever, or one blazes a trail which is, no matter the nature of the work, part of the process of becoming. I think rigor implies trusting inner experience, investigating inner experience, and so investing the work with courage. In this way the artist reveals the darkness and the wild beauty at the heart of things. Such a revelation can be a profound aesthetic experience and, simultaneously, a transgressive, a regenerating experience.

I fear we are undergoing a "fascistization" of culture and one indication of that is the idea that beauty is elitist, or somehow "soft." As if beauty didn't belong to all of us. And the idea that truth is a lump of bloody human cartilage attracting flies and not the *living being*. What I am attempting to describe here is a process toward understanding, and if I speak of rigor and imagination so much it's because I think we cannot function as free beings, as *imagining* beings, unless we have the courage to perceive the world and to name what we see, to choose clarity over opacity.

LM: Again, the way you're describing this process—this struggle between competing forces, the existence of an evil that is actual rather than just a metaphor—sounds almost Manichean.

RK: There's a connection there with Manichism, I'm sure, but I'm not talking of *cosmical* powers but worldly ones. I'm talking about the constant tension or struggle I perceive—well, it is *palpable*— between forces of enslavement and obscuration, and forces of liberation and illumination. For example, what are the descendants of the Maya fighting for now? They are fighting for what we all want and what we all must have: the right to *be* in the fullest sense.

LM: In some basic sense your books always seem to present these opposing kinds of principles struggling for control of people's minds and lives—and one thing I admire about your treatment of this struggle is that you're "old-fashioned" enough to eschew the easy relativism that's become associated with so many postmodern works. In other words you're willing to take sides and come down clearly on the side of *life*.

RD: I'm saying the side of life is the primary subversion.

Black Isis

The Death Cunt of Deep Dell

Rikki Ducornet

1. David Lynch

I cherish a particularly eerie moment in David Lynch's *Eraserhead* when a radiator metamorphoses into a miniature theater and an excessively sentimentalized Thumbelina performs in the void. As lively as she looks, she is an illusion, a lethal figment of the mind. Her stage is set in the dark heart of psychotic and sidereal space, and to see her is to be both mortal and mad. The larval boy who evokes her is as much a phantom as she; it is unclear who dreams whom, although it is likely a lesser archon is dreaming them both.

One of the Death Cunt's many disguises, she will return in the shape of some barely roasted birds which when carved evoke fecal fucking, and again as Lula's fatal mother in *Wild at Heart,* the three porno graces poisoning the evening air of Greater Tuna, Bobby's girl and Bobby's own anal mouth which sullies—but does not destroy— the morally free Lula. Infinitely mutable, the Death Cunt briefly surges again as an ecstatic and sightless woman who slides across our field of vision like a phosphene before vanishing.

A house on fire, the Death Cunt burns at the core of *Wild at Heart* and reaches quintessence in *Lost Highway*'s "Deep Dell": the acutely eroticized "glamours" Alice and Renée—spawn of the Devil's cunt-cabin (which is also the Devil's own ubiquitous eye). The cabin recalls Robert Coover's gingerbread house with its irresistible, cherry-red genital door; like Hansel, Fred/Peter the doubled hero has no chance. The devil has fucked his mind; teased to lunacy his only means of escape is to atomize.

"Do you want to fuck me?" asks the Devil as Alice. "Do you want to ask me why?"

2. Quay Brothers

The Quay's Enkidu (from a largely disguised reduction of the "Epic of Gilgamesh") is also lost embracing the promise of erotic delight. Prison cell and torture chamber, Gilgamesh's little house is suspended in limbo, ruled by rage, and like the Devil's cabin, inescapable. Drawn like a moth to flame, Enkidu leaves the safety of the cedar woods to enter it and examine Gilgamesh's dazzling poison damsel. Her peep-show genital is deep pink, a color another dreamer of satanic houses, Jean Ray, calls "bastard red, the color of shame" and, when it engenders a universe—Ray's version of Coover's "Big Bang"—"the pink catalyst." Overcome by the female seduction of spacetime (her sex is also a pendulum) Enkidu leans into her, springing the trap. He is seized, suspended in the air with wires. (In the original story, Enkidu gets to lie with the whore for seven nights before attempting to rise and finding he is as though tied down.)

Immobilized by the gorgeous stuff of dreams—a bolt of orange silk is here a marvelous metaphor for the seductions of the illusory material world—Enkidu is brutally beaten by Gilgamesh, and his wings cut from his body. The deadly dream theater has now become a cage. Gilgamesh—a species of conquistador fused to the body of his horse—maniacally circles his prisoner on his compulsive little wheels.

Lucent in the Quay's other masterpiece: *The Street of Crocodiles,* the Death Cunt reappears in the form of a pocket watch, a dressmaker's dummy and a hairy glove—seductive artifacts of a world held together by spit and string. Space and time are both so old and shoddy they are barely able to sustain the illusion of the real. By film's end the empty-headed tailor-archons of the world's dusty rag and bone shop, having exhausted their short supply of sumptuous matter—are overtaken by entropy.

3. Robert Coover

In Robert Coover's chronically ambiguous *Comedies of Terror,* chaos is exemplified by a cosmical ogress too; a Charybdis animated by opposites, she cannibalizes everything that moves. Coover engages the archetypal femme fatale, the Cabala and even the techniques of Dada cinema to create disturbingly kaleidoscopic fictions in which the Death Cunt (his term) plays a central role.

Dada was the infant of calamity and by propelling images into one another demonstrated in a most tangible way Coover's irresistible gnostic argument: Calamity is the normal circumstance of the universe ("The Phantom of the Movie Palace"). Dada, just as the cabalistic exercise of "skipping and jumping" with the mind, revealed the rents in the fabric of things and more: it argued that the world's fabric was itself made of absences. Cinema, then Dada, and above all Dada cinema, conveyed the vertiginous fact of our porous foundations. If once again the world was flat, the finite edge of Yahweh's footstool bobbing like a cork above chaos, it was also a sieve world riddled with holes. The mystic veil has become a movie screen, and the expanding universe a gleaming thicket of tangled film spooling out . . . like some mysterious birth, animated by light motes passing through a cabalistic window before igniting for an instant only in the air.

Shrinking and expanding, anorexic and bulimic, Coover's universe seesaws (now you see it, now you don't) upon a cinematic "dream cloth"—the nothing that is happening faster and faster. In Picabia's words: There is one movement and that is perpetual motion.

Like the Quays' and Lynch's hungry houses, Coover's House of Rue contains "deep dells," pits and pendulums; clocks like cunts split open, their works springing out like wild hairs (Charlie in the House of Rue)—an image which precedes and evokes the Quays exactly. The cinematic house which like a clock can be rewound, is also a sorcerer's apprentice world of waters—flooded by soup, douchebag, ink, alcohol and tears. And it is aglitter with bright, sourceless light. This illumes some emblematic pies (a reminder that no one is safe from the ultimate slapstick), a coffin surrounded by candles and a brass pendulum. In a hybrid nightmare of cabalistic Dada, a toreador maid metamorphosed into a flickering lightbulb (a beacon suggesting gnosis, it appears in the Quays' *Street of Crocodiles* as the head of a baby doll) beckons the knob of Charlie's cock into the maid's lethal closet, her hole-y terror. At tale's end, Charlie—a potential corpse just like the rest of us—embraces a cadaver above the gaping maw of feminine time.

4. Jonathan Swift

In the bed of the Death Cunt, appetite, copulation, birth, death and defecation are all contained in (and exemplified by) the vortex—and I use that word precisely because it best describes the vertiginous quality of Swift's vision, a vision informed by his chronic malaise: Ménière's disease. Characterized by precipitous vertigo and severe unbalance, the world, in seizure, appears to spin. If Gulliver in Brobdingnag is in danger of being swallowed whole by outsized vulvas, tumors, molehills and animals, the greediest orifice belongs to Time.

Perhaps the cacophony that tortured Swift's wounded inner ear translated into an exacerbated perception of the particulating world. Cossinus, that exemplary Swiftian hero, who having seen too much is undone, scorched by the sight of Celia's horrid fact. (Cossinus and Peter) Whipped by scorpions, badly stung, he has seen the Medusa's face: her serpents hiss at him directly. (The other symptoms of Ménière's is tinnitus: a rumbling and hissing in the ears.)

Once again, Time is female; female flesh epitomizes dissolution. Returning at the witching hour of midnight, Corinna (The Progress of Beauty) sits on her three-legged chair—in other words her bidet—and pulls off her hair and plucks out her eye. The passage of time accelerates to a dizzying degree; like particles in an atomic canon, matter fractures and dissolves. Corinna's macabre striptease reveals that she is in fact an upholstered coffin; tacks, tassels and padding removed, all that remains is an eager abyss. (Eager because once abed, the hag lies awake tormented by thoughts of love.)

Corinna's glass eye is a species of genital; it fits, after all, into an orifice and, with a glance can "glamourize"; like a phallus, pierce to kill. Just as cosmetics, those ointments good for scabby chops (The Lady's Dressing Room) mask the abuses of time, the eye fills the absence that contains it. Beauty is a corpse in drag, a sieve-woman riddled with holes. Magnified, her skin appears like a graveyard erupting pestilence. Sweat is a caustic, smelly substance, and love's fire brings a stench from every pore (The Description of a Salamander). Corinna's eye socket is her glass eye's casket, her mouth a reliquary that contains her dead teeth, her body melted down to an anamorphic spill. But Swift's own eye is bigger than his stomach. Having taken on more than he can chew, he cannot swallow and so will spew.

Incapable of love, Swift cannot forgive the flesh because it dies; he cannot forgive womankind the transitory physicality that defines, determines and damns him, too. In his spyglass poems—those poems in which the masculine eye burglarizes the absent Beauty's chamber, peeping into the very things that cause virility to recoil, the distinction between the real and the false, corruption and health, sex and death dissolve and decay; these ravished rooms swell and crack as in the throes of intense seismic upheaval.

The descent into the female vortex culminates in the revelation of that vile machine, that reeking chest, Celia's own Pandora's box: her chamber pot which, as Groddeck proposes, when stained with menstrual blood, is for the little boy the proof that the female is a castrated male. Celia's own chamber pot, like a Brobdingnagian wench's vulva, is a metaphor for the Medusa herself: the "Deep Dell" that turns a man to stone. It is no accident that the Nanunculus Grildrig's intimate view of a frolicsome girl's outsize cabinet of curiosities—a mirror of his own incapacities—is followed by a decapitation that in a fit of lyricism, Gulliver likens to the (ejaculating) fountains of Versailles.

Vulnerable when open and closed, the eye is a paradoxical organ.

Unlike the stomach (or the mouth) it cannot give back what it has taken in. If a bad meal can be vomited or, with difficulty, digested, a horrific vision, repressed, is made to fester. Groddeck points out that the child first sees himself reduced and contained within the mother's eye.

Hot, nurturing, pregnant with the little child, the eye is not like the mother but is the mother. Magically it has diminished and imprisoned the child, like a dwarf in the palace of the Queen. If we are struck by something—as Strephon is struck by horror—the vision has pierced the eye and impregnated it with monsters.

This phallic eye is incarnated by Swift's Salamander (Salamander). A venomous fang, a poison pendulum:

It spews a filthy froth,
(Whether through rage, or lust, or both)
Of matter purulent and white
Which happening on the skin to light,
And there corrupting to a wound
Spreads a leprosy and baldness round.

The organ of self-perpetuating and self-punishing anger, the phallic eye is also very cold:

So cold, that put in the fire
'Twill make the very flames expire.

Throughout the Travels Gulliver devours with his eyes: the Queen of Brobdingnag's prodigious mouth, the breast tumor full of holes large enough to contain him, the Yahoo's filthy Excrements, hairless Anus and Pudenda. By tale's end he is stuffed to the point of gagging. It is not surprising that Swift insists upon the mouth, the genitals and the anus, for they are emblematic of the body's dependency, a dependency that teaches the dark truth about a "Mother" Nature whose exigencies are absolute—"Truth" intolerable to a loveless and an alienated spirit. (For it seems to me that the passage of time and the limitations of mortality are bearable, even acceptable, to those who dare engage in the world fully, and unbearable to those who do not. Recall how Swift's own "Saucebox" Stella was imprisoned in the airtight cabinet of a secret and a sterile marriage.)

If in Lilliput, Gulliver's mouth and anus prove equally calamitous, in Brobdingnag the Nanunculus is more of a mouth, the suckling of a mischievous monkey whose perilous nursing brings to mind King Kong's abduction of Fay Wray. Having pulled Gulliver from his cabinet, the monkey proceeds to cram him with stuff he squeezes from his chaps—and this three hundred yards from the ground. Gulliver as Grildrig exemplifies infantilization and impotency; contained in cabinets and pockets much as the cinematic frames or Devil's eye contain and determine Coover's Charlie and Lynch's Peter/Fred, he is reduced to curiosity, a Lusus Naturae—as helpless and freakish as the fetal issues of Swift's lady friends described in the Dean's journals with loathing. And performing the favorite tricks of eighteenth-century automata, Grildrig recalls Sade's clockworks, too.

Grildrig is a rich portmanteau of provocative possibilities; grig: grasshopper, cricket, small eel; and grill and girl, of course. The outsize Queen drops her gold ring over Gulliver, girding and girdling him, and, one supposes, nearly getting rid of him. The Grildrig is something of a riddle also, as is his puzzling world. When he is dropped in cream (the onomatopoetic Splacknuck foretells this disaster) he nearly drowns; forced into a hot marrow bone he is simultaneously swaddled and reduced to stuffing.

The Queen at table offers something else to think about: if the table separates the top half of her body from the bottom, Gulliver stands right upon this Great Divide. Above him the Queen crams; beneath him she digests. No wonder the little cricket-man feels giddy. He is suspended between two horrors—the Queen's mouth and her royal bum.

Distortions, groanings, strainings, heavings . . . like Rabelais's Gargamelle's, Chloe's leavings are prodigious too . . . But: is she shitting or giving birth? One thinks of Freud's little Hans for whom all babies were "lumfs" and "born like lumfs." And Ambroise Paré's "Examples of Monstrous Things," his tales of impostures, unforgettable and obscene, such as: "The Woman Who Pretended to Have a Canker in Her Breast" and "The Fat Wench from Normandy Who Pretended to Have a Snake in Her Belly." Paré's "Example of Winds" is written in a manner that can only be called Swiftian with its descriptions of women whose bellies house colonies of frogs and whose percussive capacities are likened to artillery.

In his poem "A Panegyric on the Dean," Swift's Queen of gluttony confines her daughter Cloacine to the outhouse where she gives birth to an impious line of Godesses and Gods including Voluptuous Ease. Once again a purposeful confusion is entertained between the mouth, the anus and the womb. Cloacine's brood pay tribute to their mother in the form of turds, and Swift complains they do not leave them in nature. The sincerest turd is dropped by a peasant in a clay pot, or upon the humble branches of a bush—not into a silver vase by a Duchess. This bucolic turd is described with seeming tenderness (again bringing Sade to mind and those curious "ices" served at

Silling): it has a spiral top, or a copple-crown.

Shitting is the price we pay for being mortal, the ticket we hand to the Creator in order to participate in the spectacle that is the world. By insisting we shit in this garden, Swift may be asking we pay God in kind, to, in the great tradition of clowns secular and holy, send the pie soaring back into his face. After all, Swift might say: the trick He has played is a Dirty One.

I would suggest that if Lynch, Coover and the Quays all engage the Death Cunt knowingly and at a certain distance, Swift is its victim; I would suggest that he distrusts both voids—fore and aft—as savagely as he distrusts the "visions" or "humors" in between; that his imagination pierces to deflate; that the eye of the needle is as sharp as its tip; that the vision is a sprawling body that will not be contained: the body as "Deep Dell," graveyard, quicksand, bog; the world an ogress riddled with orifices and littered with dung in which Gulliver-Swift (just as Charlie, Fred/Peter and Enkidu, too) finds himself "in the middle up my knees" (*Gulliver's Travels*).

BIBLIOGRAPHY

Coover, Robert. *A Night at the Movies*. Elmwood Park, IL: Dalkey Archive Press, 1992.

Coover, Robert. *Pricksongs and Descants*. New York: New American Library, 1969.

Groddeck, Georg Walther. *Das Buck vom Es: The Book of the It*. Intro. Lawrence Durnell. New York: International Univ. Press, 1976.

Paré, Ambroise. *On Monsters and Marvels*. Chicago: Univ. of Chicago Press, 1982.

Ray, Jean. *Œvres Complétes III*. Paris: Robert Laffont, 1964.

Swift, Jonathan. *Collected Poems*. Ed. and intro. Joseph Horrell. Cambridge: Harvard Univ. Press, 1958.

Swift, Jonathan. *Gulliver's Travels*. Ed. Robert A. Greenberg. New York: W.W. Norton, 1970.

Swift, Jonathan. *Journal to Stella*. Oxford: Clarendon Press, 1963.

Clean

TEXT BY RIKKI DUCORNET
DRAWINGS BY T. MOTLEY

Dogs are dirty
Birds are filthy .

Fish are clean except
for the intestines
which are dirty.

People love to wash and
that's why in the eyes
of Jesus they are best.

Dogs don't go
to heaven,
they turn into
worms, but
good Christian
people stay
just the same,
younger and
smelling
good all
the time

All the people get washed
when they die and sit
at the table of
Holy Lightning
with Jesus
eating all
that
clean food.

Jesus smiles when he sees the
people washing. He knows that the
people like to be clean and that's
why he likes them better than the
animals who eat any crap dirty.

clean people who don't smell like vinegar sit at his table, only younger with new hair, teeth and skin,

all naked but no fornicating, eating all that clean food.

that's why it's important to get the old folks soaped and combed and in to bed between sheets boiled four times and ironed into nice even creases - twelve creases for Jesus - and their toenails pared.

Our old people look good, just simple folk, the color of milk and veal roast.

When it's time, Jesus calls them, he says:

O have you pared your nails?

And they answer:

O yes Sweet Lord we have pared our nails and ironed our sheets twelve times.

and Jesus says:

Are you CLEAN?

which is a joke because he knows they are and the old folks laugh a lot at this.

And Jesus says:

Do you smell good and are you the color of roast veal?

And the old folks answer

O yes, Lord, we are clean and Our thoughts are like white sauce and our blood is like water and we are ready, O Sweet Jesus.

Then Jesus gathers them up in His arms and gives them clean teeth, the better to eat at His Holy Table, and clean ears, the better to hear his Holy Music,

—and clean eyes, the better — to see and worship Him.

© 1994 DUCORNET/MOTLEY

Excerpts from Five Novels

Rikki Ducornet

In my essay for this issue of the *Review of Contemporary Fiction,* I have chosen to write about the Death Cunt in part because it is at the heart of the "gnostic vision" as I see it, and a recurrent theme in my own work. For this reason also, I have chosen brief instants from each of the five novels in which the "Death Cunt" appears or, as in the excerpt from *Phosphor in Dreamland* in which—a mere figment of the mind—she has been admirably (!) overcome.

From *The Stain* (Earth)

Look carefully at the freshly disturbed soil and you will see shining in the sun a derelict rib. The scattered remains of persons deceased are revealed after thaws and heavy rains. Here little Charlotte will accumulate a singular set of ivory pawns: vertebrae, lunates, phalanges and molars.

Charlotte is seven years old. As is usual, her birthday is celebrated by a trip to the cemetery. Charlotte, in black wool coat and stockings, a black ribbon tied to her hair, is wedged between her aunt and uncle for a morning of prayer. The late October sun is hot and the air heavy with the brute stench of boxwood.

As Edma prays and Emile dozes, Charlotte explores the cemetery with her immense grey-green eyes (changeling eyes, Edma calls them, neither here nor there). She observes that the ornate mausoleum squatting ponderously to the left of her mother's grave has a broken step that has slipped to reveal an inky crevice. And this crevice crawls with flies. The mausoleum's stained and pitted front-age is also alive with flies, swarming multitudes clinging to the defunct family's name like grapes. With a thrill, Charlotte recognizes the letters and reads the stones. And it is here, in the cemetery, that she will have her first lesson in geometry:

> *God's love is a circle*
> *Our Hearts sleep within*
> *Safe from Sin.*

and:

The triangle is perfect purity—
God, His Son, the Holy Ghost—
The Blessed Trinity.

Charlotte sees that the triangle itself stirs restlessly beneath a shifting swarm of flies.

She wonders about the grinning cavity. What is inside? She knows that a body was placed in the grave before her. Has a perfect soul escaped from that crack, she ponders, leaving in its wake perfect bones? But clean bones do not explain the flies' nagging presence. Flies are dirt-eaters, Aunt has told her often. They eat rotten things, they revel in de-compo-sition and where they settle to feed, they lay eggs—eggs that transform themselves into worms. Charlotte supposed that if the eggs of chickens were a gift of Light, the eggs of flies must be the gift of Darkness.

She thinks of all the flies she has ever seen collecting upon the indecipherable lumps of neglected chicken offal that Edma wrenches from the gaping corpses of chickens and throws into the kitchen yard—for the chickens. If chickens eat one another just as evil persons do (Edma had pointed out such people in an illustrated newspaper article she had saved—sullen creatures with extravagantly knobby knees protruding grotesquely from beneath scanty grass skirts and despised by God for having devoured all their neighbors) how can their eggs possibly be clean? That morning, Charlotte comes to the irrevocable conclusion that eggs are not fit for human consumption.

"Aunt!" she suddenly cries, forgetting that she must never interrupt Edma in prayer. "Aunt! Where does the *meat* go?"

Her question is answered by a nasty pinch on the cheek that leaves a mark, red and white, for many throbbing minutes. Charlotte wonders if cannibals eat family members and through silent tears gazes intently upon her mother's grave. For the first time she sees that the wreath of glass beads moored there is shaped like an open mouth—a vertical mouth—quite large enough for Charlotte to pass through. Is the mouth a door? Did her mother's soul pass through that door on its way to Heaven? After reflection, she decides that the mouth, having eaten and digested her mother's meat, having sucked her bones clean, allowed her soul to escape as a sigh from its lips, leaving a perfect skeleton behind. She sees that every grave has a wreath and this confirms her discovery. (No wreath is visible on the façade of the mausoleum and this very neatly explains the presence of those spectacularly numerous flies.)

Many years later, Charlotte will enter the mausoleum alone. She will find a wreath inside, but broken, its twisted wire frame having rusted and crumbled, the glass pearls, silver, blue and white, strewn across the tilted floor.

It is time to go home. Charlotte walks towards the gate sandwiched between her aunt and uncle. She sees a small bird perched naughtily on a cross; a moon-shaped stone broken in two like a wafer; smells the lush scent of chrysanthemums—those gallic flowers of death—and boxwood. And then she perceives a faint but persistent odor that, sickly sweet, frightens her and has to do with the unusually warm day, *the heat, the meat, it dies, it flies . . .* and they are passing the poorer graves, all marked off by squares of pink gravel, scalloped on the edges like fancy birthday cakes.

> *The Four Hours of the Day,*
> *Morning, Noon, Evening and Night,*
> *The Square proclaims God's might.*

Unexpectedly, Edma stoops and carefully pulls up a small grey-green plant by the roots—a perennial she intends to add to the kitchen yard's flower borders. Charlotte, choking on suppressed curiosity, takes advantage of the unexpected gesture and asks:

"Aunt, what does e.t.e.r.n.a.l. mean?"

"E-E-E-ternal!" Emile stutters.

"Eternal," says Edma, pleased to answer a question she considers worthwhile, "is Forever. Like God."

"F-F-F-" Emile adds.

"Is He *Death,* Aunt?"

"He is Death and He is Life. He takes and He gives. For example, when you were born, your mother died."

"Why did He make her *die?*"

"She sinned against Him!"

"L-L-L-Lust!" explains Emile.

Charlotte did not know what lust was, but she imagined it was not unlike cannibalism. She wished with all her heart that God would die. She would steal his wreath so that His soul and His bones and His meat would rot together. Forever. So that flies would feed upon His corpse. Forever. And that night Charlotte dreamed her own triangle.

It was immense, rising from the sands of a vast desert. When she approached, she discovered that it was actually a pyramid and so large that once she had walked around it she was terribly tired, hot and thirsty. She wondered if it had a door, so that she could enter and lie down in the shade. But looking closely, she saw that it was made of pieces of red meat, sewn together with thick black thread, and that the whole thing stank of rotten chicken offal. Suddenly the thread bloomed with blue flies, and the sound of their buzzing was deafening.

"Aunt! Aunt!" she cried, frightened. "What is it?" But a voice that was not her aunt's voice replied:

It is the House of God.

From *Entering Fire* (Fire)

Lamprias de Bergerac

Doubtless you are wondering what had precipitated my marriage with Virginie, when it is evident that I was made to wander alone, to follow intuition's thin, glimmering thread where it would lead me.

We were introduced at a garden party. The women all fiddled with fans, and the men, their moustaches carefully waxed, stood about as stiffly as their own starched collars. In evanescent brocade, Virginie, a "bibi" of tulle and whalebone perched smartly on her head, was a wonderfully long-waisted girl with large, astonished eyes and thick, black eyebrows, close set, like centipedes about to copulate. Her lips, as they folded over a creamcake, were the colour of apricots and for one wet instant divulged her tongue. She sipped her tea and silently accepted another cake. Enchanted, I watched as it too disappeared into her mouth and down a throat noosed with pearls.

"Virginie!" bellowed my mother, in taffeta, with me in tow. "My son is only just returned from the turbulence of the Guianan jungle!" And she backed off ostentatiously, leaving us alone. Virginie, her great blue irises ringed with darker indigo fixing a mysterious distance on the horizon just beyond my left ear, whispered dreamily, *"The voyager . . . The voyager pursues his road, free and contented. He possesses nothing yet the entire world is at his feet. His eyes are ceaselessly struck by new objects which give him food for thought. Our life,* don't you think . . ." and for the first time she looked into my eyes, *"our life is a voyage."*

Head over heels in love I proposed to her within the week. My mother, delighted by the prospect of my domestication, gave the de Bergerac ancestral house over to wall-paperers, and retired to one of the family's many country estates where she lived piously and in the company of harassed housemaids, and where she produced twenty-four night-bonnets and a linen altar cloth before passing on.

It was not until the ordeal of our honeymoon that I was forced to admit that my bride, for all her fetching ways with pastry, and despite the heavenly bliss of her eyes, had no soul. O! The memory of that week in Hell! Unable to bed her—for the sight of my naked body had shocked her into a froth of loathing—I attempted to talk to her. But my Virginie had no mind; her conversation was only what she had managed to memorize from her exercise books. I remember the morning of my awakening . . .

We were walking down a freshly raked path fragrant with jasmine. I commented upon the smell.

"Perfume," said Virginie, "is agreeable to the nose. The shade," she added, "is agreeable to those who walk." I mentioned Darwin.

"Books," said my wife interrupting me, "are agreeable to the wise." Our path led to a tearoom. I suggested refreshment. When our cakes and coffee were served, Virginie, brushing an éclair with the apricot lips I already loved less, said:

"The most agreeable coffee comes from Arabia."

"Virginie, dearest . . ." I took her small, gloved hand in mine, "talk to me, dearheart."

"I am talking! Yes . . . and that reminds me: The conversation of the ignorant is insipid, don't you think?"

I then asked her why she had consented to be my wife. Virginie tore a brioche in two and buttered it tenderly. "My mother bade me marry," she explained, taking a bite, "and I did." She brushed crumbs from her blouse. "Youth takes council from the aged."

By the end of the week the marriage was still not consummated. At dinner I suggested an annulment. And there in the hotel dining room, surrounded by elderly couples in retirement, a baked custard quivering in its dish beneath her eager spoon, Virginie threw herself into a fit of shrieking, the first fit of the Feast of Fits which was to punctuate our life together.

"If only," said Virginie, once we returned home and her mother had convinced her that she was, like all mortal women, sexual, "if only people could reproduce photographically." Even this bon mot was not her own, but belonged to Dr Roux, the eccentric inventor of the two-hundred-metre high battery, and then at the apex of fashion.

The week following our honeymoon, I left for China to study the Aerides odoratum and the Arundina, two particularly luscious specimens of orchids. I wanted to give my new bride time to accustom herself to the physical realities of marriage. Always an optimist, I imagined the slow awakening of desire, and passion's blossom. I hoped Virginie would come to miss me. I flattered myself that once having entered her mind I would enter her body. I never even considered what was to be Kindergarten's technique: to rub her neck, to rub her back, to massage her ribs and her buttocks, her thighs, her feet, her knees and then all over again—for an hour, for two hours—until her body, as elastic and as yeasty as teacake batter, would be ready for what she called: *The Sacrifice.*

Once and only once would this madwoman be mine and once was all she needed to conceive a Calamity.

And Dust? Dust I had pulled from the fire, only to drop her into Virginie's infernal frying pan. When I had found her sitting in the streets of Peking holding onto her little bleeding feet, banished by her mother-in-law for having stolen a peach, I chose to believe that Virginie, an obedient (if unbedded) wife and a devout Christian, would be pleased to adopt so needy, so self-effaced, so exotic a companion.

Dust was a dear, gentle thing and lovely when she smiled. I recognize that it was a blunder to get her pregnant. But so grateful was she for the kindness shown her, so anxious to please, that during our travels together she was forever posing herself in the most provocative postures, and giggling behind her plump hands in the most suggestive manner imaginable.

It was impossible for me to concentrate on my work. My head was swimming with visions of this doll-like creature, her legs like sharpened pencils in the air, her jewelled mouth a ripe fig seeded with teeth. As I fell into her bed I imagined for a fleeting, foolish instant my ancestor's dark, sprawling house transformed by two women living as sisters together, surrounded by an affectionate brood of children. And so, from foggy thinking fired by lust, I created a madhouse.

I reflected upon all this beneath a canopy of blossoming cattleyas; clusters of *Brassavola fragrans,* not visible to the eye, filled the air with savage sweetness. And I remembered that before setting himself down to his business of miracles, Savinien had needed to dispel the shadows that tempted his spirit and troubled his heart. He described his mood as one of Profound Melancholy. Reviewing my amorous history, myself heavy of heart, I felt closer to him than to any man I had ever known. I feared that I was a coward, I feared I was deluded, I feared I was, at best, a fool.

From *The Fountains of Neptune* (Water)

Christmas holidays had begun and I did not miss the schoolroom, nor my master whose name was Shelled; rather, Shelled is what we called him. He had been shell-shocked during the Franco-Prussian War and he had never entirely recovered. A man of sixty, he appeared to us as someone archaic, even biblical; there was something terrible about this moody man's yellow face ravaged by tics. In his worst moments he threatened to hurl us through the window; on better days he read us stories from Baudelaire's translation of Edgar Allan Poe. I cherish a vivid recollection of Shelled sputtering *The Gold Bug,* one arm bent at a painfully acute angle across his loosely aproned back and the other holding the book within a hair's breadth of his myopia. Further down the aisle one of the wilder boys had shat directly in his path. Shelled stepped neatly over it without changing his inflection.

This wild, scatological boy was the one friend I had made in school. I admired Maximinole who was older than the other boys and who, unlike me, had "no time for stories." Max was interested only in what he called "real things," liberty and, of course, tormenting Shelled. Fossils in pavement, shadows in fog, the beached frames of unfinished boats prodding the air like the skeletons of whales, the moon hanging in the sky like an evil face were without interest. Planets, meteors, old stones, old shells, old sailors' gibberish—what did they matter? What did they prove? Those starfish I went on about were *dead* things. Once in my zeal to win Max over I had bragged about a piece of rock I had found in the attic. Its one polished face offered a seascape perfect in every detail: grottoes, rising mist, cresting waves, reeling birds. Maximinole hotly insisted the thing was impossible, and in an excess of anger had punched me in the face. My profusely bleeding nose and pained expression were too much for him; Max ran from the schoolyard and never returned. Later I learned that he—in that city of sailors—had apprenticed himself to a baker. Someone had seen the fiery Maximinole at dawn bent in two beneath a fifty-kilo sack of flour. Although he hurt me, I've always felt that I pushed him too far, wanting him to see the world in a way he was unable to. I hate to think that this boy who had so brazenly lowered his drawers in the aisle was doing mule's work for a baker.

Companionless, therefore, on that cold December morning on the edge of Christmas, I set off in the slush—for there was a drizzle to the day and the heavy snows of Saturday night and Sunday morning were sliding off the rooftops and into the gutters with a hiss. I sloshed down the street on the lookout for marbles; I had found two favourites this way: an unusually heavy one made, I think, of hematite and a large one of transparent glass filled with thousands of pin-prick bubbles. Faithful to my habit I walked along with my eyes glued to the ground, my old wool beret pulled down over my ears making me look, I hoped, a little like a pirate. I also wore a pair of wool gloves cut off at the fingers. I did not find any marbles that day, but the sloppy water, oily in places and black, and the lumps of unmelted snow calving like icebergs in the miniature oceans of the street, had me continually dreaming. Such was the enchantment of those floating worlds that I lost all notion of place and time and wandered down to the port where the hulls of the season's deserted *sardiniers* rocked in the icy water with a sorrowful, sucking sound. Their names were marvellous: *The Free Thought, Hook's Slave, La Communarde.* Soon the wind sent me scurrying back to the protection of the streets where a thin mist followed me everywhere. The sun was already waning when, with a shiver of foreboding and delight, I recognized the side-street and the alley leading to the Ghost Port Bar. In an instant I saw the Ghost's familiar fogged panes, its ancient stone doorsteps all puddled in the middle.

To the small boy I was, the Ghost inspired awe. I pushed the door open and entered on tiptoe. At first I could see nothing but the bottles twinkling like precious stones behind the bar: the hot ice of *eau-de-vie,* kirsch, and kümmel, absinthe's green and bitter worm, a horrid toad-black beetroot alcohol, whisky, rum, and anisette, *prunelle,* a blushing peach brandy; and syrups: mint and lemon, angelica. . . . It was still early for customers and the Cod's wife was not standing in her usual place. The room smelled of roasting fish— surely the Cod's dinner. I walked over to the chimp's cage. Charlie Dee was fast asleep. His snoring made me think of walking on gravel at the bottom of a pool. Then my heart leapt, for I saw in the far corner of the room, smoke wheeling about his head, Toujours-Là. The dying sun sent a faint gleam through the nearly opaque glass and bathed his features in alarming shadows. Now I wonder what demon compelled me to navigate the dusk and to sit down at his table.

The old sailor was pouring out two fingers of Terminus brand absinthe. With as much ceremony as a trembling hand would allow, he cradled a lump of sugar in a pierced spoon, balanced this over his glass, and poured in water. When the absinthe swelled to the colour of sea water, Toujours-Là acknowledged me and greased his whistle.

The liquor in the Ghost was served in thick, hand-blown tumblers the like of which I've not seen since. They were very old and the Cod had inherited a seemingly endless quantity of them when, no longer fit for seafaring, he had bought the place, handed his wife the brass key, and gone upstairs to give himself over to toothache, piles, and melancholia. The Ghost's glass tumblers were so heavy, and the lip so sound and smooth, that they commanded love and respect. I'd heard of men throwing bottles in anger in that place, but no man had ever smashed a glass.

Toujours-Là licked his lips, cleared his throat, and said:

"I've travelled the world over and I've seen the Devil *everywhere*. But nowhere, Nini, nowhere, mind you, nowhere have I seen God." He sucked his teeth, took a drink, and twitched.

"Rose says—" I began.

"Don't believe the crap you hear!" he barked. "The universe and all its filthy planets were not created by God but by the Devil. Every morning the sun rises with an empty belly and at night she sinks bloated with blood. You've seen how the moon circles the world like a clean bone?" I nodded. "Like a skull licked clean of meat," he insisted.

"Like the face of the Ogress!" I whispered, fascinated by the gloomy colour of his words. Although I sensed that the mad steersman was about to ferry me across the starkest latitude of his imagining, already my own darkest waters were rushing out to meet his.

"War is brewing again, Nini; I feel it biting at my bones. They said Bismarck was a hound—*all* men are hounds! The Devil's hounds! And women are hornets. *When was the last time you saw your mother?*"

I was stunned. Toujours-Là, having momentarily emptied his gullet of bile, took up his pipe and for a time kept quiet. But I, at least within, was anything but quiet; my blood was in a turmoil. I tried to remember when I had seen her and could not. It was like trying to see a midnight path in a starless, moonless air. But then, unknown to me, the quicksand of my thoughts shifted, and I changed the subject.

"Tell me a story!" I breathed, curiously exalted as when once I'd leaned too close to a cage of vipers a tattered man was showing for a *centime* in the street. "Tell me another story; tell me, Toujours-Là," I rambled on as stiff in my chair as Pinnochio before he was made flesh, "tell me another one, about her—about the Ogress—"

Just then the Cod's wife came downstairs with a dish of baked tuna and pan-fried potatoes.

"So you're here, Nini!" She pecked at my cheek and striking a match lit a lamp. "Where's Totor?"

"I don't know—I'm out alone! Out exploring!"

"I'll bring you a lemonade," she said, "a hot lemonade with bitters. But no rum, Nini. Rose was in, mad as a cat—you're not supposed to be here, son."

"I'm big enough to know where I should be!" I said dramatically, and to prove it pulled off my wool cap and threw it down on the table—just one of the heroic gestures I'd stolen from Maximinole.

When she had gone Toujours-Là said:

"The woman's always mothering me and wants me to eat. I tell her: 'This is my meat!' " He held his glass to the light. "You want some supper?" The food looked good and I had been wandering since breakfast. He pulled the biggest folding knife I'd ever seen from his pocket. The tuna's flesh was so hot it hissed against the cold steel.

"I once loved baked tuna. But they say a man's a moulded river, little more than water. There's something to be said for an entirely liquid ballast." He knocked off another glass and with the ragged vocal cords of a rusty pall sang:

> "My woman's a bar lily
> with a heart of flaming whisky
> and the greenest eyes
> and the meanest ways, yes
> and the sweetest lies. . . ."

When the Cod's wife was back with my lemonade and saw the empty dish pushed aside, she gave Toujours-Là a kiss. "Good boy," she said.

"Good boy!" he spat. "I'm old enough to be your grandpa—you silly cunt!"

"You watch your language in front of the child!" she bridled, hurt.

"I can hear anything!" I cried bravely. "My brain's solid copper!"

"If the old sonofabitch wasn't ready to croak," she explained, "I'd throw him out. Owes me plenty, too!" She slammed back upstairs.

I felt something pulling at my leg; it was Charlie Dee. He looked at me from under the table and grinned. I helped him up onto my lap where he immediately stuck his finger into my lemonade. Meanwhile Toujours-Là knocked his pipe out against the heel of his shoe. The ash tumbled to the floor. He took a curious beaded pouch from his pocket and scrounged around for a few fragrant shivers of tobacco. Then he refilled his pipe lovingly. I thought: One day, like Totor and Toujours-Là, I will carry a pipe. Hung before his face the mermaid sailed the air, and, like a steamship, smoked. She made the Ghost feel homey; she was, after all, a toy hearth. Toujours-Là poured himself another. This time he made a *panaché;* he mixed his absinthe with mint syrup and a spot of anisette.

"I was never a man," he began, secreting the bottles on the floor beside his chair, "to carry dung in a pocket to exorcize misfortune. . . . One morning I woke up *nowhere at all.*

"I was young, still wet behind the ears, in fact, Nini, barely twice your age; an apprentice ship's carpenter on his first time out, shipping with the Greenland Company and eager for adventure. We was after whales in Baffin Bay and we'd anchored off what's now known as Thule—the furthest point off the North coast of Greenland a big ship can sail. The night before, I'd sat myself down in the most peculiar bar you'd ever hope to see—it squatted like a bitch taking a leak. The beams and rafters was made of the ribs of whales, the sod walls was carpeted with seal fur and the one window was the stretched bladder of a walrus.

"Outside they was those boreal constellations hanging so glassy they set my teeth on edge; why, just looking at them was like chewing sand. There was something hideously timeless about the place, and the morning looked like evening and the other way 'round so you never knew what time it was or where you was, fore or aft, sleeping or waking. Hell, you had to think twice before sitting down else sit on your own face.

"The blue-eyed Eskimo who ran things had, by the smell of it, distilled the bile of seals; too many hours before I'd taken a swig and one—the orbs of my eyes had bled, two—my ear drums had burst, three—I couldn't feel my legs from the knees down, four—I began to feel warmer than I'd ever felt since relinquishing the womb (maybe warmer), five—I'd apparently begun to sing Offenbach, six—I was dancing on the table in my socks while my head orbited the room, and seven—I was out like a candle and under the table in the dimmest corner of a dark room, a room wherein everything was barely perceptible, lit by a couple of sputtering walrus-oil lamps.

"Despite the considerable rumpus I'd made in the infancy of the evening, my mates and the polar proprietor had forgotten all about me. When I woke up I found that my granddaddy's pocket-watch was gone, but I still had my pipe." He sucked on it thoughtfully, curing the cleft between the mermaid's breasts with a filthy nail. "I ran outta there like rats from a hull on fire, but the sea was as empty as an overturned coffin.

"I stood by the water, cursing—'Devil take me!' I hollered, 'I'm marooned!' I repeat, I was *nowhere,* Nini; there was nothing in Thule, nothing but Eskimos and one crazy Dane trapper (and he's the one stole my watch for sure), and a couple of tumbledown sod wigwams, plus that damned cabaret tucked inside the ribcage of a leviathan, and the frozen heads of slaughtered reindeer marking the end of the street, their ears gnawed off by polar foxes which gave them an especial dismal appearance, *and above all ice*—ice, ice, ice—thousands of square feet of the stuff underfoot. I was standing on ice, Thule was anchored on ice—just thinking about it, even now, gives me vertigo. Water's one thing; ice another. I'd rather wed a witch than be marooned on ice!

" 'Devil take me!' I cried, 'I need a ship! Any ship!' In that beggarly light I looked with despair on a horizon larded with *ice!*

"And then, Nini, I see her. I see: Bel. She materialized like an uncorked genie in the middle of downtown Thule, halfway between a pyramid of frozen walrus guts and the public shit-house.

" 'Hello, sailor,' she mewed, 'you're wanting a ship and I have one. I'm always on the prowl for sailors, she purred, and she gave me a wink.

" 'You a ship's captain?' I asked, flabbergasted. I'd never dreamed a woman ship's master, and the wench was beautiful—if peculiarly dressed in an obsolete velvet with sleeves like bellows. She was wearing lots of jewellery; I particularly admired the wide choker of pearls. I took one sniff of her skin and the scattered pieces of my fractured skull came together.

" 'If you is a captain,' I said, 'where's your ship?' After all, I'd peeled the horizon for the *Søren Kierkegaard* and seen nothing but the bung-hole of a whale. She laughed and her black eyes gazed towards the ocean.

" 'I'll be damned!' I said again, because I seen a ship, Nini, such as I'd never seen before, and thank Lucifer, never since!"

"What was she like?"

"A species of barquentine but bloated, writhing with shapes indeterminate, ugly and obsh . . . obscure. Despite her size she was somehow volatile . . . a hammered air . . . a . . . what's the word? Coagulum, yes, a coagulum of night, suspended between the sea and the sky like a cathedral on fire."

"A cathedral!"

"From stem to stern she was carved like some hermetic cabinet with all manner of occult ribaldry: naked witches straddling billy goats and lunatic carpenters wielding their privates like hammers. There was queens kicking the posteriors of valets and kings with the vish . . . the visages of maniacs copulating with mitred bears; and preaching foxes and farting preachers—in short, a thousand devils and devilish devices, an encyclopaedic chaos wreathed with the names of rebellious spirits: Lucifer, Beelzebuth, and Astaroth; and magical words such as ZAITUX and TROMADOR in a muddle of griffins—but all rendered with such foh! felicity that though she could have looked ridiculous, in fact, the monstrous vessel commanded—in her wild and gloomy way—respect. Especially her mammoth figurehead."

"Oh!"

"She appeared, Nini, wading knee-deep in the brine, which, with each passing instant, looked less like water and more like a filthy chowder. She confronted us full-on, a giantess of blackened madder, so wonderfully carved she must have been the work of sorcery. Her haggard beauty was worried by a century of high wind and salt. The throat was thrown back in silent laughter, the teeth as big as casks of rum, the feral nostrils flaring, the orbits of the eyes like planets, the tangled mane of hair blazing with the phosphorescent algae that gave the ship the semblance of burning. The cleft of her bosom was so deep it could have held the bodies of three men; her nipples were broad enough to straddle."

I laughed.

"Laugh, will you! Little sprat! Only *listen!* At those massive thighs, the spheral knees, the foam sputtered and died. Suddenly the sea was still. So much *dead water,* a gum, a pitch—"

"A co-agulum!"

"A clotted pitch! 'She suit you?' Bel asks. 'Her name's *Great Babylon.* And mine's Bel. Now let's drink to seal our contract.' I find myself standing in a richly appointed cabin on board, Bel proffering a brimming cup. As I drink, a story I heard long ago rattles in my head: *The woman was dressed in purple and scarlet trimmed with gold and gems and pearls: in her hand she held a golden cup filled to the brim with abomination. . . . On her forehead was inscribed a mysterious name: Great Babylon. . . . And I saw that she was drunk on blood.*"

"And was there blood in the cup?"

"No, boy, sweet wine. One taste and a whirlpool is spinning in my mind and before nodding I am sleeping. I awaken in the belly of the *Babylon* in a hammock next to twelve others, all empty. Sticking my head up the hatch I smell roasting and baking, and follow my nose to where Bel and her crew is feasting. I'm greeted with raised cups and pull up to a table set like an altar with all my favourite dishes: veal stuffed with prunes, and duckling with sauerkraut, and egg pudding swimming in caramel—"

"Rose makes that!"

"So I've heard. . . . We is a motley crew in our stained monkey jackets keeping company to a captain who looks more like a countess. Coopers, harpooners, blacksmiths, common sailors—sea-dogs all, and who, from what I gather, have all been saved from calamity: bedlam, suicide, starvation, shipwreck—even hanging for murder. Bel is like a mother to us, that fondant bosom heaving as she passes the platters.

"Then the cook staggers in with a flaming Alaska. He's the strangest character imaginable. Looks like a hyena trotting around on hind paws and swathed in an apron. I needs look twice to see a man; yet swear I hear claws clattering like meat forks on the deck.

" 'Tell these worthy tars tomorrow's menu,' beams Bel. 'A menu's like a lullaby,' she confides to me. 'I like my men to sleep.'

" 'We sleep a lot,' a deck-boy yawns. 'A-a-a-a.' He drops off then and there, his forehead in his pudding.

" 'Eggs Rosita!' the cook attacks the menu with a yelp. 'Eggs Rossini. Baron of lamb *à la byzantine,* Scarlet Beef, fried *animelles,* moussaka of mutton, a partridge *estouffade,* a salad *arlésienne,* braised salmon, pigs' trotters with mustard sauce, sea-bream served in melted butter, scallops Mornay, stuffed shoulder of veal, smothered—'

" 'Stop! Stop!' we all cry together as if afraid to die of too much happiness.

" 'I, ah . . . uh, eat when I, ah, sleep . . .' the deck-boy sighs, still sleeping. 'I sleep when I, e—'

" '*Cèpes!* Fruit *rissoles,* rhubarb pie, pudding *à l'anglaise,* jam omelette, Bourdaloue pears, soufflé Erzsebet, frangipani, Devil's food—' howls the cook. It comes to me that all my mates look like sucking pigs—their faces so round and plump and their colour so high.

" 'A Sauterne will be served with the Devil's food,' Bel flashes her teeth, 'and with the pigs' trotters, a Moselle. And now,' she breathes, 'our toddy before tucking in!' Bel smiles at me and winks. To tell the truth, I think this winking's vulgar for a captain; then again I suppose a captain can never be a *lady.*

"Bel, it is clear by her attributes and attitudes, has been around. She is no white lily, but more your scarlet poppy, and her petals, lovely as they is, is mussed. Sounding my thoughts she gives me a slow, sideways glance which causes my stomach to sink. But then she's handing me a fragrant cup. Inside I see a ring of imps cracking whips and leaping hoops of fire."

"Oh! Don't drink it, Toujours-Là!"

"It smells so pungent and delicious, I quaff it down and I'm sent flying into the familiar whirlpool to the sound of trumpets and more prosaic the baaa baaa baaaing of a thoush—thousand sheep. I awake the next morning feeling unstrung and queer. But the smell of frying beefsteaks and fresh coffee has me and my mates leaping to our feet.

"Each day at breakfast Bel gives us our orders: retracing her chalk tetragrams (and the Devil knows their purpose), and scraping the rust off these iron coffins she cherishes, their insides fitted out with sharp nails, and swabbing down the timbers of the ship, those huge, hot decks. But scrub with bucketfuls of elbow grease and good, brown soap, still a dreadful phosphorated mould is always growing back, coating everything in a luciferous sheen. Yet there is never much else to do as the *Great Babylon* sails herself, her canvas groaning day and night in an unceasing wind. We is going somewhere very fast, but in a haze so thick only Satan could say where. I fear we'll hit ice, but Bel says she knows no finer helmsman than the Infinite and His wind. I figure that the Infinite of whom she speaks is no other than His Highness of Infinite Hell. In the mist I sometimes think I see His furies knotting the latitudes and longitudes that net the globe, tugging, and twisting, and dredging for our souls.

"Since I am a carpenter, Bel has me repair the *Babylon's* ancient witcheries—those lewd emblems worried by the salt of time. Some of these—the griffins and the bears—is badly worn about the rumps and muzzles as if in their static race around the bulwarks they has been tearing one another to pieces. Some is lost their noses, some their teeth, others is featureless. Sculpture were never my line and the stuff the *Babylon* is made of is dreadful dense. I wonder how, despite the outlandish humidity, the wood is so hard and dry. An unworldly fire consumes the ship from within.

"Nights I dream the *Babylon* is made of rotting flesh, and fractured bones and tiger's breath and tar," Toujours-Là continued, pouring out another *panaché,* "but Bel likes me and shows it by cuffing my ear in this kittenish way she has. Once, young fool that I am, I grabs her and gives her a kiss. For this I get a scratch from my temple to my chin what don't heal for weeks. She is a demon, no doubt; keeps her pronged tail tucked beneath her petticoats.

"We all feel poorly. Some complains it is for lack of exsh . . . exsh . . . Oh! Hang it! Or blame it on the constant wind wish, dammit! DAMMIT! For a polar wind ish Goddammed hot *and getting hotter all the time!* I, for my part, blame it on my su . . . sup—"

"Supper!"

"Shhh! Suppurating cheek which ish badly inflamed, and a nasty rat bite I've got on the neck, which gets to hurting worse as the days pass. The others—why, they's bitten too; the *Great Babylon,* scrub and scour as we do, is infested with rats and it maddens us that if we hears them scuttling all the time, and all of us bit—*we never see a one of 'em!*

"THAT MONKEY STINKS!" he shouted then for no apparent reason. "THAT MONKEY STINKS TO HELL!" Startled, Charlie Dee tucked his head down under the table. "Speaking of in—fah!—*infested*—I can see his lice from here! SET HIM DOWN!"

"He's clean," I said. "The Cod's wife gives him a bubble bath each Saturday and rubs him down with lavender water. Totor told me. What happened then?"

"Time . . ." he said, shivering, "time is speeding by unstoppable. Time's a broom bewitched, straddled by a hag. Have we been given the Devil's red shoes to dance our lives away? Are we eating the

Devil's pudding?"

"We is!" I shouted, tremendously excited. "We is!"

"SHUT YOUR TRAP!" the sailor barked. "Each day when I awakes I try to think, but the pain in my head is too horrendous, and the hunger in my belly has me stumbling with the other fools to that charmed table.

"STOP TOYING WITH THAT CRITTER, LAD!" he shouted savagely. "Set it back down on the floor or stick it in its cage. You want to hear the tale or fuss with animals?"

"But I *am* listening, Toujours-Là, I *am*! Charlie Dee's not doing anything. Please. And then? What happened then? It's the Ogress! I know it is she! Bel and the Ogress—one and the same!"

"Yeah," he said. Then, in a low snarl I did not like at all: "Yeah, Slyboots! I could tell you another story. . . ." He lifted his glass to his lips and delved for the last few drops of liquor with his tongue.

"Listen to me, boy," he hissed. "Listen at the chinks. Listen if you want to know what hides beneath the tides, the shhh . . . swiftly ebbing tides of air you breathe. Prick your ears, my suckling; I want to hear your ear-bones crack! Listen sharply! ARE YOU ALL EARS?"

This tirade ended when Toujours-Là was seized by a painful spasm. When he took up the story again, his voice, thick and rumbling, was hardly recognizable.

"We is all growing weaker. Despite all that sleep and fancy fare we look like starvelings. All my mates is ulcerated at the throat— the punctures are deep and ugly. Did I say we was thirteen at table? Thirteen counting Bel?"

"I don't recall, Toujours-Là."

"You recall! Little bugger! Heed me! I am dreaming. . . ."

He waited. I was angry and did not ask about his dream. He looked at me intently and, only after a long pause, continued:

"I am dreaming about black widow spiders what eat their mates, you know. Mantises do it, too. In the act. Eat the male's head clean off *in the act*. You ever seen that, little bugger? Ever seen the Act?"

"Toujours-Là," I whispered, my head swarming, I think I should go home. Rose—"

"THE STORY AIN'T OVER!" He reached down and plucked a bottle from the shadows. "I consider throwing myself into the sea, but Bel, always so good at leeching onto my thoughts says: 'These waters are swarming with sharks.' Now, if the thought of drowning is beginning to appeal to me, I have no desire to be eaten alive. It takes all the courage I have left to ask: 'What waters, ma'am? *Where are we?*'

" 'Where is not your concern,' she says. 'I hired you as ship's carpenter, not as ship's philosopher. How dare you ask *where? There is no where.* Nor will there ever be.' Throwing back her gorgeous head and exposing her long, white throat bound in its pearl bandage, she roars with laughter. Outside the wind swells and echoes her hilarity.

"One morning I awake slick with sweat, a shrill shriek, possibly my own, tearing through my ears. I've been wrenched from a vivid nightmare of a winged and whiskered creature crouching heavy on my chest, its barbed proboscis boring into an artery, its thread-like tongue worming into my brain. The pain at my neck is esh . . . excruciating. Near mad, I see the others in a haze, sleeping still as Death, each one bleeding a thin, yellow blood at the neck. Despite my horror and my weakness, I know I must solve the riddle of Bel's floating *Babylon*."

"Did you? Did you, Toujours-Là?"

"No! Her griffins have kept their secrets, and if it was they what steered her, or Satan's own shadow—neither you nor I will ever know!" He circled his tumbler's rim with his thumb. "I penetrate to the heart of her; I explore the hull's baleful maze. So tortured by fear and pain, I have to stop each step to hold my aching head in both my hands and weep. I find nothing! Nothing in the main hold. Nothing in steerage. Nothing in the afterhold, or the captain's store. She carries no cargo but these empty iron coffins and I am sorely baffled that with no ballast in a gale, which by the second doubles in velocity, the *Babylon* doesn't rise into the air.

"I come at last to the galley—there is nothing there—not an onion, nor an apple pip; nothing but a sinking feeling and, Heaven help me, a mangy cur, scaled and patchy, outlandishly filthy and seemingly exuding a noxious green sss . . . smoke. He's sleeping in the centre of a chalk circle I've retraced myself. He opens one rheumy eye and, curling back a purple lip, shows a set of teeth I know I have no use for. When I see his shadow rising on the wall, I leap for a ladder and, pushing through the scuttle, find myself looking up into my captain's cabin."

I must have squeezed the chimp too tightly in my arms then, for he squirmed and, pulling away from my embrace, sprawled across the table and knocked over the sailor's glass. Toujours-Là gave Charlie Dee a slap which sent him sliding to the floor. He stood whimpering and stealing angry looks from behind his fists. Stunned, I mopped up the absinthe with my handkerchief.

"I see," he continued, pouring out another, "I see—hanging from the rafters in the dim glow of that evil ch . . . chamber, hanging heavy and sodden from its feet, its wet muzzle glistening in the darkling air, *an abomination*—the creature of my dream. She is the offspring of a mantis and a bat, her teeth like prongs, her furry belly pendulous and swollen. Had she been a creature of the sea, no matter how hi . . . hi . . . hideous, I would not have been so afraid; it is the wedding of insect and mammal in the middle of the ocean what strikes me as particularly hidsh . . . hidsh . . . horrible. A bead of fresh blood ish hanging from her snout and this thing, this frenzy escaped from some lunatic's reverie is"—Toujours-Là hesitated and, squinting at me, I think gleefully—"is *wearing a pearl choker.* And the blood she is drooling, child, *is my own.*" For emphasis, Toujours-Là jabbed at the air before my face with his pipe. Charlie Dee reached out and struck his thumb down its incandescent bowl. Grunting surprise and pain, he knocked the pipe to the floor where it shattered.

Toujours-Là leapt from his chair and swept the chimp up by the ankles. He raised him high and sent him fracturing, head first, against the wall. With a sickening thud, Charlie Dee collapsed in a heap, spitting blood.

Having scrambled to my feet, I fought for breath. Upstairs, the Cod lifted himself out of his tub.

"what's going on?" he shouted. "what's going on down there?" The Cod's wife pushed him back into the suds and pounded downstairs. Charlie Dee lay knotted in spasms. With a trembling hand, Toujours-Là polished off his glass.

When the Cod's wife screamed, I ran. I ran as fast as I could away from Toujours-Là and the Ghost Port Bar. But the Ghost Port Bar and Toujours-Là have always followed me.

After the murder of Charlie Dee, Toujours-Là disappeared.

"Good rubbish," said Rose. "May he never be seen again!" Two slow days passed before I returned to the Ghost with Totor for the monkey's funeral.

From *The Jade Cabinet* (Air)

When I think of the *Hungerkünstler,* I cannot help but think of Angus Sphery's study, that magical place where, little girls, Etheria and I spent so many happy hours. I cannot help but recall with bitterness how, in order to appease the *Hungerkünstler*'s appetites (and so her temper) our father sold all those precious artefacts that had so deeply informed our hearts and our imaginations. First the beetles went, then the penguin eggs, next the albino mole, then Dr. Johnson (Father sold him to a French collector who also bought the Nigerian crocodile); he sold the butterflies to buy the *Hungerkünstler* one dozen pairs of shoes, the Small Blues and Painted Ladies, the Great Peacock Moths and the Small Angel shades. . . . He sold his stuffed tanagers, his lyrebird, his Quetzal; sold his six hawkbill tortoise shells, the pearl in the shape of a pig, the skull of a wistiti. . . . He sold everything, even the bottle of honey that had been procured from a hive built upon Thomas More's tomb, and the beautiful egg of a dodo. ("What," Dodgson had mused with wistfulness upon making its acquaintance, "is emptier than the egg of a dodo?")

But what is hardest to tell, and what shows above all else the piteous colouration our father's mind had taken: *he sold the jade:* the cane pommel once the pride of his youth; the cicada from Tubbs's cabinet and the chimera too; sold the earrings he had given to our mother, Margaret Sphery, to celebrate Etheria's birth!

I tell all this so that you will appreciate the power the *Hungerkünstler* wielded over men; her nefarious influence. When she left our father's house for the New Age, its redundant footmen, bellpulls, and puddings, nothing remained in our father's study but a few fossilized clams and a coconut. Even the books were gone. Had his own devastation been less terrible, I know I should have hated Angus Sphery; as it was I could not. He was a ruined man, abandoned by the world. Having stung him to the quick and strung him up, the *Hungerkünstler* had sucked him dry. That winter he died a husk.

Alone I cared for our mother who did little else but stare at taches on floor and ceiling. She seemed to have grasped that her husband had perished for she carried articles of his clothing about, knotted to the hems of her petticoats, or stuffed down the front of her dress. And if by nature forgiving, as I write this—I freely admit it—I am consumed with hatred for Tubbs and the *Hungerkünstler* for the manner in which they annihilated my family and squandered its treasures.

In Egypt the *Hungerkünstler* grew fat. She sat in the centre of her camel hair tent surrounded by dishes of honey and whey, devising methods to torment Tubbs—including the attempted seduction of Baconfield whose whole being, as we have seen, was taken up elsewhere. Both Radulph and the *Hungerkünstler* became weightier: she in body and he in mind. Tubbs darkened also: it was as if his centre had somehow imploded; he absorbed light. In fact, he was as plagued by my sister's absence as by the souvenir of the sound Feather's body had made when it struck the pavement. That absence, that sound, were the very air that scorched his lungs, the terrible gravity that kept him earthbound. In his memoir Tubbs writes that in Egypt his sorrow *contained him as a cage*—as did his flesh. His flesh seemed an alien substance and yet it ruled him. He loathed the *Hungerkünstler*, yet perpetually desired her. She led him by the horns, those same horns which in his dreams had been transformed into the double crown of Egypt and which burdened him like a dunce's cap of solid lead. In a recurrent dream that plagued him throughout the month of March, Tubbs wore that dreadful crown and nothing else and the *Hungerkünstler,* a bloated, red spider, straddled his neck so tightly with her eight legs that he was barely able to breathe. Whipping him mercilessly with her cane, she precipitated him into a foaming maw of quicksand.

Tubbs always awoke screaming from this dream which he blamed on Baconfield, who had filled his mind with visions of tombs like gutted encyclopaedias submerged in sand. And more than once Baconfield had wagged that all the kings of Egypt had been horned by the greed of thieves and the stealth of time. How unsafe the pharaoh's sarcophagal house! How treacherous a man's vanity. Egypt was nothing more than one vast, pillaged jade cabinet!

"The Land of the Nile is a pudding," Tubbs writes in his memoir, "truffled with the grisly artefacts of human pride, heaving with mummies tarred and bound, and yawning with funerary chambers. BOUNDLESS PAGANISM! The mythical imagination is inescapable in Egypt, all pervasive: everywhere one turns one sees kings with the heads of lions, queens with the faces of crocodiles, hippopotamuses wearing dresses. Every article—obelisk, throne, and sphynx—is but a garish furniture which clutters death's antechamber. . . . And everywhere pyramids pustulating like the blebs on a plague-ridden beggar!"

It is a pity Tubbs was not an Egyptologist enamoured of the kings or even an enlightened collector, for he had an uncanny gift and could not walk two feet without kicking up an outsized alabaster thumb, a tauricornous amulet, a gold needle, an unnameable something-or-other black with tar (the matted viscera of a princess, the paw of a sacred cat), or the wee clay figure of a king defaced by sorcery or neglect. The entire country, as far as Tubbs could see, was one heaving cemetery hideously jumbled by the dance of time. He often felt the whole world listing, tilting, and on sleepless nights imagined that not only was the world as flat as Baconfield argued, it was a dustbin filled to the brim with trash. Which explains his firm resolve to grind to a fine powder whatever he could, mummies and tumble-down temples alike, an attitude mirrored by the *Hungerkünstler.* I explain:

The *Hungerkünstler* alarmed Baconfield (who was skittish among women to start with); more than once he had witnessed the fits of servants whom she had crazed with her incessant screeching and slaps. Inconvenienced by her hot advances, having oft, he hoped, with tact rejected her, and in an attempt to mollify her,

Baconfield gave her a green peridot scarab of uncommon size and exquisite workmanship, which had dwelt in the chest cavity of a priestess for three thousand years and which he had bought from a *fellâh* in rags. The *Hungerkünstler,* who feared death and believed in magic, gave it to a servant who, before her eyes, reduced the precious thing to dust and fed it to her dissolved in wine sweetened with honey. So convinced was the *Hungerkünstler* of the amulet's uncanny powers that she pressed Baconfield for others. As it turned out the *fellâh* lived in a hovel which straddled a tomb; it sufficed that he lift a stone from a hole in the floor to enter into the mastaba of a corpse which swarmed with priceless scarabs of opal, peridot, *fayrûz,* onyx, and coraline. Some had the faces of rams, others of bulls, others had human faces. All of these were swallowed and digested by the *Hungerkünstler.* When a colossal *scarabaeus sacer* was uncovered by Baconfield himself as he rooted under his pyramid, he had it carried by four men to the *Hungerkünstler's* tent. Rather than eat it, she turned it over to Tubbs who had ordered a second machine from Baconfield's nephew, very much larger and more powerful than the first, its purpose to crush the limestone temples which littered the environ landscape. Tubbs, who hated disorder (and so created it where'er he went), had all the temples he could seize—their columns in the lovely shapes of exotic plants, their carved friezes of undulating maidens—dismantled and transformed into chalk which was sent by barge downriver to the port of Boulak and sold to the masons of Cairo.

Thus as a plague of locusts did Tubbs and his party descend upon Egypt. Had Tubbs a pudding-pan large enough, he should have steamed the whole country with currants and eaten it up with a runcible spoon.

From *Phosphor in Dreamland* (Light)

Dearest Ved—Having now read all of the poet's vast opus, I can with certitude say this: When Phosphor made love to Extravaganza, the vortex of his cowardice, the gaping maw of his alarm vanished, and it was as if he had come into the world fearless, staff in hand. In Extravaganza's arms, his torment was melted down and reduced to a sweet honey that she extracted fearlessly. Her tender body gave itself utterly and unabashedly; being simple and having no notion of evil, she was Edenic animal seized by heat. Her eyes and cunt wept with happiness; her breasts filled the poet's mouth like those magical fruits that are renewed as they are eaten. The feast was an eternal feast, or so it seemed, and the nights they spent together, all too swiftly done, somehow sprawled into infinity, abolishing not only terror but self and time.

Because it seemed to Extravaganza that, in her poet's embrace, her body dissolved and reorganized into infinite series of animate and inanimate things—sea urchins and clamshell rattles, ivory clappers, ferns and fishskin drums—once she had surfaced from the oceans, lakes, burrows, nests, marshes, mud, sand pits, oyster-beds, and whirlpools of love, she battled bewilderment, unsure of where she was and, for that matter, *what* she was. Standing stark naked and quivering before her mirror, and slapping her sweet ass with her open palms, she would cry, as if surprised: "I am a human female!"

The poet entered into a loving and living dream; it claimed him, even when awake. All day long Phosphor was haunted by the nights, which, as the seasons progressed, hung strung together like amber beads on a golden wire. These he gnawed and worried in his mind. Dazzled by love, Phosphor's cock and his heart had become one and the same animal.

These were blissful days and weeks—the most delightful of their lives. Phosphor, himself transformed, abandoned his epic—a pretentious and patriotic work—to devote himself to an inspired poetic revery on the nature of sensual love. Convinced that he had entered the secret chamber of an occulted mystery, he took it upon himself to reveal the prodigy to the vast world. His verse was a steaming milk, a wizard's ink—and it rained upon the page, page after page. As Extravaganza slept, or sucked a plum, or beside the open window combed her hair—which, free of ribbons, tumbled to her toes—Phosphor described in amorous detail love's multiplicitous vocabularies of salutations and smiling receptions, overturning the natural realm in order to ambush the metaphorical creatures that would do desire justice; for example, *the Gazelle* (or *When the Beloved Attempts to Flee the Arrow*), *the Lion* (or *Embracing, the Lovers are Encircled by an Invisible Yet Palpable Mane of Fire*). And because he had not forgotten how a fish had unlocked his once solitary heart, Phosphor called his favorite embrace (although hard-pressed to name a favorite, as in bed with Extravaganza each act of love precipitated and included all the others)—that embrace during which the female, mounted from behind and knowing that the molten ring of her delight has moored her lover utterly, brings her thighs together as best she can, and the male, pushing his way in even deeper—as if that were possible—clutches his mistress' breasts to further anchor himself—this position the poet called *the Carp*.

After a convoluted correspondence with the university rector and the chief librarian, Phosphor was given permission to contemplate—in the company of a Consultant to the Holy Office of the Inquisition—an ancient manuscript from India proposing entire zodiacs of love in the shapes of copulating animals and mythic beings: blue gods and mortal women, black and white; red goddesses and mortal men, white and black. As the poet contemplated the book in a fever, the Consultant groaned and agitated his censer.

In the fragrant mornings, the garden ablaze with butterflies, parrots rioting in the trees, Phosphor would return to work:

> My beloved's body is a delirious moon
> A garden where foxes* paw and suck the grapes.
> Her body is a vine plundered by foxes,
> A tempest in a forest, a rain of black honey.
> Her body is my darkness, total, luminous.
> Her body is a rose of beaten gold;
> It burns against my heart.

Extravaganza was dreaming and nothing could stop her; enchantment bubbled forth to inundate her soul with an effervescent water. Rather than eat breakfast, the lovers lay together until late, their tongues touching—and she would whisper the tumult of visions that, flooding the night, had submerged her. The poet listened to her eagerly, his cock throbbing between the buttocks of his beloved, his fingers lovingly investigating her wet fur.

Often, as she would describe some astonishing dream of thunderstorms and weirdly horned and pelted animals, or floating cities constructed of mother-of-pearl and brass, or harems wherein all the houris had the faces of ibises or tigresses, yet were in all their other parts human and sweetly formed, the poet would grasp his bride by the thighs and pull her to him. Compliant, already yielding, she would yield further, and for a time the telling of the dream would cease. Then, save for the sound of their breathing and the acute hammering of their blood, and the creaking and thudding of their windswept vessel, their chamber would fall silent.

Once, Extravaganza awoke wildly laughing. As she explained to Phosphor, in her dream she had seen the face of God. She recognized the nose at once—it was her lover's cock; the apples of His cheeks, Phosphor's balls. The Lord's beard, hairs upon hairs, curls upon curls, and the place from which He spoke and breathed the breath of life was her own splendid cunt.

---

*Says Ombos: There are no foxes in Birdland. This is, evidently, a reference to Pliny.

HECTOR

BY Rikki Ducornet & T. Motley

NOT MANY DAYS BEFORE HER NINTH BIRTHDAY, SCRUBBING IN THE BATH, SHE DISCOVERED A PART OF HERSELF TUCKED AWAY LIKE THE TENDER FIRM BUD OF A ROSE.

GENTLY CARESSED WITH THE SPONGE, OR, BETTER STILL, HER OWN MIDDLE FINGER, IT GAVE HER INTENSE PLEASURE.

TRANSMUTED FROM DOCILE TO WACKY, SHE RETIRED EARLY TO BED WHERE, ONE HALF-HOUR LATER, HER FATHER WOULD FIND HER IN DEEPEST SLUMBER GROUNDED AS IF BY LIGHTNING.

HE WOULD RETURN DOWNSTAIRS ON TIP-TOE AND PERPLEXED. IT DID NOT OCCUR TO HIM THAT HIS DAUGHTER HAD DISCOVERED ECSTASY.

EVERYTHING EXCITED HER. SHE POURED OVER HER FAIRY BOOKS, IGNITED BY THE BAROQUE FIGURES OF EVIL WITCHES LEANING UPON THICK RODS, BOW-LEGGED ELVES WITH LONG, TURGID HATS, AND LEAN, HARD PRINCES STEADILY ADVANCING THROUGH UNDERBRUSH AND BRAMBLE.

AND COMING SHE CRIES OUT, HER PILLOW TRANSFORMED TO THE STALLION'S BACK, CARRIED AWAY BY THE PRINCE OF FIRE HIMSELF, HER OWN MASTER-ELF-OF-TEN; SHE NAMES HIM:

FAIRY FINGER

SHE HAD NOT BELIEVED IN FAIRIES UNTIL NOW. THEIR LAUGHTER ROUSED HER IN THE MIDDLE OF THE NIGHT AND SHE SAW THEM CAVORTING IN THE DARK:

the tiny two!?

WEE

RAM & Coldenrod

SAUCEPAN-RUST

POLISHING SHOES AND SEWING ON BUTTONS, SHINING LIKE THE EYES OF A STALLION WHINNYING NOW TROTTING QUICKENING NOW CHARGING, STRADDLED BY PRINCELY LEGS, HIS NOSTRILS FLARING BREATHING FIRE HIS HEAD STEAMING, MOUTH FOAMING BODY STEAMING

LITTLE NED NEEDLE

DRAGON HORSE

DEAR FLY

...BUZZING, STINGING, RINGING...

© 1994 DUCORNET/MOTLEY. adapted with permission, from THE COMPLETE BUTCHER'S TALES (DALKEY ARCHIVE PRESS) 1994

Ducornet and Borges

Raymond Leslie Williams

Like Gabriel García Márquez, Salman Rushdie, and Carlos Fuentes, Rikki Ducornet fully understands that writing fiction is essentially the rewriting of other texts. Ducornet apparently learned this important lesson from her mentor Jorge Luis Borges, the Argentine master who has also served as a model for García Márquez, Fuentes, and a plethora of other neo-Borgesian writers, including John Barth. Several generations of Latin American writers have been engaged in a dialogue with Borges since the Argentine master published his now classic stories (*Ficciones* and others) in the 1940s. Indeed, several novelists associated with the 1960s "Boom" of Latin American literature have spoken of their considerable debts to Borges.

For these Latin American writers, who were young intellectuals in the 1940s, Borges's stories, such as "The Secret Miracle," "The Library of Babel," and "The Aleph," represented a reaffirmation of the right of invention in a region bound by traditional aesthetic norms. Consequently, Borges's fiction has been a revolution and a liberation for three generations of writers who have felt bound to realism and the need to write fiction exclusively to denounce the social ills of Latin America.

But Borges's creative genius seems to have resonated far beyond the most immediate circumstances of Latin American writers who felt stifled in the 1940s, 1950s, and even early 1960s. His metafictional musings and linguistic tours de force were translated and widely read in English and numerous other languages in the 1960s. Along with John Barth, Nabokov, and Calvino, Borges became a figurehead of a self-reflective and cerebral fiction that not only entertained but also invited readers to reflect upon language and literature themselves. Even French literary theorists in vogue at the time, Roland Barthes and Michel Foucault, turned to Borges as a source and an example.

The situation of literary culture in the U.S. has probably changed as much since the 1940s as it has in Latin America. Nevertheless, the presence of Borges is palpable in both American and Latin American writing. Rikki Durcornet's fascination with Borges is not a matter known only to academic specialists: she has illustrated a volume of Borges's writing, and the back cover of her recent *Phos-*

phor in Dreamland declares boldly that the novel "can be described as Jonathan Swift meets Angela Carter via Jorge Luis Borges." Ducornet's dialogue with Borges is evident from her early fiction; in this essay I will comment briefly on an early and later work—*The Stain* and *Phosphor in Dreamland*—in the context of Borges.

Borges and Ducornet, unlike García Márquez and Fuentes, make a playful farce out of rewriting history. For García Márquez and Fuentes, Latin American historiography has betrayed and failed the citizens of the Americas, and one important role of the writer is to recoup, with a fiction that is more real (as well as sometimes more unreal) than classical historiography, the supposed truth of history. Ducornet and Borges obviously are interested in history, but they tend to eschew the very concept of truth in writing. The two writers are far too fascinated with the playful and humorous possibilities of perverting history and historiography to engage in such historical projects as those of Fuentes and García Márquez.

Although their similar approaches to history are notable, perhaps the firmest alliance between Borges and Ducornet is found in their attitudes and uses of language. Ducornet's language itself is frequently arresting, and the two writers' simultaneously stunning and subtle uses of language suggest more than mere coincidence in style. In some cases Ducornet's language involves relatively simple, yet playful twists—a sideshow for the reader consisting of phrases such as "gelid grasp" and "saturnine spouse" used in *The Stain*. But just when the unsuspecting reader might believe that Ducornet cultivates only the precious and the Borgesian, she drops a phrase such as "dog turds" (from *The Stain*) or "It seemed to them that the entire cosmos reeked of mildew, stagnant pooks, the shit of fish, the saliva of snakes, and the sulfurous flatulence of saints" (from *Phosphor*). Her indulgence with language in *Phosphor in Dreamland* occasionally pushes the limits of linguistic tour de force and the celebration of the word. Borges pushed similar limits. In the end Ducornet's language has much of Borges's erudition and self-consciousness, but little of his prudishness.

The Stain is the story of a young girl named Charlotte born of a woman who had been raped and then died in childbirth. In this novel Ducornet portrays a sordid and monstrous (essentially un-Borgesian) world in which Charlotte attempts to survive. Like many of the fictional settings of Borges and Ducornet, the dominant ideology (which here is basically the local mindset) in *The Stain* is Catholicism; in *The Stain* the repressive forces of institutional religion work in opposition to the liberating forces of other forms of spirituality that Charlotte seeks, such as gardening and painting. In the end, she finds refuge in nature, where she lives in isolation and paints.

In her wildly imaginative novel *Phosphor in Dreamland,* Ducornet sets the action on a Caribbean island called Birdland and rewrites Borges, García Márquez, and Jonathan Swift. The narration consists of letters about an island that seems vaguely Spanish without ever bothering to be specific about geographies or nationalisms. (Borges was frequently very specific about geography and nations in his fiction, but he never considered these matters important, either.) Frequent digressions and occasional images of terror keep the reader from ever getting too close to this island or imagining it as real. Obviously, Ducornet does not sympathize with realism.

Phosphor in Dreamland tells the story of Nuño Alpha y Omega, an unorthodox young man also known as Phosphor, who is born clubfooted with crossed eyes and who aspires to be a photographer and a celebrated poet. But Phosphor's story is just one of multiple tales that weaves in and out of several levels of dreams, for the island is populated with the eccentric: lôplôps (huge birds with human screams), a tyrannical scholar named Fogginus, Phospor's beloved Extravaganza, some "clean sweepers" (proponents of ethnic purity), and an imposing Grand Inquisitor.

As interesting as exotic Birdland might be, the reader actually luxuriates in language and dreams more than this fake state. The digressions, playful and entertaining footnotes, and terror prevent the American reader from lazily falling into the stereotypical image of the Caribbean island as tropical paradise. (The footnotes and letters to Ved make this text a most Borgesian metafiction.) Even though Ducornet seems more interested in language than the representation of society, she does adroitly satirize a hierarchial and superstitious colonial state.

Ducornet's response to the local dominant hierarchy is the celebration not only of language and story but also of the erotic and the body. When she gets momentum (which happens frequently), language and body become transgressive and even a little perverse. Her description of Phosphor embracing his lover, for example, is an incredible linguistic tour de force. Unexpected juxtapositions, surreal turns, and magical transformations permeate everyday life and virtually every page.

As metafictionists who are highly conscious of language itself and whose writing constantly reaffirms the right of the fiction writer to invent, Borges and Ducornet have much in common. There are important differences, too. Borges scorned writers concerned with society, but social relevance is a high priority in Ducornet's fiction. *The Stain* and *Phosphor in Dreamland* contain numerous passages of satire directed toward traditional institutions, institutions about which Borges was basically indifferent. When Ducornet's characters search for meaning in life, they find possibilities for fulfillment beyond the intellectual reflections and dreams that are the typical destiny of the characters in Borges's fictional world. As a satirist and as a master of language, Ducornet is a powerful writer. Like the young Latin American writers who write today as Borges's cultural grandchildren (e.g., Ricargo Piglia and Diamela Eltit), Ducornet is as concerned about social relevance as she is about language.[1] There are telltale signs that in her previous existence, she was probably a Cuban postmodern writer greatly envied by Borges. And she would read as well in Spanish in Latin America as Borges does in English in the United States.

NOTE

[1] I have studied Piglia, Eltit and other postmodern writers in Latin America with social and political agendas comparable to Ducornet's in *The Postmodern Novel in Latin America* (New York: St. Martin's Press, 1995).

Rikki Ducornet's Tetrology of Elements: An Appreciation

Allen Guttmann

If my mode were analysis rather than appreciation, I'd attempt to place Rikki's work—"Rikki" is the pen name that Erica Ducornet preferred before Chatto and Windus insisted on something more conventional—in relation to that of the writers whose work seems most similar to hers: Borges and García Márquez. Her narratives, like theirs, move back and forth across the line that separates realistic fiction from fantasy. In *The Stain,* for instance, the children tormented by the Mother Superior are recognizable children, but strange things happen to them. Consider this moment. Mother Superior's lover, the Exorcist, is breakfasting. " 'Oysters,' he explained . . . as he spooned shallot vinaigrette onto the creature's exposed and quivering parts, 'are simply gorged with good intentions. They mollify Mind.' " He is interrupted by the Mother Superior's cry ("The attic!") and both of them rush off to discover the impossible. "Eulalie was floating above the attic's bare board floor, her body listing to the left as her chain tugged at her ankle. Her blanket lay in a heap beneath her, and although the attic was freezing she was hot and vapor rose from her breasts and thighs. She gazed down upon them all with an expression of unabashed merriment.[1]" One never knows, when reading the Tetrology of Elements, when the more-or-less realistic narration is likely to ascend, like Eulalie, into the realm of the impossible.

The reader accepts these moments because Rikki's prose is never prosaic. In an afterword to the tetrology Rikki explains, "I was infected with the venom of language in early childhood when, sitting in a room flooded with sunlight, I opened an alphabet book. **B** was a Brobdingnagian tiger-striped bumblebee, hovering over a crimson blossom, its stinger distinct."[2] Sweet are the uses of the venom of language! A few examples will have to suffice. Like Henry James, who refers in *The Ambassadors* to Waymarsh's "matutinal beefsteak," Rikki plays with the Latinate and Germanic sources of the English language. An unsavory woman who eyes Charlotte, the heroine of *The Stain,* emits a "mucilaginous grunt" (194). Setting that story in a French village not unlike Nôtre Dame le Puy, where she lived for a number of years, Rikki indulges in bilingualism: referring to a werewolf, a woodsman plays with words: "One little *sou* for the *loup-garou*" (211). All of the novels are marked in this fashion by Rikki's second language.

There is also the linguistic exploitation of cultural diversity. *The Stain* is enlivened by the antics of a charlatan named Ali-Hassan Popa and *The Jade Cabinet* includes some adventures among the Bedouin. Cûchla, the Amazonian Indian who is the heroine of *Entering Fire,* becomes enchanted by British and American popular culture. She thwarts Senator Joseph McCarthy with a medley of allusions from *The Hunting of the Snark, The Wind in the Willows, The Wizard of Oz, Krazy Kat,* etc.:

Senator McCarthy: Have you, uh, read subversive books. . . .
She: (Interrupting him!) Are you a Snark or a Boojum?
Senator McCarthy: Now let's get this straight, here I ask the questions.
She: OK, Boss, I admit to everything. Poop! Poop! I borrowed the motorcar while the owners were at lunch; Ding Dong the witch is dead; sir, I stole the tarts; I threw the brick at Krazy too.[3]

Subversive books indeed!

In naming her characters, Rikki draws on the resources of several languages. In *The Stain* we encounter Sister Malicia (who is as mean as they come), Madame Cloche (who sounds not at all like a bell because she suffers from lockjaw), Père Archange Poupine (who is fatherly, angelic, and childlike[4]), and Ali-Hassan Popa (who seems in his con-man's behavior to combine Islamic with Roman Catholic fraud). *Entering Fire* introduces us to a phallophobic bride named Virginie, an entomologist named Cletis Twigger, and a pair of Nazi officers named Roll and Möpse (German names which, taken together, refer to a variety of pickled herring). In *The Fountains of Neptune* there is an amiable monkey named Charlie Dee (who sets the reader to thinking of Victorian debates about Charles Darwin and his evolutionary theories) and an elderly psychiatrist named Venus Kaiserstiege (who encourages us to believe in the human ability to rise towards the empire of eros[5]). The fourth novel, *The Jade Cabinet,* introduces us to the ethereal young Etheria and the weighty husband, Radulph Tubbs, from whom she takes flight. Rikki's multilingual vocabulary can cause problems: the *OED* explains "conopic jars"[6] (*Jade Cabinet* 120), but my French dictionary doesn't include *"pedzouille"* (*Entering Fire* 145).

Distinctive speech patterns particularize the characters. Charlotte's kindly but ineffectual Uncle Emile stutters while his hysterically conventional wife Edma speaks in meanly pious platitudes ("Extravagance and vanity! Vanity and waste!" [43]). In *The Fountains of Neptune* Rose, who is also known as "Other Mother" because she and her husband have adopted the orphaned Nicolas, speaks in malapropisms; she met her husband at a fair, "in that insomnic device the ferret wheel."[7] Kindhearted, she sympathizes with women who suffer from "various veins" (18). Writing or speaking, ponderous Radulph Tubbs thumps out bombastic imperatives; his wife has disappeared, he complains, **"FIND HER!"** (110). In each of the four novels descriptions are more often than not a medley of images: Sister Malicia is "a cadaverous creature as human as a broom handle, her arms knotted across her flat chest to protect the inverted nipples that dented the flesh like the cruel traces of tacks, her pale blue eyes lying loosely in their sockets like faded minerals in sagging boxes." She has "a voice tortured by a tight larynx into the nightmarish urgencies of a twisted bassoon" (124).

Rikki's characters are often endowed with imaginations akin to their creator's. Charlotte, heroine of *The Stain,* has no toys (because Aunt Edma disapproves). She is allowed to play in Uncle Emile's vegetable garden: "With her pastels she drew faces on the smooth pebbles Emile had laid down years before in the garden path. She gave them names and personalities, and acted out the life of Jesus. . . . Joseph, like Emile, was a stutterer and did not do or say much. . . . Jesus did not eat . . . vegetables but took His nourishment directly from the sun." The pebble-people embody and enact Charlotte's desires and her fears. "One day Joseph was accidently kicked into a flat stone designated as the Pope. God-the-Father punished this perversity by dropping Joseph down the well." Divine punishment leaves poor Charlotte so riddled by guilt that she imagines God as a "monstrous wing" that blots out the sun (43-44). In *The Fountains of Neptune,* stories told to young Nicolas by his foster-father Totor become the boy's reality:

Once on my way to school I find a ring fallen, Totor tells me, from the body of a fish. I would not have missed a tribe of pious tuna reading psalms as they vanished two by two down Fools' Alley had I been quicker. . . .

The scales, tails, tongues of sea monsters are secreted, then revealed in the shadows of the floating clouds; the smiles of mermen are scattered on the water, and above the doors of houses Totor points out impressions of webbed fingers. (26)

By the end of the novel, Nicolas, recovered from the sleep of decades, imagines a young companion named Olivier, someone with whom to share his waking fantasies.

Inevitably, Rikki's own reference to these four novels as the "Tetrology of Elements" (*Jade Cabinet* 157) raises questions about symbolism. *The Stain* is associated with earth, with *this* earth, *this* world, as opposed to the heaven toward which Aunt Edma's thoughts are obsessively directed. It is hard to imagine a raunchier wedding than Cousin Nestor's, drunkenly celebrated while Aunt Edma sulks in a privy. Charlotte's birthmark, the image of a hare upon her cheek, is meant to establish her as humanly imperfect. There can be no doubt about which element pervades the story of *Entering Fire*. Symbolic flames—lust, hatred, warfare, purgation, purification—flicker through the entire book. "Its fires," comments Rikki, "are sexual, intellectual and political, and its tensions Manichean" (*Jade Cabinet* 158). Metaphorical ambiguity characterizes *The Fountains of Neptune* as well. Water takes the life of Nini's father. Water holds the secret of Nini's lost mother. In water he seeks her—and very nearly loses his life in the effort. As Rikki herself has explained, "Water is conjured as unstable weather; furiously boiling one moment, ice the next, it takes on the shapes of pools, whirlpools, downpours, oceans and tears" (*Jade Cabinet* 157).

Concluding the tetrology, *The Jade Cabinet* hints at hardness but, in actuality, is filled with what Rikki refers to as "an animating air.... Radulph Tubbs, so weighty, is, when he rises, inflated by vanity" (*Jade Cabinet* 157).

These four works are, then, *poetic* novels. Are they also poetic *novels?* If one takes seriously E. M. Forster's *faux-naïf* definition ("the novel tells a story"), there can be no generic doubt. Rikki's fiction is modernist rather than postmodernist. The narrative element is as strongly present as in an adventure novel. The poet is a storyteller.

The Stain, set in a nineteenth-century French village, begins with Charlotte's mother. Beneath an image of Christ, whose "infinitely drear eyes" (7) look down in disapproval, she gives birth to her illegitimate daughter. When the midwife arrives, too late, she finds "the dead woman, the baby caked with blood and screeching, and the man dead drunk and moaning in a chair" (13). Charlotte, reared by her rigidly Catholic Great-Aunt Edma, is taught to believe that her birthmark—the stain—is the sign of her mother's sin and of her own worthlessness. When Charlotte asks why Christ made her mother die, Edma tells her, "She sinned against Him!" (58). No match for Edma armed with her dogma, Great-Uncle Emile has retreated into the world of his beloved vegetables. The most he can do for Charlotte is to teach her to read from seed catalogs, "the only books in the house apart from the Bible, a pamphlet from Lourdes about Bernadette Soubirous, and a cookery book which contained lurid diagrams demonstrating how to bleed, gut and truss fowl" (41). No wonder that Charlotte eats seldom, and sparsely, and vomits often. In search of salvation she smashes the glass of her clock, stopping time, and swallows the shards. "As

Edma enters [Charlotte's room], the little porcelain porringer glowing like the Grail between her hands, Charlotte vomits blood, ropes of it, exultant" (62).

Edma summons an Exorcist and the Mother Superior of the local convent, St.-Gemmes aptly located in the town of La Folie. The Mother Superior agrees with Edma about the le diable au corps and goes to extremes to overcome her sexual impulses: "Penitent, she had rubbed her clitoris with nettles and crept about naked on all fours in the cold of her unkept rooms until ill, but her illness only led her further astray, or so she believed, for then her thoughts became disconnected, ragged flags flapping in the wind, and the nettle's sting excited her" (69).

She is excited again when she and the Exorcist have dinner with Edma and Emile; at the table, the Exorcist, who is a hypocrite, a glutton, a libertine, and a wonderfully comic user of extravagant language, goes after the Mother Superior: "And having removed his left boot, he explored the Good Mother's ample skirts with his foot. Meeting with no resistance, he continued to probe, rooting at last between her conveniently spread thighs" (89). When the dazed nun begins to hum a tune to which the Exorcist supplies some suitably obscene lyrics, Edma cries out, "You're all drunk!" At this, "The Mother Superior hiccuped and began to cry" (91).

In time, however, Edma delivers Charlotte to St.-Gemmes, where the Exorcist is happily ensconced as the Mother Superior's lover. For the eleven-year-old girl, life with Sister Malicia, Sister Purissima, and an assortment of similar sadists is a Dickensian horror. Shortly after Eulalia's levitation, Charlotte discovers the power to work some magic of her own. She casts a spell that heats Sister Malicia's false teeth, made of metal, until they feel like "living coals burrowing into her flesh" (150). Charlotte escapes from the convent and flees to the woods.

There she finds refuge with Archange Poupine, the fairy-tale hunter. When Charlotte is attacked and nearly raped by a werewolf who has terrified the neighborhood, Archange rushes to the rescue. The werewolf turns out to be the Exorcist disguised by a wolf-skin. The Exorcist escapes from Archange but is killed by pursuing villagers. A few months later, Charlotte, safe from harm, "sees the golden hare once again." He casts a spell, presumably a protective one, "from which she will never entirely awaken" (221). This may not be an entirely happy end, but Charlotte has, at least, escaped the metaphorical and literal clutches of Aunt Edma, the Mother Superior, and the Exorcist. If this enchanting book has a flaw, it is that the characters—like those of a fairy tale—are figures in an allegory of Good and Evil, but the excitement of this satirical romp through the follies of La Folie more than compensates for any lack of realistic characterization.

Much the same can be said of *Entering Fire*. The story is narrated, alternatively, by Lamprias de Bergerac, a romantic adventurer who leaves his native France in quest of exquisite flowers and exotic women, and his neglected and embittered son Septimus, whose Oedipal rage takes the form of a frenzied commitment to French fascism. In the power of their imaginations, the two narrators seem equally talented. Lamprias overwhelms readers with lyrical language; Septimus stuns them with crazed invective: "The Occident—too big-hearted for her own good—writhes beneath a rash of hobos, Bagel-Barons and leeches. The Occident has a tapeworm, a tapeworm named Liberalism. The Occident is being bled to death by the ghoul bats of Jewry; the sticky spermatozoa of long-dingled black men, yellow men, red men contaminate the virtuous Mother Race, perhaps irretrievably" (78-79).

Lamprias married Septimus's mother because he was charmed by her epigrammatic speech. He soon discovered (a) that Virginie's frigidity approaches zero degrees Kelvin and (b) that her conversations consists entirely of platitudes drawn from clerical textbooks.

> We were walking down a freshly raked path fragrant with jasmine. I commented upon the smell.
> *"Perfume,"* said Virginie, *"is agreeable to the nose. The shade,"* she added, *"is agreeable to those who walk."* I mentioned Darwin.
> *"Books,"* said my wife interrupting me, *"are agreeable to the wise."* (51)

Lamprias's response to the disappointment of his marriage is a voyage to China, from whence he returns with a concubine named Dust and a son named True Man. Virginie is, quite understandably, resentful. Her son Septimus, the physically unattractive consequence of her unique experience of marital sex, is jealous. When True Man commits rape and pays the judicial price—death by hanging— Virginie and Septimus are gratified.

Lamprias scarcely notices. He visits with friends who share his scientific interests. He heads for Brazil, there to encounter Evangelista (a criminally destructive entrepreneur), Tarantula Jane (a prostitute), and a medley of other unlikely types. In the rain forest he comes upon the love of his life, an Indian maiden named (credits go to the television series of Rikki's childhood) Cûcla. Since Cûcla is a "primitive," it is only appropriate that she—like the wise savages of romantic fiction—instruct Lamprias about nature, but her instruction takes an unexpected turn. When Lamprias assumes that she *believes* the myths that inform her life, she lets him know, in good humor, that she is anthropologically sophisticated about signifiers and the signified. " 'The snake is only an *idea*,' she teases, 'and like all good ideas He expands' " (33).

While Lamprias seeks wisdom in the Amazon, Septimus is convinced that he has found it in fascist ideology. Nurtured by his mother with the doctrines of fin-de-siècle anti-Semitism, Septimus evolves an even more crazed form of racism based on the difference between the Brachycephalic man and the Dolchycephalic man: "The Dolchycephalic's root syllable, *MOG* (still evident in the early Chaldean) means magician. Mog, Mogol, Molog, M'grel, Mo'b—the evolution is self explanatory" (79). While Lamprias experiments with the hybridization of orchids, Septimus raves about the mongrelization of races. In 1940 his dystopia materializes. He is thrilled by the sight of Nazi storm troopers arriving to rescue France from the clutches of Jewish communists. (He is, however, disappointed by Maréchal Pétain, who falls asleep during the audience.) Like Marcello in *Il Conformista* (novel by Albert Moravia, film by Bernardo Bertolucci), Septimus projects his own psychic trauma upon the Other and imagines that fascism can restore the *normalità* that never was. Among those whom Septimus betrays to the Nazis is Marta Strada, one of his father's many loves.

After the war, which father and son both survive, the scene shifts to the Hudson Valley, where Lamprias has taken Cûcla, where Septimus pursues them, intent as always on revenge. When Cûcla, child of nature, doffs her dress, she is arrested and brought before Judge Schuyler. She is bewildered that anyone can be offended by nudity: "Who could take offence at my little nipples . . . ?" (105). Worse trouble follows when Septimus, who has contacts with the FBI, arranges to have Cûcla and Lamprias accused of un-American activities and then summoned to appear before Senator McCarthy. The encounter, in which the inquisitor is confounded by Cûcla's deft deployment of American popular culture, is the most hilarious in the book. She goes to the hearing armed with a brick because a brick is the weapon of choice in George Herrmann's *Krazy Kat*. By the time she has hit him with quotations from Lewis Carroll and other "subversives," the bewildered senator is ready to release the "loony broad" and go fishing for real fish with "a shifty looking man named Dick Nixon" (145).

Despite this sweet moment, all is not well with Lamprias and Cûcla. She conceives a child—another instance of "hybridization"—and then miscarries. Septimus, utterly crazed by the syphillis he contracted from visits to prostitutes, dies in a delirium of hatred for his father. Lamprias, who is now a very old man, will never have an

heir. That, presumably, is the punishment for his having chosen romantic adventure rather than bourgeois responsibility.

Septimus wanted a real father. Young Nicolas, the orphaned protagonist of *The Fountains of Neptune,* is driven by the need to discover what happened to his mother. With his foster-father Totor,
Nicolas frequents the Ghost Port Bar, where alcoholic old salts like
Toujours-Là tell tantalizing stories of mermaids, the Ogress,
and other strange creatures of the sea. Totor's wife Rose—Other
Mother—tries to counteract the influence of the Ghost Port by preparing some of modern literature's most temptingly described
meals, but baked chicken stuffed with lemon, onions, and sorrel are
no match for stories that hint at the secret past that Nicolas wants
desperately to know. "I am tormented," says Nicolas, "by a mad desire to laugh at the sudden poverty of Rose's bottled eggs, her cher-
ries in vinegar, the brash, bare bellies of her copper pots; her efforts
to create order in what Toujours-Là had that very hour exposed as a
riotous universe" (43). Sexuality is one aspect of that universe.
Toujours-Là, whose name suggests the ubiquity of woe, shows
Nicolas "the castle of love." It is a room in which the Cod's Wife, pro-
prietress of the Ghost Port Bar, can be seen "naked on her knees and
thrashing in a weird forest of arms and legs." To Nicolas, who is
"horror-struck, perplexed, unsure of what I have seen," the cynical
Toujours-Là remarks, "Now you know what women are, Nini. But
you ain't seen the worst. Blue Beard's closet is *fathomless*" (88).

The worst, which Nicolas discovers decades later, is that his
mother, Odille, was a promiscuous woman who conspired with a
lover to murder her husband. This they accomplished by drowning
him. The deed was seen, accidently, by the Cod, who happened to be
looking to sea with his telescope. When Odille and her lover
beached their boat, they were set upon and beaten to death by the
furious villagers.

Before Nicolas can hear this horrific story, he must experience
something akin to his father's death. While boating on a pond with
"the Marquis" (a black sailor whom Totor and Rose have be-
friended), Nicolas imagines that, below the surface of the water, *"I
saw my mother's face"* (113). Into the water he goes. When the Marquis pulls him out, he is nearly dead. He has fallen into a comatose
state that lasts for decades.[8]

Nicolas is revived, some fifty years later, by "the world's only
Freudian hydropothist" (121), Dr. Venus Kaiserstiege. She has
cared for him at her Proustian spa, A la Recherche du Paradis
Terrestre. (He is her only patient. During the war, the Nazis had
seized and murdered all the others.) In this sequence of chapters,
part 2, the narrative technique changes from the Chinese boxes of

stories told within stories told within stories to something akin to the case history. Questioning Nicolas, telling him about her correspondence with Rosa and her interviews with Totor and the Marquis, bringing him back to the fishing village, where the museum exhibits photographs taken by his father, Venus Kaiserstiege helps Nicolas to recover and "work through" his traumatic past. While she is in America on a lecture tour, Nicolas and his imagined friend, Olivier, build a fantasy world—the Kingdom of d'Elir[9]—in the deserted mansion.

Like *The Stain* and *Entering Fire*, this extraordinary novel concludes rather inconclusively. In Venus Kaiserstiege's absence, the villagers, led by a repulsive female hate-monger, storm into the mansion and destroy Nicolas's lovingly constructed Kingdom of d'Elir. Venus Kaiserstiege returns from America, but she has bad news for Nicolas: "I know I shall join the Marquis soon beside that deepest fountain of all, which is Death" (215). When she is gone, Nicolas feels like the fetal monster in a glass that Toujours-Là had shown to him when he was only a child. Like "the floating monster," Nicolas is "of the world and not of the world, and—as long as I can hold fast the glass wand of reverie—somehow eternal" (220).

After the psychological complexities of *The Fountains of Neptune,* the final novel in the tetrology seems amazingly lucid, which is clearly appropriate for a work associated with air rather than with water. As in *Entering Fire,* the Manichean opposition between the (mostly) Good and the (mostly) Evil is quite obvious. The embodiments of this dichotomy are Etheria, the beautiful daughter of Professor Angus Sphery, a mid-nineteenth-century Oxford don, and Radulph Tubbs, an industrialist. She is "a creature of air and light" (*Jade Cabinet* 41); he is a Dickensian character whose traits and attitudes resemble those of Mr. Gradgrind (from *Hard Times*). "I firmly believe," writes Tubbs in his memoirs, "that if a thing cannot be said once and for all with *clarity,* then it is best left unsaid." Having "*done* Italy and Greece," he appalled by the "accumulations of rubble for which those countries are notorious." Why doesn't someone replace, with tidy factories, "the *uselessness* of all that riddled marble" (27-28)?

Angus Sphery is an eccentric polymath convinced that all known languages are corruptions of the language of Eden. He tries to raise his daughter so that she never hears a spoken word. "just as the philosophers of Swift's *Travels* communicate by showing objects to one another, so Angus Sphery made Etheria acutely aware of the affinities between the eyes upon a moth's wing and a human eye, the woolly head of a sheep and a cauliflower, an oddly forked carrot pulled up in the garden and the human figure" (12). When Etheria is six, a second daughter, Memory, is born and the girls' mother "insisted that the charm be broken; words entered, whispered at first, into the house" (13). Too late. The wonderfully perceptive Etheria never learns to speak.

She and her sister become favorites of Charles Dodgson, the mathematician-photographer better known to posterity as Lewis Carroll. He was "so different," Memory remembers, "so unlike the others! *He was like us!*" (64). Dodgson provides the girl with their favorite toys: "miniature kites to fly in the kitchen above the steaming kettle, a paper bird that whistled when dropped from the laboratory windows and a lily pond of painted cardboard containing paper crabs and sirens and one magical fish: *Ask! Ask! Ask me a wish!* penned on his two sides . . ." (17). The sisters are not at all disturbed by "Dodgson's inclination to photograph little girls in the nude" (130). His affections are untainted by sexuality.

The same cannot be said for rich and handsome Radulph Tubbs. He falls in love with Etheria but suffers by comparison to Dodgson. Instead of miniature kites and paper birds and cardboard fish, he presents Etheria with "a large volume bound in dark brown leather, published at his own expense and containing photographs of all his . . . spinning factories, mills, bleach and dye-works" (30). (Visiting one of these factories, Margaret Sphery contracts cholera and goes mad.)

Unfortunately for Etheria, Tubbs inherits a collection of jade. The exquisite carvings mean nothing to him, but they dazzle Angus Sphery, to whom Tubbs gives one of the most perfect pieces. In a moment of panic, when his wife's madness drives him to despair, Sphery begs Tubbs to marry Etheria and take her away, a service that Tubbs hastens to perform. He truly loves Etheria and there are moments when she seems to care for him (he is handsome), but their life together in his mansion, New Age, is a disaster. In his inability to control himself, he repeatedly commits what we now refer to as marital rape. The worst assault involves a jade phallus that he "thrust . . . into the very depths of her. . . . From that day on she was cold but pliant . . ." (55-56). One recompense, for Etheria, is the pleasure she derives from a garden whose path suddenly becomes "a picture pavement" (43) upon which are portrayed Arachne, Perseus, and other mythic figures. (They are, of course, the equivalent of the pebble people in Emile's garden.) In this "Wonderland" (43) of garden, pergola, and grotto Etheria seeks refuge—until Tubbs has it destroyed and replaced by geometrical forms designed by his architect friend Baconfield. (Tubbs dreams of pyramids.)

In response to this final desecration, Etheria "vanished forever in thin air like a puff of smoke" (56). The last two-thirds of the book are devoted to his frantic search for her, which does not prevent him from industrial enterprise in Egypt, where he and Baconfield grind ibis mummies into fertilizer. The Egyptian episodes are enlivened by the architect's adventures among the pyramids and by the presence of a character even stranger than Etheria.

The *Hungerkünstler,* whom Rikki has borrowed from Kafka's story, *Ein Hungerkünstler,* first appeared to Tubbs and Etheria at an English fair, where a hawker "informed the crowd that [she] had not eaten for two months" (68). Her anorexic shape fascinates Etheria, her unintelligible babble excites Angus Sphery, still searching for the primal language, and after Etheria's "vanishment" her voracious sexual appetite attracts Tubbs: "When Tubbs and the *Hungerkünstler* were not fornicating on swings suspended from the beams or in bathtubs filled with stout they fought together like wild beasts" (80). In Egypt the *Hungerkünstler* becomes a glutton, grows hideously obese, and is abandoned by Tubbs when he returns to England.

There Tubbs intensifies his search for Etheria, his love for her having finally overcome his lust for industrial profits. He is certain that he has found her in the guise of a magician named Zephyra, but, after the jealous *Hungerkünstler* has murdered Zephyra, Memory discovers that the magician was really "not my sister; Zephyra was a man" (152). She keeps the secret to herself. The plot, which has never been linear, now takes another wholly unexpected turn when the bereaved Tubbs, bearing orchids and other gifts, asks Memory to read his memoirs. She does (which is how she is able to quote extensively from them in her narration). Moved by his adoration of her sister and softened by "the Spanish nougat I have never ceased to love" (153), she marries him. After five peaceful years, Tubbs dies and is buried, as he wished, next to Zephyra, whom he believed to the end to have been the lost Etheria.

In the afterword that follows, Rikki writes, "All four novels investigate the end of Eden and the possibility of its reconstitution" (158). The loss of Eden seems clear enough. Charlotte is still an adolescent when *The Stain* concludes, and her fate is undetermined, but what hope is there for the other protagonists? Lamprias and Nicolas are old, Cûcla longs to return to her rain forest, Venus Kaiserstiege is dead, and Memory has lived for years without a sign of the lost Etheria. The possibility of Eden's reconstitution seems very remote. The Tetrology of Elements is wonderfully comic—and strangely sad.

NOTES

[1] Rikki Ducornet, *The Stain* (1984; Normal, IL: Dalkey Archive Press, 1995), 157; hereafter cited parenthetically.

[2] *The Jade Cabinet* (Normal, IL: Dalkey Archive Press,1993), 155; hereafter cited parenthetically.

[3] *Entering Fire* (San Francisco: City Lights, 1987), 144; hereafter cited parenthetically.

[4] "Poupine"; adjective: "childlike." Does the feminine form suggest motherly qualities as well?

[5] "Stiege"; noun: "a set of stairs."

[6] "Canopic vase: a vase used in Egypt, chiefly for holding the entrails of embalmed bodies."

[7] *The Fountains of Neptune* (1989; Elmwood Park, IL: Dalkey Archive Press, 1993), 19; hereafter cited parenthetically.

[8] In a prefatory note to the novel, Rikki explains that "Oliver Sacks' *Awakenings* came to my attention shortly after I conceived *The Fountains of Neptune,* and if I chose not to make the book a medical history—having perceived it from the start not as an historical novel but a work of the imagination—his beautiful book has informed my own."

[8] The name, like much of the book, was inspired by Rikki's father, Gérard DeGré, who was in her childhood the "Emperor of d'Elir."

"The Tantalizing Prize": Telling the Telling of The Fountains of Neptune

Richard Martin

> His knowledge of the story behind all stories is the
> tantalizing prize he holds up in the half-light again and
> again and always Just beyond my reach.[1]

Although the central story of Rikki Ducornet's 1989 novel *The Fountains of Neptune* is narrated consistently by its protagonist Nicolas, within the dominant narrative many other stories are told. The novel thus becomes a tale of embedded fictions and the fictionalization of their tellers. One such is the disreputable old sailor/storyteller Toujours-Là, "a man of keys" (93) the reader is told, the magical spinner of yarns, who can open the secrets of the past. Yet however much "the story behind all stories" may tantalize the listener/reader, one should not fall into the trap of expecting the key to meaning or awaiting the shimmering appearance of one of what Lyotard has called *grands récits* from the waves of narrative. Far more, like the novel's central character, the reader will learn only to be "interested in the allusive messages of . . . dreams" (219). Whoever reaches toward those "tantalizing prizes" may find herself or himself fated, like the originator of the word, forever to reach out in vain, convinced that the prize offered bears resemblance to Scheherazade's treasure in John Barth's *Chimera:*

> "I've read a thousand tales about treasures that nobody can find the key to," she told me; "we have the key and can't find the treasure." I asked her to explain. "It's all in here," she declared. . . . it comes down to particular words in the story we're reading, right? . . . This is the key, Doony! And the treasure, too, if we can only get our hands on it! It's as if—as if the key to the treasure *is* the treasure!"[2]

Scheherazade's statement is, however—how could it be otherwise?—equivocal: on the surface Barth seems to be suggesting through her words that the key to the treasure of meaning or understanding lies on the surface of the text, in the language itself. However, it might well be permissible to repunctuate the statement to read, "the treasure . . . it's, 'as if'—'as if,' the key to the treasure." In other words there is a twin key that will unlock the text which is nothing less than submission to the imaginative act implicit in the stance of "as if."

The approach to the textual world of Ducornet's novel thus bifurcates into an examination of language and a penetration of the demands made upon the reader to accept imaginative premises. I intend to begin by exploring the trail offered by the second of these passageways first.

The Fountains of Neptune proposes to the reader the acceptance of the facts of the neurological case study of the Sandman: a pre-teenage boy falls out of a boat and is almost drowned; under the care of Dr. Venus Kaiserstiege, "the world's only Freudian hydropothist" (121), he recovers but remains in a coma for fifty years, briefly waking after forty. When he finally regains consciousness, he assists Dr. Kaiserstiege to write up his own case history (also entitled *The Fountains of Neptune*) and ends as the caretaker of her deserted spa-clinic, "the curator of silence" (218), alone with his visions of a past that remains a set of dreams. The novel—and so, too, our reception of it—also rests upon the fundamental tenets of Dr. Kaiserstiege's therapy as laid down in one of her letters to Nicolas, the narrator/patient, which become the theoretical basis of Ducornet's fictional practice: *"I insist that the self is rooted in nostalgia and reverie, and that they are the fountains of Art. I argue that Art reveals the real. That the existential is always subjective. All that is true is hidden deep in the body of the world and cannot be taken by force. It must be dreamed and attended and received with awe and affection . . . To survive the world we must all be lucid dreamers"* (190; italics in original). If it could be the task of art to "reveal the real," then it fulfills this aim by employing the imagination to stimulate memory; if then that, too, is true, it is presumably only logical to add, as Ducornet does, that what is revealed will inevitably be, of the subject, subjective. There is nothing particularly unusual in the suggestion that the artist is a visionary, a seer, nor that the seen is peculiar to this one seer. However, Dr. Kaiserstiege's formula embraces more than the productive dimension of the text, for she focuses also upon the receptive: if the artist both dreams and cultivates ("attends") the product of this activity, then of the recipient it is expected that she or he should treat the text with "awe and affection"—further attributes of subjectivity—a combination of attitudes which will render the dreams "lucid." Thus the rules which are to condition the reception of the fictional text are generated from within the text itself. The reader is called upon both to respect and to love what she or he reads. Since one can only respect something or someone that has in a certain measure "earned" this response and similarly can only love someone who possesses those features and qualities that subjectively inspire love, it would seem that Ducornet awaits personal involvement, which can, in the terms of the novel, only be aroused by immersion in those dimensions that present themselves as the key to understanding: language and the imagination. For the moment, we have come full circle and can only return into the inviting maze that is, once more, the text.

In what follows I propose to scrutinze the telling of tales rather than the narrating of the novel, since within the context of the book's governing metaphor, water, tales told by sailors of the sea become insiders' voyages through the oceans of the world of fiction. At one point, Nicolas relates that he felt exhilarated "and clean" because of his sense that "all the old stories had been written on water" (183). To examine the tellers and the telling of their tales is to attempt to penetrate the significance of that purgative metaphor. If the first part of *The Fountains of Neptune* is, among many other things, a fluidum of stories which, once told, elude retention, the second part, in which Nicolas discovers/invents his real/phantom playmate Olivier, not only presents the reader with a liquescent narrative of the unstable invasion of the everyday world by the realm of fantasy but also reinvents storytelling when Nini himself, by acting the part of Toujours-Là telling a story, becomes the re-membered narrator of his childhood. As Dr. Kaiserstiege points out on the final page of her case history of the Sandman (the bringer of dreams): *"The Sandman created a dream-child which was his way of creating a self, and a dream-world because he was a stranger to this one. . . . By bringing together disparate times and places, the Sandman had dissolved history"* (216; italics in original). Within the context of tale-telling in a setting dominated by water, it is important to note that the juxtapositioning of dreamworld and daily world results in the literal dissolving of history, in the liquefaction of the solidity of a past that has already been codified and should thus be unchangeable. Among other things, *The Fountains of Neptune* celebrates the power of narrative not merely to make but also to *unmake* history.

As it is the telling rather than the tales themselves which interests me here, let us turn our attention to the compilation of the narratives of sailors ("All sea-talkers," [15]) out of a past that, as the name of the site of many of the tellings ("The Ghost Port Bar") suggests, defies any identification beyond the confines of its fictional context. The trinity of tellers Ducornet employs cover a whole range of possibilities governed by the watery metaphor of her narrative. The nickname of Nini's foster father, Totor, calls up echoes of various French words and phrases: *toto,* the louse, *le toton,* the small top inscribed with letters which can form random messages, *le taux tort,* the false rate subverting the exchange of communication, and, finally, *le taud tort,* the twisted tarpaulin, the nautical covering which denies its promise to grant shelter. It is of no interest here whether such echoes were in Ducornet's mind; suffice it that Totor, the storyteller, can be seen as embodying in his name alone such a range of associations which in their turn affect his tales. Then there is Toujours-Là, the narrator as absinthe drinker, who is always there but never here, and whose view of mankind is symptomatic for an aqueous text: "they say a man's a moulded river, little more than water" (56). The third narrator of improbable fictions is Aristide Marquis, known simply as the Marquis, who, by rejecting his given name, elevates himself to a rank to which he is only entitled by name. It is perhaps only logical, given this foundation, that the Marquis's tales emerge as non-narratives in which nothing happens, "just a lot of twitteration," as Toujours-Là puts it (38); tales which rely heavily on the wiles of the illusionist for their success.

It is Totor—himself an ambivalent figure whom Nini sees as "the perpetual glamour of the sea made flesh" (15)—who introduces the fictional figure that dominates the symbolic level of the novel's story: La Vouivre, variously identified as a woman, an ogress, and a temptress. She, too, is a figure of ambiguity in an essentially ambiguous fictional universe, both the *vœu ivre,* the drunken vow, the promise given under intoxication, and the accusation, *vous ivre.* In terms of the thematic discourse of the novel, "She is enchantment— a warm-blooded aquatic animal" (20), and the incarnation of Nini's destiny: "If you look well and hard, Nicolas, you may—if you are lucky (and I believe you are)—see her, see her *just once,* for she can't be seen twice, else you pay for your curiosity with blindness or your life" (21). This prevision of Nini's fateful boating expedition at the village of Paradis-sûr-Loire, where in seeing the face of La Vouivre in the water he sees, too, his mother's face, is, in the context of Totor's tale, merely a typical storyteller's trick to fascinate his juvenile listener. Characteristically, however, the impact of the all-too-realistic fulfillment of his fiction (Nicolas's virtual drowning) upon the storyteller serves to underline the symbolic significance that the imaginative plaything has taken on. In recalling her visit to Totor in the fall of 1914, Dr. Kaiserstiege tells Nini that she had found him "an empty husk . . . bewildered by what had happened," for "in his mind, Odille [Nini's mother] had grown into mythical proportions, Ogress and Vouivre combined" (147). In other words, what began for the teller as a fiction to frighten the listener has become the narrator's own horrifying obsession, involving retribution and attempted infanticide.

Totor's two other tales in part 1 of the novel concern the mythical seaman Bottlenose, who in the first is the conventional storybook seaman dreaming of treasure, "all in a solid gold box deep in the mud of the banks of the river Congo" (73), a locale which places him in the uncertain company of imperial mythmakers: Conrad *(The Heart of Darkness)* and Kipling *(Just So Stories*[3]*)*. The second tale concerns Bottlenose's theory that the world—in particular people's moods and the weather—could be influenced by wind, so that he who could "make his own wind" would be master of all (108). This piece of whimsy is presented to Nini shortly before his decisive accident, suggesting that the wind of words is that which plots the trajectory of the narrative into the world of action. In contrast, Totor's stories that the adult Nini remembers and tells to Olivier in part 2 are both concerned with death and are thus somber reversals of the stories of part 1. In the first all but one of a load of treasured monkeys destined for the zoos of Europe die at sea; the survivor is tormented by the captain whose ear she bites off in fury. With a hint at Melville's *Billy Budd,* the marmoset is executed, but her tormentor dies of brain fever. Totor's last tale is of the discovery of a lonely spinster who was found poisoned dressed as a bride with the corpse of a monkey dressed as her groom beside her: " 'You see,' Totor explained to me, 'their love was impossible, but it was pure, I think, and somehow admirable' " (213). The sense of impossible yet admirable purity itself pervades the final scenes of the novel with Nini in solitude at the spa; it is that which is most closely associated with the boy-become-man-become-himself as child. Yet it is a part of the ambiguity of such narratives that the reaction of Totor's wife Rose to his interpretative remark is both violent and ridiculous: "Pure! . . . Their love was Peruvious, Victor! And all your stories Peruvious, too! You only tell them to taunt me" (213). Her agitated malapropism is a particularly felicitous coinage which brings together "pernicious," "spurious," and the exotic overtones of "Peruvian" to add the ambiguity of reception to the indeterminacy of narration. Nor should we ignore the notion of storytelling as provocation was as central to Melville as it is to Ducornet.

When we turn our attention to Toujours-Là, we find that his first story combines many of the elements we have already become familiar with: fantasy, humor, and the ambiguous power of narrative. He tells of being forced to dock in a strange port where he hears rumors about a mermaid; he attempts to obtain information from a man in a bar:

So I stopped a fella and said: "Hey! Where's this mermaid I've heard about?"
  "A Myth!" he lisped. "A fairy-tale!" (31)

The combination of the word "myth" and the information "he lisped" immediately sets up the by-now familiar evasiveness of the narrative: Are Toujours-Là and his interlocutor talking about the same thing? Is the mermaid fantasy or is she a real girl? Toujours-Là eventually traces her with the aid of a dwarf whom he meets at the significantly named bar the Scheherezade. It turns out that the creature is a maimed girl and not a mermaid, but a girl who lived the impossible fictitious existence of a marine animal in the local canal. Thus, once more fiction, the horrific ("Cut off her hands and feet and cauterized the wounds with fire" [32]), and the grotesque combine in a tale which, like its characters, dwindles into nonexistence at its conclusion: "Now Nini . . . The story was the fault of Master Punch and no reality" (33).

Toujours-Là prefaces the centerpiece of his narrative art, the tale of the vampire ship *Great Babylon*[4] with the statement: "One morning I woke up *nowhere at all*" (57; italics in original). The narrative that develops within this fictional void is the most literate in the novel; Toujours-Là begins with a narrational nod to *Moby-Dick* with his account of a bar where "the beams and rafters was made of the ribs of whales" (57-58), which he continues in his description of the nightmare vessel "carved like some hermetic cabinet" (60).[5] Throughout, Toujours-Là's accents are those of Coleridge's Ancient Mariner while his story combines Bram Stoker and the *Flying Dutchman* legend. It is significant, however, that this tale relies for its effect upon the deliberate accentuation of its reception. In answer to Nini's conventional listener's question "What happened then?" Toujours-Là goes into an irrelevancy about time and continues:

"Have we been given the Devil's red shoes to dance our lives away? Are we eating the Devil's pudding?"
    "We is!" I shouted, tremendously excited. "We is!"
    "SHUT YOUR TRAP!" the sailor barked. (64)

Here the narrative floats between the extremes of active listener participation or involvement and narratorial externalization of the same listener. Similarly, when Toujours-Là himself gets caught up more in the telling than in the tale, thus breaking the narrative thread, it is the narrator himself who forcibly recalls his listener:

"I am dreaming about black widow spiders what eat their mates, you know. Mantises do it, too. In the act. Eat the male's head clean off *in the act*. You ever seen that, little bugger? Ever seen the Act?"
    "Toujours-Là," I whispered, my head swarming, "I think I should go home. Rose—"

"THE STORY AIN'T OVER!" (65)

When the narrator breaks the narrative flow, the listener is immediately recalled to the conditions governing his extranarrational
life. Again it is Toujours-Là who, having brought the story to a satis-
factorily suspenseful conclusion with the revelation of the beautiful
woman captain transformed into "an abomination" of drooling
blood, spans the gap to the "reality" of his listeners by murdering
the chimpanzee who is the pet of the Ghost Port Bar. In *The Fountains of Neptune* the reader is continually confronted by the stress-
ing of this fluid frontier between the narrative and its context, between the worlds of narrator and reader, of contrived fiction and
accidental fact.

The final story ascribed to Toujours-Là is in fact an act of sus-
tained mimicry when Nini pretends to be his old friend in a game of
make-believe with the illusionary boy Olivier: "Today I am
Toujours-Là . . . and you, *you are me*" (197; italics in original). Since
the essence of mimicry is to create a superficial resemblance, Nini's
version of a Toujours-Là narrative relies heavily on surface approximation; characteristic phraseology and the occasional inter-
weaving of drunken pronunciations receive Olivier's praise: "You
sound just like him!" (198)—a remark which serves to emphasize
the identity of the Sandman and the playmate he has created.
Apart from such superficialities, the outstanding feature of Nini's
mimicry is that he chooses to tell episodes from Toujours-Là's own
childhood, thus underlining the flowing of the former listener into
the personality of the quondam spinner of yarns, both merging into
a new narrating voice. At the heart of these tales is once again an
episode concerning a treasure, this time a polished lump of dung
surrounding a larval beetle: "I did not know they was a worm inside
but I was sure they was a *power* in there. Poor, ignorant Toujours-
Là! The most powerful thing in my life has been my own bewilderment!" (200; italics in original). This not only summarizes the childhood friend viewed from the perspective of late adulthood but also
appears as a self-indictment on the part of Nicolas as narrator and
human being. Just as he has created the boy, Olivier, to be his old
self, so too he hides behind the assumed drunkenness of Toujours-
Là to utter his own final statement of belief: "I return, see, to what I
knew as a small, filthy child: the essence of the universe is ignorance! If there ish a God sh-she's as my mother was—stumbling
blindly through a dark room and thrashing out in anger . . . Tell me
N-Nicolath—wash ish more presch-precious then the dreamsh of
childhood?" (202). This act of imitation is a final affirmation that
narratives result not in insight and knowledge but in nonknowl-

edge,[6] and that as such the act of narration creates an idea of God in its own image. The dreams of childhood now become themselves symbols of order and informed care rather than escapes from the empirical world. Nini tells Olivier—more perhaps in his own voice than in that he has assumed for the narration—how the young Toujours-Là first read the Bible and loved "the notion that the world had been constructed purposely." However, the tale does not end there but continues: "I came to question that; it seems the only sense is the sense we give it" (201). Here the reader arrives at the logical conclusion to this fictional edifice of the telling of tales: meaning depends not so much on authorial or narratorial structuring as on the nature of the reader's receptivity and reception. It is this that is implied very early in the novel when the Marquis is not only entertaining the young Nini but also acting as a demonstration of the transient and contingent nature of medium or form: he begins by reciting lists of names which he repeats in song and then again in action as he mimics rowing in a boat round the room. Then in response to the admiring listener's comment, "It's magic," the Marquis replies: "Everything, Tit-Z'oreilles, is magic" (37). Thus have we truly come full circle, for what else can the tantalizing prize of Ducornet's novel be but its own telling.

NOTES

[1]Rikki Ducornet. *The Fountains of Neptune*. (1989; Elmwood Park, IL: Dalkey Archive Press, 1992), 93; hereafter cited parenthetically.

[2]John Barth, *Chimera* (1972; London: Quartet Books, 1977), 7-8.

[3]I am thinking here of Kipling's story "The Elephant's Child" with its refrain of "the banks of the great grey-green, greasy Limpopo River" (*Just So Stories* [London: Macmillan, 1926], 58). The parallel between the Elephant's child and Nini is significant: the young elephant remains firmly on the river bank, struggles with the creature that lives in the water (the crocodile) and is changed for life for the benefit of all around him.

[4]It is perhaps not irrelevant to point out that not only did the biblical Babylon function negatively as "a metaphor for certain forms of degeneracy," but—closer to the topic of this article—was also known in Hebrew as Babel, which is explained in the Bible as meaning confusion of speech (Bruce M. Metzger and Michael D. Coogan, eds., *The Oxford Companion to the Bible* [New York: Oxford Univ. Press; 1993], 70-71; Genesis 11.9).

[5]The bar of Melville's Spouter-Inn is described as "a rude attempt at a right whale's head," whereas Ishmael's first impression of the Pequod is of "a thing of trophies. A cannibal of a craft" (*Moby-Dick* [Harmondsworth: Penguin, 1972], 105, 165).

[6]"Reduced to non-sense, non-signification, non-knowledge, the world is no longer to be known or to be explained, it is to be EXPERIENCED as it is

now recreated in the New Fiction . . . as a newly invented, newly discovered reality—a real fictitious reality" (Raymond Federman, "Fiction Today or the Pursuit of Non-Knowledge" 1978, in *Critifiction: Postmodern Essays* [Albany: State Univ. of New York Press, 1993], 16).

Rikki Ducornet

Photograph by Victoria Straub, 1998

Gender Derision, Gender Corrosion, and Sexual Differences in Rikki Ducornet's Materialist Eden

Giovanna Covi

Rikki Ducornet's novels propose a critique of Western cosmology through a visitation of what were once considered the constitutive elements of the material universe: earth, analyzed in *The Stain* (1984); fire, in *Entering Fire* (1986); water, in *The Fountains of Neptune* (1989); and air, in *The Jade Cabinet* (1993).[1] Ducornet considers them "as Books of Nature and, because they are descriptive and painterly, as *Vanitas* and *Archetypa,* too" (*JC* 158). They also must be read as tales of magic—the magic of language and memory which exposes the politics of the human condition. "If fiction can be said to have a function," states Ducornet, "it is to release that primary fury of which language, even now, is miraculously capable—from the dry mud of daily use. So that furred, spotted and striped, it may—as it did in Eden—scrawl under every tree as revelation" (*JC* 157). Thus magic turns into politics by virtue of its alchemical character, of its connection between mystery and natural science. By rejecting the distinction between nature and human society, a distinction which was never made in alchemy, these texts participate in the politics of discourse of such postmodern hybrids as global warming, deforestation, and black holes; this type of discourse compels us to rethink the definition and constitution of modernity itself.

As magic books of nature, these novels foreground both the ornamental discourse of temporality and the explicative discourse of origin: they inhabit the borderland between nominalism (or constructivism) and essentialism, between rhetorical and foundational interpretive theories; in other words, they occupy the space in which the deconstruction of the traditional nature/culture dichotomy finds its articulation. In this way Ducornet, along with other feminist artists and theorists engaged in refiguring the contemporary epistemic horizon,[2] gives us the words to say our condition of errant, temporal being-in-the-world as sexed subjects liberated from the normative binarism of the masculine-feminine dichotomy. In fact, the descriptive and painterly and thus solid and evanescent space she provides is fruitful terrain for a critique of the notion of gender, which constitutes the focus of my reading.

The dominant definition of gender as cultural construction presents three major problems[3]: it implies the existence of a prediscursive, natural sex, a dependence which is an absorption and displacement of the historicity of nature and of the position that sex occupies within such a history. Furthermore, the concept of gender is anchored to a fixed identity: as a construction, in fact, it presupposes an agent. Finally, such agency is conceived as subject, which in turn is constituted by the matrix gender: thus it is an "I" "subjected to gender, and subjectivated by gender" (Butler 7) which imposes the domination of heterosexism as a norm and point of origin. This is why I am convinced that the diffusion of "gender studies" is not only the domestication of "feminist studies" but also a cultural operation that traps our notions of subjectivity within the traditionally obligatory choice between nature *or* culture; gender invariably reduces and essentializes sexuality—complex, contradictory, changing, and unlimited like desire—either to a relationship between the two biological sexes or to a purely linguistic, idealized, mythically androgynous indifference. It reduces the temporality of the subject to a fixed identity. As I have argued elsewhere, this critical operation represses the efforts to articulate in positive terms the crisis of modernity which characterizes our age; gender as an interpretive parameter favors the conservation of traditional epistemic discourse, because gender is among the founding categories of humanist binarism. I agree with Judith Butler that it would be much more fruitful to abandon the question of how gender interprets and constitutes sex and explore instead how norms regulate the materialization of sex itself. To put it somewhat differently, gender metamorphosizes into what I call sexual differences[4] and identity becomes a feminist subjectivity[5], when the subject is defined not in terms of "who am I?" but rather in terms of "who am I in relation to others in a given sociopolitical context?" The abandonment of gender as an ontological category contributes to the definition of a prismatic, fluid, relational identity whose power is defined by the temporality of being.

Ducornet's postmodernist books of nature[6] provide the means for remapping our idea of subjectivity in this sense. They offer not only delightful pages of comedy in which identities constituted according to the fixed parameters of feminine and masculine are the target of a devastating derision but also tragic scenes of violence in which gender is subjected to a radical corrosion. Thus Ducornet explores the roots of violence in our culture through descriptions which always inscribe the traces of gender logic. Such traces, in turn, expose the semiotic function of description—how appearance and signification partake of a Derridean supplementary logic, a

situation made explicit by the following metanarrative passage in
The Jade Cabinet:

> I believe it was Sam Johnson . . . who, having asked one of his small
> sons to count some objects in the street, whipped the boy severely for
> claiming there were four when there were three. Had Dr. Johnson been
> my father, surely I would have been beaten too. For to make the present
> tale stand up and wag, oft must I take three for four and four for three.
> And more often than not there are *no* objects to be seen because the fog of
> forgetting or unknowing is so thick I perceive but vague lumps floating in
> the stew.
>   Furthermore, even if I describe things exactly as they were, the lan-
> guage I use is not divine, but a poor imitation, a stew overcooked and
> lacking salt. Imagination is the only spice I have. . . . (126-27)

It is precisely by means of this double logic of addition and sub-
stitution, which foregrounds the complicity of gender with violence
and renders imagination a necessity, that Ducornet's discourse finally pushes beyond the exposure of the forces which have caused
what she calls "the end of Eden," or the reduction of the subject to a
fixed identity. In proposing the magic of language as a revelation
which translates into social agency, Ducornet's fiction envisions the
possibility of Eden's reconstitution (*JC* 158) and thus moves beyond
a nihilistic deconstruction to point the way toward a feminist subjectivity which, like sexuality itself, is provisionary, temporary,
changing, fluid, and multiple.

As Ducornet writes in "Waking to Eden," the afterword to the
fourth novel, "the world is a ceremonial dialogue to be actively engaged, and life's intention the searching out of the fertile passages
and places, a fearless looking for the thorny **A** and **B** in everything"
(*JC* 156). According to the Kabbalists, the former is the masculine
Aleph, "vigorous" and "confident," and the latter is **B**eth, "female
and passive—a little house waiting to be prodded by the thrusting
dart of letter **A**"; **B** "will always be there, her door open in expect-
ancy, boldly confront[ing] the universe" (*JC* 155). But when the dart
reduces its target to a stranger in this world, Ducornet's fiction suggests that history must be dissolved and Eden rebuilt as "a metaphor of the world-self as it might have been, had it been ruled by
love" (*FN* 216). Eden stands for the alphabet which allows us to see
that even the depth of the abyss can be inhabited by truth and virtue (*FN* 170). Eden, indeed, is the language of the voiceless and the
damned who speak outside of the logic of the domination that has
previously emarginated and silenced them. In this sense Ducornet's
Eden is what I call the feminist subject, a subject who is at home
with the unattainable, enigmatic nature of the world, the real as

well as the imagined. This Eden has nothing to do with nostalgia for a fully comprehensible, transcendental, and whole paradise, a position which Ducornet defines in *The Fountains of Neptune* as "pathetic," because it was "the universe reduced to sign" (216-17). In contrast, her Eden expresses the awareness that, although "no book can contain an entire life, nor explore an entire brain" (*FN* 218), language—and thus fiction in its political function—offers the possibility of a reconstitution. This strategic political hypothesis of a materialist Eden foregrounds Ducornet's "scornful anger" and "feminism" ("R.K.") over what some reviewers have called her "wild imaginings" (Morlock), "bizarre characters," and "exotic fiction" (Antonucci); it is the feminist politics of her discourse, her hypothesis of Eden, which confers to her stories "of magic, imagination, language, memory and other elements illusory" also an "essential" character ("Mar."), and turns "what could easily have become a farrago of the arbitrary works" ("R.K.") into a sociopolitical proposition. For this reason, Ducornet's figuration of Eden corresponds to what Angela Carter has called "the slow process of decolonializing language" (*Nothing Sacred*): Eden only becomes possible after gender has undergone a process of derision and corrosion; from the ruins of such an operation, "a dream-child" (*FN* 216)—*Unheimlich*, groundless—can be conceived.

Ducornet's tetralogy presents an amusing, but ultimately grim picture of modern society. The focus on language throughout exposes the absurdity and violence of a world ruled by the antagonism between the letter A and the letter B, an opposition shown in *The Fountains of Neptune* to be responsible for the fact that "the human race continues to castrate its children" (192).

Gender derision is evident in *The Stain* when the transvestite Exorcist enters a convent of nuns to have sex with the Mother Superior. Disguised as the Visiting Sister of the Bird, Rosa Mystica, whom the other nuns find attractive more for her daring use of rouge than for her masculine profile, he upsets the Mother Superior, who complains that he never takes off his female clothes even when they are alone. The Exorcist replies that "Sexuality is deceptive," and adds: "All living creatures carry the promise of both genders. You, my dove, disguised as a cavalry officer, would be irresistible!" (177). The irony of this scene mocks the fixity and hierarchy of the two sexes. But it is when the Exorcist becomes a werewolf later in the novel that gender corrosion occurs.

When a scandal forces the nuns to evacuate the convent, and the following day the building itself collapses due to a flood, the Exorcist feels guilty for his "female impersonation" (179), an act which has offended even Abraxas. The Exorcist then decides that the time has come for him to marry. His intended is Charlotte, a young orphan girl who bears a birthmark, the sign of her mother's sin, on her cheek—the stain, which has banned her from village life. Since marriage is ritual, the Exorcist finds no better way to redeem himself from his previous sin of gender transgression than to sacrifice the twins born on the same day as Charlotte. In fact, marriage, based on the difference of gender, can occur only after the mythical identity of individuals has been erased. In his notebook he writes: *"Ritual Murder is the Absolute Arm of Pleasure. A Totalitarian Magic! I must invent it!"* (182). This determination marks the beginning of his murders and rapes, as if violence followed necessarily from obedience to the law of gender. In fact, as he attempts to possess Charlotte, he declares: "Aggression, my lamb, is an art! The art of desire. . . . Desire and death" (219).

All of the acts of violence in the novel are either triggered or connotated by a sexual tension, a hostility which is reiterated in the juxtaposition between the rhetoric of pure logical rationality and that of silence. For example, the Exorcist and the Mother Superior are attracted by each other's rhetorical skills, while Charlotte has a fragmented voice after she reacts to her emargination by eating glass, her good uncle Emile stutters, the twins speak an incomprehensible secret language, and the cook of the convent, Sorberina, who as a child had been repeatedly raped by her father and brothers, is speechless and her mouth is fractured.

The verbosity of the powerful is laughable, just like their gender shifting, and the silence of their victims is tragic, just like the violence they are subjected to. Fortunately, derision and corrosion are not all there is in the world. The "spice of imagination" allows us to see through the ruins of this devastating picture an inkling of a possibility for the reconstitution of Eden. This is evident already in the convent, where—despite the rule of silence—Eulalie is punished and severely tortured precisely because of her silence. This subplot demonstrates that values can be turned upside down: the imposed silence of submission can become the determined silence of resistance; it can originate a new language—the magic ambiguous language of the voiceless. Charlotte will speak this language in the last pages: once saved from the violent verbosity and physical cruelty of the Exorcist, she will be free to accept her body together with her mind. To show that a sexed subjectivity is possible outside the nature-culture and thus the female-male cleavage, Charlotte will no longer exist as a sign of feminine sin and becomes a "normal young female" (198), who enjoys creating words and painting nature with colors made of earth, water, fire, and air.

In *Entering Fire* gender is parodied by the bourgeois de Bergerac family. The wife Virginie is a virtous, proper, and pious lady, whose conversation consists entirely of maxims out of conduct manuals. She is the impersonator of the image of the woman as "angel in the house," a pure example of the patriarchal moralism of bourgeois culture: at the discovery of sexuality on her wedding night, she shockingly observes: "The ultimate Insanity! I still cannot believe that this was His intention in the First Place, but an Aberration of a later epoque when the Devil had taken command of the Material World" (19). According to the genderized culture of modernity, her asexual feminity is coupled with the sensual virility of her husband Lamprias. An amateur botanist, he leaves his frigid wife and his Chinese concubine, his sons Septimus and True Man for the Amazon forest, where, in the language of the libertine who reduces sex to graffiti icons,[7] he claims that, "every fish is the spirit of a penis in search of an orchid. And every orchid is the spirit of a woman's vagina" (20).

This paradise of sexuality is juxtaposed by the hell of Nazism and colonialism that have marked the modern world and which Lamprias's legitimate son fervently supports. Born "white and male" (12), Septimus loves his virginal mother and hates his libertine father; a ferocious misogynist and racist, he spends his life sending women, Gypsy children, and Jews to gas chambers and singing "Of masculine energy. Of the regenerating power of Truth" (117) in a monomaniacal pursuit of order, before dying ironically of syphilis. Also in *Entering Fire* the descriptions of violence are governed by the logic of gender, as shown in the scenes of the execution of the Amazon boy and of True Man. Along with his mother, Septimus takes pleasure in the spectacle of the decapitation of his half-brother True Man and comments:

His raven hair, and delicate, flared nostrils, the sculpted lip (and True Man had the mouth of a Khmer effigy) all kindled in my heart a paroxism of revulsion, of anger, of envy—yes! For I could not help but remember the countless scented love-notes that fell like the petals of camellias from the letter-box to the floor and all for him, the lice-ridden, panting, sperm-stained scoundrel who spent his summer afternoons in the beds of unscrupulous bourgeoises, in ditches in the arms of seamstresses, in the dim cheese-cellars of languorous groceresses (and among the women in the milling crowd I believe I may have recognized the wife of a Député!). (97-98)

And this is the way that the assassination of the Amazon Indian boy by Rosada's colonial army is described: "He looked like your lady, fine-featured, gentle. . . . The object of Rosada's game was to sacrifice parts of the boy without actually killing him. One of Rosada's

thugs shot off his thumbs. He was an accomplished marksman—
they all were, and he razed them clean. But that's nothing. They
shot at the boy's penis next. So that Rosada could aim at the boy's
balls" (68).

In *Entering Fire* it is gender corrosion rather than derision that
dominates the narrative. The dismantling of gender as division and
not only as patriarchal superiority is underlined in the pages in
which Septimus pontificates over the superiority of the circle,
which he sees as the symbol of the myth of the virginal mother. It is
a far more important universal principle for him than that expressed by the phallic triangle of scientific progress, and he states:
"The exemplary totem of the Master Race, the round-headed race, is
the globe. It signifies the moon, the aureole of saints, the Maternal
Teat. Did not a shining sphere protect and guide Napoleon? The
Brachy invented the spoken word and the first sound he uttered
was *AM*. (Maman, Adam, Am, Amen, etc.) *AM* lies at the roots of all
Indo-European languages" (79).

It is thus the fantasy of the Mother Goddess which sustains the
superiority of the White Race. The opposite view is expressed by
Cûcla, Lamprias's Amazon woman, who "felt that the chatter of
cats, cows, ducks, rascals and mice filled tragic gaps. Without the
beeps! and Wows! and moos and honks, English was no better than
a mouth full of missing teeth" (104), and who praised Krazy Kat,
because "languages without twitters, grunts and howls could not
capture and create worlds" (105). This juxtaposition demonstrates
that the creation of a mirror image does not imply any new order:
the horrors of Nazism spring rather from the impossibility of comprehension between Septimus and Cûcla, from the division separating the virginal feminine from the sexual masculine, rather than
from Septimus's theories. The novel consists entirely of letters, the
last of which is written by Septimus to his father. Septimus laments: "Frankly I could do with a letter. Why is it you have never
written?" (158). The son's accusation foregrounds Lamprias and
Virginie's joint responsibility for their son's beliefs, which originates in the opposition between their two separate worlds and his
consequent blind love for the one and obsessive hate for the other.
That Lamprias does not represent the positive pole set up against
Septimus is underlined by the final comment on the implications of
his monomaniacal pursuit of scientific research. Following the clas-
sificatory method of natural science[8] during the "feverish years of
[his] exploration" (91), Lamprias eventually manages to clonate hybrid flowers from the seeds he gathered in the Amazon. His orchids
in vitro make him a successful and famous man in Paris and New
York, but fame is followed by introspection, and finally the pre-

sumed freedom of his pursuit is exposed by his own meditation as being complicitous with the logocentric, colonialist attitude by which ontological difference is domesticated and reduced to the graspable One: "I fear I have thoughtlessly turned Mystery out into the streets, like a heartless father a wayward daughter. Treasure has become a streetwalker; anyone who can pay her price can have her. At the weddings of emirs she is scattered on the ground like common rice. . . . Now that my colleagues talk of duplicating men, I shudder and wonder if it would not have been better to have left Mystery alone altogether . . ." (*EF* 92-93). *Entering Fire* thus ends in ashes, the ashes of Nazism in which there is no space for reconstituting Eden.

In contrast, the search for Eden occupies the entire second half of *The Fountains of Neptune.* In fact, the protagonist, Nini, sleeps through both World Wars after being plunged into a fifty-year coma by a vision of his dead mother at the bottom of the sea; he awakes and constructs the Kingdom of d'Elir, a fantasy world and identity. As a boy, all he knows of his parents are terrifying stories told by a drunken misogynist; when he gets old and has to create his own life, stories are all that he has of himself. His mother was killed, drowned by villagers for having helped her lover kill Nini's father. This faceless woman represents love and death: her head is that of an ogress, a medusa, and her body that of a seducing mermaid, for in the sea "Arm in arm, light and darkness dance upon the water" (101). The final acceptance by Nini of her paradoxical nature will allow him to be at home with the enigma that is the world and by which virtue can inhabit even the depth of the abyss.

World War II destroyed the places of the past, denying even the right to memory. This wiping clean of one's history produces a continuous deferral of the objects, which leaves Nini only with a photo of someone who merely resembles the mother of his dreams, and his psychoanalyst, Doctor Venus Kaiserstiege, and only with a letter written by a friend of her lover who dies in the trenches. This Venus' Eros further deepens the relationship between Nini and Doctor Kaiserstiege, because he is the Marquis of his infancy who used to tell the young boy plotless stories, which were meant for the eyes and not the ears—i.e., stories which abandoned the linearity of narrative language to embrace the dance in the air of the body of their narrator. As Robert Coover has observed, *The Fountains of Neptune* "might aptly have been titled by the name of their favorite inn in a nearby riverside village: *A la Recherche du Paradis Terrestre*"; instead, it bears the title of the case book written by Doctor Kaiserstiege in collaboration with Nini, the Sandman, in which a life "reduced to potent signs" (*FN* 133) is recreated thanks to the woman doctor. Her tenderness and beauty encourage the building of a "world-self as it might have been, had it been ruled by love" (216) had it not been violated by the trauma of one's father being killed by one's mother and in turn then being herself killed by one's community—a trauma which determines the boy's understanding of gender. The Doctor's conviction that children have a right to Paradise convinces the Sandman that the Virtuous Abyss is nothing other than the female aspect of Neptune, and this allows him to appreciate not only the "something uncommonly soft and feminine about [his] appearance" (*FN* 146) but also makes him accept that it is impossible for language to grasp an entire life or mind and allows him to be at peace with the paradoxical idea of a limited eternity. At home with the temporality of being and with the aporias and proliferation of stories, he concludes his casebook/novel as follows: "I am only interested in the allusive messages of my dreams, the innumerable spaces of my memories, and the perpetual wanderings of my thoughts. . . . [T]he Sandman is very like the floating monster, both of the world and not of the world, and—as long as I can hold fast the glass wand of reverie—somehow eternal" (219-20).

The controlling metaphor of air in *The Jade Cabinet* allows for the possibility of Eden from the very beginning. Paradise is Etheria, the daughter of Angus whose "insatiable desire for knowledge" has caused her muteness. Angus, an entomologist, pushes the critique of natural science sketched in *Entering Fire,* with reference to the character of Lamprias, to a devastating conclusion. In his obsessive urge to classify and comprehend everything, in his scientific search for the Universal Primal Language, Angus decides to raise his daughter in complete isolation from any exposure to human speech; subsequently, he gives her away in exchange for a collection of jade, and finally he sells also this collection in order to satisfy the insatiable appetite of the *Hungerkünstler,* a creature exhibited at the Saint Giles Fair who "lives on air and converses with angels" (68) and whom Angus buys to demonstrate that she speaks the Universal Language, that she beholds "the Roots of Adam's Tongue" (76). In chapter 10 Etheria vanishes: she "evaporated" (75) with the jade—"the very objects which had enslaved her she used to buy herself wings" (76)—and she managed to succeed thanks to Feather's help. Feather is the servant who had printed calling cards in the name of Mr. Marx and would periodically bring them "on a silver dish" to his master, the industrialist Tubbs; Feather "knew the principles of magic. He knew that the magician plays with the public's perceptions and memories" (74), and he taught Etheria that "Men like Radulph Tubbs . . . who believe only in what can be seen, or touched, or eaten, are not the exception but the rule" (75). This is

214 REVIEW OF CONTEMPORARY FICTION

what turned her into a wizard—"famished for space, Etheria became a master at creating its illusion" (75). What volatilizes with her are her silent beauty, her uncanny quality of expressing herself "with wonderful little idiosyncratic ideograms of her own invention," which her plain sister Memory, her "chief interpreter," deciphers "at a glance" (14), her riddles created in the company of Charles Dodgson, and her magic jades. All this vanishes when Tubbs, her misogynist husband and Dodgson's principal enemy, destroys their garden and rapes her with one of the jades: "I remember how I thrust the object into the very depths of her, how I invaded her as she had never dreamed possible, possessed her so unnaturally that had it lasted a moment longer, surely her heart would have broken. Spent, I kneeled, then stood. Etheria lay in ruins at my feet. Thus for the third time, I had made her mine. . . . [A] few months later, Etheria vanished forever in thin air like a puff of smoke" (55-56).

Etheria, who already only existed in translation in the novel, from this moment on exists only in the minds of Memory and Tubbs, the narrators of the entire text. When, at the end of the book, she seems to reappear on stage as the magician Zephyra, she is killed by the anorexic-bulimic *Hungerkünstler*. At this point, Memory discovers that her sister's body is that of a man; nevertheless, Tubbs will spend the rest of his days bringing flowers to Zephyra's tomb. Thus Etheria/Zephyra is killed by the violent figure which in the novel stands for the myth of a universal Adamic language, for the Oneness which is equally and monomaniacally pursued both by Angus and Tubbs. Similar to the ritual murder of the twins in *The Stain,* her sacrifice stands for the cost of attaining an impossible monadic, sexually determined identity.

The concluding novel of Ducornet's cosmology, although substantial like air, manages thus to envision a world in which Eden is always possible. But air is indeed substantial—it is one of the four elements of the natural world—and thus the materiality of Ducornet's Eden forecloses all possibilities of a teleological reconstitution. Eden is the reality of Etheria's world of silence, which offers a magic escape from the violence of gender's hierarchy and a mysterious overcoming of gender's heterosexism.

NOTES

[1]Hereafter cited in the text as *S, EF, FN,* and *JC,* respectively.

[2]I am convinced that the most exciting provocations in this sense come from those writers and philosophers who have confronted Luce Irigaray's

claim that it is necessary to create a new language in order to say the world anew. The fusion between the practice of writing and the expression of theory, the crossing over of the boundary which traditionally separates poetry from philosophy, have become common features of feminist discourse. I am not only thinking of widely quoted feminist theorists who write in a poetic language—such as Gloria Anzaldùa, Hélène Cixous, Luce Irigaray, Audre Lorde, or Adrienne Rich—but also of the innovative theories expressed in the poetry and prose of some contemporary artists. Among these, I would include Jamaica Kincaid's figuration of the subject as a "prism" and Kathy Acker's articulation of relational identity as "sympathizing."

[3]See Judith Butler, *Bodies that Matter,* for a comprehensive discussion of these points.

[4]My argument for preferring the term *sexual differences* to *gender* is that the former focuses on the plurality of differences which, according to the sociopolitical evaluation of sexuality in a specific context, concur to separate, to divide, to make a difference (*sex* comes from the Latin, *secare,* to divide). On the contrary, the latter is etymologically linked to a rigid biological dualism by way of its kinship with the word *generare,* and it either invariably reduces and essentializes sexuality to a biogical relationship between the two sexes or denies it altogether in a purely linguistic, androgynous leveling of difference. When a text forces the boundaries of language and reality beyond the deconstruction of logocentrism and toward the rethinking of a new episteme, it metamorphosizes *gender* into *sexual differences.* I have elaborated this position in articles on Keri Hulme's *The Bone People,* Jamaica Kincaid's *Lucy,* and Kathy Acker's *Don Quixote* and *Great Expectations.*

[5]I am referring here to Rosi Braidotti's definition of "feminist subject," which is conversant with Teresa de Lauretis's discussion of identity as positionality.

[6]Ducornet's books of nature are here defined as *postmodernist* in the sense of a politicized and historically committed discursive experimentation—i.e., of texts which engage the effort, however provisional, of calling into question the received forms and discursive practices of the canonical tradition in order to retrieve the temporal dimension of art and the differences which it disseminates. See, for example, William Spanos, *Repetitions,* especially chapter 5.

[7]For this definition of sexuality reduced to pornography, see Angela Carter, *The Sadeian Woman,* especially chapter 1.

[8]For a critique of Linnaeus's method, in the context of a wider analysis of the various logocentric discourses which concur in reducing difference to sameness, see William Spanos, *Repetitions,* especially with reference to his interpretation of Melville's *Moby-Dick.*

WORKS CITED

Acker, Kathy. Introduction. *Boxcar Bertha: An Autobiography.* New York: Amok, 1988.

Antonucci, Ron. Rev. of *The Jade Cabinet,* by Rikki Ducornet. *Library Journal* 1 Feb. 1993.

Braidotti, Rosi. *Patterns of Dissonance: A Study of Women in Contemporary Philosophy.* Cambridge, UK: Polity, 1991.

Butler, Judith. *Bodies that Matter: On the Discursive Limits of "Sex."* New York: Routledge, 1993.

Carter, Angela. *Nothing Sacred: Selected Writings.* London: Virago, 1982.

———. *The Sadeian Woman: An Exercise in Cultural History.* London: Virago, 1979.

Covi, Giovanna. "Keri Hulme's *The Bone People:* A Critique of Gender." *Imagination and the Creative Impulse in the New Literatures in English.* Ed. Maria Teresa Bindella and Geoffrey V. Davis. Amsterdam: Rodopi, 1993. 219-32.

———. "Kathy Acker's Corrosive Fiction: Deconstructing Postmodernism and Gender." *Methodologies of Gender.* Ed. Mario Carona and Giuseppe Lombardo. Rome: Herder Editore, 1993. 361-70.

———. "The Islands in New York: Jamaica Kincaid's *Lucy.*" *Traditionalism vs. Modernism.* Ed. Erhard Reckwitz, Lucia Vennarini and Cornelia Wegener. Essen, Germany: Die Blaue Eule, 1994. 257-70.

de Lauretis, Teresa. *Feminist Studies/Critical Studies.* Bloomington: Indiana Univ. Press, 1986.

Ducornet, Rikki . *The Stain.* 1984. Normal, IL: Dalkey Archive Press, 1995.

———. *Entering Fire.* San Francisco: City Lights, 1986.

———. *The Fountains of Neptune.* 1989. Normal, IL: Dalkey Archive Press, 1992.

———. *The Jade Cabinet.* Normal, IL: Dalkey Archive Press, 1993.

"Mar." Rev. of *The Jade Cabinet,* by Rikki Ducornet. *Publishers Weekly* 4 Jan. 1993.

Morlock, Eric. Rev. of *The Fountains of Neptune* and *The Jade Cabinet,* by Rikki Ducornet. *Small Press* 11.3 (1993).

"R.K." Rev. of *The Jade Cabinet,* by Rikki Ducornet. *Times Literary Supplement,* 14 May 1993: 25.

Spanos, William V. *Repetitions: The Postmodern Occasion in Literature and Culture.* Baton Rouge: Louisiana State Univ. Press, 1987.

Phosphor in Dreamland

Lynne Diamond-Nigh

In the preface to his "archeology," *The Order of Things*, Michel Foucault tells us that that book was inspired by a passage in Borges, in which the entry in a Chinese encyclopedia under *Animals* divided them into the following categories: "(a) belonging to the Emperor, (b) embalmed, (c) tame, (d) sucking pigs, (e) sirens, (f) fabulous, (g) stray dogs, (h) included in the present classification, (i) frenzied, (j) innumerable, (k) drawn with a very fine camelhair brush, (l) *et cetera*, (m) having just broken the water pitcher, (n) that from a long way off looks like flies" (xv). It was not just the incongruity of those juxtapositions that fascinated and delighted Foucault but the cathartic laughter that welled up inside of him, as our familiar ordering and cataloging processes imploded to where the sole locus that remained of them, for them, the only place where "that" could be thought and exist, was the oracular space of language. These heterotopias, he further tells us, go beyond the incongruous, to that lawless place where myriad disparate orders exist side by side without causal connection, where they "desiccate speech, stop words in their tracks, contest the very possibility of grammar at its source; they dissolve our myths and sterilize the lyricism of our sentences" (xviii). Utopias, on the other hand, although as fabulously unreal as heterotopias, "permit fables and discourse: they run with the very grain of language and are part of the fundamental dimension of the *fabula*" (xviii).

Rikki Ducornet's novel *Phosphor in Dreamland* (1995) pits utopia (Birdland) against heterotopia (Pope Publius), poetry against dogma, sensuality against asceticism, myth against history, love against fear, fragmentation against unity, man against nature, in an initiatory romance journey that has many a stop by way of Jung.

My first clue to the connection with Foucault, however, came from the inordinate quantity of lists, about fifteen (though not in list format, but presented as unnumbered and unlettered sequences in a sentence), which were either heterotopic or utopic, depending on from whom they emanated. Fogginius, an obnoxious pedant and a constant babbler, would "stop words in their tracks," allowing of no dialogue, no lucid clearing from which an interchange could flow. Instead of conversation, he pronounced lists; one, for example, chronicling his deathbed watch of Yahoo Clay, names all the topics he discourses upon, and which finally led Clay, in a mad frenzy, to abandon speech for weeks: "the circuitous legend of Saint Sousmyos . . . the progressive and retrograde motions of the stars, the nature of the souls of animals, the divinity of the number six . . . the bones of the body" and the "magical paraphernalia of Simon Magus . . . rotting at the bottom of the sea" (50). The chapter ends, "Shield and Shadow, Clay's voice had always been superfluous" (50). Fogginius's stepson Phosphor, on the other hand, inventor and poet, wrote words that had the opposite effect: they created love and sensuality, communion and dreams. And it was the pointed use of the term *shadow,* this emphasis from the title onward on dreams, that led me from Foucault's lists, utopias, and heterotopias to Jung's mythic world.

Indeed, the first list in the book points the way: a definition of the word *chromosomes* produces the following (short) list: the Minotaur's maze, the face of the Medusa, the map of Milano and Mars seen from space, all places and creatures that harbor mythic associations. But it was the bird of the title, as well as numerous subsequent birds throughout the work, that pinpointed a more explicit connection to Jung: birds, according to him, are symbols of transcendence. Birdland, Ducornet's utopia, is the place where such transcendence can and does occur, just on the other side of the romance threshold, for it is indeed where the romance, not the novel, can unfold. In contradistinction to Pope Publius, the space of commerce, exploitation, linear historicity, and stultifying, death-dealing dogma, all qualities we have come to associate with bourgeois, masculine hegemony and hence the traditional novel, Birdland unfolds itself as the mythic arena of magic, a commons where man and animal meet in one admirable creature, the lôplôp bird, who sounds like a human when it screams and begs for mercy when it is captured. More admirable even, is its opposition to brutality by song: "One blow of that great beak could have shattered Clay's skull; instead, the creature had continued to sing, *as if a voice could still ferocity! * Phosphor wondered: *Could a voice inspirit the world? Embellish it and change it for the better?* Privately he feared that all poets would one day go the way of the lôplôp. *We are all birdmen,* he shuddered, *doomed"* (99). We hear the echoes of Baudelaire's "Albatross" and intuit the shaman whose power lies in his ability to leave his body and fly around the universe, the holder of prophetic visions, the medium through which a person comes into the fulfillment of his true being and transcends his existence as he has known it before. For Jung, this creature unites the male and female aspects of the psyche; in Birdland, the place of "and," Phosphor finds his anima: *"I am now penetrating . . . with joy and terror, the Eternal*

Feminine: moist, mossy, hidden nameless. I hurry into darkness. In the margin he penned *nameless/darkness.* The rhyme would serve him later" (86).

Phosphor, then, is Jung's mythic or, if you will, in literary terms, romance hero. The quest that leads him away from Pope Publius follows the path of all other initiatory voyages. He starts as a reputed photographer, Nuño Alfa y Omega, called Phosphor, hired by Fango Fantasma, the island's ruling aristocrat, to "capture," that is photograph and fix, the diversity and complexity of the island they inhabit. Disappointed in love, ignored by Professor Tardanza's daughter, Extravaganza, he leaves Pope Publius with Fogginius, Fantasma, and little Pulco, a younger version of himself. He loses his self: "*My life,* he thought, *has come full circle. I am not my own master. . . . I am a mere thing of Fantasma's fantasy*" (106). As he penetrates more and more deeply into the primeval area (Birdland), he sheds the carapace of individuality and self-aggrandizement and realizes that it is only through spiritual (which here also means erotic) union with the Other—the feminine, nature, animals, and even the hated Fogginius—that he can reach and take hold of the hidden and mysterious powers of the unknown, the unconscious, the source of profound creation. Renouncing ambition and realizing that love is the supreme value and goal, he returns to Pope Publius, winning not only the hand of Extravaganza but also her heart, body, and soul, for it is he who liberates her, he who breaks the cycle of her family's curse, their damnation as people who cannot dream.

Fango Fantasma, on the other hand, try as he might, cannot avail himself of Birdland. He sets off by himself and returns announcing, "I have had enough! . . . If I can little stomach the company of men, the forest is far worse. There really is nothing there I want" (121). And with this language of commerce, he initiates their return to Pope Publius where "We shall devote ourselves to an Entire Itinerary of the Civilized World as Perceived by Fango Fantasma. We shall create a Theory and Practice of Order. We shall meditate upon Harmony in the shape of *my beautiful house.* Its gracious quadrangular rooms! *Why didn't I think of this sooner? . . . Why did I inflict this detour in chaos upon myself?* . . . My house! . . . is smack in the center of the visible universe. . . . It has a left side and a right side and a roof that does not leak! It contains venerable objects that *all have names.* . . . My house! . . . how I miss its *measurable rooms!*" (122).

It is very soon after this experience in primitive Birdland that Ducornet solidifies what is one of the major themes of her work, the magic and power of the word. There, Fantasma has stilled Clay's insensate mimesis of Fogginius's lists with musket fire and this desperate cry wrung from him, comparable to the one longing for order, harmony, names, and measurable things, in direct counter-point to Phosphor's musings of the voice "inspiriting" the world: "If I hear the sound of another human voice . . . if anyone dares speak, *I will blow out his brains too*" (101).

In the beginning, of course, was the Word. Phosphor clearly marks the distinction between his roles as photographer and poet as that of the difference between a documenter and a fixer (solidifier), and that of a creator: " 'My black box seizes reality . . . it does not *reveal* anything.' It seemed to him that words evoked more than images. 'In the beginning was the *word*. . . .We are still waiting for the *light*' " (38). Words for him, and for other mythologizers, far sur-pass their imitative function by becoming instruments of cognition and vehicles of transcendent creation: "Phosophor then turned to poetry to satisfy a need—the heart's need, perhaps, and the need that mirrored his mind's acute hunger for gnosis" (18). The biblical Genesis myth beginning with the word resonates with other genesis myths, Virgil's *Aeneid,* and the more contemporary Latin American ones of Gabriel García Márquez's *One Hundred Years of Solitude* and Alejo Carpentier's *The Lost Steps.* The importance of the word as foundation for the founding of a city/the establishment of a civili-zation is axiomatic, most specifically, in its function of naming. Hence, Fantasma's insistence on returning to a world where every-thing could be securely identified and categorized, where every-thing had its proper name: objects without names signified the void, the abyss.

Proper names: blatantly transparent and parodically character-istic of the people holding them. Mere literal translations or asso-ciations render their absurd caricaturesque properties instantly: Phosphor, light; Fogginius, fog and obscurity; Señora Portaequipajes, the landlady who carries luggage; and so forth. In the mythic arena names denote essences, but these names embrace a double mythic function because, as the time of myth is circular, rather than linear, the use of allegorical names circles back to unite this contemporary romance with ones of many centuries previous to it, in which such names were a staple of the narrative tradition. And other literary resonances and allusions that reach across the ages are explicitly evident in *Phosphor,* a characteristic that Northrop Frye noted as peculiar to romance rather than novel. These resonances echo most profoundly with the modern Latin American novel, as has already been noted, but even more specifically with the writer who so strongly contributed to the very possibility of that novel, Jorge Luis Borges. With Alejo Carpentier, the author of the already-named *Lost Steps,* who viewed Latin American culture as indigenously ba-roque and fantastic, a viewpoint with which postcolonialists have overtly quarrelled, Borges initiated a cataclysm in Latin American literature by rendering that reality in mythic rather than Western terms. At times, I felt that I was reading Borges modulated into a comic tonality; not only did he resonate in Birdland's world outlook, but just as strikingly in Ducornet's turns of phrases: "Not only would he be his island's first poet laureate and photographer, he would be its first geographer and cartographer! His endeavor was greater than epic: it was encyclopedic!" (63).

In the same time that these words lightly mock Borges, they also refer to the overarching cathedral of his world, made up of libraries, books, and, of course, words. But there is one primal area where Ducornet and Borges part, and that is her belief in, and his virtually total neglect of, the central importance of the sensual and the "merely" physical. For Ducornet, eroticism pre-exists the significant, signified world and leads to an understanding of language: "Now that Phosphor was ready to love, he was also ready to speak and *so to write*— . . ." (140). The heterotopians, primarily represented by the priest Secundo of the Inquisition, want only to silence men, eviscerating them of their corporeality, their will, and their voice. In one of Phosphor's poems to Extravaganza, the lines that damned and silenced him connected the natural, physical, erotic, sacred, and linguistic worlds:

> *Arboreal, aerial goddess*
> *riding the phallic beaks of toucans;*
> *goddess of the waters*
> *copulating with clams; squid woman*
> *daughter of the sacred scallop sheathed in*
> *your codpiece of shell*
> *more lovely than the miters of popes*
> *the bloody crosses, the insipid wafers*
> *of popes . . .* (132)

Secundo's report to the Inquisition, as a counterpoint of style and content where polarities are inverted, comments on this as well as his other poetry:

He speakes, Secundo continued, *of gazing into his beloved's eyes where, juste as a sorcerer reads the future in bowls of quicksilver and in the palpitating viscera of slaine beastes, so doth he reade his destinie. He would have us believe that his beloved's part speakes to him in the voice of prophecy, that the moles upon her boddie form an alphabet, and the lines of her bellye map Paradise. He names love a transcendent magick and sayeth the lovers' boddies are the crucibles which transforme the soule. . . .*

Luste and dreaminge, I have ascertained, are inexorably joined.
(157-58)

Like the path of Joseph Campbell's mythic hero, the path of Phosphor's quest takes the form of separation, renunciation, and return: as we have seen, the exterior form of this quest takes him from Pope Publius to Birdland and back again where he claims Extravaganza and the dream. But his quest to become a poet, that leads to his posthumous apotheosis by educated and noneducated alike, entails a period of apprenticeship (the renunciation stage) that sets the scene for his understanding of the connectedness of all living things and the conflation of the corporeal, sacred, and unconscious worlds with the world of the word; he learns to understand and accept the paradoxically ephemeral and eternal quality of life. On his honeymoon he falls in love with a carp, "more syllable than animal" (137); Ducornet says: "the poet recognized the carp's corporeality *and his own* . . . [and] was forced to reflect upon physicality and to accept the nature of the world in its entirety. His beloved . . . more the stunning consonant of some divine alphabet, more scroll than living creature—" (138). It is through this apprenticeship, when he learns to love the fish, that Phosphor is able to discard the belief that his wife Extravaganza is innocent and pure, dumb and incapable of thought, unreal; he then can enter into a physically and emotionally symbiotic relationship with her, whereby each acts as the muse and catalyst for the other's fulfillment and transcendence. It is from this union of body and soul that Extravaganza's erotic genius flowers, as does the best of Phosphor's poetry.

And so, we come back full circle to words and the importance of fabulation in the mythic world. To return to Foucault's division, the world of Phosphor and Extravaganza is a utopian world, going with the "grain of language," and depending on that grain to flourish in its plenitude, heaping up possibilities and piling up connections that meander and digress to ever-infinite branches and paths. The lovers, too, form part of that multiplicity, for Phosphor and Extravaganza are taken over by Polly and the narrator, who themselves must rely on the story for their existence.

WORKS CITED

Ducornet, Rikki. *Phosphor in Dreamland*. Normal, IL: Dalkey Archive Press, 1995.

Foucault, Michel. *The Order of Things: An Archaeology of the Human Sciences*. 1971. New York: Vintage, 1994.

Desiring Words

Warren Motte

With five bold, original, and deeply ingenious novels to her credit, as well as several volumes of short fiction and verse, Rikki Ducornet should be regarded as one of the major figures of the American avant-garde. Her latest book will confirm and amplify that reputation. *The Word "Desire"* is a collection of twelve stories, each of which questions human (and in one case canine) sexuality through a different perspective and a different approach. What I would like to propose here is a trip through the collection, at a pace varying from the quick trot to the dilatory stroll, along some of the sunlit straightaways and the shaded meanders this book offers its readers.

The settings of the stories range as broadly as desire itself: Egypt, Quebec, India, France, Mexico, Algeria—and even the Vatican, that most apparently *un*sexual place, where a doomed wet nurse suckles a dying pope.[1] Quirky, pleasantly idiosyncratic characters stride through these stories: a French Orientalist who falls in love with a four-armed Hindu goddess; a neurotic spinster who is ravished in a dream by two hunky—and wingèd—men; Josephine's dog "Fortuné," who dreams of following Napoleon into Egypt, but immolates himself instead in the jaws of a bull mastiff because of an unhappy *affaire de coeur*. The manner of the telling in these tales is as richly various as what is told. The writing here is characterized by the lexical virtuosity, the narrative resourcefulness, and the gift for the utterly incongruous yet utterly convincing image that have come to be the hallmarks of Ducornet's work. In many of these stories Ducornet seems to have wagered on exoticism and alterity, but it becomes clear that she has done so strategically, in an effort to persuade us that desire is a vital thread in the fabric of every human experience.

Or rather, in the story entitled "Fortuné," canine experience, through which Ducornet eloquently adumbrates the exemplarity of the exceptional. Fortuné himself is a singularly lucky dog on the face of it: spoiled rotten by Josephine, he conceives a passion for the opera and Egypt alike when his mistress takes him to see Mozart's *The Magic Flute*. He recognizes that his creative vision is likewise singular, for he sees things as an artist would: "After that vivid night I knew that though I *looked* like any number of little dogs, I, Heaven help me, did not *imagine* as they imagined."[2] Fortuné has a box seat for the viewing of contemporary history, too, but the Egyptian campaign inflames his imagination less, finally, than his personal campaign to win the favors of the fickle Mina, Madame Menfous's lapdog. He is constant in his love, even if Mina—the bitch!—is not; inexplicably, she prefers the muscular, grunting, slow-witted, proletarian Creon, the cook's bull mastiff. When Fortuné acts out his constancy out on the bloody stage of his rival's maw, he gives us a noble lesson in desire and its consequences. As writers of "cynical" tales from Cervantes's *Coloquio de los perros* to J. R. Ackerley's *My Dog Tulip* have suggested,[3] we humans have much to learn from dogs.

Constancy is also a salient characteristic of Vertige Doré, an eminent French Orientalist and scholar of the ogress myths. As a young boy, he had fallen in love with an image of Sri Lakshmi, a goddess whose supernumerary arms wove a tight embrace around Doré's imagination: "Her face was immeasurably beautiful, her eyes almond-shaped and black, and her lips smiling. I was captivated by the full orbs of her breasts and her little naked feet. But what seized my imagination above all were her *four arms*. I decided then and there that I would find her" (75-76). His desire will take him to India, where fakirs worship idols of dung and elephants crush condemned criminals to death with their feet. Doré is a fundamentalist of desire, reading his fantasy literally in spite of all exhortations to abandon it (even one from the Archbishop of Canterbury). And because of that admirable constancy, he will eventually find consummation. Such is not the case of Gertrude, a prudish, anti-Semitic, middle-aged woman who experiences her erotic nature as neurosis. She is scandalized by reports of African sexual customs, yet she finds herself dreaming of her sister's vulva. When, in yet another dream, two handsome and seraphic men—whose angelic character is trumped by their virility—ravish her, she screams herself awake, claiming for the sake of appearances to have heard burglars in the house. It's a logical thing to do, for such sexual pleasure as she may experience is, in a very real sense, stolen pleasure.

In "The Foxed Mirror" Guillermo, a three-year-old Mexican boy, is forced to kiss a glass coffin with a Christ figure in it. Later, he will study for the priesthood and go to Niñopan as village priest at age nineteen, where he will grapple with his vexed sexuality. Like the representation of the Christ, the vivid paintings of a local boy named Saturnino Atl fire Guillermo's erotic imagination. The way the image mediates desire is at the center of this story, which deals, too, with the tenuous relations between signs and their referents. In "Opium" a dying pope asks to suckle a wet nurse's milk directly, rather than from a cup (a mise-en-scène that will recall, to readers as debauched as yours truly, any number of dreadful pope jokes). On the surface, that wish is simple enough, and yet the wet nurse recognizes immediately what it portends for her: "when she hears the Pope's request she knows she is doomed" (180). The power of desire is what is at issue here, but of course that is a script which is read very differently, according to whether one is empowered, like the Pope, or disempowered, like the wet nurse.

"I have what you call a sexual soul," an analysand tells her therapist in one of these stories (87). The way that soulful sexuality may often lie latent, until it manifests itself in unexpected ways, is one of the major themes of The Word "Desire." But to suggest that eroticism is the "theme" of this collection and to leave it at that would be reductive. As J. H. Matthews has argued, "Rikki does not look upon eroticism as self-indulgent daydreaming. It appears to her just the way surrealism shows that it must be, a revolt against the human condition, a means for surmounting the limitations of pedestrian living and for asserting the irresistible power of desire to release men and women from oppressive contingent circumstance."[4] Nor is eroticism merely a convenient lens through which the writer may view human experience here. On the contrary, it is the very motor of these stories, and of the collection as a whole. "Sex is at the center of the self," Rikki Ducornet suggested in an interview published in 1982. "Identity is rooted in our sexuality, as is our hunger for being and becoming."[5]

For desire is one of the ways we bring ourselves into being. If we do see the other through our desire, we nonetheless see ourselves, too—and we see ourselves desiring. "I am the bright mirror of desire," a woman tells her companion in "The Many Tenses of Wanting" (93). Like any specular image, our desire constructs a semblance of the real, one which may be more or less consonant with its reflected subject. Yet that gap between appearance and reality affords us significant room for maneuver, and allows us to imagine a correspondence between the way things are and the way things ought to be. We play meaningfully and articulately, for a moment at least, in the space that our desire furnishes. As a character in the final story puts it, "Desire is a figment swiftly fleeting, an ephemeral enactment upon the finite stage of the mutable world, and flesh a flame and a seeming" (192).

In that sense, desire is liberating. Rikki Ducornet recognizes the emancipatory potential of desire. Like the Surrealists, she subscribes to the dictum, "To each according to his desire!" (Hancock 15)—and she puts that notion into play, in one fashion or another, in every story in this collection. She also believes that art is intricately and necessarily bound up in human desire, not only as a vehicle to express that desire, but as a force to stimulate and enable it: "Because it does more than fulfill human needs, it inspires human desires. Art is more than a reflection of life; it is above all a *giver* of life" (Hancock 16).

Desire can be emancipatory, then; but it can also imprison us. And Fortuné is not the only character in these stories who realizes that desire has its dark side. In "The Chess Set of Ivory" a cuckolded husband unburdens himself, obliquely but nonetheless entreatingly, to his young daughter: "Father's words came quickly now; they spilled from his mouth with such urgency I could barely follow: 'Evil is a *lack,* you see,' I thought I heard him say. 'A lack, a void in which darkness rushes in, a void caused by . . . by thoughtlessness, by narcissism, by insatiable desire. Yes, desire breeds disaster' " (15). The father's reflection bears not only upon the sort of desire that leads his wife to dance, naked, with a stranger, and to befriend what seems like the entire Egyptian officer corps, "including the young Nasser" (8); he is also—and perhaps particularly—thinking of his own desire for her, and of the way that human emotion sets the terms of human catastrophe.

As the title of this book reminds us, however, desire is also a *word.* Commenting on Rikki Ducornet's early writings, Geoff Hancock remarked, "What makes Rikki's work unique is a particular vision of poetry and prose that attempts to raise the word to the level of talisman" (Hancock 13). That talismanic status accorded to the word is apparent throughout *The Word "Desire."* Each of these stories insists, in different but mutually complementary manners, upon the word as a vehicle of desire, and upon language as a vector of sexuality. André Breton once argued that the reciprocal relations of words in combination could be thought of as erotic in nature,[6] and a similar suggestion is put forward in *The Word "Desire."* Words and the tales they tell are objects of intense longing here, where storytelling is cast as a dynamic of desire. Simply stated, what this book proposes to its readers is a meditation on desiring words.

The title story is about a couple who have been lovers for two years. As the woman considers their life together, she reflects upon the word "desire": "She is luxuriating, gazing out, thinking how the word 'desire' illuminates their lives; how far the word 'desire' has taken them" (188). Ducornet's strategy in this story is emblematic of her broader praxis in the book as a whole. Here, her writerly gaze is focused closely upon a word. She scrutinizes that word from a variety of angles, turning it now this way, now that, each time grafting different connotational possibilities to it. "She thinks: *How far the word "desire" goes! How it tugs us along! How it worries us, daggers us! How it lights our path!*" (191). As her text iterates that word and invests it with more and more meaning, the word assumes a sort of incantatory power, and begins to *perform* what it denotes. In that perspective Ducornet's writing in *The Word "Desire"* is animated by the same impulse that the heroine of the title story experiences: "the will to *be* desire, to be the infinite faces of desire; to be one word and that word is 'desire' " (193).

Gradually, though, it becomes apparent that the role of the word *desire* is vaster still. Massively overdetermined, performative, promoted from lexical integer to talisman, the word functions here as a different sort of sign. Each time we see it, we are reminded that it figures in the title of the book, and we are thereby coaxed to read these stories as metaliterary fables. That is, whatever other tales they may tell, all of the texts in *The Word "Desire"* stage a narrative of literary desire. The many images of extraordinary fictional books embedded in the text confirm that impression. *Das Wunderbuch,* a book containing the "marvels of nature" (57), is a good example, as is the equally marvelous work of an archaeologist who *desires* to write about her life in the desert and the desert of her life: "This time her project is a book, the visions of a dreamer, the dreamer of the Sahara she has become" (110). The metafictional discourse in *The Word "Desire"* is insistent (as indeed it is in all of Rikki Ducornet's writings[7]), yet it is elaborated with great subtlety and nuance. It hinges, moreover, firmly upon the word, for each of these texts is a parable of literary desire. Or, more specifically, of the way writerly desire—the desire to tell—and readerly desire—the desire to be told—find articulation in a tale.

Here again, there are many images in the text that serve to emblazon that dynamic pungently. A young boy begs a girl whom he loves to tell him a scary story; a woman and her analyst pursue their desire for truth in the narratives of psychoanalysis; a mother tells Madame Roseveine de la Roulette's tale of a hermit crab who has abandoned his shell in order to inhabit an ivory pipe, as her children listen raptly; two friends from very different cultures meet and connect closely with each other on the isotopical and infinite ground of the story: "they will exchange the stories of their lives, which, now that they have begun to tell them, could prove to be without end" (112-13). In each case, narrative offers people the same sort of marvelous possibility through its desiring words, a possibility that the narrator of "The Many Tenses of Wanting" formulates to her companion in the following manner: "You see—I expect wonders of another sort from you, from us; yes: our minds will catch fire" (94).

Like her, each of the stories in this book is a "bright mirror of desire." But on both sides of the mirror, that image is doubled—and indeed cannily duplicitous, in the highest specular tradition.[8] For one of the ideas that *The Word "Desire"* promotes most convincingly is the notion that sensual desire and creative desire, the needs of the body and the needs of the mind, erotic longing and narrative longing, cannot be disintricated, if one wishes to consider them in their plenitude. "All things of importance have a tendency to inscribe themselves on the sensile pages of our vivid histories," muses a character after listening to the story of the hermit crab (40). Like him, Rikki Ducornet recognizes that narratives are both textual and sexual, an encoding and expression of both writerly and readerly desire. More indelibly than anything else, that is what is inscribed on the "sensile pages" of this luminous book.

NOTES

[1]See Charlotte Innes's remarks about Ducornet's fiction in "Through the Looking-Glass," *Nation* 258.22 (6 June 1994): "If Ducornet's stories have the sturdy legs of social relevance, their dress is fantastic. All the novels are set in the past, mostly in the late nineteenth century or the first half of the twentieth. All are set outside the United States—in France, England, South America, Egypt—though a few short stories are U.S.-based and treat modern themes. Yet even when the books mention real events like the German invasion of France in *Entering Fire* and *The Fountains of Neptune,* or real people like Charles Dodgson in *The Jade Cabinet* (which is indebted to his playful style), they seem to be set not quite in those times or places but in some imagined, timeless, dreamlike version of them. It's as if Ducornet needs this distance, as a paper with a vague wash on which she can freely paint her own ideas and question some age-old notions" (811).

[2]Rikki Ducornet, *The Word "Desire"* (New York: Henry Holt, 1997), 162; hereafter cited parenthetically.

[3]My thanks to Ross Chambers for drawing my attention to Ackerley's writings.

[4]J. H. Matthews, "Rikki Ducornet's Non-Nonsense Almost-Fairy Tales," *Symposium* 42.4 (1989): 319.

[5]Geoff Hancock, "An Interview with Rikki," *Canadian Fiction Magazine* 44 (1982): 21; hereafter cited parenthetically.

[6]See Gabriel Bounoure, *Edmond Jabès: La demeure et le livre* (Montpellier: Fata Morgana, 1984), 36.

[7]See her remarks in the Hancock interview. Questioned about the influence of the surrealists on her work, she suggests that surrealism is for her more a "life force" than a literary model, "But the writers who have *affected* me the most are the metafictionists: Coover, Gass, Borges, Beckett, Nabokov, Angela Carter, García Márquez and Asturias" (15).

[8]See Ducornet's observation about metafiction's subject: "As I see it, metafiction is concerned with the multiple aspects of perception and so the *duplicity* of perception . . . the transience of truth. Perceptions may replace action. Or subvert it. Distort it. Transform it" (Hancock 17).

A Rikki Ducornet Checklist

Novels

The Stain. London: Chatto & Windus, 1984; New York: Grove, 1984; rev. ed., Normal, IL: Dalkey Archive Press, 1995.

Entering Fire. London: Chatto & Windus, 1986; San Francisco: City Lights, 1986.

The Fountains of Neptune. Toronto: McClelland & Steward, 1989; Elmwood Park, IL: Dalkey Archive Press, 1992.

The Jade Cabinet. Normal, IL: Dalkey Archive Press, 1993.

Phosphor in Dreamland. Normal, IL: Dalkey Archive Press, 1995.

Collected Short Fiction

The Butcher's Tales. Toronto: Aya Press, 1980.

Haddock's Eyes. Les Editions du Fourneau, 1987.

The Butcher's Tales (short version). London: Atlas Press, 1991.

The Volatilized Ceiling of Baron Munodi (with illustrations by the author). Les Indes Oniriques, 1991. Includes French translation as *Les Plafonds volatilisés du Baron Munodi.*

The Butcher's Tales (selections). Toronto: Aya Press, 1980; London: Atlas Press, 1992.

Saida. Editions du Fourneau, 1993.

The Complete Butcher's Tales. Normal, IL: Dalkey Archive Press, 1994.

The Word "Desire." New York: Henry Holt, 1997.

Poetry

From the Star Chamber. Fredericton, New Brunswick: Fiddlehead Poetry Books, 1974.

Wild Geraniums. Actual Size Press, 1975.

Weird Sisters. Intermedia, 1976.

Knife's Notebook. Fredericton, New Brunswick: Fiddlehead Poetry Books, 1977.

The Illustrated Universe. Toronto: Aya Press, 1979.

The Cult of Seizure. Erin, Ontario: Porcupine's Quill, 1989.

Children's Books

The Blue Bird. New York: Knopf, 1970.

Shazira Shazam and the Devil. New York: Prentice-Hall, 1972; Junior Literary Guild, 1973.

Illustrations

Robert Coover. *Spanking the Maid.* Columbia, SC: 1981.
Jorge Luis Borges. *Tlön, Uqbar and Orbis Tertius.* Erin, Ontario: Porcupine's Quill, 1983.
Karen Elizabeth Gordon, *Torn Wings and Fauz Pas.* New York: Pantheon, 1997.

Rikki Ducornet

Photograph by Forrest Gander, 1997

Book Reviews

Franz Kafka. *The Castle*. Trans. and preface by Mark Harman. Afterword by Malcolm Pasley. Shocken, 1998. 328 pp. $25.00.

This new translation of Kafka's *The Castle* comes heralded by its publisher as "a Kafka for the twenty-first century," a claim made with one eye cast uneasily backward at the famous and earliest English translation of 1930 by Willa and Edwin Muir. It is the Muirs' translations of Kafka's stories and novels, after all, that first brought international acclaim, in the English-speaking parts of the world, to a then relatively unknown writer of highly idiosyncratic and demanding German prose. Arthur Samuelson, whose publisher's note is otherwise filled with valuable information regarding Max Brod's German edition, has almost nothing to say about the Muirs. Mark Harman, in his translator's preface, passes brusquely over the Muirs' considerable accomplishments; his somewhat misleading reference to the Muirs as "a gifted Scottish couple" can only be seen as an attempt to escape his rivals' shadow. Who can blame him? In addition to being an accomplished translator, Edwin Muir was himself a poet of extraordinary power. One can hardly do better than to pick up a copy of his *Collected Poems* to recall exactly how good a poet he was.

Nonetheless, there is good reason to support the claims regarding Harman's translation. First, there is the matter of the Muirs' translation. To start with, that translation is now nearly seventy years old and, yes, it is beginning to show its age. Often the Muirs' language looks old-fashioned on the page—sometimes quaint. Secondly, the Muirs' explicitly religious interpretation of *The Castle* (via Max Brod) inevitably influenced their own writing and editorial decisions to a degree that is perhaps undesirable in the art of translation. Thirdly, and through no fault of the Muirs, their translation of *The Castle* is based on Brod's heavily edited German edition. Brod saw it as his primary editorial obligation to bolster and protect his dead friend's literary reputation. In regard to *The Castle,* he wanted to turn a fragmentary and unfinished manuscript into a whole and unified novel to the degree this was possible. He therefore excised material that didn't fit his own limited understanding of *The Castle* and lopped off the last chapters of the manuscript to bring the narrative to what he felt was a more logical conclusion. Furthermore, he regularized Kafka's punctuation in an effort to make the "finished" novel more readable, inserting semicolons and breaking up longer sentences; nor did he always honor Kafka's intentions regarding chapter breaks.

In the 1970s an international group of scholars led by Malcolm Pasley began reassembling the German text of *The Castle,* essentially undoing all of Brod's editorial and stylistic interventions and fixing transcription errors. Harman's translation is based on this restored text, which was finally published in 1982. His translation therefore more closely mirrors Kafka's lightly punctuated German, which makes for a book that is both stylistically less pure and unified than the Muirs' *Castle*. Unconventional punctuation, a certain stylistic unevenness, and word repetition all serve an oral function in Kafka's German. By and large, I think, Harman has successfully rendered the breathless quality of Kafka's own prose. When Harman's writing falters, as it does occasionally, it's through a desire to remain close to Pasley's German text. This new translation, which owes so much to the old one, will likely be the preferred translation for years to come. [John Kulka]

William H. Gass. *Cartesian Sonata and Other Novellas.* Knopf, 1998. 274 pp. $24.00.

William Gass regularly demonstrates how the artist's devotion is best measured by his concern for the language he cultivates; his scruple and injunction is that beauty, vision, and morality require the precision and ingenuity of sentences lovingly constructed. Indeed, the dry prairie solitudes that dominate these four novellas prove to be rich soil for linguistic enterprises. Disappointments and hatreds still sparkle with imagery and inspire alliterative runs that belie the conditions of the characters, whose funks and futilities recall those of Gass's previous Midwestern populations in *Omensetter's Luck* and *In the Heart of the Heart of the Country*.

The title novella features a poisonous marriage reminiscent of the Kohlers in *The Tunnel*. It pits airy, clairvoyant Ella Bend Hess against her abusive Caliban of a husband, Edgar—mind and matter, recoiling from one another, yet inevitably knotted together in mutual complaint. Gass again makes exquisite rhetorical capital out of such unsentimental motives as blame, anger, misogyny, guilt, and disaffection. Thus, even as "Cartesian Sonata" steeps the human spirit in a muddle of primal urges, it strives to redeem our creatureliness through style.

While "Cartesian Sonata" reworks writings going back over thirty years, the other three novellas are of recent vintage. Gass's consistency of theme and method over that period suggests that his fictions elaborate the artistic philosophy of his renowned essays. Walt Riff, an itinerant accountant and cooker of books, finds religion in the abundant, meticulously cared-for kitsch at a rural "Bed and Breakfast." Pinched, despairing, arid Emma Bishop beats a retreat into an obsession with poetry in "Emma Enters a Sentence of Elizabeth Bishop's." And Luther Penner, "The Master of Secret Revenges," refines an aesthetic of retribution in the fevered tradition of Jethro Furber, to name another of Gass's prominent fascists of the heart.

A lavish imagination is all that is lovely about any of Gass's isolated minds. In each novella, meanness or poverty sets us up for ambushes by lines too marvelous to miss. [Arthur Saltzman]

Mario Vargas Llosa. *The Notebooks of Don Rigoberto*. Trans. Edith Grossman. Farrar, Straus & Giroux, 1998. 259 pp. $23.00; Efraín Kristal. *Temptation of the Word: The Novels of Mario Vargas Llosa*. Vanderbilt Univ. Press, 1998. 256 pp. $34.95.

Erotic fiction in Latin America remains confined to the margins of cultural production. While the reader may find strategically placed erotic encounters in "mainline" fiction, the idea of focusing a work on the erotic is still not widely appreciated. *Notebooks* is a notable exception: a masterful exploration of the abyss of erotic endeavors. Such explorations constitute an abyss in that, by challenging the conventional morality that narrowly circumscribes them—and the genius of conventional morality is that a modicum of sexual life is constantly transgressing it—one must live with the constant panic of the loss of a legitimate relationship to constituted society. The fact that Don Rigoberto is more of an intellectual eroticist than a Sadeian activist provides the novel with a metafictional dimension which can be viewed as either taming erotic desire by inscribing it with complex narrative structures or as leading to a contemplation of how erotica must necessarily be an intellectual undertaking, since the brain is the one human organ most capable of unlimited sexual fulfillment.

Kristal points out in his fine study that Vargas Llosa's recent writing, including *Notebooks*, is concerned with "the importance of imagination and fantasy in curbing those irrational elements that can endanger social coexistence," that it, I assume, is better to create cultural texts of enormous erotic depth rather than to seek to pursue an erotic program with other bodies, certainly a reendorsement in favor of the latter of eros versus civilization. However, the value of Kristal's comment is, as he goes on to demonstrate in this finely nuanced examination of Vargas Llosa's literary output, that the project of containment in *Notebooks* fails and the irrationality that underpins the pursuit of eroticism cannot ultimately be contained by literature or any other form of sublimation. This may end up effectively challenging the popular image of Vargas Llosa as the 1960s committed-writer-gone-reactionary. But that depends on whether one wants to see this investment in the "inevitability of irrational propensities" as stridently challenging bourgeois decency and order and the authoritarianism they require or as doing little more than entertaining pessimistic, and therefore potentially quite dangerous, male fantasies. [David William Foster]

Anne Carson. *Autobiography of Red: A Novel in Verse*. Knopf, 1998. 149 pp. $23.00.

Translator, poet, and professor of classics Anne Carson has written a work which challenges many long-held literary oppositions: prose vs. poetry, epic vs. lyric, ancient vs. modern. This text retells the story of Geryon, a winged red monster, moving from his childhood to his love for and loss of the young boy Herakles. A parallel narrative follows the career of the ancient poet Stesichoros, original author of the myth. But the narrative appropriates

myth only to reinvent it. Notably, the book begins with an epigraph from
Gertrude Stein: "I like the feeling of words doing as they want to do and as
they have to do." Here we are immediately alerted to the fact that Carson's
"autobiography" has a Steinian twist: it is less an exploration of individual
subjectivity than an explosion of the conventions and codes on which autobiography as a genre depends. Geryon composes his own autobiography
(which begins before he can write, as a cigarette glued to a tomato), but it
is his camera that becomes increasingly important to him as the text
proceeds. The sections of the text that concern photography are the book's
most compelling and beautifully written moments. When Geryon photographs Herakles, Carson writes: "It is a photograph of the future, thought
Geryon months later when he was standing in his darkroom / looking down
at the acid bath and watching likeness come groping out of the bones." And,
despite all its masterful formal innovations, what I admire most about this
book is its emotional power. *Autobiography of Red* is an extremely moving
story of love and loss and the powers and failures of language. [Nicole
Cooley]

Julián Ríos. *Loves That Bind*. Trans. Edith Grossman. Knopf, 1998. 246 pp.
$23.00.

Ríos is the author of *Poundemonium* and *Larva: Midsummer Night's
Babel*—both published by Dalkey Archive—and he now gives us another
complex text full of wordplay (in several different languages). This elaborate, arcane fiction consists of a series of letters from Emil, the narrator,
to his missing lover. The letters are arranged alphabetically—each is a
commentary on other "love" stories: we have *Lolita, Zazie, The Good Soldier,
The Sound and the Fury, The Great Gatsby,* et al. Emil recognizes that
his life cannot be removed from the words he has read. They are, indeed,
salvation.

The letters are startling because they are filled with wild transformations of language. Puns abound: "I made so many wily wordplays with
apples and pears in pearadice, remember? that you had to plant your feet
firmly and protest. Enough! Another pearouette, no . . ." In the same letter,
based on *The Great Gatsby,* he writes: "Save me the last waltz, please,
though it's three o'clock in the morning, before the embalming begins.
Another danse macabre?" Notice that Zelda's novel is mentioned; it is
joined to Scott's remark about the dark night of the soul at three o'clock
(*The Crack-Up*).

It is easy to claim that Emil—and Ríos—cannot control his life; he,
therefore, must shape language. His letters serve as anchors because he is
drowning. The letters are desperate pleas. They are written so obsessively
that they begin to control him. He becomes, if you will, their text.

Ríos structures his complete text so that his narrator's letters seem to
take on a life of their own. The alphabet cracks when "Z," the final letter, is
reached. The letter is full of ellipses, disturbances: "Zz . . . at first it was the
buzz. That didn't let me sleep a wink last night. My fault for leaving the

window open. It was one of those Dutch mosquitoes that always buzz Zuider Zee . . . Zuider Zee . . . And when I turned on the light, it hid, I don't know where, probably beside the papered-over fly on the wall. Zz . . . when I turned the light off again."

The text remains incomplete because Emil never embraces his beloved. Although he manages to end his text with "angels"—which, of course, was the first word he used—he remains suspended. Thus he recognizes that language fails him: it cannot bind love. [Irving Malin]

Raymond Queneau. *Children of Clay*. Trans. Madeleine Velguth. Sun & Moon, 1998. 434 pp. Paper: $14.95.

Raymond Queneau's fifth novel is best known for being the outcome of his lengthy research into the obscure works of French nineteenth-century "literary lunatics": writers, philosophers, cosmologists and amateur mathematicians whose misguided ideas never succeeded in finding an audience. While such a collection would appear to be of particular interest today given the enthusiasm for raw art and post-postmodern displays of inspiration, Queneau's anthology never succeeded in finding a publisher in the 1930s, so he instead sowed these discoveries into this Depression-era novel, chronicling the Claye family's plunge from riches to rags. These motley and interwoven characters include a handful of grocers and servants, a satirically reactionary political group typical of the '30s, and, at the forefront, the research on literary lunatics undertaken by the curious master/slave dialectic of the purulent Purpulan and Chambernac, a retired professor who would bear comparison with Queneau if it wasn't for the fact that Queneau himself turns up as a character.

Craftsman that he was, Queneau managed to make all these characters tie into the novel's multiple allegories of megalomania and regeneration, but one cannot help but feel that *Children of Clay* would ultimately have served better as two books, with his original, unrecycled anthology of lunatics standing on its own. Perhaps not the best novel with which the newcomer to Queneau should start, *Children of Clay* has nevertheless been a crucial absence from his presence in English, an absence due at least in part to the translation difficulties which the book must have posed (lunatics don't always make for lucid writing). However, Madeleine Velguth, whose inventive rendition of Queneau's *Chêne et Chien* slipped by unnoticed a few years ago, has done an admirable job, and her own appendix of Queneau's lunatics is in itself an invaluable bibliography. [Marc Lowenthal]

Steven Millhauser. *The Knife Thrower and Other Stories*. Crown, 1998. 256 pp. $22.00.

After winning the Pulitzer for *Martin Dressler*, Millhauser returns to the short-story genre with a most impressive collection. The stories in *The*

Knife Thrower are reminiscent of his short work of the past (I think of *The Barnum Museum*) as well as his latest prize-winning novel. Yet even in the most familiar stories in *The Knife Thrower,* Millhauser breaks new ground.

Seamlessly stitched but intriguingly complex, the stories explore the fantastic and the subterranean, while relying on description and detail rather than plot development. Although some stories could be considered variations of other Millhauser themes, they expand upon the complexities of his past stories (from this collection and other works by Millhauser), informing—and thus adding to—the complexities of each new story. The ever-expanding, ever-developing department store in "The Dream of the Consortium" recalls the hotels built by Martin Dressler, as does the theme park in "Paradise Park." They are the products of obsessive-compulsive capitalists who exhaust the possibilities of consumerism by creating absurd, elite versions of "superstores" which seek to create an environment that will fulfill—even surpass—our consumer needs. Paradise Park, for example, becomes an abyss for its mysterious proprietor, Charles Sarabee, as well as its visitors. The park's popularity increases as new "rides, new spectacles, new thrills" are added, at least five every year. Sarabee continues to create increasingly elaborate rides and spectacles until he extends the park to an enormous underground level, featuring "thrills" and pleasures that seemingly transcend reality—merry-go-rounds with bucking broncos, rollercoasters with gaps in the tracks. He digs deeper, literally, and adds yet another level where visitors discover lakes and woodland areas, waterfalls, but also Turkish palaces, concubines, Spanish galleons, the experience of being buried alive in a coffin. Paradise Park is development turned decadence.

Other stories in this collection succeed on their simplicity. "Clair de Lune" and "Balloon Flight, 1870" are dreamlike, playing on more intimate desires and anxieties. Still other stories, such as "A Visit" and the title story, are masterfully surreal and bewildering. *The Knife Thrower* is, indeed, a brilliant collection. It is vintage Millhauser: chimerical, disturbing, immaculate, sublime. [Christopher Paddock]

Marguerite Duras. *Writing.* Trans. Mark Polizzotti. Lumen Editions, 1998. 78 pp. Paper: $14.95.

"My books come from this house," Marguerite Duras writes in the title essay of this her last book. "From this light as well, and from the garden. From the light reflecting off the pond. It has taken me twenty years to write what I just said." If this essay tells us what a lifetime of writing has taught Duras about what it is possible to say, the brief memoir in the book, "Death of the Young British Pilot," returns us to its genesis and we see how everything was there from the beginning. "I know it isn't a story," she writes of the pilot. "It's a brutal, isolated fact, without reverberation." The memoir is an account of a twenty-year-old British pilot whose plane has been shot down over Duras's town during the Second World War and who is killed by the Germans. Several years after the war an older Englishman visits the town to find out what has happened to the pilot, and it is from him that the town learns his name and age. As the Englishman visits the grave year after year, the town learns, as Duras makes clear, something about love, and Duras writes of the pilot to remember her own love for her younger brother who died during the same war half a world away and whose body was shoveled into a mass pit. In her account half a century later, we find everything that was ever to interest Duras: some early trauma that would mark a lifetime; loss never resolved; love almost always inextricable from loss; memories one would never forget. We also see, briefly, in this memoir of the pilot and extensively in the title essay, how Duras writes. To make of anything, story, literature, fiction, call it what you will, is to compromise the experience she writes about. All her writing draws our attention to what cannot be said: her words evoke silence, her sentences isolate the space between. Once the writer ceases to doubt everything she has written she ceases to be a writer. "There are often narratives," Duras writes, "but very seldom writing." Only if one is alone facing the empty page that words can never fill can one make sense of the persistence of memory, the inevitability of loss, the tenacity of love. [Robert Buckeye]

Charles Bukowski. *The Captain Is Out to Lunch and the Sailors Have Taken Over the Ship*. Black Sparrow, 1998. Illustrations by Robert Crumb. 144 pp. $27.50; paper: $14.00.

These intermittent journal entries (8-28-91 to 2-27-93) provide literary insights and personal glimpses. Many dwell on the boredom, ugliness, and depression of racetracks. The author encounters common cybernetic setbacks (cat spray in the hard drive) as well as welcome convenience. He has become a model of professionalism in manuscript preparation. More nihilist than Marxist, he suggests that he "never wrote any social protest stuff" because "you really can't make something good out of something that isn't there." A sequence detailing a zany project for a sitcom based on Bukowski's life has the understated hilarity of his funnier stories, as have the recurrences of a curmudgeonly senile neighbor. A mellower misanthropist, Buk drinks in moderation, suffers television for his wife's company, and enjoys a productive year of what he considers (and I concur) the best poems and stories of his life. There are lapses, inevitably, into the same old shinola: hell is a poetry reading. Most humans are either "subnormals" or their defenders. He's run out of good books to read. Unwitting postmodernist, he laments having missed the '20s, while paradoxically continuing to exhibit Harold Bloom's "anxiety of influence" towards Hemingway. Gradually, though, the book takes on tragic overtones with the first symptoms of leukemia in June, 1992. He struggles with his hard-boiled parody/fantasy, *Pulp*. He begins to put his house in order. Having survived so much, he can barely credit his mortality. It would be instructive to be told how much, if at all, these journals were posthumously edited. Nevertheless, these reflections approaching endgame reveal the complex humanity of a too-often-caricatured figure who beat seemingly prohibitive odds to achieve the destiny he came to embrace as a world-class writer of uncompromising novels, stories, and poems. Robert Crumb's illustrations are perfect. [Gerald Locklin]

Michel Tournier. *Gemini.* Trans. Anne Carter. Johns Hopkins Univ. Press, 1998. 452 pp. Paper: $15.95.

One important question we ask concerning an artist is this: to what degree does his description or interpretation of the world intend to transform it? Repeatedly Tournier has taken up the hat of some conventional story of our culture, Robinson Crusoe, Jeanne d'Arc, and resewn it into gloves.

Gemini (*Les Météores,* 1975) is Tournier's third novel and, in its integration of conflicting impulses and its lisibility, perhaps his most successful. *Friday* emerged in 1967 to win the Grand Prix de l'Académie Française; *The Ogre* took the Prix Goncourt three years later. Only with *The Four Wise Men* (1980) did Tournier gain attention here in the States. At home, for all his award winning, he remains a bowl-sized lump in the literary oatmeal, an earnest didact at odds with both the modernist tradition and the gospel of human progress.

That there is in Tournier a compulsiveness of intellect often in conflict with his brief as a novelist, only a fool would contest. In *The Mirror of Ideas,* he sketched the world as a rain of dualities. *Gemini,* with its tale of twins so indistinguishable that even their parents refer to them collectively as Jean-Paul, hangs from the same branch. The twins are a world to themselves, speaking their own language, minds and bodies intimately bound. But as they mature, Jean rebels, sailing off into that shadowy, besieged outer world. Paul, deeply rent, follows. Where once was unity, now everything bespeaks the twin's separateness: Venice's mirrored halls, Japanese Zen gardens, the Berlin wall.

In all Tournier's work, it is as though on one hand he longs to diagram the world, to reduce it to schemata, and on the other, taking up again these old stories, somehow to remythologize them, to make them large again. From the pitched battle between these two urges, when he is at his best, Tournier generates tremendous energy. And in *Gemini* he is, make no mistake of it, at his best. [James Sallis]

Milorad Pavić. *Last Love in Constantinople: A Tarot Novel for Divination.* Trans. Christina Pribichevich-Zorić. Dufour, 1998. 184 pp. $23.95.

Milorad Pavić cannot help but create a text that extends the conventional boundaries of the novel: his *Dictionary of the Khazars* is perhaps the most genuinely realized example of hypertext this side of cyberspace, allowing the reader to begin virtually at any point in the novel and digress ad infinitum; *Landscape Painted with Tea* is a novel that takes the form of a crossword puzzle; *The Inner Side of the Wind* can be read from front to back as well as back to front. Equally ambitious in its ingenuity is *Last Love in Constantinople,* which proves to be a worthy addition to the impressive oeuvre of a literary pioneer.

Last Love is a novel divided into the twenty-two cards, or "keys," of the Major Arcana, which together with the fifty-six cards of the Minor Aracana comprise the Tarot. Provided in the novel's three appendixes are the actual cards of the Major Arcana, instructions as to how the reader can set up the cards for a reading, and interpretations of the cards/keys. The reader has the option of reading the novel straight through or reading it as designated by a Tarot reading. The latter option is clearly the more intriguing of the two, especially after it is understood that each card can have two completely different meanings depending on whether it is right side up or upside down. The structure alone implies a stunning multiplicity: the book is potentially ordered in a different way every time it is engaged. Such engagement is further enriched by the process of interpretation, wherein lies the most ingenious result of the novel.

Each card/key is already supplied with multiple interpretations: a narrative and what one must assume are traditional "meanings" of the cards (depending on their respected positions) supplied in appendix 2. When the reader lets the cards decide the order of the novel, the meanings of the cards complement and/or complicate the corresponding passages which make up the novel, and vice versa. Furthermore, the cards and their corresponding narratives must be interpreted in relation to the order they compose. Not only does this structure rival Pavić's *Dictionary* for its postmodern inventiveness, it also provokes the reader to reflect upon conventional modes of interpretation. Nothing can be left unevaluated.

Pavić is known for his idiosyncratic style; beautifully lucid yet non-sequential sentences enhance the magical-realist quality of his work. But at times, the prose in *Last Love* is too abstract, even awkward. Still, the wit and charm of Pavić's writing outweigh the inconsistencies. [Christopher Paddock]

Milan Kundera. *Identity.* Trans. Linda Asher. Harper Flamingo, 1998. 168 pp. $22.00.

Chantal and Jean-Marc take a holiday. After a series of both comic and bitter misunderstandings, but most of all French as in farce, the two grow apart. Everything they interpret, they mistake: politeness for protective-ness, caring for manipulation, and so on. In any other Kundera novel the two would be among a number of couples, but in *Identity* they are alone. Even the narrator abandons them, to think thoughts a Kundera narrator would think. I counted one small narrative intrusion, at the end, rounding out what reads like an especially wicked, ironic fable minus the moralizing.

The reader of Kundera's longer novels inhabits large houses of fiction. The rooms are furnished in various styles, with characters coming forward or blending into the wallpaper as needed. *Identity* and the 1995 novel *Slowness* are, by comparison, single rooms. They are chamber works to the earlier symphonies. Where the other novels are in parts (five of the novels have seven), the two newest novels are divided into fifty-one short chapters. Determining what accounts for this aesthetic isn't easy. It may be language: Kundera wrote both in French and the other novels in Czech. Or it may be expectations. In an interview Kundera says although he admires Robert Musil's *The Man Without Qualities,* he cannot admire its endless length, comparing it to a castle too big to be seen. Since Kundera's short novels are pessimistic works, soaked in anger but leavened by irony, and written against the fate of the self caught in the epidemic of speed, the crush of boredom, and the culture of dissatisfaction, it may be that Kundera sees his seven-section symphonies as exceeding our limits. A third possibility exists: the two newest novels are part of an on-going body of shorter works, a suite of fictional rooms, each centered on an existential question—what happens to the self; first in the age of speed, then when it's stripped of identity? [Paul Maliszewski]

John Edgar Wideman. *Two Cities.* Houghton Mifflin, 1998. 256 pp. $24.00.

In many ways, *Two Cities* feels like a culmination of Wideman's earlier work, and is especially reminiscent of *Philadelphia Fire.* In fact, one of the narrative strains in the book revisits the story of the Afrocentric group MOVE which Wideman so powerfully told in his earlier novel. However, *Two Cities* is more narrativistic and contemplative than the more textually complex and perhaps angrier *Philadelphia Fire.* The result is a novel that maintains the thematic intensity of Wideman's earlier fiction and essays, yet adopts a softer, more haunting tone. This shift in tone feels perfectly suited to what is at stake in *Two Cities.* The novel ponders the disparities between perception and memory. Everywhere there is slippage; nothing is as it was. As the character Robert Jones says in one of his never-to-be-sent letters to the sculptor Alberto Giacometti, "When you turn from the model to shape a portrait or clay figure, it's memory and habit, not sight, that guide your hand." As with this sculptor, the characters of the story are constantly confronting their pasts, coming to grips with their memories and habits in hopes to overcome their limitations. As the relationships in this novel demonstrate, such struggles themselves may indeed be works of art. This concern with the motion of memory is also embodied in the novel's structure. It opens with Jones reading, tasting the definitions of words in the dictionary. The last he reads is "Zugunruhe . . . A noun—the migratory drive." The word is picked up again by Wideman as the title for a page-long postscript, thus framing the novel with the sense of instinctual movement across space and time. The novel comes to reside, then, within the crux of how to reconcile this impulse toward newness with the persistence of memory and habit. [Robert Zamsky]

Marcel Bénabou. *Jacob, Menahem & Mimoun: A Family Epic.* Trans. Steven Rendall. Preface by Warren Motte. Univ. of Nebraska Press, 1998. 222 pp. $30.00.

This is a book about the book Marcel Bénabou was trying to write. Originally Bénabou (a member of the Oulipo group, founded in 1960 by Raymond Queneau and joined by writers such as Italo Calvino and Harry Mathews) chose as his title "One Always Writes the Same Book," in the playful spirit of his earlier *Why I Have Not Written Any of My Books.* In this book he describes so many approaches, schemes and structures taken up and abandoned. In a chapter called "Resources" he writes of a plan wherein "Moroccan Judaism would be put through the sieve of all the disciplines." In "Models" he describes how he surveyed the Jewish tradition looking for heroic figures, contemplated the use of the synagogue as an architectural device, and reflected upon literary antecedents (Homer, Virgil, Joyce, Proust) for what they could supply. What genre was appropriate to his subject? Epic, novel, family history, tragedy? In the end, he realizes a "different goal": to make "the unfinished and unfinishable book not an unfortunate result of my incompetence, but rather a genuine literary genre with its own norms and rules." What we have before us then is the very book he was trying to write all along, in a language whose clarity, luminosity and beauty call to mind Proust, Leiris and Jabès.

   This is a book about memory and history, the way personal memory and family history intersect and depart from a collective, historical memory and experience of a specific people at a specific moment in time. Bénabou, a Moroccan Jew, tries to make sense of the Holocaust and the amazing logic sparing him that fate. And, upon migrating to Paris, he ponders his relation both to Morocco and to Western Europe. Particular memories resonate: recollections of family members (especially his mother), celebrations of the high holy days, special foods, the influence of the West on the Jewish community of Meknès, learning Hebrew.

   This is, thus, a book that through language seeks in some essential way to recreate what no longer exists: a childhood, the life of the Moroccan Jewish community in the first half of this century, before Moroccan independence. Memory is the means of consolidating and preserving wholeness of self, and writing is the process by which memories are shaped, given meaning, disseminated so they will endure beyond the remembering subject. [Allen Hibbard]

W. G. Sebald. *The Rings of Saturn.* Trans. Michael Hulse. New Directions, 1998. 296 pp. $23.95.

The narrator of *The Rings of Saturn* (who both is and is not W. G. Sebald in this combination of fiction, travel writing, historical study, and memoir) makes clear again and again his fascination with the life and work of Thomas Browne. He admires, in particular, Browne's "Musaeum Clausum," a "catalogue of remarkable books . . . listing pictures, antiquities and sundry singular items." What distinguishes this catalogue for the narrator, in addition to its eclectic scope, is that, like another of his favorite texts, Borges's *Tlön, Uqbar, Orbis Tertius,* it deals with "our attempts to invent secondary or tertiary worlds"; the items in Browne's text "may have formed part of a collection put together by Browne but were more likely products of his imagination, the inventory of a treasure house that existed purely in his head and to which there is no access except through the letters on the page." In turn, Sebald's book is a similar treasure house of items. As well as being the narrator's account of a walking tour through England's East Anglia, it is a map of the author's brilliantly wandering mind, which throughout the book takes flight in various ways: into biographical sketches of the famous, the eccentric, and the forgotten; into remembrances of momentous events and places disappearing now from our world(s) and minds; and into critical analyses of artworks, treasured and fringe, as well as the possible compulsions of their creators. Binding these disparate subjects, as they commingle through past and present, are Sebald's haunting meditations on the human desire for transcendence and the limitations of the earth, the relationships between human systems and natural patterns, the frightening immediacies of and possibilities in change, and the nebulous line separating life and death. *The Rings of Saturn* is strikingly intelligent. It is beautifully written and utterly captivating. [Matthew Roberson]

Nicholson Baker. *The Everlasting Story of Nory.* Random House, 1998. 226 pp. $22.00.

Nicholson Baker, well-known for his phone-sex novel *Vox* and his voyeuristic fantasy *The Fermata,* here attempts what in some ways might be his most risky book yet. *The Everlasting Story of Nory* depicts a year in the life of a nine-year-old American girl attending school in England; its quiet, pastoral tone is more evocative of children's authors such as Robert McCloskey (whose *Make Way for Ducklings* is cited early on) than of the famed Anonymous. Yet *Nory* rigorously avoids the cliches of both the innocent childhood remembrance and the darker coming-of-age story, instead chronicling its young protagonist's chaotic thoughts and internal world at the age she is *now.* This is Baker's forte, of course; as in all his novels, which stretch and pull a single moment of time like taffy. *Nory* offers an absurdly detailed glimpse of the present, thus showing it to be rich and strange in its very ordinariness.

Baker pulls this off not through plot (of which there is virtually none here) but through his attention to language. While simple enough to be believable coming from a nine-year-old girl, Nory's verbal dexterity shows how both the scientist and the surrealist inhabit a child's consciousness. The book tumbles with hilarious self-explained concepts, self-defined words, self-told stories—in short, with *self.* As an intriguing foil to Nory's struggle to make meaning, Baker offers the background character of her younger brother Littleguy; his linguistic repertoire of dump trucks and bulldozers serves to remind us that "his head was still basically a construc-

tion site." Although puzzlingly scattershot at first, and verging on sentimentality throughout, Baker's latest novel rewards the reader who sticks
with it with an acutely sculpted prose that offers sheer and unabashed
delight. [Eric Lorberer]

Fleur Jaeggy. *Last Vanities*. Trans. Tim Parks. New Directions, 1998. 95 pp.
Paper: $11.95.

Jaeggy's novel, *Sweet Days of Discipline,* which was published by New
Directions in 1993, still haunts me. Although it is about the "sweetness" of
"bondage" in a convent school, it rises above its perverse themes; it becomes
a philosophical meditation on the limits of the codes of love. It is oddly
religious.

The seven stories of *Last Vanities* confirm Jaeggy's artistry. She offers
eerie, menacing relationships—of parents and children, of siblings, of
husbands and wives—and she refuses to hide the ambiguous nature of
these relationships. Her characters seem to walk through a dreamscape, an
environment in which unexpected motives and actions occur. Even nature
is strange: "The Föhn is dangerous, sweet and dangerous. It makes people a
bit crazy. There are even murders. For nothing. When the west wind blows.
The filth of sweetness, that's the Föhn."

The title story is especially shocking. An old married couple is bound by
obscure needs. They balance each other for almost fifty years; they do not
want to change—nor can they. The husband begins to see his wife as ill and
even though she is not, his view unsettles their disciplined, usual "roles"
(Jaeggy regards them as "actors"). Does he fear for her life? Is he afraid that
he will be alone? We are told that "Kurt leans his hands on the windowsill.
The bird seems to be dancing, tracing out an ellipse. He has already thrown
one leg over the sill, and now he lifts the other over too. His body is lighter
than a thought." Why does Kurt, the husband, kill himself? Does he recognize that he can never regain the happiness of his long marriage? Does he
want to "kill" his wife by radically changing her condition as wife? The
questions become as "thoughtful" as his falling body (Jaeggy assumes that
mind and matter are balanced in a secretive way). The story ends on an
ambiguous note: "Verena is happy. Now she too stares at the sky, as her
husband did before her. One day perhaps, to be even nearer the sky, she too
will throw herself down." Does she want to find Kurt and renew vows?

I have probably lingered on this last story because it violates the norms
of old age, of marriage; but this story seems to be the ambiguous end of the
other six stories. All of them employ paradox, oxymoron, and irony as they
"sweetly" violate our perceptions of "normal" behavior. [Irving Malin]

Ken Kalfus. *Thirst*. Milkweed Editions, 1998. 205 pp. $16.00.

Ken Kalfus dedicates his first collection of fiction to his wife, but he follows her name with thirteen street names, ranging from "Route 202" to "Rue de la Sorbonne" to "Kutuzovsky Prospekt." This unusual overture to geography makes sense after the first few stories in the collection. Kalfus's fiction is unwilling to sit still for very long. No two stories take place in even remotely the same location, but beyond that, they take on a range of perspectives, subjects, and styles so broad that they threaten to break out of their two hundred pages. The author and his characters are in perpetual motion, and as a result the collection reads quickly.

This restlessness is welcome; a first collection of fiction should be ambitious and discontent with any single niche. It would be impossible to label Kalfus, whose stories are about topics as familiar to short fiction as infidelity and a young woman confronting her sexuality for the first time while traveling abroad; but also as unusual as the choices that go into choosing a suit for a young man accused of dealing heroin, or the mind of a Florida retiree whose death takes the form of a return trip to a New York blanketed by an eternal snowstorm.

For all of its experimentation and inventiveness, the stories in *Thirst* occasionally bear too strong a mark of another author. "Rope Bridge," for instance, takes its style, subject, and characterization directly from Updike, and "Invisible Malls" is similarly indebted to Calvino. These writers are, of course, excellent teachers, and these stories could be considered Kalfus's homage to them. Yet it is most exciting to see the author doing his own thing. His fiction is confident and imaginative, and although it is impossible to tell where he will go from here, it is bound to be worth the trip. [D. Quentin Miller]

Charles Olson. *Call Me Ishmael.* New afterword by Merton M. Sealts, Jr. Johns Hopkins Univ. Press, 1997. 158 pp. Paper: $13.95.

In 1938, Charles Olson publishes "Lear and Moby Dick" in *Twice-a-Year* and months later withdraws from the doctoral program in American studies at Harvard University. During the war years, he works in the Roosevelt administration, but in 1945, he resigns his office and within weeks is at work on *Call Me Ishmael*. Lewis Mumford and F. O. Matthiessen advised Harcourt, Brace not to publish the Olson book, while T. S. Eliot thought there was little interest in Melville among the British. When it was published in 1947, Mumford thought it a failure, Carl Van Doren a disappointment, Stanley Edgar Hyman half coherent mumbo jumbo. Ostensibly a critical study on Melville in which Olson establishes the influence of Shakespeare and others on the writing of *Moby-Dick*, particularly Melville's reading of *King Lear* between the first version of the novel and the second, the Olson book is, in addition, something more, something else. It is, in the first place, his response to formal academic study, including his own "Lear and Moby Dick," left unsaid when he left Harvard. It is also his effort to reposition literature in relation to the life of the republic. Finally, it establishes Olson's own paternity in the line of Melville, which would become increasingly clearer in the years after the publication of *Call Me*

Ishmael, when Olson, like Melville before him, had become "homeless in his land, his society." Guy Davenport begins his memoir of Olson in his last years with, "In Gloom at Watch-House Point."

The thing is to be of use, Olson repeated over and over, in whatever context. Literature, its criticism, was a means to address the actual, make contact, put our house in order. Any work was charged with the life, the life with the land, the land with its past. Melville was our original, Olson writes, aboriginal, a dreamer, and thus it was crucial for him to be saved from the resentfully competent, the bean counters. The challenge set down by Olson in 1947 remains, and the reprint of *Call Me Ishmael* a half century later is a call we need to heed, a reminder of what yet needs to be accomplished. "One is fighting for one's life," Robert Creeley says, "and always was." [Robert Buckeye]

Calvert Casey. *The Collected Stories.* Trans. John H. R. Polt. Ed. and introduction by Ilan Stavans. Duke Univ. Press, 1998. 193 pp. Paper: $16.95.

Duke University Press has done a great service in bringing our attention to the writings of Calvert Casey (1924-1969), an author who, despite early praise from Italo Calvino and others, has been lost to us. Casey was born in Baltimore, worked in England, India, Canada, Turkey, Switzerland, and Italy (he committed suicide in Rome), but he identified primarily with Cuba. Cuba is the place that preoccupies most of his writing. In fact, several stories, but especially "The Walk," feel like a darker version of *Dubliners* transplanted to Havana. But what a difference a city makes.

The collection contains all of Casey's known fiction (sixteen stories and one novella). However, this brief sample encompasses a vast world; it gives us a glimpse into the mind of a visionary stylist. I'm not sure that I would describe Casey's stories as magical realism, but each piece does peek into a mysterious world where people and their environs seem ordinary at first, but are then overcome by a veil of the vague, bizarre, troubling, and incomprehensible. These are tales of mystery and menace. They are less character studies or well-drawn-out plots than misty etchings of disturbed moods and desires. Most of the stories are passionate interludes describing obsessive yearnings and romantic matches that always fail. Other stories explore the sleazy beauty and beautiful sleaze of life on the fringes of Havana. Viewed together, all the pieces owe much to Kafka in their haunted, nightmare aesthetic. Tales like "Homecoming," "The Sun," "Piazza Margana," "The Visitors," and "The Execution" are powerful works of the imagination that should be read, reread, and included in prominent anthologies. Let's not lose Calvert Casey again. [David Ian Paddy]

Jerome Charyn. *Death of a Tango King*. New York Univ. Press, 1998. 242 pp. $21.95.

This is Charyn's first novel to diverge from his New York series centered on police officer Isaac Sidel. But even here New York gives us our point of departure. A Latina prison inmate, Yolanda, is given a chance of release when a visiting professor invites her to join an organization called the Christian Commandos, a bank of free-ranging ecologists. This episode sets a keynote for a novel where nobody is quite what s/he seems. The professor is not accredited, his organization is not quite civil servants and they operate in a "no-man's-land." The plan is to take Yolanda to meet her long-lost cousin Ruben Falcone, now king of the Medellín drug cartel. For her to turn informant? she asks. No, to protect the Colombian forests which the security agencies are destroying in their pursuit of Falcone. Yolanda is trained apparently for covert action and then taken to Colombia and from this point on the novel becomes increasingly fantastic. Yolanda's role is as a well-meaning witness to the extremes of Colombian wealth and poverty, and to the shifting relations between the rival drug barons. With the rapid pace typical of Charyn's narratives, she hears of Gaudi the legendary tango dancer turned political boss; Bailen the novelist turned president; and above all meets her cousin Ruben, the most fantastic of them all. He is an artist of guises, shifting in a flash from thug to latter-day Robin Hood, a companion with equal ease to street urchins and the president of the United States. If Ruben is Charyn's Kurtz whom Yolanda encounters on her journey into the heart of darkest Colombia, he remains as ambiguous and elusive as his prototype. [David Seed]

Wang Chen-ho. *Rose, Rose, I Love You*. Trans. Howard Goldblatt. Columbia Univ. Press, 1998. 183 pp. $22.95.

Originally published in 1984, this is the first novel by the noted Taiwanese writer Wang Chen-ho to be translated into English. From a variety of perspectives and narrative voices, it recounts the preparations made in the seaside town of Hualien, Taiwan, for the arrival of three hundred American soldiers on R & R from combat during the Vietnam War. Ending before the soldiers even arrive, the novel can be read as a satirical fable of what happens when a small non-Western economy decides to join the game of modernization and international free enterprise. Wang presents an amusing handful of main characters, chief among whom is the obese, mercilessly flatulent English teacher Dong Siwen. With the help of his friends—Councilman Qian, who was elected because he dared to pull down his pants in public, and Dr. Yun Songzhu, a married Christian man whose medical examinations are excuses to fondle young men—as well as the grudging cooperation of Hualien's "Big 4" brothel proprietors, Dong initiates an outlandish and costly enterprise. His self-appointed mission is to turn Hualien's "raw material," its prostitutes, into a marketable "product" by training them in conversational English, modern hygiene, and American culture. The novel's title refers both to a popular Mandarin song and to "Saigon Rose," a notorious strain of VD that represents one of the many forms of pollution that preoccupy Wang's characters. The pollution, however, threatens to work both ways: not only do Dong and his associates fear the disastrous results that would follow from offering the Americans "polluted raw material," but the prostitutes, pimps, and madams of Hualien uneasily anticipate the pollution that American bodies and cultural practices promise to bring to their community. This scatological, episodic, ambivalent narrative offers several hilarious yet complex dramatizations of attitudes toward Western economic and cultural influence, and it well deserves the attention of anyone interested in postcolonial fiction. [Thomas Hove]

Alison Bundy. *DunceCap*. Burning Deck, 1998. 126 pp. Paper: $10.00.

A truly epigrammatic prose can be difficult to pull off in English—not least because it's a French specialty, to which anglophone writers have to find their way indirectly. The thirty-one fictions contained in *DunceCap* average between one and five pages in length (and they're small pages, in Burning Deck's pocket-sized edition); their economy is at once playful and finely controlled, reticent and suggestive. Bundy's miniatures include terse monologues ("Meanwhile—I stand,—or think I stand—in the middle of the road,—eagerly,—oh tenderly . . ."), cameos, prose poems, and parables with wry, Stevens-esque titles ("Restrained Theory on the Disappearance of Women," "Primary Rule for Writing Popular Romance," "Unsolicited Commentary"). Bundy is at her best in these last, tracing the persistence of desire with a mournful wit reminiscent of the best work of Lydia Davis: "I stood still on the path for a minute, thinking I heard a creature moving behind us, or alongside us, and my heart beat rapidly, as if I were in a movie. I looked up through the branches to the sky." A mysterious infant interrupts a narrator's morning walk; a mock-essayist objects to the pampering of chihuahuas; a group of diners interrogate a steak—these configurations verge on allegory even as they deflect it with ironical apostrophe and mock high diction: "He stood by the fence and sucked on a stone and called it companion, and was notorious." The real virtues of *DunceCap,* though, are formal. It reads like the contents of a costume jewelry box—each item oddly wrought in a new way, with a philosophic modesty that's rare in self-conscious "play." [Brian Lennon]

Kristin Prevallet. *Perturbation, My Sister.* First Intensity, 1997. 80 pp. Paper: $10.00.

In its preface, this book offers itself as a reading of surrealist Max Ernst's collage novel *The Hundred Headless Women* (1929). Prevallet defines her writing strategy as "writing one paragraph for each collage, and then rearranging the order of paragraphs to fit into my own chapters." Thus, the text does not simply appropriate Ernst's use of collage but rather it re-invents the art form itself. Prevallet does not narrate Ernst's collages—in other words, she does not perform an explanatory function—but rather she complicates and unsettles Ernst's terrain. Structured into nine parts, the book follows an associative rather than a linear logic; as if it were a long poem, elliptical and full of silences, we can track motifs and tropes through-out the text. Prevallet writes: "She fainted at the sight of so many frag-ments, for she thought her mind was frazzled. Luckily, it was just the world, crumbling around her." Fragments function as textual poetics, yet this text takes enormous pleasure in its brokenness. In fact, everywhere in the book is a sense of play. Interestingly, the preface employs the language of psychoanalysis—with references to Freud's work on dreams, jokes and the unconscious. Indeed, the dreamlike world of this book includes not only people but also phantoms, birds and wolves, and the settings are various, among them a garden full of plastic flowers, the winter Alps and the Seine. *Perturbation, My Sister* raises a number of compelling questions, such as what is the relationship between text and image? between modernism and postmodernism? and, finally, between dream and the act of writing? [Nicole Cooley]

———————

Jason Schwartz. *A German Picturesque.* Knopf, 1998. 133 pp. $21.00.

A German Picturesque, Jason Schwartz's first book, takes as its central topic the static objectification of what is seen. With many of these stories either devoid of actions and characters or with these elements taking only a secondary role, small things—the curve in a sleeve, a winter scene on a dish, a shining spot on a doorknob—take on a curious power that somehow is equal to that of the grander events these narratives hint at. The narra-tors themselves, too, are hinted at, partly visible but never quite completely visible.

Behind this stasis a sense of history and of accumulated tradition gathers. In "Staves" for instance, an effigy is discussed in ways that hint at Judas Iscariot. A postage stamp can lead to a submerged discussion of a king. The formal occasions vary as well, the stories sometimes seeming to be based on a museum tour or on where the gaze goes in the gaps of writing a letter at one's desk or on movement through an architectural space, sometimes almost partly digested descriptions of paintings or landscapes (similar to what Robbe-Grillet does in *In the Labyrinth*).

While there is some variation in scene and in the occasions each story appropriates for its form, *A German Picturesque* insists on similar devices and similar narrators from story to story, varying them only slightly, subtly. While most first books of stories tend to be a showcase for an author's range, Schwartz's book very deliberately maps an enclosed stylistic space, exhausting all its possibilities. At their best, these are striking pieces, simple yet opaque. An unusual, interesting, and somewhat claustrophobic book, *A German Picturesque* shows Schwartz operating in a style entirely his own. [Brian Evenson]

Jonathan Baumbach. *D-Tours*. FC2, 1998. 172 pp. Paper: $12.95.

Jonathan Baumbach's tenth work of fiction chronicles the Homeric detours of a Hollywood producer making his way back to the lover he left years ago at the Paradise Hotel. Each episode of this life, lived as a series of movies, is told via the topspin Baumbach puts on the cliches of movies. For example, accused of being a spy, the producer's interrogators finally elicit his true story, a tale of alien abduction which blends *The Day the Earth Stood Still*, *E.T.* and a dozen similar pictures and includes extraterrestrials landing at Disney World to return Judy Garland, Lee Harvey Oswald, Jimmy Hendrix, and other icons. Other chapters reference detective movies, movies about vampires, psychos, zombies, femme fatales, kung fu masters, huge apes, human experimentation on lost islands—all of Hollywood B-dom. In fact, the genius of the book is its ability to evoke precisely these stock films. It shares the logic of David Axel Baumbach's photo series *Stills from Imaginary Movies*, which a dedication says inspired the novel: elements of a film genre are combined in such a way as to evoke its mythologies, if not any particular movie. Its weakness is that in episodically taking on all of these genres, the point to which the gags are put isn't so much developed by the book as used as a framing device. Just as time has made these movies simultaneously cornball and arch ("I vant to drink your blood" evokes laughs of recognition), the novel reads like an extended comedy routine, one that might have worked better as a novella. When the story does come out the other end of its murders and chase scenes, though, it borders on the profound. A final narrative jujitsu flip forces the reader to reconsider the episodes as cultural consciousness, autobiography, shadow memory—the constituent components of self. [Steve Tomasula]

Orhan Pamuk. *The New Life*. Trans. Güneli Gün. Vintage, 1998. 296 pp. Paper: $13.00.

Have you ever read a book that was so overwhelming, so utterly life-changing that you had to find everyone else who has read it and force it upon those who haven't? This impulse provides the basis for Turkish writer Pamuk's latest novel: in *The New Life* a man, Osman, encounters a book so earth shattering that it changes his entire life. He seeks out others who have read the same book, and he sets out on a bizarre journey to find in this world the new life proposed within the book.

Pamuk's novel may strike readers as strongly reminiscent of many other works (but in a book about books this should come as no surprise). The stunning opening chapter, which details Osman's experience of reading the eponymous novel, echoes Calvino's *If on a winter's night a traveler.* Osman's subsequent quest for the new life leads him to a number of conspiracies (one bent on destroying the book itself) that read like plots by Pynchon and Eco. Finally, Osman's fascination with bus accidents as the apocalyptic means into the new life feels much like *Crash*-era Ballard. Despite these similarities, Pamuk weaves these voices and ideas into a unique style that addresses particular concerns of contemporary Turkish culture.

The New Life is another volume in the postmodern library of books about books, or to be more precise, books about the experience of reading books. In this wing of the library, *The New Life* sits a little distance from Borges's *Labyrinths* and a little closer to Nabokov's *Pale Fire* and Pavic's *Dictionary of the Khazars*. But *The New Life* doesn't sit on a shelf. The book lives and moves. It moves this reader as the book within the book moves the reader within the book. [David Ian Paddy]

Helen Stevenson. *Mad Elaine.* Anchor/Transworld (Ealing: England), 1998. 236 pp. £9.99.

Helen Stevenson's third novel, *Mad Elaine,* is a hilarious and touching look at the life of a social misfit. An intelligent and sensitive librarian, thirty-year-old Madelaine Butcher is a little on the heavy side, lives with her parents, and has a mole on her chin with which she has a close personal relationship, because, it seems, she can find no real human contact. Until the day she meets Martin Bradfield, who is able to make her feel noticed and anything but ordinary.

Part attempted romance, part murder mystery, this novel is reminiscent of Fay Weldon's *The Life and Loves of a She-Devil* in its postmodern, postfeminist look inside the mind of a woman—with neither the model figure nor future of a classic heroine—who is foreign in her own rapidly changing world. Yet Stevenson's is a much more sympathetic narrator whose imagination, while as lively as that of Weldon's Ruth, allows her to escape the pain and humiliation of her life without having to resort to returning the unkindness that is bestowed upon her every day. Madelaine creates a vivid fantasy world—so vivid, in fact, that it's difficult to be certain whether the last third of the novel is indeed fantasy or reportage—whereby she is able to be at once strong, willful, bitingly funny, and *nice.* Much like her own personal heroine, Maria von Trapp of *The Sound of Music,* Madelaine wishes to find the best in every situation, whether the good she finds is real or not, lending alternately to sadly ironic and darkly funny results.

This fast-paced novel (comprised of short, headlined vignettes) offers a witty yet honest look at an abject, unnoticed, and lonely everywoman who may not find a place for herself in the modern world, but certainly tells an intriguing story. [Rebecca Kaiser]

Cormac McCarthy. *Cities of the Plain.* Knopf, 1998. 293 pp. $24.00.

The third volume of *The Border Trilogy,* McCarthy's *Cities of the Plain,* brings together Billy Parham from *The Crossing* and John Grady Cole from *All the Pretty Horses.* Beginning in 1952 and set in New Mexico, *Cities of the Plain* concerns itself with the end of the West. It explores the decline of the cowboy life as Billy and John Grady work on a struggling ranch near El Paso which is about to be bought up by the military. As in *All the Pretty Horses,* a romance plot gradually gains importance. John Grady falls in love with a young epileptic whore and Billy struggles to keep him from getting enmeshed in trouble.

The novel suffers in the way many movie sequels do: it fails to measure up to either of the two previous volumes. Though McCarthy's style remains sharp and often breathtaking, the book as a whole lacks the accumulated drive of McCarthy's earlier work. In one sense this is intended in that the book is about the death of the cowboy and as a result is more about memory of and reflection on a form of life in decline.

Nevertheless, as always is the case with McCarthy, there are some exceptional manipulations of prose here. There's a dog-hunting scene, for instance, which contains the strengths of McCarthy's best writing, and a knife-fighting scene that is as strong as that in *All the Pretty Horses.* The dialogue between McCarthy's ranchers is nicely clipped and possessed of quiet humor and sincerity, and there is a great deal of poignancy in his depiction of a dying lifestyle. It has many strengths, and were it written by anyone but McCarthy (who with *Blood Meridian* has set an extremely high standard for himself), it would be hard not to see the book as an enviable success. Though a mixed book, moments here rank among McCarthy's best work. [Brian Evenson]

Randie Lipkin. *Without.* Fugue State, 1998. 152 pp. Paper: $7.00.

I have been eagerly waiting for Lipkin's second novel. It confirms her rare talent. This novel, like her first one, *Untitled (a skier),* is a daring, wise, beautiful exploration of the "cruelty of everyday living," of mysterious loss. It explores Wittgenstein's vision of language's limitations, mysterious "reality."

The novel is set in Japan. There are many characters who are haunted by the need to achieve stability (of love, faith, art) but who discover that instability, change, rule them. There are references to death, divorce, separation (of family, gender, rituals). The dialogue is elliptical, as if language itself is without certainty. Here, for example, are some typical sentences: "Marriage and children are no indication of anything"; "I never know when you mean what you're saying"; "I won't be able to hear what he's saying. I can't listen to someone I don't know."

There are descriptions of a Finnish film and a traditional Japanese drama. The film (its very nature consists of "moving" image) is described in a haunting, disturbing way. Lipkin uses odd syntax—there are missing verbs, few declarative sentences. Language, like perception, is without fullness. It reads like an incomplete translation (one of the characters is a translator, always aware of deadlines). There are allusions to "backs," "unfolding fans," "shadows," "edges," "lines of descending fabric." Objects are not solid, complete, fixed.

The novel then suggests that change rules reality, that reality itself is an edge; although some of the characters can endure change, they need to do the same things again and again, as if to stabilize their identities. But these solitary rituals, vigils, cannot ward off panic. If we recognize the odd syntax—the symbols of fading flowers, flashing signs, ticking clocks—the present participle recurs: we are prepared for the wonderful complexity (perplexity?) of the last two sentence/paragraphs: "She pushes her cloth forward, half-standing, half-running." The final sentence: "As they reach end of corridor, he's ahead of her, passing her as he returns." The sentence conveys in its very movement, that "passing" "returns." Nothing stands still except the artistic "act of attention." *Without* is, then, a brave attempt to capture and shape change. It sanctifies absence. [Irving Malin]

Julia Kristeva. *Possessions*. Trans. Barbara Bray. Columbia Univ. Press, 1998. 211 pp. $27.50.

I'm afraid that Julia Kristeva's excursion into the genre of the thriller is not terribly thrilling. *Possessions* returns the reader to the mysteriously corrupt world of the fictitious Santa Varvara, overrun by allegorical wolves in Kristeva's previous novel, *The Old Man and the Wolves*. That book introduced the theme that Kristeva pursues more insistently here: the single murder eventually determined to have been perpetrated by multiple murderers, all with equally cogent motive and convenient opportunity. In both books, the murder (of the Professor in the first and the socialite/translator Gloria Harrison here) is "solved" by the French journalist Stéphanie Delacour, who occasionally narrates in the first person, thus suggesting that she speaks for Kristeva herself in her end-of-millenial musings on love, decadence, politics, art, language and motherhood. Certainly Ms. Delacour's adventures in Santa Varvara, where she had spent her childhood as the daughter of the French ambassador, constitute an interior voyage of discovery meant to parallel the unravelling of the murder mysteries, the first time done on her own, and the second in company of a pompous official inspector, one Nicholas Rilsky, who tempers his professional interest in crime with a passion for the violin.

Yet it is hard to determine exactly what Kristeva/Delacour wishes us to discover here. Despite her well-detailed manias, such as for the good scotch unavailable in repressive Santa Varvara and for sleeping, coffinlike, in trundle beds, Stéphanie Delacour is rarely more than wispy as a character or narrator; that the stories she files are not always those her editor is interested in, is perhaps indicative of a problematic status of narrative itself in fin-de-siècle culture. The best part of *The Old Man and the Wolves* was the reworking of the father/daughter relationship evoked by the death of the Professor; the best part of *Possessions* is its opening description of Gloria's decapitated corpse and Kristeva's reflections on the human madness revealed by such deliberate mutilation. The suggestion, however, that we all are mad, that we all are potential murderers, strains the imagination even as Kristeva hints at it in these novels that sit like the brittle tip of the iceberg atop her massive works in psychoanalysis and semiotics.

It is on these latter that Kristeva's reputation rests, and despite the occasional moments of insight and ingenuity in her novels, will probably continue to rest. [Renée Kingcaid]

John Yau. *My Symptoms.* Black Sparrow, 1998. 203 pp. $27.50; paper: $15.00.

Throughout *My Symptoms* male and female narrators surprise us with unusual, shifting colloquialisms, with playfully enlivened cliches, pleasing turns of phrase such as this one for shouting, staring, mocking kids on a school bus: "a bus load full of parrots beating the windows with their beaks and laughing." Yau's narrators speak into voids and though we hear them, we are not the addressee and cannot act or answer their plea. Communication is off the hook; life, off-line and going nowhere. Yau's characters, his poetic paragraphs, talk of guilty pleasures and masks of innocence, of various freedoms and a multitude of constraints. One man has an ambivalent relationship with his post-office box, he both depends on it and denies his dependence. That man is an emblem of the reader; the post box, the book: these are stories that recount the symptoms of many, if not most.

The book has six sections. Part one has seventeen stories ranging in length from two to six pages; the shorter pieces are more poetic and less plot or character oriented than the longer ones. Parts two and three, entitled "Lives of the Artists I" and "Lives of the Artists II," are sequences of non-narrative prose sketches. The next two sections, "Snow" and "Lives of the Poets," are also sequences, but return the book to the narrative impulse of its first section and to the subject matter of contemporary relationships askew, sexuality, and the stimulation and denial of desire. The final section contains thirteen stories ranging in length from a single page to six pages. These narratives bring the book full circle, but here the failings of memory and the passage of time are emphasized more than the failure and passing of desire.

A student instructed me to look at the first word and the last word of any book and in that combination, she guaranteed, a key to the text could be found. For Yau's book you get "my" / "room," which does seem central to the work if not fully explanatory. A room that belongs to someone as the space in which stories exist, the mind as room, or the room as a space which the reader enters. [Dennis Barone]

Jean Ray. *Malpertuis.* Trans. and introduction by Iain White. Atlas, 1998. 172 pp. Paper: $16.99.

The new English translation of *Malpertuis,* a novel of gothic delights by Jean Ray first published in France in 1943, offers a sojourn to a literary landscape not much cultivated these days—a dark place of rich language and imagery where the concerns of the contemporary (be it existential angst or complex psychological entanglements) are subordinated to a more ancient and—in some ways—exuberant approach to storytelling. This is not to say that the book lacks psychological depth; indeed, its primary narrator, a young man named Jean-Jacques, ultimately tells a tragic story of family relations and coming-of-age with a distracted unself-consciousness that makes these elements all the more powerful. Rather, it is simply that *Malpertuis* is so unabashedly a tale best told "on a dark and stormy night," which sets it apart from what we expect of most modern literary fiction. This is the novel's greatest charm: its willingness to revel in its own gothic excesses.

Malpertuis is the name of an ancient stone house that is haunted by creatures whose true nature is not revealed until the book's dramatic and satisfying conclusion. Like Poe's *House of Usher, Malpertuis* embodies the darkness of its inhabiting family's secrets. Nonetheless, doom and darkness does not make reading the book a gloomy experience. As in the best gothic fiction, the vitality of the author's imagination and language insures against that. Truth is, reading *Malpertuis* is fun. "The horrible stench of anagyris, the thrice accursed plant," Ray writes in the novel's first pages, wherein a mariner encounters a mysterious island, "came to him from that mortal land, already so close at hand, and he knew that impure spirits were involved in his adventure . . ." What's not to like about a story of impure spirits, well told? [Gordon McAlpine]

Don Webb. *The Explanation and Other Good Advice.* Woodcraft of Oregon, 1998. 120 pp. Paper: $9.95.

The Explanation and Other Good Advice, Don Webb's latest collection of short fiction, promises and delivers dreams worth dreaming, where the sheer weight of language lies squarely on the reader's chest and she is asked to breathe, where the author gets lost in the pleasure of creating worlds simply for the Heideggerian joy of it, and where fiction is governed only by secrets that can be discovered through an actual engagement with the Big Whatever that fiction is anyway.

While Webb's forte remains psychedelic science fiction shot through with a hefty dose of H. P. Lovecraft, *The Explanation* takes exciting risks with language that are hard to come by in most genre fiction. Webb uses genres like wild marionettes, creating worlds and questioning them with the same What Have I Done? awe-anguish that plagued Victor Frankenstein. I don't know if Blake was right about the entire universe in a grain of sand, Webb writes, but you can have an entire world in ten blocks.

And the worlds are seemingly bottomless; from forty telestatic channels of *History of Ballooning,* an *Al Azif* sticker book, and a quasi-academic dialogue concerning Barthelme's *Come Back, Doctor Caligari,* Webb challenges us to download smarter, slicker and quicker fiction by offering us the same thirty-nine-cent Magic Marker he uses to conjure the pages before our very eyes. Webbs dreamworlds are intelligent, engaging and surprisingly inviting. *The Explanation* encapsulates the results from a wide spectrum of creative experiments and serves them up without grudge or agenda, allowing readers rare access to the actual processes by which fictions are made. [Trevor Dodge]

Paola Capriolo. *The Woman Watching.* Trans. Liz Heron. Serpent's Tail, 1998. 214 pp. Paper: $13.99.

The eponymous woman of Paola Capriolo's new novel is watching a play about the life of Casanova; an actor known to us only as Vulpius has a small but important role, and night after night he feels her eyes follow his every gesture. Under her enigmatic gaze he hones and refines his technique, showing signs of becoming the great actor that his girlfriend, Dora, is certain he will be one day. Finally he attempts to meet the woman who has taken over his life—only to find her box empty and a wristwatch left waiting on a seat, like Cinderella's slipper. The woman does not appear in the theater again. Capriola uses the beautiful wristwatch, which cannot tell time, and the romance that never was as a springboard for discussion of fictional reality: is the watching woman "real"? What, in this community of actors and actresses, writer and readers, can pass for real? What is the nature of fiction, of what gestures and words is it composed, and how can we tell the difference between them and reality? Such timeless questions, however, remain secondary to the story itself, as a monomaniacal Vulpius takes over the theater after hours, compelling his besotted but uncomplicated girlfriend to try on costumes, roles, and lines, all for his analytical eyes alone. The real power of *The Woman Watching* lies in Capriolo's tracing of the psychological effects the ghost-muse woman's manifestation has on these two lives, effects that pass all but undetected by the community of actors in which Vulpius and Dora live. The ending of this postmodern gothic is as gripping as it is inevitable; like Vulpius, Capriolo "prepares for [each] moment with care" and "celebrates it like an apotheosis." [Susann Cokal]

Patricia Duncker. *Monsieur Shoushana's Lemon Trees.* Ecco, 1998. 197 pp. $22.95.

With this, her first collection of stories, Patricia Duncker returns to the sun-drenched French settings and themes of love and power that characterized her first novel *Hallucinating Foucault.* Many of these stories are meditations on love—primarily between women—and the emotional and sexual struggles for control and emancipation between lovers. Duncker's handling of these themes, however, is uneven. Some of her parables of sexual subversion feature characters who are little more than vehicles for a heavy-handed "message" or poles of a sexual conflict. However, when Duncker allows her characters to grow beyond allegorical gender roles, her stories exhibit wit, compassion, and a wicked sense of sociosexual satire.

Several of Duncker's best stories explore supernatural dimensions, a surprise after the intellectual passions of *Hallucinating Foucault*. Often the world resonates with sympathy for the protagonists, as if the women in question tap a deeper, natural force of expression and action. But there are ghostly moments in the collection as well, and intimations that some women are much more than they seem: archetypes of female freedom, power, and vengeance who walk unrecognized amongst us. In the concluding and longest story, "The Arrival Matters," magic is worn lightly in a world of quotidian errands, arthritic joints, and the exhausting pleasures of child minding. The story follows the last days of a kind and cantankerous old woman who is, in fact, one of a group of magicians linked as much by love as by their supernatural secrets. As her life draws to a close, she prepares to pass on her art to the young girl who will be her inheritor, while reuniting for the last time with her lifelong lover. This novella is by far the most engaging piece in the collection, a rumination on life, death, tempestuous, undying love, and the hope we vest in children. Stories such as this confirm Duncker's talents as a writer. *Monsieur Shoushana's Lemon Trees* is a varied and captivating collection. [Graham Fraser]

———————

Todd Shimoda. *365 Views of Mt. Fuji: Algorithms of the Floating World.* Illustrated by L. J. C. Shimoda. Stone Bridge, 1998. 356 pp. $19.95.

What's striking about *365 Views of Mt. Fuji* is this first novel's very look. Bordering the main text throughout are eye-catching, italicized sidebars and up to five postage-stamp sized drawings suggestive of the Japanese Ukiyo-e style central to Shimoda's story. The novel has an aesthetic quite apart from its text (one thinks of chic restaurants where as much attention is paid to presentation as to cuisine). Some spreads look crowded and are reminiscent of technical users' manuals, but typically the artwork is suggestive, hip, even haunting.

There's more to the look than aesthetics. Yes, the central text presents a linear chronology—a novel of contemporary Japan concerning an art curator who leaves Tokyo to head a private museum devoted to the views of Mt. Fuji painted by a little-known nineteenth-century Ukiyo-e master, Takenoko. But Shimoda breaks free of the linear mode through his sidebars, using them to move the reader through time and point of view. These operate, at times, like footnotes or hypertext links, presenting now Takenoko's own story, now history, and now the hidden truths of the chimerical Ono family, collective owner of the Takenoko paintings.

The novel explores what it means to be creative and unique in Japan, today and during the late shogunate. By its conclusion, curator-hero Keizo Yukawa reaches a new understanding, especially of self and art. This is, in fact, a novel of enlightenment. Yet, because the protagonist carries throughout his journey something of an excess of ego baggage, readers might find his an enlightenment with the accent on "lite." [Rod Kessler]

———————

Beth Partin. *Microgravity*. Livingston, 1998. 128 pp. Paper: $9.95.

In her first novel, *Microgravity,* Beth Partin provides a smart investigation into both the realm of cults and the realm of the mind by exploring the societal structures that allow cults to exist. A cult, Partin recognizes, is not simply individuals acting in concert, but rather an aggregate of individuals acting under the providence of a "higher authority." The authority in *Microgravity* is blood. Theresa, a scientist who has discovered how to use hormones to increase red blood cell production, and her husband have been murdered, presumably by a cult obsessed with blood.

 Microgravity follows Justine, Theresa's daughter, and Margaret, Theresa's sister, as they unfurl and reorder their lives while coming to terms with the unsolved cult murder. Margaret and Justine, who are both photographers, deal with the deaths by employing techniques of classification and collage, respectively. Margaret, who had earlier in her life toured the country with a lover while working on a story about evangelism in America, wonders why she was not aware enough to prevent the murders. Justine, who has fewer experiences to help her cope with the loss, closets herself to make a collage out of photos taken from her aunt's stockpiles. Together, they follow the blood trail to a fringe group within the Last Faith Church of Love. Lucy, the congregation's leader, provides additional clues while admitting, "I have spent my whole life doing nothing but staring," not unlike, of course, photographers.

 While *Microgravity* is overwritten at times, the inventive structure provides support for Partin's investigation into cults and, more importantly, the workings of the mind. [Alan Tinkler]

André Breton, Paul Eluard, Philippe Soupault. *The Automatic Message.* Trans. David Gascoyne, Antony Melville, Jon Graham. Introduction by Gascoyne and Melville. Atlas, 1997. 223 pp. Paper: $16.99.

An old maxim has God worrying over what happens when the last Frenchman's gone: who will then be left to explain everything? André Breton, decrier of reason and logic, steward of mystery, champion of the unconscious, nourished that genius for explanation in himself. For half a century he turned out a stream of manifestos, letters and commentary, creating the very sea upon which he set sail, and kept on course against all odds, the good ship surrealism.

 Surrealism's formal history runs fifty years, too, 1919 to 1969. It was, like punk, both art and weapon, an assault at the barricades of the commonplace, of stultification. Its role, and its influence, are immeasurable. But how many of us have actually read its texts? That date given above, 1919, derives from publication of Breton's and Philippe Soupault's "Les Champs magnétiques"—the book (Aragon said) "through which everything begins."

 The current volume pairs "The Magnetic Fields" with another seminal automatic text by Breton and Paul Eluard, "The Immaculate Conception." Both evidence the chance encounters, quests, contradictions and surprise—

as well as the profound reliance on image—that are surrealist trademarks. Breton's "The Automatic Message," offered as introduction, extolls the generative powers of phrases that come just before sleep, and of concepts of free association come across in his medical studies. Taking up the promise of liberation from Freudian psychiatry, Breton and his surrealist crewmen turned that promise towards a total liberation of the imagination. For Breton, as for Pushkin, poetry was always a form of action. Man must become ungoverned: bury all towers, cast off all bondage. He wished to change the whole of mankind, profoundly, from within each individual human being. [James Sallis]

———————

Aidan Higgins. *Dog Days*. Secker & Warburg, 1998. 286 pp. £15.99.

This middle volume of a trilogy which began with *Donkey's Years* (1995) and will conclude with *The Whole Hog* dwells mainly on the winters of 1985 and 1986, which the author, or Rory O'Hills, as he calls himself, spent at Ballymona Lodge, outside the town of Wicklow, thirty miles or so south of Dublin. There are interruptions—a sojourn in Connemara; there are digressions—reminiscences of Spain, as ever, and material on the death of his father, and some more Berlin background for the novel *Lions of the Grunewald* (1993). The opening sequence recounts an unconsummated affair between the inordinately horny Rory, age twenty-two, and a woman nearly twice his age, the no-longer-summery landscape of which is just a train-stop away from his present lodgings. He's homeless (his assumed name ironically echoes Ned of the Hills, the archetypal Dispossessed One in eighteenth-century poetry in Irish). He's in the country. Everybody has a dog, except Rory. What Rory has is difficult to describe. It certainly has bite. And it's kind of a mongrel—an album, a rant, a confession, a history, a book of (decayed) hours . . . I suppose the best name for it is a life.

Apart from the novel *Bornholm Night-Ferry* (1983) and two collections of mostly already available material—*Ronda Gorge and Other Precipices* and *Helsingør Station and Other Departures* (both 1989)—Higgins published little in the '80s. He tells a local nosy parker here that he's writing for radio, but he often refers to his set's poor reception. Too bad his radio pieces haven't seen book form, though. And the same must be said of his American publishing fate: he hasn't had a book published in this country since *Balcony of Europe* (1973). One of the most interesting—that is, penetrating, literate, infuriating, sardonic, gossipy, stylish—Irish writers around surely deserves better. [George O'Brien]

———————

Nathalie Blondel. *Mary Butts: Scenes From the Life.* McPherson, 1998. 553 pp. $35.00.

Mary Butts is, perhaps, the most obscure of major modern writers. Although she wrote wonderful fiction, she was also a brilliant critic admired by readers of *The Dial, The Bookmen,* and *Time and Tide.* (Blondel's bibliography is valuable because it fully documents Butt's criticism.)

Here are some details about Butts (1890-1937). She was a descendant of the Butts who was William Blake's patron. The Blake connection is significant because it demonstrates the wealth of the Butts family and the influence of Blake upon Butts. Butts often struggled with her mother; she did not want to be a loyal daughter who kept her place. Her art was more important than family loyalty. Butts was a believer in hermetic theology; she believed in "astral projection," occult revelation. Butts was a cocaine and heroin addict; she used drugs to heighten her awareness of "the other world." These "scenes from the life" would not matter if she didn't write remarkable prose. Here is an example from one of my favorite stories: "With or Without Buttons": "Through walls and glass, through open doors or shut, a tide poured in, not of any light or dark or scent or sound or heat or coolness. Tide. Without distinction from north or south or without or within; without flow or ebb, a Becoming: without stir or departure or stay: without radiance or pace. Star-tide. Has not Science had wind of rays poured in from interstellar space?" The passage conveys the movement of the tide—a suggestive word—with it's rhythm. The simple one-syllable words give clarity; but they are balanced by "interstellar," "Science," and "Becoming." The entire passage is, in its way, about "within and without." It is eerie and beautiful. I am grateful to Blondel. Her bibliography is detailed, clear, forceful; it is, like Carolyn Burke's biography of Loy, a revelation of an extraordinary artist. [Irving Malin]

The Unbearables. *Crimes of the Beats.* Autonomedia, 1998. 223 pp. Paper: $12.00.

By and large, the growing corpus of academic scholarship on the Beat writers has not been matched by writers' own critical reappraisals of the American '50s. *Crimes of the Beats* gives those years the attention they deserve, and its contributors take Kerouac, Ginsberg, Burroughs, et al. very seriously indeed, as measured by the harshness of their rebukes. In parodies, memoirs and feuilletons—some viciously dismissive, most confidently critical, and a few semi-reverent—such contemporary avant-gardists as Lynne Tillman, Ron Sukenick, Lance Olsen, and Sparrow reexamine the literary mythmaking of the writers who rolled "along the highway of dreams," as Tillman puts it in the voice of Kerouac, feeling "the cool American breeze rush crazily over my American skin." Kerouac the egoist, Ginsberg the mercenary, and Burroughs the reptile take heavy blows here; Gregory Corso, Diane DiPrima (whose erotic memoirs are parodied to devastating effect), and Amiri Baraka come up for pokes and jabs too. The tone is generally light—this is no manifesto—but a serious and considered critique of Beat ideals surfaces often enough amid the mockery. Those ideals were spontaneity ("I Tried to Write Spontaneous Prose but All I Ever Got Was Tired," counters Carl Watson), sexual profligacy ("What if [Neal Cassady] *wasn't* the greatest fast-speaking, bebop-loving, accelerator-pressing, woman-leaving hipster who ever lived?" asks Sparrow), and a romanticized Buddhism ("Transcending the ego," Tom Savage observes of Kerouac's dipsomania, "was not intended to mean destroying its container"). Perhaps the most potent revisioning in *Crimes of the Beats,* however, comes in the pieces, such as Tsaurah Litzky's "Reflections on Beat Sexism," that confront the all-too easy identification that a work such as *On the Road* offers to one half of its potential readership. [Brian Lennon]

John Fowles. *Wormholes Essays and Occasional Writings.* Ed. and introduction by Jan Relf. Henry Holt, 1998. 416 pp. $25.00.

This volume offers a selection of Fowles's nonfiction from 1964 up to 1997, presented under four thematic headings "Autobiographical Writing and the Self," "Culture and Society," "Literature and Literary Criticism," and "Nature and the Nature of Nature." An in-depth interview conducted in 1995 closes the collection.

Defiantly egocentric and unsystematic in his approach, Fowles shares the "magpie" curiosity he ascribes to the seventeenth-century amateur scholar John Aubrey. Fowles repeatedly pits creative authors against professional academics, setting up an extreme dualism that recalls the struggle between the artistic girl and her monstrous abductor in *The Collector* (1963). Fowles recoilingly implores novelists and poets to steer clear of universities: "One doesn't apprentice a would-be celebrator of life to a college of morticians."

If the cost of Fowles's vigorous dilettantism is a certain rhetorical excess and lack of analytical rigor, the payoff is ready accessibility and liveliness of expression. Admirers of the synthesis of self-awareness and narrative drive in *The Magus* (1966) and *The French Lieutenant's Woman* (1969) will find here a wealth of anecdotes and local insights, but no systematic authorial manifesto. Instead, *Wormholes* comprises an archive of Fowles's lifelong preoccupation with feminism, ecology, left-wing politics, the Victorian mind, existentialism, and French literature and culture.

Fowles is particularly strong on the psychology of authorship, which he theorizes, in essays on Hardy and Alain-Fournier, as the compulsive reworking of an abiding sense of loss (with a nod at the psychoanalytical critic Gilbert J. Rose). The psychology of nationalism is the subject of two brilliant essays, "On Being English but Not British" and "The Falklands and a Death Foretold," the last-mentioned a withering indictment of the jingoistic war between Argentina and Britain in 1982. [Philip Landon]

Joseph Heller. *Now and Then From Coney Island to Here.* Knopf, 1998. 259 pp. $24.00.

This memoir is titled *Now and Then,* but if you're interested in Joseph

Heller as he is now or as he's been the last forty years, this isn't the place to go. The emphasis here is on Heller as a young man—growing up in Coney Island, going to war, finding his first jobs—and really less on young Heller than on the world around him. This might have been subtitled *What Life Was Like When I Was Young.* The result is that Heller has very little to say about the art of his novels but quite a lot to say about the comparative advantages of the Coney Island amusement parks, the history of the hot dog, and strategies for getting a seat on the IND. Unfortunately, much of the material here is treated better and more interestingly in the novels: the war—famously, brilliantly—in *Catch-22;* office work in *Something Happened*; and Coney Island in the best parts of *Closing Time.* There's a nostalgic charm here, some good jokes, and a wealth of information for historians of Brooklyn, but less Joseph Heller than I think most readers will expect. [Robert L. McLaughlin]

———————

Jerome Klinkowitz. *Keeping Literary Company: Working with Writers since the Sixties.* State Univ. of New York Press, 1998. 226 pp. $24.50; Richard Elman. *Namedropping: Mostly Literary Memories.* State Univ. of New York Press, 1998. 277 pp. $24.50.

To set the record straight: Jerome Klinkowitz, when he was a young professor at Northern Illinois University and I was an even younger graduate student, did a few very nice things for me that I have never forgotten and for which I have kept silent over the years about his critical writings because I would not have had anything positive to say about them. Over the last ten years, as the publisher of Dalkey Archive, I have rejected two books by him, one of them, being the above, which I rejected as far back as 1992; looking at the few chapters that were sent me by his agent (but not the one in which I was a partial subject), I could quickly see that he was doing more of what he had been doing for years: slick, sloppy writing that seems to serve no other purpose than to promote himself, usually at the expense of the poor writers who are his subjects. To call his criticism superficial would be to compliment it. Some years ago, he seemed to get it in his head that criticism should consist of anecdotes and read like a story in *People* magazine. The self-proclaimed champion of "innovative" fiction, along the way he lost all sense of aesthetics and critical standards; any and every writer somehow seemed to fit under his ever-expanding umbrella of what constitutes innovation, resulting in one of his more embarrassing critical inventions called "superrealism," a term that allowed him to claim that even the most realistic of writers are also (strike up the band!) innovative.

The problems (to use a gracious term) with this book range from A to Z (why, at times like these, do we have such few letters in our alphabet?). It is self-indulgent, self-congratulatory (its basic thesis is that, without Professor Klinkowitz, none of the writers would have "made it," carrying them on his back but rarely given credit by them for what he had accomplished on their behalf), and self-serving. For the writers who somehow could endure his self-promotionalism, he remains kind and has fond memories; for those who finally told him to take a hike, he remembers hurts and assaults, though never attributing their desire for him to stay away as a sign that his criticism was in fact a disservice, something amounting to having a used-car salesman promote their work.

Over the past several years, I have had friends call me to ask if I had heard about this manuscript, saying that what was said about me bordered on the libelous (as I said above, when the manuscript was sent to me to consider for publication, the chapter on Gilbert Sorrentino and Clarence Major, in which my name comes up a number of times, was not included). But how can anyone be offended by nastiness from this critic when the alternative fate is to be foolishly praised and made to be part of his mythology that you "made it" only because of his efforts? In any event, it has taken several years for this manuscript to find a publisher, and finally a university press went for it and found outside readers who apparently were ill-informed enough to swallow its inaccuracies.

For example, I was there the night Professor Klinkowitz met Gilbert Sorrentino, and in fact am the one responsible (God help me) for introducing them. Half of what the Professor records about the event is made up out of whole cloth. The scowling Sorrentino that the Professor portrays didn't exist that night, though in retrospect I can imagine that such was imagined as the Professor made his usually stupid argument that if you could get kids hooked on Vonnegut, one day they would step up to more serious writers. Later in the chapter the Professor imagines that a character in Sorrentino's *Mulligan Stew* is based upon him, as though Sorrentino hadn't met enough hick professors in his time to have to rely on this one as a model. And still later the Professor claims credit for getting Sorrentino his job at Stanford University, making him, by my count, the nineteenth person to make this claim. But to return to the evening when Sorrentino and the Professor met. The line that the Professor uses to describe Sorrentino's appearance at the door is lifted word for word (without any attribution) from an essay I wrote about Sorrentino years ago: need anything else be said for the level of scholarship in this book?

As to the Professor's claim that he was able to escape the domineering influence of Sorrentino while I was not (e.g., under Sorrentino's influence I became "stern" and "abrupt"), all that I can say is that the Professor is being kind here. The fact is that I have always been an opinionated asshole who has no time for fools. The Professor credits Sorrentino for these qualities in me. As to Sorrentino's influence on my sensibilities, that's a matter of record. But as both Pound and Shklovsky argued many years ago, one chooses those influences, and indeed I did. And that influence, which I have talked about extensively in interviews over the years, was and is at work in both the *Review of Contemporary Fiction* and Dalkey Archive Press. This should be news to no one, and in fact some other professor years ago wrote a long article complaining about the same thing, that Sorrentino greatly influenced the *Review* and that the *Review* is not "objective [whatever this might mean] scholarship." Indeed, nor was it ever intended to be. It has always represented a cause that says *this* writing is good and *that* writing is bad. If there is problem with the *Review* along these lines, it is that the *Review* does not draw these distinctions often enough.

But more curious than what the Professor has to say about Sorrentino is what he does with Clarence Major, a writer who has nothing whatsoever to do with Sorrentino's aesthetics but gets wrapped into the same chapter; the only thing that seems to unite them here is that they both grew rather unfond of the Professor: Major is another example of a writer not being properly appreciative of what the Professor did for him. The Professor brings me into the fray and is indignant on my behalf that Clarence Major was somehow ungrateful both to him and me. In 1971-72, I interviewed Clarence Major for a book called *Interviews with Black Writers;* I believe that I reviewed one of his novels at about the same time for the *Chicago Sun-Times;* and I invited him to give a reading at the college where I was teaching in 1973-74. The Professor's indignation is that Clarence Major abandoned both him and me, choosing to have the likes of Toni Morrison blurb his books rather than us. After that one review, I am sure that there is nothing that could have been used as a blurb from me, but even if there were, who in the hell would want *my* blurb when he could get Toni Morrison's? And one certainly need not ask the same question in regard to the Professor. But once again, this all seems to settle with the Professor as a slight after all he had done for Major's career.

Just a few more observations about the Professor's book. First, the bibliography is one of the shoddiest imaginable, overlooking many essential pieces written about these writers and their aesthetics, but including almost everything the Professor has written in book form, even his (this is not a joke) baseball fiction. Second observation: the Professor writes about Sorrentino's later work: "Lacking the motivation that anger and crankiness provide, novels such as *Crystal Vision* and *Blue Pastoral* . . . take the lyricisms of *Steelwork* and its actual subjects as well and amplify them to the point of self-exaggeration." Well, in fact, *Crystal Vision* uses the materials from *Steelwork,* but *Blue Pastoral* uses the materials from *The Sky Changes,* retracing the characters' journey from New York to San Francisco. This is a rather basic error to make about a writer's work, especially when the point of the paragraph suggests that this fiction represents a decline in Sorrentino's work. But who's to notice, who's to care? It sounds fine, sounds right, just as long as the reader doesn't know anything, or apparently the editor of this book. One final observation. In his chapter on Ronald Sukenick (that is, "Ron": the Professor obnoxiously keeps using the first names for these writers to assure us what good buddies he was or is with them all), he recalls a kind of falling-out he had with Sukenick (the poor Professor once again being slighted), but that several years later he hooked up with Sukenick in Paris. Leaving aside the content of this meeting, I want to point out that the Professor says that they "walked across part of town to Ron's neighborhood" and that, along the way, they "paused" "for some fresh country wine." Well, let's see here. Paris is not a city that is referred to as "town"; Cedar Falls and Milwaukee are such cities. And, though I do not drink very much wine and know next to nothing about it, I can't imagine what "fresh country wine" might be: grape juice? Perhaps it is such things as these that caused, according to the Professor's lights, Gilbert Sorrentino to think of the Professor as a hick.

This book might have been interesting (a la *People*) if the Professor would have been forthright enough to entitle it thus: "How I Made Careers for So Many Writers and How I Imagine They Have Scorned Me," and then proceed to give up the veneer of providing even a glimmer of critical writing. It would have also been interesting (again a la *People*) had he told a number of anecdotes he could have, like the time that . . . but I will leave that to what will no doubt be another volume of his memoirs; after all, the guy is only in his early fifties. As it stands, the book is an incredible embarrassment.

Which editor at State University of New York accepted the above title? I don't know, but it might be the same one who accepted Richard Elman's appropriately titled *Namedropping* (which would also have been a good title for the Professor's book). It has the same self-serving, ax-grinding quality that the Professor's book does, and (what are the chances?) one of the chapters is about Gilbert Sorrentino. Before taking a look at the Sorrentino chapter, I want to point out a very peculiar omission: nowhere does the book mention—not on the copyright page, the jacket copy, or on the acknowledgements page that provides a chronology of where the writer was/is when he wrote these things, ending with a list of places where ("to the present") he has been a visiting professor—that Richard Elman died about a year ago. A useful, or at least interesting, piece of information, especially for a book of this kind? Is anyone awake in the editorial department at SUNY?

At any rate, we have a three-page assessment of the personality and writing career of Gilbert Sorrentino, and once again we get the picture of the wounded, "difficult," reclusive personality ("the Prince of Aquitaine in his ruined tower"). Let's check the chapter for accuracy. Among the first items, we find out that Sorrentino was hurt and wounded when his old friend LeRoi Jones (Amiri Baraka) went radical and abandoned his white friends: "Sorrentino seemed to regard his act as a special hurt. He would not say anything at all about Baraka." I am not sure how Elman knows the first part of this if the second part is true, but this is probably beside the point. I knew Gilbert Sorrentino very well in those years and frequently heard stories about and critical assessments of Jones; they were all warm personal anecdotes or very positive views of his work, from the plays to the poetry to the fiction. Just prior to this statement about Sorrentino and Jones, Elman says how uncomfortable he felt around Sorrentino: "It was hard to relax in his company. He always seemed to be scrutinizing you for errors or illiteracies . . . ." If Sorrentino was refusing to comment on Jones, my guess is that the conversation had already hit the point where Sorrentino knew to whom he was talking, and perhaps had stumbled across enough "illiteracies" for the day. Two paragraphs before, Elman says that Sorrentino "had a hard time bringing out his novels with trade publishers." Since Elman does not provide any dates for anything, one has to guess as to what period this statement might apply; given the few facts he does make available, the period would seem to be the early to mid-1970s. By that time, Sorrentino's fiction had been published, in this order, by the following publishers: Hill & Wang, Pantheon, Pantheon, and New Directions; if we move up the timetable a bit, the next two novels came out from Grove and then Random House. Are these or are they not *trade* houses? Are they or are they not what one would consider, especially in the 1970s, among the most distinguished trade houses in New York? Either Elman didn't know who had published Sorrentino's work, or more likely, he did, and yet these facts would not fit his argument about the embittered novelist who couldn't get published by a serious trade house. Strangely, or not so, the piece rhetorically unfolds in a way similar to how the Professor's does: praise amid the covert attacks, so that someone who really doesn't know the facts, will take the assessment as a fair, perhaps even more than fair. The chapter ends with Elman making reference to the only time he "ever saw Gil smile easily and happily." This may be true, but then we have to see this in the context of Richard Elman having been there.

The misfortune of both of these books, but especially the first, is that they are so badly done and represent fragile egos at work. While many of the writers that Klinkowitz covers still remain unrecognized in contemporary American literature, and since yet another university is willing to give him space in its catalog, the book could have been an opportunity to provide much-needed discussion; instead, it becomes an occasion for the author's self-imposed illusion that he made them well known.

One final note: Gilbert Sorrentino *is* the most important American novelist since the late 1960s. This fact is always worth keeping in mind. [John O'Brien]

New and Recommended in Paperback

• E. M. Cioran. *History and Utopia*. Trans. Richard Howard. Univ. of Chicago Press, 1998. 118 pp. $11.00.
——. *Tears and Saints*. Trans. and introduction by Ilinca Zarifopol-Johnston. Univ. of Chicago Press, 1998. 128 pp. $18.00.
——. *The Temptation to Exist*. Trans. Richard Howard. Introduction by Susan Sontag. Univ. of Chicago Press, 1998. 224 pp. $14.00.
• Cyrus Colter. *City of Light*. TriQuarterly, 1998. 423 pp. $17.95.
• Millicent Dillon. *A Little Original Sin: The Life and Work of Jane Bowles*. Univ. of California Press, 1998. 464 pp. $17.95.
• Shusaku Endo. *The Samurai*. Trans. Van C. Gessel. New Directions, 1997. 272 pp. $10.95.
• Guillermo Cabrera Infante. *Three Trapped Tigers*. Trans. Donald Gardner & Suzanne Jill Levine in collaboration with the author. Marlowe, 1998. 487 pp. $14.95.
• Jack Kerouac. *On the Road*/Fortieth Anniversary Edition. Viking, 1997. 307 pp. $24.95.
• Thomas Mann. *Death in Venice and Other Tales*. Trans. Joachim Neugroschel. Viking, 1998. 366 pp. $25.95.
——. *Doctor Faustus: The Life of the German Adrian Leverkühn As Told by a Friend*. Trans. John E. Woods. Knopf, 1997. 534 pp. $35.00.
• Rick Moody. *Purple America*. Back Bay, 1998. 298 pp. $13.95.
• Bradford Morrow. *Giovanni's Gift*. Penguin, 1998. 325 pp. $12.95.
• Tayeb Saleh. *Season of Migration to the North*. Trans. Denys Johnson-

Davies. Lynne Rienner, 1997. 169 pp. $12.95.
- David Shields. *Dead Languages.* Graywolf, 1998. 244 pp. $12.95.
- David Foster Wallace. *A Supposedly Fun Thing I'll Never Do Again.* Back Bay, 1998. 353 pp. $13.95.

School of Stupidity

We have received numerous complaints and letters of concern from readers that no one was elected to the School of Stupidity in the last issue of the *Review.* As with everything in life, there is a story behind this. Although the Committee meetings have a marked tendency to rouse ill-feelings and rancorous statements that members later regret having made, the spring meeting was characterized by a quite unusually high degree of angry exchanges and, I am sad to say, a few unnecessary, though quickly interrupted, bursts of slapping (women) and punches (men). The issue, quite simply, was whether the award could be given to a corporate entity or should be reserved for individual accomplishments. One member shouted at one point, "If we begin to attack corporations, then *Nation* magazine will win hands-down every time, and there's absolutely no point in our meeting again!" Another member agreed with, "And who is more deserving than *Nation,* that hypocritical rag that fronts as a liberal, anti-corporate magazine while reviewing only books from corporate publishers??!!" Well, this led to several suggestions for other corporations that were, in the minds of the Committee members, just as deserving, from the *New York Times* to the *Chicago Tribune* to *Bloomsbury Review,* though no one else on the committee recognized the latter and accused the nominator of making up names. At this point, one member, in a rather high-handed fashion, made a motion to give the award to the Germans, but this brought immediate and heated objections by other Committee members who pointed out that the award could not be given to an entire country, though all agreed that the country merited the honor. "Fascist," "hun," and "barbarian" were some of the unpleasant words bandied about in a rare moment when the Committee seemed in complete agreement. After two days of such turmoil, all was happily resolved, with eight of the nine members resigning in protest, although all for different reasons, with one member objecting to the quality of sweet rolls available to Committee members during meetings. The one-member Committee then adjourned, voting beforehand to postpone the election until the fall.

Now that late summer has descended upon Central Illinois (temperature 93, humidity 140), we had hoped that cooler minds would prevail. Needless to say, there were still disagreements about the sweet rolls, but finally, even with a new Committee in place, all hell broke loose. The nomination for the Germans came up once more, with much the same result as last time, with two abstentions. With 38 members voting, representing a full range of the political and aesthetic spectrum, there turned out to be, inevitably, many different nominees, among them:

Chip McGrath of the *New York Times*
Elizabeth Taylor late of the *Chicago Tribune*
John Leonard late of *Nation*
Art Winslow of *Nation*
The entire *Nation* staff
Germany
Agents
Subsidiary Rights People
Ex-wives
Lawyers
City of Chicago
Printers
Tom Le Clair
Young People
College Administrators
Hip Critics
Jonathan Yardley
Washington Post Book World
All Book Review Editors
Representative Tom Ewing
The Pulitzer Committee for Criticism
The Pulitzer Committee for Fiction
The National Book Award
The National Book Critics' Circle
Writers
Humanity

Well, needless to say, this just won't do. Just won't do at all. Once again, the hostilities began. Blacks against whites, whites against Chicanos, Chicanos against Asian Americans, urbanites against rural folks, rural folks against intelligence, Modernists against Postmodernists, Postmodernists against Minimalists, Minimalists against intelligence, Christians against Jews, Jews against the token Nazi German on the Committee, the Christian Right against itself, Bulgarians against Hungarians, the Italians against everything except red sauce, the drunken Irish against the undrunken Irish, the French against hot dogs, the Swiss refraining from saying anything but strangely looking for any stray change that may have been dropped on the floor, and the Feminists against everything and everyone. What a wonderful day!

It has now become clear that the School should close its doors, unable to use the democratic process to reach any kind of consensus. Correct, trustworthy opinion must originate from one person, and one person only. Beginning in the next issue of the *Review,* therefore, a new column will begin: ASK THE EDITOR. We encourage people to write in for advice on sundry matters.

Books Received

Al-Hakim, Tawfiq. *In the Tavern of Life and Other Stories.* Trans. William Maynard Hutchins. Lynne Rienner, 1998. $38.00; paper: $18.95. (F)

Amburn, Ellis. *Subterranean Kerouac: The Hidden Life of Jack Kerouac.* St. Martin's, 1998. $27.95. (NF)

Ammons, A. R. *Glare.* Norton, 1998. Paper: $15.99. (P)

Anderson, Perry. *The Origins of Postmodernity.* Verso, 1998. Paper: $16.00. (NF)

Annesley, James. *Blank Fictions: Consumerism, Culture, and the Contemporary American Novel.* St. Martin's, 1998. $55.00; paper: $18.95. (NF)

Arnold, Stephen H, ed. *Critical Perspectives on Mongo Beti.* Lynne Rienner, 1998. $59.95. (NF)

Badian, Seydou. *Caught in the Storm.* Trans. Marie-Thérèse Noiset. Lynne Rienner, 1998. $25.00. (F)

Baker, Keith. *Inheritance.* Morrow, 1998. $24.00. (F)

Barrett, Andrea. *The Voyage of the Narwhal.* Norton, 1998. $24.95. (F)

Barry, Sebastian. *The Whereabouts of Eneas McNulty.* Viking, 1998. $23.95. (F)

Bataille, Christophe. *Hourmaster.* Tran. Richard Howard. New Directions, 1998. $17.95. (F)

Bataille, Georges. *The Bataille Reader.* Ed. Fred Botting and Scott Wilson. Blackwell, 1998. $45.00; paper: $14.99. (NF)

Begley, Louis. *Mistler's Exit.* Knopf, 1998. $22.00. (F)

Bennett, Guy. *Last Words.* Sun & Moon, 1998. Paper: $9.95. (P)

Bergsson, Gudbergur. *The Swan.* Trans. Bernard Scudder. Mare's Nest/Dufour, 1998. Paper: $14.95. (F)

Berman, Sabina. *Bubbeh.* Trans. Andrea G. Labinger. Latin American Literary Review, 1998. Paper: $12.95. (F)

Berriault, Gina. *Afterwards.* Counterpoint, 1998. Paper: $12.50. (F)

———. *The Son.* Counterpoint, 1998. Paper: $12.50. (F)

Bird, Stephanie. *Recasting Historical Women: Female Identity in German Biographical Fiction.* Berg, 1998. $55.00; paper: $19.50. (NF)

Blagg, Max. *Pink Instrument.* Photographs by Ralph Gibson. Lumen Editions, 1998. $21.95. (P)

Bloom, Clive, ed. *Gothic Horror: A Reader's Guide from Poe to King and Beyond.* St. Martin's, 1998. $59.95; paper: $19.95. (NF)

Blythe, Will, ed. *Why I Write.* Little, Brown, 1998. $23.00. (NF)

Booker-Canfield, Suzanne, and Rosemary M. Canfield Reisman. *Contemporary Southern Men Fiction Writers: An Annotated Bibliography.* Scarecrow, 1998. $55.00. (NF)

Booker, M. Keith. *The Modern British Novel of the Left: A Research Guide.* Greenwood, 1998. $89.50. (NF)

Borinsky, Alicia. *Dreams of the Abandoned Seducer.* Trans. Cola Franzen in collaboration with the author. Univ. of Nebraska Press, 1998. $40.00; paper: $15.00. (F)

Boyd, William. *Armadillo*. Knopf, 1998. $24.00. (F)

Braschi, Giannina. *Yo Yo Boing*. Latin American Literary Review, 1998. Paper: $15.95. (F)

Bryant, Dorothy. *Confessions of Madame Psyche*. Afterword by J. J. Wilson. Feminist, 1998. Paper: $15.95. (F)

———. *Ella Price's Journal*. Feminist, 1998. Paper: $14.95. (F)

———. *Miss Giardino*. Feminist, 1998. Paper: $11.95. (F)

Butts, Mary. *Ashe of Rings and Other Writings*. McPherson, 1998. $24.00. (F, NF)

Campbell, Elaine, and Pierrette Frickey, eds. *The Whistling Bird: Women Writers of the Caribbean*. Lynne Rienner, 1998. $49.95; paper: $19.95. (F)

Campana, Dino. *Orphic Songs*. Trans. I. L. Salomon. City Lights, 1998. Paper: $12.95. (P)

Chandra, G. S. Shanrat. *Sari of the Gods*. Coffee House, 1998. Paper: $13.95. (F)

Chang, Eileen. *The Rice-Sprout Song*. California Univ. Press, 1998. Paper: $14.95. (F)

———. *The Rouge of the North*. California Univ. Press, 1998. Paper: $14.95. (F)

Cheung, Martha P. Y., ed. *Hong Kong Collage: Contemporary Stories and Writing*. Oxford (China), 1998. Paper: HKD 95.00. (F)

Cixous, Hélène. *FirstDays of the Year*. Trans. with preface by Catherine A. F. MacGillivray. Univ. of Minnesota Press, 1998. Paper: $16.95. (NF)

Coleman, Wanda. *Bathwater Wine*. Black Sparrow, 1998. $27.50; paper: $15.00. (P)

Cowen, James. *Troubadour's Testament*. Shambhala, 1998. $20.00. (F)

Dahl, David Rains. *The Blue Deer and Other Fictions*. Capra, 1998. No price given. (F)

Davidson, Toni, ed. *Intoxication: An Anthology of Stimulant-Based Writing*. Serpent's Tail, 1998. Paper: $13.99. (F)

Davies, Catherine. *A Place in the Sun?: Women Writers in Twentieth-Century Cuba*. Zed/St. Martin's, 1998. $65.00; paper: $22.50. (NF)

Delville, Michel. *The American Prose Poem: Poetic Form and the Boundries of Genre*. Univ. of Florida Press, 1998. $39.95. (NF)

Desai, Kiran. *Hullabaloo in the Guava Orchard*. Atlantic Monthly, 1998. $22.00. (F)

Diaz, Alejandro Hernandez. *The Cuban Mile*. Trans. Dick Cluster. Latin American Literary Review, 1998. Paper: $13.95. (F)

Diaz, Tony. *The Aztec God of Love*. FC2, 1998. Paper: $12.95. (F)

Donoghue, Denis. *The Practice of Reading*. Yale, 1998. $30.00. (NF)

Duffy, Jean H. *Reading Between the Lines: Claude Simon and the Visual Arts*. Liverpool Univ. Press, 1998. Paper: £15.95. (NF)

Dunmore, Helen. *Talking to the Dead*. Back Bay, 1998. Paper: $12.95. (F)

———. *Your Blue-Eyed Boy*. Little, Brown, 1998. $23.95. (F)

El-Bisatie, Mohamed. *A Last Glass of Tea and Other Stories*. Trans. Denys Johnson-Davies. Lynne Rienner, 1998. $24.00. (F)

Elkhadem, Saad. *Two Avant-Garde Egyptian Novels: The Great Egyptian Novel / From Travels of the Egyptian Odysseus*. Trans. by the author. Bilingual edition. York, 1998. Paper: $15.95. (F)

Ellingham, Lewis and Kevin Killian. *Poet Be Like God: Jack Spicer and the San Francisco Renaissance.* Wesleyan/New England, 1998. $35.00. (NF)

Erhart, Margaret. *Old Love.* Steerforth, 1998. Paper: $13.00. (F)

Evenson, Brian. *Father of Lies.* Four Walls, Eight Windows, 1998. $22.00. (F)

Farah, Nuruddin. *Secrets.* Arcade, 1998. $23.95. (F)

Farrell, James T. *Chicago Stories.* Ed. Charles Fanning. Univ. of Illinois Press, 1998. Paper: $17.95 (F)

Fell, Alison. *Dreams, Like Heretics: New and Selected Poems.* Serpent's Tail, 1998. Paper: $13.99. (P)

Ferguson, Jon. *Farley's Jewel: A Novel in Search of Being.* Cinco Puntos, 1998. Paper: $11.95. (F)

Field, Edward. *A Frieze For a Temple of Love.* Black Sparrow, 1998. Cloth: $27.50; paper: $15.00. (P)

Fonseca, Rubem. *Vast Emotions and Imperfect Thoughts.* Trans. Clifford E. Landers. Ecco, 1998. $24.00. (F)

Ford, Richard. *Women with Men.* Vintage, 1998. Paper: $12.00. (F)

Fuller, Henry Blake. *Bertram Cope's Year.* Turtle Point, 1998. Paper: $14.95. (F)

Gaggi, Silvio. *From Text to Hypertext: Decentering the Subject in Fiction, Film, the Visual Arts, and Electronic Media.* Univ. of Penn. Press, 1998. No price given. (NF)

Gilmore, Lyman. *Don't Touch the Poet: The Life and Times of Joel Oppenheimer.* Talisman House, 1998. $21.95. (NF)

Gorup, Radmila J., and Nadezda Obradovic. *The Prince of Fire: An Anthology of Contemporary Serbian Short Stories.* Foreward by Charles Simic. U of Pittsburgh Press, 1998. Paper: $19.95. (F)

Grapes, Jack, ed. *13 Los Angeles Poets.* Bombshelter, 1997. Paper: $13.95. (P)

Grenier, Roger. *Another November.* Trans. Alice Kaplan. Univ. of Nebraska Press, 1998. $40.00; paper: $12.00. (F)

Gretlund, Jan Nordby and Karl Heinz-Westarp, eds. *The Late Novels of Eudora Welty.* Foreword by Reynolds Price. Univ. South Carolina Press, 1998. $22.95. (NF)

Gunesekera, Romesh. *The Sandglass.* The New Press, 1998. $21.95. (F)

Hadas, Pamela White. *Self-Evidence: A Selection of Verse, 1977-1997.* TriQuarterly, 1998. Paper: $14.95 (P)

Hardwick, Elizabeth. *Sight-Readings: American Fictions.* Random House, 1998. $26.00. (NF)

Harington, Donald. *When Angels Rest.* Counterpoint, 1998. $24.00. (F)

Harrison, William. *The Buddha in Malibu.* Univ. of Missouri Press, 1998. Paper: 16.95. (F)

Harsch, Rick. *Billy Verité.* Steeforth, 1998. $22.00. (F)

Hart, Josephine. *The Stillest Day.* Overlook, 1998. $23.95. (F)

Haverty, Anne. *One Day As a Tiger.* Ecco, 1997. $22.00. (F)

Hensley, Dennis. *Misadventures in the (213).* Weisbach/Morrow, 1998. $24.00. (F)

Herriges, Greg. *The Winter Dance Party Murders.* Wordcraft of Oregon, 1998. Paper: $13.95. (F)

Hill, Geoffrey. *The Triumph of Love.* Houghton Mifflin, 1998. $22.00. (P)

Holoch, Naomi. *Offseason.* Faber and Faber, 1997. $23.95. (F)

Houston, Pam. *Waltzing the Cat.* Norton, 1998. $23.95. (F)

Hugo, Lynne and Anna Tuttle Villegas. *Swimming Lessons.* Morrow, 1998. $21.00. (F)

Husain, Intizar. *The Seventh Door and Other Stories.* Ed. and introduction by Muhammad Umar Memon. Lynne Rienner, 1998. $45.00; paper: $19.95. (F)

Hustvedt, Siri. *Yonder.* Henry Holt, 1998. $20.00. (NF)

Hutchisson, James M, ed. *Sinclair Lewis: New Essays in Criticism.* Whitston, 1997. $29.50. (NF)

Irving, John. *A Widow for One Year.* Random House, 1998. $27.95. (F)

Jamison, Fredric. *The Cultural Turn: Selected Writings on the Postmodern, 1983-1998.* Verso, 1998. Paper: $16.00. (NF)

Jancar, Drago. *Mocking Desire.* Trans. Micheael Biggins. Northwestern Univ. Press, 1998. $44.95; paper: $14.95. (F)

Jeffers, Alex. *Safe As Houses.* Gay Men's Press, 1998. Paper: $14.95. (F)

Jhabvala, Ruth Prawler. *East into Upper East.* Counterpoint, 1998. $24.00. (F)

Jones, Gail. *Fetish Lives.* George Braziller, 1998. $20.00. (F)

Karlin, Wayne. *Prisoners.* Curbstone, 1998. $19.95. (F)

Keifetz, Mandy. *Corrido.* Fleabites, 1998. Paper: $12.00. (F)

Klinkowitz, Jerome. *Here at Ogallala State U: The Collected Effusions (With Commentary) of Our 'Milt' Elliott.* White Hawk, 1996. Paper: $10.00. (F)

——. *Vonnegut in Fact: The Public Spokesmanship of Personal Fiction.* Univ. of South Carolina Press, 1998. $24.95. (NF)

Koja, Kathe. *Extremities.* Four Walls Eight Windows, 1998. $22.00. (F)

Kramer, Kathryn. *Sweet Water.* Knopf, 1998. $24.00. (F)

Kundera, Milan. *Farewell Waltz.* Trans. Aaron Asher. HarperCollins, 1998. (F)

Labiner, Norah. *Our Sometime Sister.* Coffee House, 1998. $22.95 (F)

Larson, Wendy. *Women and Writing in Modern China.* Stanford Univ. Press, 1998. Paper: $19.95. (NF)

Lawlor, William. *The Beat Generation: A Bibliographic Teaching Guide.* Scarecrow, 1998. $42.00. (NF)

Lounsberry, Barbara, et al, eds. *Tales We Tell: Perspectives on the Short Story.* Greenwood, 1998. $55.00. (NF)

Makanin, Vladimir. *The Loss: A Novella and Two Short Stories.* Trans. Byron Lindsey. Northwestern Univ. Press, 1998. $44.95; $14.95. (F)

Makine, Andrei. *Once Upon the River Love.* Trans. Geoffrey Strachan. Arcade, 1998. $24.95. (F)

Maraini, Dacia. *The Silent Duchess.* Trans. Dick Kitto and Elspeth Spottiswood. Afterword by Anna Camaiti Hostert. Feminist, 1998. $19.95. (F)

Marsh, Nicholas. *Virginia Woolf: The Novels.* St. Martin's, 1998. $55.00; paper: $19.95. (NF)

Marsigli, Annalita. *The Written Script.* Overlook, 1998. $24.95. (F)

Martin, S. I. *Incomparable World.* George Braziller, 1998. $20.00. (F)

McAlpine, Gordon. *The Persistence of Memory*. Peter Owen, 1998. $29.95.
(F)

McCann, Colum. *This Side of Brightness*. Henry Holt, 1998. $23.00. (F)

McCormick, Mike. *Getting It in the Head*. Henry Holt, 1998. $23.00. (F)

McFerrin, Linda Watanabe. *Namako: Sea Cucumber*. Coffee House, 1998.
Paper: $14.95. (F)

McGraw, Milena. *After Dunkirk*. Houghton Mifflin, 1998. $24.00. (F)

Minot, Susan. *Evening*. Knopf, 1998. $23.00. (F)

Modiano, Patrick. *Out of the Dark*. Trans. Jordan Stump. Univ. of Nebraska
Press, 1998. $40.00; paper: $12.00. (F)

Moore, Lorrie. *Birds of America*. Knopf, 1998. $23.00. (F)

Neville, Susan. *In the House of Blue Lights*. Univ. of Notre Dame Press,
1998. $35.00; paper: $14.00. (F)

Nieh, Hualing. *Mulberry and Peach*. Trans. Jane Parish Lang with Linda
Lappin. Afterword by Sau-ling Cynthia Wong. Feminist, 1998. Paper:
$12.95. (F)

Norman, Howard. *The Bird Artist*. Farrar, Straus & Giroux, 1998. $23.00.
(F)

O'Brien, Tim. *Tomcat in Love*. Broadway, 1998. $26.00. (F)

Ortese, Anna Maria. *A Music Behind the Wall: Selected Stories, Volume Two*.
Trans. Henry Martin. McPherson, 1998. $22.00. (F)

Oser, Lee. *T. S. Eliot and American Poetry*. Univ. of Missouri Press, 1998.
$29.95. (NF)

Owens, Louis. *Mixedblood Messages: Literature, Film, Family, Place*. Univ.
of Oklahoma Press, 1998. $27.95. (NF)

Ozeki, Ruth L. *My Year of Meats*. Viking, 1998. $23.95. (F)

Perloff, Marjorie. *Poetry On and Off the Page: Essays for Emergent Occasions*. Paper: $19.95. (NF)

Pessoa, Fernando. *Poems of Fernando Pessoa*. Trans. and edited by Edwih
Honig and Susan M. Brown. City Lights, 1998. Paper: $15.95. (P)

Petsinis, Tom. *The French Mathematician*. Walker, 1998. $24.00. (F)

Ridley, John. *Love Is a Racket*. Knopf, 1998. $24.00. (F)

Roberson, Susan, ed. *Women, America, and Movement: Narratives of Relocation*. Univ. of Missouri Press, 1998. $37.50. (NF)

Rogers, James. *Savage Life*. Serpent's Tail, 1998. Paper: $12.99. (F)

Ross, Robert, ed. *Australia: A Traveler's Literary Companion*. Whereabouts,
1998. Paper: $13.95. (F)

Roth, Philip. *I Married a Communist*. Houghton Mifflin, 1998. $26.00. (F)

Rothenberg, Jerome, and Pierre Joris, eds. *Poems for the Millennium: The
University of California Book of Modern and Postmodern Poetry*. Univ. of
California Press, 1998. No price given. (P)

Ryman, Geoff. *253: The Journey of 253 Lifetimes*. St. Martin's, 1998. Paper:
$14.95. (F)

Sadlier, Darlene J. *An Introduction to Fernando Pessoa: Modernism and the
Paradoxes of Authorship*. Univ. of Florida Press, 1998. $49.95. (NF)

Saramago, José. *Blindness*. Trans. Giovanni Pontiero. Harcourt Brace,
1998. $22.00. (F)

Schoemperlen, Diane. *Forms of Devotion: Stories and Pictures*. Viking,
1998. $24.95. (F)

Schwartz, John Burnham. *Reservation Road.* Knopf, 1998. $24.00. (F)

Selby, Jr., Hubert. *The Willow Tree.* Marion Boyars, 1998. $25.95. (F)

Simmons, Charles. *Salt Water.* Chronicle, 1998. $19.95. (F)

Smith, Mary C. *The Undesirables.* Black Heron, 1998. $24.95. (F)

Spicer, Jack. *The House That Jack Built: The Collected Lectures of Jack Spicer.* Ed. and afterword by Peter Gizzi.Wesleyan/New England. Paper: $18.95. (NF)

Spiegel, Alan. *James Agee and the Legend of Himself: A Critical Study.* Univ. of Missouri Press, 1998. $34.95. (NF)

Stark, Marisa Kantor. *Bring Us the Old People.* Coffee House, 1998. $22.95. (F)

Stavans, Ilan, ed. *Prospero's Mirror: A Translators' Portfolio of Latin American Short Fiction.* Curbstone, 1998. Paper: $17.95. (F)

Stern, Mario Rigoni. *The Story of Tönle.* Trans. John Shepley. Northwestern Univ. Press, 1998. $26.95. (F)

Stone, Robert. *Demascus Gate.* Houghton Miflin, 1998. $26.00. (F)

Swensen, Cole. *Noon.* Sun & Moon, 1998. Paper: $10.95. (P)

Thai, Ho Anh. *Behind the Red Mist.* Ed. Wayne Karlin. Curbstone, 1998. Paper: $13.95. (F)

Thompson, Alice. *Justine.* Counterpoint, 1998. $18.00. (F)

Tlili, Mustapha. *Lion Mountain.* Trans. Linda Coverdale. Lynne Rienner, 1998. Paper: $15.95. (F)

Troutt, David Dante. *The Monkey Suit and Other Short Fiction on African Amcericans and Justice.* The New Press, 1998. $24.00. (F)

Troy, Mary. *Joe Baker is Dead.* Univ. of Missouri Press, 1998. Paper: $16.95. (F)

Tusken, Lewis W. *Understanding Herman Hesse: The Man, His Myth, His Metaphor.* Univ. of South Carolina Press, 1998. $29.95. (NF)

TuSmith, Bonnie, ed. *Conversations with John Edgar Wideman.* Univ. of Mississippi Press, 1998. Paper: $17.00. (F)

Kenneth Tynan: Letters. Ed. Kathleen Tynan. Random House, 1998. $30.00. (NF)

Kenneth Tynan: Profiles. Random House, 1998. Paper: $20.00. (NF)

Updike, John. *Bech at Bay.* Knopf, 1998. $23.00. (F)

——, ed. *A Century of Arts & Letters: The History of the National Institute of Arts & Letters and the American Academy of Arts & Letters.* Columbia Univ. Press, 1998. $39.95. (NF)

Welsh, Irvine. *Filth.* Norton, 1998. Paper: $14.00. (F)

Wimmer, Dick. *Boyne's Lassie.* Zoland, 1998. Paper: $12.00. (F)

Wood, Michael. *Children of Silence: On Contemporary Fiction.* Columbia Univ. Press, 1998. $22.95. (NF)

Wydeven, Joseph J. *Wright Morris Revisited.* Twayne, 1998. $28.95. (NF)

Yablonsky, Linda. *The Story of Junk.* Back Bay, 1998. Paper: $12.95. (F)

Yáñez, Mira, ed. *Cubana: Contemporary Fiction by Cuban Women.* Foreword by Ruth Behar. Beacon, 1998. Paper: $12.95. (F)

Zong-Pu, Feng. *The Everlasting Rock.* Trans. Aimee Lykes. Lynne Rienner, 1998. $35.00; paper: $16.95. (F)

Contributors

GIOVANNA COVI, researcher in English, at the University of Trento-Italy, has recently edited *Critical Studies on the Feminist Subject* (Trento: Labirinti, 1997) to confirm her interest in feminist theory, women writers, and translation.

GREG DAWES is Associate Professor of Latin American and World Literature at North Carolina State University. He has published numerous articles on Latin American and U. S. literature and literary theory. His book *Aesthetics and Revolution: Nicaraguan Poetry 1979-1990* (University of Minnesota Press) appeared in 1993. Since then he has been preparing a manuscript on the poetry of Pablo Neruda.

JOSEPH DEWEY, Associate Professor of American Literature at the University of Pittsburgh, is the author of *In a Dark Time: The Apocalyptic Temper in the American Novel of the Nuclear Age* and has recently completed *Locked in Magic Kingdoms: Spectacle Realism in the Novels of Reagan's America.*

LYNNE DIAMOND-NIGH is the editor of the *New Novel Review*. She teaches at Elmira College and is currently writing a book titled *Confla (gra) tions,* on the relationships between the visual arts and literature.

SINDA GREGORY teaches American literature at San Diego State University. She's the author of *Private Investigations: the Novels of Dashiell Hammett* and co-editor with Larry McCaffery of various interviews with contemporary American and Japanese writers.

ALLEN GUTTMANN teaches English and American Studies at Amherst College.

CHARLES B. HARRIS is the author of *Contemporary American Novelists of the Absurd* (1971) and *Passionate Virtuosity: The Fiction of John Barth* (1983). He directs the Unit for Contemporary Literature at Illinois State University.

JAMES HURT is Professor of English at the University of Illinois, specializing in modern literature. His books and essays deal with modern drama, Irish literature, and the literature of the Midwest.

RICHARD MARTIN retired as professor of English and American Literature at Aachen University, Germany, earlier this year.

LARRY MCCAFFERY has recently published *Some Other Frequency: Interviews with Innovative American Authors* (Univ. of Pennsylvania Press) and *Federman, A to X-X-X-X A Recyclopedic Narrative* (co-edited with Doug Rice and Thomas Hartl, San Diego State Univ. Press).

WARREN F. MOTTE, Jr. teaches in the Department of Spanish and French at the University of Colorado-Boulder. His book *OULIPO: A Primer of Potential Literature* has recently been reissued by Dalkey Archive Press.

JIM NEILSON, a regular contributor to *minnesota review* and co-editor of *Cultural Logic,* teaches English at Trident Technical College (Charleston, SC). *Warring Fictions,* his book on the cultural politics of the Vietnam War narrative, is forthcoming from the University of Mississippi Press.

ANN PANCAKE is Assistant Professor in creative writing at Penn State Erie, the Behrend College. A recipient of an NEA grant for her short fiction, she has published in *International Quarterly,* the *Virginia Quarterly Review, Antietam Review,* and *Shenandoah.* She is working on both a collection of short stories and a book about the interrelation between social class and temporality in American literary culture.

SHARON SNYDER teaches courses in literature and film studies at Northern Michigan University. She most recently co-edited *The Body and Physical Difference: Discourses of Disability* for the University of Michigan Press, where she is also series editor for a line of books—*Corporealities.*

TREY STRECKER, a doctoral student at Ball State University, is completing a dissertation on contemporary American encyclopedic fiction.

RAYMOND L. WILLIAMS chairs the Department of Spanish and Portuguese at the University of California-Riverside. His most recent books are *The Writings of Carlos Fuentes* and *The Postmodern Novel of Latin America.*

Annual Index

References are to issue number and pages, respectively

Books Reviewed

Reviewers' names follow in parentheses. Regular reviewers are abbreviated: IM=Irving Malin; JO=John O'Brien; CP=Christopher Paddock; TH=Thomas Hove; SC=Susann Cokal; JS=James Sallis; RB=Robert Buckeye; KW=Kent D. Wolf

Auster, Paul. *Hand to Mouth: A Chronicle of Early Failure*, 1: 228 (Stephen Bernstein)

Axelrod, Mark. *Cardboard Castles*, 2: 259 (Gordon McAlpine)

Babel, Isaac. *1920 Diary*, 2: 227-8 (TH)

Baker, Nicholson. *The Everlasting Story of Nory*, 3: 242-3 (Eric Lorberer)

Barone, Dennis. *Echoes*, 2: 247 (Matthew Roberson)

Bartheleme, Donald. *Not-Knowing: The Essays and Interviews of Donald Barthelme*, 2: 226 (Monique Dufour)

Baumbach, Jonathan. *D-Tours*, 3: 249 (Steve Tomasula)

Beard, Richard. *X20: A Novel of (Not) Smoking*, 1: 236 (KW)

Bellen, Martine, Lee Smith, and Bradford Morrow, eds. *Conjunctions 29: Tributes: American Writers on American Writers*, 2: 257-8 (Brooke Horvath)

Bénabou, Marcel. *Jacob, Menahem & Mimoun: A Family Epic*, 3: 241 (Allen Hibbard)

Benedetti, Mario. *Blood Pact and Other Stories*, 1: 250 (Andria Spencer)

Bercovitch, Sacvan, ed. *Nathanael West: Novels and Other Writings*, 1: 221-2 (John Kulka)

Bergman, Ingmar. *Private Confessions*, 2: 248-9 (Darryl Hattenhauer)

Bernhard, Thomas. *The Voice Imitator*, 2: 241-2 (Jeffrey DeShell)

Blondel, Nathalie. *Mary Butts: Scenes From the Life*, 3: 258-9 (IM)

Breton, André. *Anthology of Black Humor*, 2: 235 (JS)

Breton, André, Paul Eluard, and Philippe Soupault. *The Automatic Message*, 3: 257-8 (JS)

Brodkey, Harold. *The World Is the Home of Love and Death*, 2: 251-2 (IM)

Bruns, Gerald L. *Maurice Blanchot: The Refusal of Philosophy*, 1: 230-1 (Thomas Lecky)

Bukowski, Charles. *The Captain is Out to Lunch and the Sailors Have Taken Over the Ship*, 3: 237-8 (Gerald Locklin)

Bundy, Alison. *DunceCap*, 3: 247 (Brian Lennon)

Burgess, Anthony. *Byrne: A Novel*, 1: 236-7 (Jack Byrne)

Burgin, Richard. *Fear of Blue Skies*, 2: 249 (IM)

Calvino, Italo, ed. *Fantastic Tales: Visionary and Everyday*, 2: 234-5 (David Ian Paddy)

Capriolo, Paola. *The Woman Watching*, 3: 255 (SC)

Carey, Peter. *Jack Maggs*, 2: 239-40 (Philip Landon)

Carrère, Emmanuel. *Class Trip*, 1: 244-5 (CP)

Carson, Anne. *Autobiography of Red: A Novel in Verse*, 3: 233-4 (Nicole Cooley)

Casey, Calvert. *The Collected Stories*, 3: 245 (David Ian Paddy)

Chamoiseau, Patrick. *Solibo Magnificent*, 2: 237-8 (Marc Lowenthal)

Chapman, Stepan. *The Troika*, 1: 251-2 (Grant Hier)

Charlebois, Lucile C. *Understanding Camilo José Cela*, 2: 262 (David William Foster)

Charyn, Jerome. *Death of a Tango King*, 3: 246 (David Seed)

Chen-ho, Wang. *Rose, Rose, I Love You*, 3: 246-7 (TH)

Cherkovski, Neeli. *Bukowski: A Life*, 2: 244 (Gerald Locklin)

Chin, Sara. *Below the Line*, 2: 256-7 (SC)

Cixous, Hélène, and Mireille Calle-Gruber. *Hélène Cixous Rootprints: Memory and Life-Writing*, 1: 234

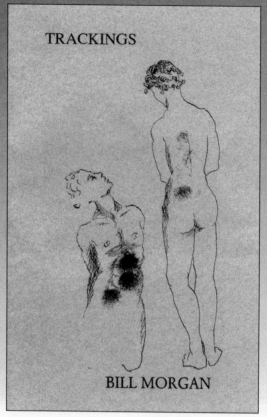

Trackings by Bill Morgan

"The work is carefully, painstakingly executed and there seems to be no word, no phrase in excess. Each piece seems an integral part of the whole and moves steadily to the tragic conclusion. There is a lot of pain here, something we can relate to."—Carolyn Page

"We were both immensely moved by *Trackings*, an anatomy of an involved love relationship that moves from heights down to despair." —Robert Peters & Paul Trachtenberg

"The very old story, truthfully, poignantly told. These poems manage a remarkably reflective accuracy while keeping their own authority, and one is moved to become a compassionate witness. Simply put, Bill Morgan has a lot of heart."—Robert Creeley

To order this book, send $5 plus postage ($1.25 for one book, $1.75 for two or more) to
Dead Metaphor Press, P.O. Box 2076, Boulder, CO 80306
1-303-417-9398

southside rain
by
Quraysh Ali Lansana

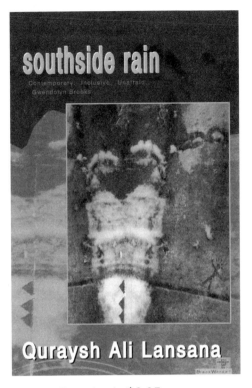

Paperback $9.95

"Contemporary. Inclusive. Unafraid."
Gwendolyn Brooks

"Quraysh Ali Lansana's poems are rhythms in ample beat and heart
beat. They are reckoned assaults against the decadent & deceptive
social cloth interlaced with the delicate thread of our skins. With the
word, Lansana tears off this mantle of oppressiveness. This poetry
that resonates with ancient and fresh liberation song."
Luis Rodriguez

Blackwords/
A Division of Alexander Publishing Group, Inc.
P.O. Box 21
Alexandria, VA 22313-0021

V Q R
THE VIRGINIA QUARTERLY REVIEW
A National Journal of Literature and Discussion

SUMMER 1998   *Volume 74, Number 3*

FIVE   DOLLARS

THE VIRGINIA QUARTERLY REVIEW
ONE WEST RANGE
CHARLOTTESVILLE,VA 22903

SUBSCRIPTION RATES:
INDIVIDUAL $18.00
INSTITUTION $22.00

Leonardo's *St. John* (Paris, Louvre), whose "treacherous smile" was
famously described by Walter Pater

ANTIOCH
the REVIEW

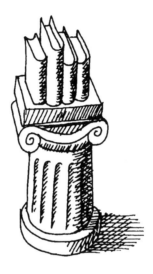

Advisory Board

 # Eclectic Literary Forum

A quarterly of contemporary literature

chosen by *Writer's Digest*
as a "Top Mainstream Market for Poetry"

*Regular & special features*_____

Poetry, short stories, essays on literary themes, in-depth reviews, *special issue interviews*, editorial commentary, Native American and other ethnic folklore, Rotten Apples wit, Quick Pro Quotes . . .

Contributors include: Gwendolyn Brooks, William Stafford, X. J. Kennedy, Allen Ginsberg, Joyce Carol Oates, Dana Gioia, Nikki Giovanni, Hayden Carruth, John Haines, Rachel Hadas, Michael Bugeja, R.L. Cook, Martha Vertreace, Lucien Stryk . . .

Visit *ELF on the Web* @ http://www.pce.net/elf

Order Form

☐ Yes! I want to subscribe
   Subscriptions: $16/yr

   Institution Rate: $32/yr

☐ Please send me a sample copy: $5.50

Send Order Form and payment to:

ELF Associates, Inc., P. O. Box 392, Tonawanda, NY 14150

CLARA ORBAN

The Culture of Fragments
Words and Images
in Futurism and Surrealism

Amsterdam/Atlanta, GA 1997. 210 pp.
(Textxet 11)
ISBN: 90-420-0111-9   Hfl. 65,-/US-$ 34.-

Works of art such as paintings with words on them or poems shaped as images communicate to the viewer by means of more than one medium. Here is presented a particular group of hybrid art works from the early twentieth century, to discover in what way words and images can function together to create meaning.

The four central artists considered in this study investigate word/image forms in their work. F.T. Marinetti invented *parole in libertà*, among other ideas, to free language from syntactic connections. Umberto Boccioni experimented with newspaper clippings on the canvas from 1912-1915, and these collages constitute an important exploration into word/image forms. André Breton's collection of poems *Clair de terre* (1923) contains several typographical variations for iconographic effect. René Magritte explored the relationship between words and images, juxtaposing signifiers to contradictory signifieds on the canvas. A final chapter introduces media other than poetry and painting on which words and images appear. Posters, the theater, and the relatively new medium of cinema foreground words and images constantly.

This volume will be of interest to scholars of twentieth-century French or Italian literature or painting, and to scholars of word and image studies.

EDITIONS RODOPI B.V.

USA / Canada: **All Other Countries:**
2015 South Park Place   Keizersgracht 302-304
Atlanta, GA 30339   1016 EX Amsterdam, The Netherlands
Phone (770) 933-0027 / **Fax** 933-9644   **Tel.** ++ 31 (0)20 622 75 07
Call toll-free (U.S.only) 1-800-225-3998   **Fax** ++ 31 (0)20 638 09 48
e-mail: orders-queries@rodopi.nl — http://www.rodopi.nl

UNIVERSITY OF DELAWARE PRESS

presents a reader's guide to
William H. Gass's *The Tunnel* :

INTO *THE* TUNNEL

edited by
Steven G. Kellman
and Irving Malin

The diverse essays in this
volume are an attempt to
guide the reader through the
prolixities and perplexities of
William H. Gass's *The Tunnel*, perhaps one of the
most significant American novels published since
World War II. *The Tunnel* both defies and
demands commentary, and will be read as a land-
mark of postwar American fiction. Despite its preoccupation with Nazi atrocities, the clash it trails is the Cold
War more than World War II. The novel deconstructs history
as a contrivance with a counterfeit past and a doubtful future.

$35.00

University of Delaware Press -- 326 Hullihen Hall -- Newark DE 19716
(302) 831-1149 -- Fax: 302/831-6549 -- udpress@odin.english.udel.edu
http://www.english.udel.edu/udpress/
Address orders to: AUP -- 440 Forsgate Dr -- Cranbury NJ 08512